The Maculate Muse

The Maculate Muse

OBSCENE LANGUAGE IN ATTIC COMEDY

SECOND EDITION

Jeffrey Henderson

New York   Oxford
Oxford University Press
1991

Oxford University Press

Oxford   New York   Toronto
Delhi   Bombay   Calcutta   Madras   Karachi
Petaling Jaya   Singapore   Hong Kong   Tokyo
Nairobi   Dar es Salaam   Cape Town
Melbourne Auckland

and associated companies in
Berlin   Ibadan

Copyright © 1975 by Yale University
© 1991 by Jeffrey Henderson

Published by Oxford University Press, Inc.
200 Madison Avenue, New York, New York 10016

First published by Yale University Press
First Oxford University Press edition 1991
First issued in paperback 1991

Oxford is a registered trademark of Oxford University Press

Library of Congress Cataloging-in-Publication Data
Henderson, Jeffrey.
The maculate muse : obscene language in Attic comedy /
Jeffrey Henderson.–2nd ed., 1st Oxford University Press ed.
p.   cm. Includes bibliographical references and indexes.
ISBN 0-19-506684-7
ISBN 0-19-506685-5 (pbk.)
1. Greek drama (Comedy)–History and criticism.
2. Words, Obscene, in literature. 3. Greek language–Obscene words.
4. Scatology in literature. 5. Sex in literature.
6. Sex–Terminology. I. Title.
PA3166.H4   1991   882'.0109–dc20   90-42489

1 2 3 4 5 6 7 8 9 10

Printed in the United States of America
on acid-free paper

For Ann

Preface

In 1971, when I began the dissertation that would become *The Maculate Muse*, scorn of the old taboos about human sexuality and its social expressions had become socially fashionable among many members of my generation, even a badge of cultural liberation. For me, an academic who had never thought that human sexuality should be a shameful secret and who had always been amused and fascinated by erotic art and literature, that era of "sexual revolution" seemed an opportune time to explore the sexual dimensions of my favorite classical artform. But there was little to build on: the sexual organization of the Athenian polis, and therefore the specifically Athenian meanings of its erotic art, were still largely unexplored subjects. Investigation of the whole system would have been beyond my capacity even if I had given myself more than one year to write a dissertation. But I wanted to start, and obscenity seemed to be the category that could most easily be defined and analyzed by a novice scholar and that would be most useful as philology. And I saw nothing improbable in Aristophanes' claim (e.g., *Nu.* 518–62) that obscenity, like other features of his art, whether considered as poetry, as wit, or as characterization, should ideally be not merely enjoyably shocking but also creatively original, aesthetically dynamic, and even liberating. For me Aristophanes often attained this ideal, as have other major writers in forms both elevated (Shakespeare, Rabelais, Joyce) and proletarian (Charles Bukowski, William Burroughs).

At the time few of my colleagues felt the same way. Friends warned me that I was unlikely to get the dissertation published even if I did manage to find something worthwhile to say about comic obscenity, which they doubted. One professor was sympathetic but suggested I write the dissertation in Latin, while another angrily asked, "How could you do this to Aristophanes?" Fortunately, Zeph Stewart, my advisor, and later Edward Tripp, my editor at the Yale University Press, provided the support and encouragement I needed to bring off the project. As it turned out, *The Maculate Muse* did manage to show that obscene language was a more central and interesting feature of Old Comedy than had been supposed, even in light of the groundbreaking work by K. J. Dover (in *Clouds*) and Jean Taillardat (in *Les Images d'Aristophane*). Since then, obscene language in comic and other Greek poetry has begun to be acknowledged by translators[1] and to receive the same kind of scholarly interest and attention as other kinds of language. And we now have Adams (1982) and Richlin (1983) on the Latin side.

Also, since then, new approaches to the study of sexuality,[2] which see it as a phenomenon central to every culture, though always in different ways, have begun to stimulate the interest of classicists, with some impressive results.[3] In addition, new cultural approaches to the study of gender and gender-roles have forced a reappraisal of our own discipline and its cultural dynamics. Here the Women's Classical Caucus has played a leading role, and the formation of a Gay/Lesbian Caucus has recently been announced. In light of these developments of the past twenty years I would certainly do some things differently were I writing the book now.

My use of psychoanalytic theory—the most powerful tool available in any study of the sexual and emotional dynamics of language and narrative— would be more sophisticated now, largely as a result of my association, since 1982, with Richard Caldwell.[4] My analysis of the aggressive and regressive dynamics of comic obscenity was adequate, but we still need a refined psychoanalytic study of comic plots and situations, especially in their mythopoeic dimensions[5]; such a study would further illuminate the dramatic codes at work in comic obscenity. Greater awareness of the role of comic drama as a social and political institution[6] sheds additional light on the power of comic obscenity to expose and degrade, and thus to play a role (analogous to but distinct from that played by lawcourts, *dokimasiai* and

---

1. Noteworthy are the translations that accompany Alan H. Sommerstein's edition of Aristophanes (Warminster and Chicago 1980—).

2. See the Introduction to Halperin/Winkler/Zeitlin (1990) for a survey. The University of Chicago Press recently announced the debut in 1990 of the *Journal of the History of Sexuality*.

3. I have added a selection of recent works on texts and material remains to the bibliography.

4. Classicists, when they know anything about psychoanalytic theory at all, do not so much reject as misunderstand it. I hope this situation will change now that Caldwell (1989, 1990) has provided lucid descriptions of the theory and examples of its application to myths and mythic language. For a feminist reappraisal of the psychoanalytic approach see du Bois (1988).

5. I should have made more extensive use of P. Rau, *Paratragodia* (Munich 1967), who often discusses comic usurpation of the erotic in tragedy. The extent to which a comic poet could mythologize in his own right is shown by H. Hofmann, *Mythos und Komödie. Untersuchungen zu den Vögeln des Ar.* (Hildesheim 1976).

6. See the essays in Winkler/Zeitlin (1990).

euthynai) in the corporate surveillance of sexual behavior.[7] In this field,. incorporation of the evidence of erotic art—more ubiquitous in classical Greece than in any other society except Japan—is a desideratum, but (in my case at least) would require collaboratior with an expert iconographer.[8]

The accomplishments of recent gay and feminist scholarship have alerted us to the degree to which Attic comedy expressed, and helped to enforce, the norms of an exclusively androcentric and in certain ways homophobic public regime. But at the same time there was an "other" Athens—the spheres of home and cult, the world of "detached" *apragmones*, foreigners and slaves— that was more traditional and inclusive, whose principles and protocols were often at variance with those of the official polis, and whose rival claims could be (uniquely) expressed, even championed, at the comic festivals. More attention should be paid to such points of social and ideological conflict, lest we end up fabricating yet another oversimple picture of a complex society, replacing the Athens that could be held up as an ideal for men by an Athens that can play sinister "other" to a gay or feminist ideal. If *The Maculate Muse* seems in retrospect to reproduce the vocabulary and assumptions of the androcentric and homophobic sides of Attic comedy too uncritically, then it remains to be seen to what degree these may in fact have been subversive (as would befit Dionysos and the negative and deflationary biases of his festive comedy); whether in the end there is any more benign and less degrading way to make public humor out of sex; and whether indeed erotic art or literature can ever do without guilt, taboo, violence, conflict, and degradation and still be erotic.[9] The study of sexuality still needs to investigate not merely the behavior of people in groups and in relation to institutions like marriage, but also their behavior in sex. For philologists, critics, and historians obscenity, being a way to express sexuality that every society tries to define and then suppress in its own ways, is of particular value.

These are some of the questions that would inform *The Maculate Muse* were I (re)writing it today. But on balance it seems best simply to reprint the original text, adding a new preface and some necessary *addenda, corrigenda*, and *retractanda*. Historical interest and cost-efficiency aside, the book remains a basic starting-point, and is offered again in hopes of contributing to the ongoing investigation of an aspect of Greek culture that continues to fascinate in new ways.

7. See Winkler (1990) 45–70.

8. Various approaches can be found in Bérard et al. (1990), Boardman (1978), Bowie/ Christenson (1970), Hofmann (1978), Johns (1982), Keuls (1985), Marcadé (1965), Sutton (1981; forthcoming), Taplin (1988).

9. In this connection it is worth mentioning the feminist debate over the social and political aspects of pornography and the desirability of its censorship: see Ellis et al. (1986) and, from the classicist's point of view, Richlin (forthcoming), Introduction.

In another way 1991 is an opportune time for re-release, in view of what seems to be a national reversion to sexual conservatism (I would say intolerance), as witnessed, for example, by this chilling notice to humanists from our government:

> None of the funds authorized to be appropriated for the...National Endowment for the Humanities may be used to promote, disseminate, or produce materials which in the judgment of the...National Endowment for the Humanities may be considered obscene, including but not limited to, depictions of sadomasochism, homoeroticism, the sexual exploitation of children, or individuals engaged in sex acts which, when taken as a whole, do not have serious literary, artistic, political or scientific value.[10]

One can only hope that the art of classical Greece, which frequently depicts each one of these banned subjects, will be among the materials judged "serious" even when we are studying Old Comedy. At any rate, to reissue *The Maculate Muse* in such a climate gives me an agreeable feeling of rebelliousness reminiscent of my student days.

I am grateful to my editor, Rachel Toor, for suggesting this new edition and for her many helpful suggestions, and to the reviewers and friends (Amy Richlin and John J. Winkler particularly) who over the years have alerted me to the book's strengths and weaknesses.

May 1990   J. H.

---

10. Sent to all applicants for funding as of November 1989. For a Greek word to describe this kind of censorship I can't help but recall Aristophanes' coinage (*Eq.* 878) πρωκτοτηρεῖν [make surveillance of assholes], applied by the Sausage Seller to Kleon, who had boasted of "putting a stop to homosexual fornication".

Contents

Introduction

Obscene humor has always been something of an embarrassment to writers on ancient comedy, from Aristotle, Plutarch, and Longinus to scholars of the present day. Everyone knows that Aristophanes and his fellow comic poets included in their works a great abundance of obscene words, allusions, double entendres and visual bawdiness, but to this day there has been no study that attempts comprehensively to elucidate, evaluate, or even to discuss the nature and function of sexual and scatological language in Attic Comedy. Occasionally an article will appear explaining an obscene word or passage. The older commentaries, when they take note of obscenities at all, usually follow the scholiast's laconic and often inaccurate definitions.

The work of modern scholiasts, like J. Taillardat's *Les Images d'Aristophane* (Paris, 1962) and C. Charitonides' ΑΠΟΡΡΗΤΑ (Thessaloniki, 1935), are merely reference lists, and quite incomplete ones at that, which paraphrase the scholia and tell us nothing about the function of obscene language in the comedies. The attempts to acknowledge and understand comic obscenity in such treatments of individual plays as Dover's commentary on *Clouds*, MacDowell's on *Wasps*, Ussher's on *Ecclesiazusae,* and Wit-Tak's book on *Lysistrata*[1] suffer from the absence of any comprehensive study of obscenity in all the remains of Attic Comedy. The same can be said for the well-meaning but inadequate treatment of the subject in the standard reference works and in books of literary criticism, like those of Cedric Whitman, *Aristophanes and the Comic Hero* (Cambridge, Mass., 1964)

---

1. *Lysistrata: Vrede, Vrouw, en Obsceniteit bij Aristophanes* (Groningen, 1967). This book makes some valuable observations, although the author's reliance on modern sociological and psychological theories at the expense of philological accuracy gravely mars her conclusions: see P. Rau's trenchant critique in *Gnomon* 40 (1968): 568 ff. Miss Wit-Tak's sequel, "Obscenity in the *Thesm.* and *Eccl.* of Aristophanes," *Mnem.* 21 (1968): 4 ff., suffers from the same methodological imperfections.

and, most recently, K. J. Dover, *Aristophanic Comedy* (Berkeley and Los Angeles, 1972).

Contributing to the natural disinclination of scholars to study Aristophanic obscenity is the notion that none of this material has any relevance to the actual meaning and value of the plays; it is usually assumed that the plays would be better without it. Scholars seem to feel that they may on the basis of that assumption safely ignore the obscenity, and the explanations they give for its presence in the plays in the first place are similar to those given in the case of other authors, Shakespeare being perhaps the closest parallel:[2] the obscenity, they say, must be traditional and thus, we must suppose, indispensable, an inheritance from lower forms of art such as the hypothetical Dorian or Megarian farces[3] or the cults; or it must have been an extra morsel tossed in on the principle *his plebecula gaudet;*[4] or the poet had to use every kind of humor available to him in order to win prizes or sweeten his moral messages.[5] Conversely, the obscenities are explained away through the popular notion that they were not really obscene at all, since the ancients were uninhibited children of nature who looked on all human functions without shame:[6] therefore there is no need for more discriminating people to discuss them, for their presence in the plays is merely the consequence of artful innocence.

But a thorough study of the evidence will reveal the incorrectness of such assumptions. The obscenity in Aristophanes is almost always integrally connected with the main themes of the plays; it is an important part of the stage action, the development of plots, and the characterization of personae, and can no more readily be excised from the plays than can any other major dramatic or poetic ingredients. Far from being merely an artist's concession to the rabble, the obscene jokes and allusions in ancient comedy often reach a level of sophistication equal to the cleverest allusions to poetry or philosophy, and are composed as much for δεξιοὶ θεαταί as for the groundlings. We must keep in mind that the very spectacle of Attic Comedy was, at least until well into the fourth century, thoroughly

2. As Eric Partridge observes in his amusing book, *Shakespeare's Bawdy* (London, 1968).

3. W. Schmid, *Geschichte der griechischen Literatur* (Munich, 1929–46), 1: 637, nn. 1, 2; 4: 8, n. 1, 22 ff.; P. Mazon, "La Farce dans Aristophane," *Rev. d'hist. du théâtre* 3 (1957): 7 ff.

4. See the discussion by Wit-Tak (n. 1, above), pp. 109 f.; M. Croiset, *Histoire de la littérature grecque*[3] (Paris, 1913), 3: 484, 606; W. Süss, *Aristophanes und die Nachwelt* (Leipzig, 1911), pp. 78 f.; F. Wright, *Feminism in Greek Literature from Homer to Aristotle* (London, 1923), pp. 150 f.; G. Murray, *Aristophanes* (Oxford, 1933), chap. 1; van Daele at Pl 703.

5. Schmid (n. 3, above), 4: 400 f.

6. See, for example, N. Dracoulides, *Psychanalyse d'Aristophane* (Paris, 1967), pp. 38 f.; H. M. Hyde, *A History of Pornography* (London, 1964), p. 10.

obscene: the male actors were grotesquely padded in the rump and belly and wore the phallus;[7] the female parts (even if played by men) usually involved nudity and much sexual byplay;[8] the dancing was often highly suggestive; the abusive, parodic, and satirical thrust of the comedies relied heavily on obscenity for its impact. In other words, the ethos of Attic Comedy, as well as the traditions it carried on, included obscenity in all its forms as an indispensable element.

It is the purpose of this study to offer as comprehensive a consideration of sexual and scatological language in Aristophanes and the other poets of Attic comedy as seems feasible in the present state of our knowledge.

The first three chapters, which are more or less theoretical, appraise the nature of obscenity as it appears in Attic Comedy and attempt to understand the historical, cultural, and literary factors which led to the elevation of obscene language to the prominent position it holds in the artistic repertoire of Aristophanes and his fellow comic poets. Since ancient critics and literary historians, all of them writing at a time when Old and Middle Comedy and public indecency in general were relics of the past, offer nothing worth discussing in this connection, our evidence in chapters 1–3 must be the remains of comedy itself, archaeological evidence, the cults, and obscene language as it appears in other contemporary literature.

The subsequent chapters attempt to identify and discuss all the obscene terminology I have been able to find in the extant remains of Attic Comedy. In these sections, as in the introductory chapters, I have translated all Greek, not only to make the discussion available to those who are without Greek or who are not specialists in this field, but also because passages quoted from Attic comic poets (especially fragmentary passages) often

7. It is now generally agreed that the phallus was worn by male actors, except in cases like that of Cleisthenes in *Thesmophoriazusae*, where its absence adds to the humor. All the relevant arguments can be found in the following series of articles: W. Beare, "The Costume of the Actors in Attic Comedy," *CQ* 4 (1954): 64 ff.; "Aristophanic Costume Again," *CQ* 7 (1957): 184 f., with Webster's reply (p. 185); "Aristophanic Costume: A Last Word," *CQ* 9 (1959): 126; T. B. L. Webster, "South Italian Vases and Attic Drama," *CQ* 42 (1948): 15 ff.; "Attic Costume: A Reexamination," *Eph. Arch.* (1953/54): 192 ff.; J. F. Killeen, "The Comic Costume Controversy," *CQ* 21 (1971): 51 ff. See also R. Ussher's Introduction to his commentary on *Ecclesiazusae* (Oxford, 1972); T. Gelzer, "Aristophanes," *RE Supplbd.* 12. 1515.44 ff.; A. Willems, *Aristophane* (Paris-Brussels, 1919), 3: 381 ff.

8. The costumes of women characters who were supposed to be naked probably included simulated sexual organs and pubic hair: e.g. V 1373 ff., P 891 ff., L 87 ff. On the question of nudity vs. costuming, see C. H. Whitman, *Aristophanes and the Comic Hero* (Cambridge, Mass., 1964), p. 311, n. 31; Willems (n. 7, above). For the question of nakedness in general, cf. Schmid (n. 3, above), 4: 23, n. 2, 286, n. 7. In Aristophanes, see Eq 1390 ff., V 1342 ff., 1373, P 886 f., Av 670, L 1114, T 1181 ff.

contain terminology and allusions which even the experienced scholar
might find difficult. I hope that the translations will save every reader
from the annoyance of frequent trips to *LSJ*.

In order that these chapters will have an interest and value beyond that
of the usual glossary, I have arranged the terminological entries by num-
bered paragraphs in groups that can be read as independent essays on the
various aspects of comic obscenity. A straight lexical approach would
have made it impossible to do justice to the material: the terminology
must be explained as it occurs in each individual context and in relation to
typologically similar terminology; definitions alone would be neither
accurate nor enlightening. Readers who wish to consult this book as a
reference work may use the indexes, which have been designed for use as a
glossary.

For readers who have little or no Greek but wish to make use of the
Greek terminology, I suggest the key to transliteration given by K. J.
Dover, *Aristophanic Comedy*, pp. xii ff.

In translating Greek obscenities I have regularly used the nearest English equivalents. I hope and trust that no one will be shocked by these
words. In any case, the reader will soon perceive that it would be at least
cumbersome, and often impossible, to explicate the Greek texts by means
of clinical, euphemistic, or Latin terminology.

I would like to thank C. H. Whitman and A. Lowell Edmunds of
Harvard, K. J. Dover of St. Andrews, Charles Segal of Brown University,
and Edward Tripp and Barbara Folsom of the Yale University Press for
their interest and helpful suggestions, and to express particular gratitude
to Zeph Stewart of Harvard, not only for his patient and painstaking
criticism of several drafts of this book, but for the friendship and encouragement he so freely extended to me during my four years in Cambridge.
Whatever faults remain are entirely my own.

J.H.

New Haven, Connecticut
June 25, 1973

Abbreviations

Authors and works are abbreviated as in *LSJ*. The plays and fragments of Aristophanes are abbreviated according to the following list:

A	*Acharnians*	L	*Lysistrata*
Eq	*Knights*	T	*Thesmophoriazusae*
N	*Clouds*	R	*Frogs*
V	*Wasps*	E	*Ecclesiazusae*
P	*Peace*	Pl	*Plutus*
Av	*Birds*	Fr	*Fragment*

The Maculate Muse

1 Obscene Language and the
Development of Attic Comedy

The plays of Aristophanes burst with jokes and buffoonery of all kinds: in the service of satire, abuse, parody, irony, and surrealistic absurdity are countless plays on words, comic distortions of proper names, ludicrous and extravagant compounds, constant shifting between different proprieties of diction, verbal surprises, equivocations, deceptions. Although the physical action must have been fast-paced and colorful, it is primarily in his verbal pyrotechnics that the genius of Aristophanes (and the writers of Old and Middle Attic Comedy in general) resides.[1] The Athens of the middle fifth century was itself fascinated, even infatuated, with words and their power;[2] its citizens listened intently and with great sophistication to the clever speakers who mounted the *bema;* to be a polished and urbane orator and debater was a highly prized accomplishment; to be slow and clumsy with words meant second-class consideration.

Already the ground was being prepared for the great studies of rhetoric, dialectic, linguistics, and genre that would appear in a constant flow from the late fifth century on. Playwrights were required, no less than the public speakers, to be verbally entertaining, to use the great subtlety and flexibility of Attic Greek to its best advantage. The audiences at Aristophanes' plays were the same quick-witted public that attended the tragedies; they expected the same sophistication in both genres—more so, perhaps, from comic poets: in comedy there is no mythological grandeur and high emo-

---

1. For systematic discussions of Aristophanes' comic methods, see W. Starkie, *Acharnians,* pp. xxxviii ff., an analysis from the pseudo-Aristotelian *Tractatus Coislinianus* (in Kaibel, pp. 50 ff.; Cantarella, 1: 33 ff.); L. Grasberger, *Die griechischen Stichnamen* (Würzburg, 1883), pp. 11 ff.; C. Holzinger, *De Verborum Lusu apud Aristophanem* (Vienna, 1876); O. Froehde, *Beiträge zur Technik der alten attischen Komödie* (Leipzig, 1898).

2. Cf. Grasberger (n. 1, above), pp. 11 ff.

1

tion to absorb the audience's attention, little opportunity to dilate upon a theme. The action must move quickly, and one joke must give way to another as soon as its brief impact disappears. While tragedy kept to a single, stylized verbal plane, a comedy that hoped for success had to draw on any and all resources of the language, from the highest to the most mundane and vulgar.

The sexual and excremental areas of human activity figure prominently in the comic material of early Attic Comedy; there is no type of joke or comic business, however sophisticated, which does not make use of them to provoke laughter. Alongside the constant use of unadorned obscenity—words like πέος, cock, κύσθος, cunt, and πρωκτός, ass-hole—is an even greater abundance of double meanings, both invented by the poet for the occasion or already common in Attic slang. These are important elements of Aristophanes' art and contribute just as much to the meaning of his plays as any other;[3] but before we attempt to identify and discuss the particular varieties and literary uses of obscene language in Attic Comedy, which is the task of the following chapters, we must first try to analyze the impact of obscenity in general on the spectator of Old Comedy. Why did obscene language figure so prominently in the plays? Where did it come from and why does it appear to be an exclusively Attic phenomenon? Why did it die out so quickly as an acceptable part of comic writing?

We must begin by clarifying our terms. By "obscenity" we mean verbal reference to areas of human activity or parts of the human body that are protected by certain taboos agreed upon by prevailing social custom and subject to emotional aversion or inhibition. These are in fact the sexual and excremental areas. In order to be obscene, such a reference must be made by an explicit expression that is itself subject to the same inhibitions as the thing it describes. Thus, to utter one of the numerous words, to be found in any language, which openly (noneuphemistically) describe the tabooed organs or actions is tantamount to exposing what should be hidden. Our ability to expose the forbidden by using words gives these words a kind of magical power. I shall return to this point soon.

The Greeks did not have a special term for this kind of language as distinguished from any language considered insulting or for any reason socially unacceptable. Our concept of the obscene derives from the Latin *obscenus*. It might be worthwhile to sketch briefly the difference between our ideas of obscenity and those of the Greeks.

Obscenus, whether originally from *caenum* (Priscian 9.54, followed by W.-Hofmann s.v. *caenum*), or *scaena* (Varro *LL* 7.96, quare turpe ideo

---

3. A full treatment of the dramatic and poetic uses of obscenity in Aristophanes will be given in chapter 3.

obscenum quod·nisi in scaena palam dici non debet; see Ernout-Meillet), or *scaeuus* (Varro *LL* 7.97, followed by Thierfelder, p. 107 ff.),[4] clearly means filthy, repulsive, hateful, disgusting, offensive, and possessed of the power to stain and contaminate.[5] In the moral realm it meant exactly what most of us mean when we say *obscene*: filthy, indecent, offensive. Thus it could describe lewd pleasures (Cic. *ND* 1.40. 111), adultery (Ov. *Tr.* 2.212), pictures (Prop. 2.5.19, 6.27), verses (Prop. 1.16.10), gestures (Tac. *An.* 15.37, cf. Suet. *Calig.* 56), jokes (Cic. *Off.* 1.29.104), shameful things generally (Quint. 8.3.38, Cic. *Off.* 1.35.127, quodque facere non turpe est, modo occulte, id dicere obscenum est; cp. 1.35.128), even the genitals themselves (Ov. *M* 9.347; Mel. 3.7; Suet. *Calig.* 58). Obviously, the Roman word shared with ours the notion that words which describe tabooed sexual or excremental organs or functions are somehow dirty as well as shameful; the natural induction is that the organs and functions are themselves dirty and shameful. It is no secret that such a feeling was present in Roman culture, though perhaps not in the degree to which the stringent prohibitions of Puritanism and Victorianism have influenced modern feelings. Undoubtedly the term *obscenus* entered popular speech from its original use as an augural term meaning inauspicious, unfavorable, or evil-boding;[6] thus the idea of *res mali ominis* passes to the tabooed areas, which then become, along with the words which describe them, *obscena*.

The Greek words that come closest to being *voces propriae* for what we have described as obscenity are those which derive from the root *aizd-: αἰδέομαι, αἰδώς, αἰδοῖος, αἰσχρός, αἶσχος, αἰσχύνομαι, and so on. All seem to imply shame, fear, reverence, or ugliness.[7] Any activity, person, or thing which is shameful, ugly, fearful, or to be revered can be described by using one of these words; the valuation of sexual and excremental organs and functions is but one area of their utility. There seems to be no suggestion of filthiness or harmfulness, as there is in *obscenus* and *obscene*. The primary notion is that of shame and modesty. Thus in the Nausicaa episode

---

4. A. Thierfelder, "Obscaenus," *Navicula Chilonensis. Studia Philologica F. Jacoby Oblata* (Leiden, 1956), pp. 107 ff. For complete citations, see Kuhlmann in *ThLL* IX.2 s.v. *obscenus*.

5. Cf. Vergil *A.* 3.241, 262; 7.417; Pliny 10.29.44, etc. Of excrement itself, Sen. *Ep.* 8.1.20; of urine, Ov. *RAm* 437.

6. Cf. Vergil *A.* 12.876 (birds); *G.* 1.470; Suet. *Galba* 4 (dogs); Cic. *Dom.* 55.140 (omens); Hor. *Ep.* 5.98 (old woman); other citations in Thierfelder and Kuhlmann (n. 4, above).

7. Cf. the cognates *aistan* (Goth. = fear); Ger. *Ehre*; Lat. *aestimo*; Goth. *aiwiski* (= αἰσχύνη). See Frisk, Chantraine s.v. The fullest treatment of the concept is C. von Erffa, *ΑΙΔΩΣ*, *Philol. Supplbd.* 30 (1937). See also Th. Hopfner, *Das Sexualleben der Griechen und Römer* (Prague, 1938), pp 17 ff.

of the *Odyssey* the young maiden says she is afraid (αἴδετο) to tell her father of her θαλερὸν γάμον (6.66 f.) or to be seen accompanying Odysseus back to the city (6.273 f.). Similar is Odysseus' reaction to bathing with the young ladies (221 f.),

> αἰδέομαι γὰρ
> γυμνοῦσθαι κούρῃσιν ἐϋπλοκάμοισι μετελθών

[For I am ashamed to be naked among fair-haired young ladies.]

Compare the goddesses' unwillingness to look on Ares and Aphrodite (8.324) and Penelope's to be with the suitors alone (18.184). Someone who *is* willing to do these things is, of course, ἀναιδής: his actions are immodest, shameless, and therefore ugly and offensive, αἰσχρός.[8] The same rationale lies behind the use of αἰδώς to indicate the genitals,[9] as in *Il.* 2.262, 22.75. The more common αἰδοῖος seems to have meant something close to "worthy of respect."[10]

Two more specifically sexual passages are worth mentioning. In Pindar's *Ninth Pythian,* Apollo has come across the huntress-maiden, Cyrene, in the glens of Pelion and has conceived a strong passion to deflower her on the spot (36 f.). But the centaur Cheiron admonishes him that gods and men alike must have the modesty and restraint (αἰδέοντ', 41) not to consummate a marriage in the light of day, that is, without the ceremonies proper to a wedding. These, as Pindar tells us (12), are properly carried out by the happy couple in Libya, where Aphrodite "cast a charming veil of modesty (ἐρατὰν αἰδώ) over their sweet union" (we may compare this with Hera's admonition to Zeus at *Il.* 14.330 ff. about sleeping out on Ida). Similar is Herodotus' story of Candaules' wife (1.8 ff.). Candaules, king of Lydia, was so taken by his wife's beauty that he forced his trusty guard, Gyges, to sneak a look for himself and thus confirm his opinion. Gyges at first tried to refuse by pointing out that a woman sheds her modesty (αἰδώς) when she sheds her clothing, but was finally forced to comply. Unfortunately, the wife saw Gyges and determined that one or the other of her admirers must die; Herodotus points out that, among the Lydians, being seen naked brings great disgrace (αἰσχύνην μεγάλην, 10), even for a man. Both of these passages emphasize a peculiarly sexual meaning of αἰδώς and its cognates

8. Von Erffa (n. 7, above), pp. 19 ff.

9. Ibid., pp. 39 f.

10. This usage seems to be confined to Greek; as for the Latin equivalent, von Erffa, p. 40, rightly points out that "im Lateinischen begegnet die Bezeichnung 'pudenda' oder 'reverenda' erst spät und wohl im Anschluss ans Griechische" [In Latin the designation *pudenda* or *reverenda* appears for the first time only late, and indeed in imitation of Greek usage].

which harmonizes with all other spheres of the word's significance: namely, the notion of modesty, restraint, and a feeling of decency and secrecy
surrounding what is private (but not "dirty," as we moderns might say).
In the Pindar passage especially, one notices an important double-edged
concept: αἰδώς denotes both the intimacy of sexual activity and an ethical
impulse to restrain its exposure.

These Homeric examples may stand as valid for the entire classical
period. The basic idea of shame and modesty, but without dirtiness, remained unchanged despite the sophistications made by poets and theorists.
In Greek, the sexual and excremental realms were categorized as a subdi-
vision of all those areas which must be treated with respect and modesty.

Contributing to this idea was the Greek conception of all passions and
drives as inborn necessities of life against which one cannot struggle successfully. This was especially true of divine Eros:[11] examples are so abundant that citation is unnecessary. Indeed, one might say that the Athenians of the fifth century viewed sexuality in almost all of its manifestations as an essentially healthy and enjoyable fact of life. There is no
indication of the kind of guilty, inhibited, and repressive feelings so characteristic of later societies in regard to this area of human life. The Athenians of this era may not have been uninhibited children of nature, but
their inhibitions concerning human sexuality were certainly less muddled
by complicated feelings of shame and guilt than our own. I shall return to
this point in the following chapter.

Φύσις was, in fact, a not uncommon euphemism for the sexual organs
(*LSJ* s.v. VII.2; see also O. Weinreich, *RhM* 77 [1928]: 112). We find
mention of these "necessities of nature" with reference to the genitals in the
comic poets: τὰς τῆς φύσεως ἀνάγκας (N 1075), τὴν ἀναγκαίαν φύσιν
(Philem. 4.6), φύσιν (Anaxandr. 33.18, Alexis 240.8), τὴν ἀναγκαίαν
τύχην (Amphis 20). When the sexual drives are regarded as natural urges
to be viewed with the proper respect and guarded by modesty, there can be
no place for the judgment implied by *obscenus*.[12]

The use of improper (noneuphemistic) words to describe these urges was
no more obscene than the urges themselves: one must guard against saying
them in public and in polite company not because they are dirty but because they stand for what one keeps to himself. One would no more say
πέος at a dinner party than actually expose himself. But there was no
special term to describe such language: to speak of anything out of place

11. The subject is well covered by H. Schreckenberg, *Ananke* (Munich, 1964), pp. 58 f.

12. See the illuminating discussion by E. R. Dodds, *The Greeks and the Irrational* (Berkeley, 1964), chap. 2, "From Shame-Culture to Guilt-Culture." Also excellent is K. Latte,
"Schuld und Sünde in der griechischen Religion," *Arch.f.Rel.* 20 (1920–21): 254 ff.

was to speak shamelessly or insultingly (αἰσχρολογεῖν). Gentlemen did
not speak of such things, but only of noble, or at any rate high-minded,
matters (cf. Xen. *Lac.* 5.6). A common way of illustrating this was to say
that, had our maker wanted us to flout our intimate parts, he would not
have put them out of the way; therefore we ought to keep our language
similarly concealing.[13]

By way of contrast, compare Cicero *Off.* 1.35.128: latrocinari fraudare
adulterare re turpe est, sed dicitur non obscene, it is in fact base to deceive,
to commit adultery, to pillage, but one may speak of these things without
being obscene. To a Roman certain sexual and scatological expressions
were themselves unclean, but if one used the proper language, talk of
morally reprehensible matters was permitted. But a Greek would consider anything reprehensible to be αἰσχρόν and therefore an unfit topic for
conversation. That is, the Greeks had no word that could make the distinction Cicero makes: αἰσχρολογεῖν (e.g. at Pl. *Rep.* 3.395e) has a much
wider coverage, as well as a very different meaning, than *obscene*. A man
who does not possess tact is characterized by qualities that put him outside
the pale of proper society: βδελυρία, disgusting behavior (Thphr. *Ch.*
11.1 f.), ἀγροικία, rusticity (ibid., 4.4), ἀπόνοια, tactlessness (ibid.,
= μηδεμίαν αἰσχρὰν ἐργασίαν ἀποδοκιμάσαι, the readiness to commit
any shameful act).

This feeling of shame that comes from being exposed or listening to
words that expose what should be covered up is crucial to our understanding of obscenity in Old Comedy, indeed for the understanding of obscenity
throughout the history of Greek literature up to the end of Old (and some
Middle) Comedy. For the obscenity used in this early literature is different in character, purpose, and social function from what was written
later in Greece, and from obscenity as it appeared in Roman and subsequent literature.

To explain the difference it is necessary first to differentiate between
pornography and obscenity.[14] Both may refer to the sexual and excremental (although true pornography seldom refers to the latter) but their
motivation and effect are completely different. Pornography plays upon
our sexual fantasies by constructing dream worlds in which our longings

13. The best description is Longinus 43.5 f.; the first appearance of the idea is Xen.
Mem. 1.4.6. See D. Russell, *Longinus* (Oxford, 1964), ad loc. and A. Pease, "Caeli Enarrant," *HThRev* 34 (1941): 163 ff.

14. Perhaps the best study of the two as literary phenomena is E. Mertner and H.
Mainusch, *Pornotopia: Das Obszöne und die Pornographie in der literarischen Landschaft* (Frankfurt am Main, 1970); see also P. Gorsen, *Das Prinzip Obszön. Kunst Pornographie und Gesellschaft* (Reinbeck bei Hamburg, 1969) and, from an author's standpoint, D. H. Lawrence,
Pornography and Obscenity (London, 1929).

for sexual gratification are satisfied with no effort on our part. We are allowed to look at and enjoy the objects of our sexual desires; they and rendered passive and gratify us automatically. All the initiative, hazards, and responsibilities that must be faced in real life are bypassed. Thus pornography is introverted; its target is autoeroticism and private imaginings.[15] It goes without saying that pornography is best suited to books that can be read in private. It is difficult to imagine a pornographic play or social function in the style of Greek theater: the emotions aroused by pornographic actions or descriptions cannot be shared with others and cannot produce comedy.[16] Pornography demands a darkened theater or the privacy of an easychair. The pleasures it offers are the vicarious pleasures of sexual acts themselves.

Obscenity is by nature extroverted; that is why pornography usually avoids it, preferring the stimulating effects of suggestive language to the naked impact of obscene words.[17] The effect of obscenity is to break through social taboos rather than to escape them in fantasy.[18] Thus obscenity is most often used to insult someone; to emphasize what one is saying in the most forceful possible way; to make curses; to add power to comedy, jokes, ridicule, or satire.[19] Its efficacy in all these functions resides in its ability to uncover what is forbidden, and thus to shock, anger, or amuse. The pleasure afforded by obscenity lies in our enjoyment at exposing someone else or seeing someone else exposed without having to effect the exposure physically.

Very often this exposure is hostile and serves to degrade its object, but sometimes it is used only to excite amusement or pleasure in the audience by arousing their sexual feelings, for instance, by describing sexual intercourse with a young girl. The difference between the latter

15. Mertner and Mainusch (n. 14, above), p. 120.

16. Ibid., p. 40: "Ganz im Gegensatz zur Pornographie ist das Obszöne in der Lage, sich vom Bezirk des primitiv Sinnlichen zu befreien, ohne ihn zu verlassen. Im Bereich des Komischen ist das augenfällig. Es gibt den obszönen Witz, aber keinen pornographischen" [Obscenity, in complete contrast to pornography, is in the position of being able to free itself from the limited range of the primitively sensual without actually abandoning it. This is conspicuously true of the realm of the comic. There are obscene jokes, but no pornographic ones].

17. Ibid., p. 110. There *are* pornographic writings that make use of direct and non-euphemistic language in their descriptions, but the tendency in almost all cases is toward the avoidance of literalness or harshness of language. It was not until toward the end of the nineteenth century that pornographers began to include crass and obscene descriptions in their works, but even today the great majority aim for florid and oblique (even sentimental) language.

18. Ibid., pp. 88 f.

19. Ibid., pp. 185 f.

pleasure and pornographic pleasure is one of intention and tone: pornography seeks to arouse detailed fantasies that fulfill wishes the listener considers in some way forbidden, while the obscene allusion to sexuality in Old Comedy arouses only the amusement of a brief and uninhibited release of sexual feelings. There are no feelings of guilt and fear behind such a release because the acts described were not themselves considered dirty or illicit, but only, on all public occasions (save at comedies), private. This simple excitation of pleasurable feelings (or hostile ones) was, as we shall see, also characteristic of much of the obscenity found in the iambic poets and perhaps (although we cannot be certain) in the cults as well.

In Greek literature what can be called pornography did not make its appearance until well after the decline of Old Comedy, when the conception of love was becoming more romantic, more spiritualized, more capable of description in a way that emphasized pathological analysis and suggestive sensibility.[20] Since obscenity tends to unmask and destroy the fantasies pornography constructs, obscene language tends to disappear from the literary scene and is replaced by titillating euphemisms. The erotic intrigues of New Comedy and Hellenistic poetry (apart from the pornographic epigram) do not admit coarse, direct speech; tasteful nuance is more stimulating.

The obscenities in Old Comedy do not serve to stimulate extended or detailed sexual fantasies; they are meant to make us laugh. Thus not all of them have the character of unadorned obscenity or smut: most are retailed in the form of jokes, using all the technical properties available to any other kind of joke. The majority of these jokes are cast in the form of double entendre and allusion, a process that replaces an outright obscenity by something innocent but similar, but that in fact serves to emphasize the original obscenity in a comical way.

Naturally, not all such replacement mechanisms are comical: when Euripides (*Ph.* 18) or Sophocles (*OT* 1211) refer to a wife as ἄλοξ, furrow, we realize at once that this is a metaphor, and a grand one at that. The physical reference is unmistakable but we do not feel that it is obscene: the context, the respectable nature of agricultural terminology, and the remoteness of the image save it. The same is true of straightforward euphemisms like συγγενέσθαι, be with, or τὸ μόριον, the part, where the reference is clear but the language deliberately vague and abstract.

On the other hand, obscene double entendres derive their impact from the generally low or amusing points of comparison they employ: thus χοῖ-

20. The whole topic is definitively treated in part 1 of E. Rohde, *Der griechische Roman und seine Vorläufer*[3] (Leipzig, 1914); see especially pp. 59 f.

ρος (cunt/piggie) in popular Attic slang emphasizes the physical reference in a comical way rather than disguising or ennobling it, just as the *redender Name* Kinesias in *Lysistrata* renders a character obscenely comical by allegorizing his state of sexual excitement. In this manner the obscene double entendre has much in common with the language of slang; often the two are distinct only in that slang is common to the language, while double entendres can be invented for specific comic purposes. The use of more sophisticated joke-mechanisms is therefore due, not to inhibition or a desire to divert our attention from what is really meant, but just the opposite: to intensify the obscenity and render it more potent than the inert, blunt *vox propria* would be. The force of Old Comedy and its success in competition depended on the level of verbal sophistication attained by the poet, including (and especially) in the realm of the obscene.

It is in this light, incidentally, that we must perhaps interpret Aristophanes' continual insistence that his use of obscene comedy was different from that of his (he says) less gifted contemporaries. He maintains that he avoids κακὰ καὶ φόρτον καὶ βωμολοχεύματ᾽ ἀγεννῆ, lowness, vulgarity and sordid clowning (P 748) and πονηρὰ σκώμματα, evil scurrility (N 542), and gives examples of the kind of material that only poets like Phrynichus, Lycis, and Ameipsias would stoop to using (N 537 ff., V 58 ff., P 739 ff., R 1 ff.). His own comedy claims to be σώφρων τῇ φύσει, chaste in its nature (N 537, cf. Eq 545) because of its great "technical sophistication" (P 749), and the poet's anger is vehement when his carefully prepared jests are beaten in competition by ἄνδρες φορτικοί, vulgar people (N 524): ὅστις οὖν τούτοισι γελᾷ, τοῖς ἐμοῖς μὴ χαιρέτω, whoever laughs at such things will not enjoy my wit (N 560). These are perhaps not merely idle boasts designed to win over judges but reflect the real difference between the technical prowess of an Aristophanes and that of his fellow comic poets. Jokes "snitched from the Megarians" (V 57), which "always get a laugh" (R 2), are used only by those who cannot invent new jokes or vary the old ones in unexpected and imaginative ways.[21]

The purpose, then, of the obscenities in Attic Comedy, whether outright obscene words or comically disguised references, was not to stimulate extended and detailed fantasies in the audience, in the manner of pornography, but to open the sexual and excremental areas of human activity to public view. As we have seen, these words and expressions, like the acts to which they refer, were not felt to be dirty in and of themselves, but subject only to feelings of shame, modesty, and a certain taboo. To utter them was

21. See Th. Gelzer, "Aristophanes," *RE Supplbd.* 12 (1971), 1527.6 ff., 1541.18–1542.7, who gives as examples of typical jokes turned to new uses Eq 24 f., N 634 ff., V 1388 ff., P 871 ff., E 311 ff., 877 ff.

verbally to expose the parts to which they refer. But to whose shame? Who was exposed? Not the audience, certainly; they suffered nothing more by listening to obscenities than they suffered by looking at the exceedingly graphic pictures of sexual acts of all kinds that were depicted routinely and openly in pictorial and plastic art throughout the fifth century. Unlike the Romans and ourselves, to whom obscene words are automatically offensive because of their intrinsically evil, staining, and dirty nature, the Greeks who watched Old Comedy took great pleasure in them, just as in their private lives they took uninhibited pleasure in the acts to which the obscenities referred. The reason is that they could in the theater safely watch someone *else* being exposed, someone *else* losing his protective cover of modesty and shame. The unfortunate victims of this public exposure were in fact (*a*) the characters on stage and (*b*) other, extradramatic targets of the poet's attacks whose exposure the poet felt would amuse the audience. We must now turn our attention to the particular comic mechanisms involved in these exposures.

Obviously it is impossible in civilized societies to act out one's hostilities whenever and however one wishes, just as it is impossible to see and touch at will what is forbidden. Obscene words replace physical aggression; they compel the person to whom they are directed to imagine the part of the body or the activity they describe, and thus show that the person who utters them is also imagining these things. We note the role of smutty language in *sexual* aggression where the motive is seduction (undressing and touching) as well as in *hostility* where the motive is the exposure of an enemy's hidden parts (degradation). The inhibitions imposed on such aggressiveness by society, as well as the resistance of the listener to his exposure by obscene words, open the way for the introduction of a third person whose presence makes comic or degrading exposure possible.[22] That is, the first person, frustrated in his desire to expose the second person, toward whom his aggressiveness is directed (whether hostile or libidinous), calls on a third person to be his ally. The first person's obscene speech exposes the second before the third, who in turn derives pleasure from the effortless satisfaction of his own libido or hostility.

Now the naked uttering of obscenity is itself sufficient to bring about pleasure in the third person (and satisfaction to the first). But when the obscenity is also a joke—a play on words, an allusion or other witticism— the pleasure is increased immensely. Thus we can expose and exploit something very sensitive and vulnerable in another person, which owing to the

22. The most enlightening discussion is that of Freud in his brilliant and amusing *Jokes and their Relation to the Unconscious*, trans. J. Strachey (New York, 1960) [= *Der Witz und seine Beziehung zum Unbewussten, Ges. Werke* VI].

obstacles imposed by civilized society could not be brought out openly. Moreover, we derive further pleasure from the presence of the third party in that (*a*) the third party enjoys our joke and (*b*) takes sides with us because of his enjoyment. That is, the pleasure derived by the third party from our joke makes him disinclined to examine the grounds of our aggressiveness dispassionately and in general disarms serious or critical thought. The presence of a joke also modifies the *appearance* of aggressiveness and thus makes it easier and less potentially dangerous to laugh at someone else's expense.[23]

The same mechanism is at work at a comic performance. The role of the third person is assumed by the audience, which is thus free to enjoy the exposure of other people, particularly people whose political, intellectual, or even divine authority in the community is so great that open attack or ridicule in any other form would be out of the question. Moreover, the comic poet has at his disposal all the resources of the stage, which yield infinitely more possibilities for exposure than any personal situation. The playwright can actually bring his targets onto the stage, actually show them in their dependence on bodily parts or drives, put obscene words in their mouths, or have other characters make them the targets of obscene exposures. All the techniques of caricature, mimicry, parody, travesty, disguise, burlesque, and slapstick are available to augment the inherently humorous spectacle that is afforded by the use of obscenity to expose someone else.[24] In addition, the nature of the comic performance itself intensifies the pleasure afforded by this process: the expectation of the comic, the festival atmosphere that prevails, the playwright's license to do and say what he wants, the audience's tonic mood of cheerfulness, and the lighthearted, joking, exaggerated manner in which the exposures are effected.[25]

We can now account for the incredible abundance of obscene jokes and situations in Attic Comedy: they are there precisely because the areas of sexuality and scatology in comedy offer especially deep and satisfying pleasure and thus well serve the release of hostile or sexual aggressiveness through laughter.[26] Again, it must be emphasized that the words and situations were themselves innocuous as long as the audience was merely a spectator; obscenity was not considered inherently evil or offensive. It was the shame of exposure that made obscenity obscene for the Greeks; the goal of unmasking and degrading invented comic figures (e.g. the Sausage-

23. This may help to explain the importance of jokes and witticisms in rhetorical persuasion: see Cic. *de orat.* 2.216–289; Quint. 6.3; Gorgias Frag. B 12 (Diels-Kranz).
24. Freud, p. 200 ff. (= *G.W.* 227 ff.).
25. Ibid., 218 ff. (= *G.W.* 249 ff.).
26. Ibid., 221 f. (= *G.W.* 252 f.).

Seller, Strepsiades, Lampito, Kinesias and Myrrhine, or Blepyrus) and real-life targets of hostility (e.g. Cleon, Cleisthenes, or Ariphrades) made obscenity an indispensable and crucial mechanism in an art form whose most notable function was ridicule, satire, parody, and caricature.[27]

Thus the use of sexual and scatological detail in comic degradation and exposure was but one of several powerful methods of producing laughter through ridicule and attack. We find the same sort of obscenity in the fragments of all the other writers of Old Comedy, although the intact state of eleven of Aristophanes' plays might give the impression (probably false) that he was more obscene than the others. The basic nature of Old Comedy was negative, critical, and aggressive; the object was to expose its victims to ridicule and abuse. Although the comic poets often claim to be advising the state and delivering the clearest programs for right action (A 656 ff., V 650 ff., L 1112 ff., R 686 ff.), the tone is usually ironic and jesting. When someone or something *is* praised positively it is inevitably an abstraction like the Good Old Days or the spirit of the Marathonomachai; the salvation of the polis that we see presented on stage is a comic utopia founded by grotesque caricatures who are themselves targets of comic exposure.

Thus, in *Peace*, it is Trygaeus and his outrageous assault on Olympus which bring back peace; there is no mention in the play of the actual peace negotiated by Nicias a short time before. The poet might insert serious thought into his parabasis or (occasionally) elsewhere, but the advice itself always turns out to be most general and unadventuresome. In any case, the audience did not expect positive enlightenment on private, political, or social dilemmas;[28] it expected negative criticism and scurrilous exposures

27. Compared to Old Comedy, the indecency of the sly double entendres and off-color remarks of Roman and English Restoration comedy look very tame indeed. The social strictures, the offensive nature of obscenity itself, and the ethos of these later comic forms prohibited the kind of light-hearted and large-scale use of blatant obscenity that we find in Old Comedy.

28. See W. Schmid, *Die altattische Komödie* (= Schmid-Stählin, *Geschichte der griechischen Literatur* 1, no. 4 [1946]), pp. 14 ff. A thorough discussion of the negative characteristics of Old Comedy in its criticism of society is that of A. Meder, *Die attische Demokratie zur Zeit des peloponnesischen Krieges im Lichte zeitgenössischen Quellen* (Lengerich, 1938), pp. 15 ff. The remarks of K. J. Dover, *Aristophanic Comedy* (Berkeley and Los Angeles, 1972), pp. 52 f., are worth quoting. "The 'good advice' offered to the community by an Aristophanic parabasis, when it is not extolling the merits of the poet himself at the expense of his rivals, tends always to be advice which is acceptable at the level of popular sentiment, even if it is not always accepted and put into practice. It is acceptable because of its essentially conciliatory character, promoting that *homonoia*, 'community of mind,' which was regarded as strengthening the city against external enemies. The clearest example is the least jocular of parabases, *Frogs* 686–705 and 718–737."

of those whom the poet found risible or whom he considered to stand in the way of enlightened polity. This may account for the fact that the great majority of all the obscenities uttered in most Aristophanic comedies are uttered by the hero, whose function is usually to take comic revenge on authorities of all kinds.

That we do not find obscenity anywhere else in the surviving literature of the time, or hear it mentioned in any other connection (nor can we imagine another context in which it might have been employed), testifies to its unique appropriateness to the phenomenon of Old Comedy. There are two exceptions: the Ionian iambic poets and the cults of (above all) Dionysus and Demeter. These have a crucial importance in the development of Old Comedy and the inclusion of obscenity therein as a central method of comic degradation, abuse, and ridicule. It is to these backgrounds that we must now turn our attention.

We may begin with the cults.[29] The appearance of obscenity in cults and celebrations whose purpose is to promote fertility, make rain, initiate youths, celebrate multiple births, or mark other important occasions, is universal. The efficacy of obscenity in such activities is sometimes sympathetic, in that the naming of sexual organs and acts aids fertility, or apotropaic, in that evil powers do not like obscenity.[30] Whatever the reason, obscenity, usually restricted, is considered on these special oc-

29. Most of the evidence is given by H. Fluck, *Skurrile Riten in griechischen Kulten* (Endingen, 1931), although his conclusions, especially the one that all obscenity in cult is apotropaic, cannot be accepted. There is a critique in L. Deubner, *Attische Feste* (Berlin, 1932), p. 267.

30. Apotropaic obscenity is unlikely to have been used much in Greek cults; obscenity was not considered frightening or particularly harmful in itself. M. Nilsson's remarks on the phallus are most instructive (*Geschichte der griechischen Religion* 1³ [Munich, 1967]: 118 f.): "So wurde der Phallos von den Griechen als ein Heiltum betrachtet, nicht als ein *fascinum,* dessen Unanständigkeit böse Einflüsse abwehrt. Ein Glaube an die Wirkung unanständiger Gebärden als Gegenzauber bestand allerdings, beschränkte sich aber hauptsächlich auf die weibliche Organe. Dem Phallos und dem Geschlechtsakt standen die Griechen fast ebenso unbefangen gegenüber wie Tierzüchter; das zeigen eine ganz Anzahl Vasen, die wegen ihrer für unsere Begriffe anstössigen Bilder nicht ausgestellt werden können—von den Komödiendichtern nicht zu sprechen. Die Römer dagegen besassen dieselbe Art des Schamgefühls wie wir, und bei ihnen ist der Phallos *fascinum*" [Thus the phallus of the Greeks came to be regarded as a holy thing, not as a *fascinum* whose indecency warded off evil influences. To be sure, a belief in the efficacy of indecent gestures as countermagic did persist, but for the most part it was restricted to the female organs. In regard to the phallus and the sex act, the Greeks were as dispassionate as animal breeders, a fact demonstrated by a great multitude of vases whose illustrations are to our minds too shocking to be exhibited, to say nothing of the comic poets. The Romans, on the other hand, possessed the same feelings of modesty as we, and so for the Romans the phallus was *fascinum.*]

casions to be good luck and great fun. Its public use marks a complete departure from the ordinary: what is ordinarily forbidden is sanctioned on certain days. In our discussion we will be concerned not with such innocent magical practices as the obscenity that accompanies the planting of cumin,[31] rue, and basil,[32] or the trimming of hedges,[33] but with communal festivals of which obscenity was a major, standard feature. The importance of these cults for our examination of Old Comedy resides not simply in the presence of obscenity but in its context: obscenity is almost always cast in the form of ritual strife and abuse.[34]

When Aristotle (*Pol.* 7.1336ᵇ 17) advises men in authority to ban from the ideal polis pictures and literature with obscene content, he makes an exception for the cults for which custom prescribes scurrility (τωθασ-μός).[35] The word τωθάζειν means mock at or jeer (cf. V 1362) but undoubtedly derives from the ritual mockery of the cults. For Aristotle the mockery is synonymous with obscenity; we may compare another word for obscene mockery, στηνιῶσαι (Hsch.), which derives from the Stenia festival of Demeter. As Farnell remarks, the αἰσχρολογία of the cults was "no mere casual and licentious *jeu d'esprit*, the coarseness of a crowd of

31. Thphr. *HP* 8.3.3, 11.8.5; Stob. 2.31, 83; Pliny *NH* 19.120.

32. Palladius *de re rust.* 4.9; Pliny *NH* 19.120.

33. Thphr. *HP* 9.8.8.

34. Like other ancient and certain modern societies (e.g. Japan), which consider a man's good reputation among his fellows of the highest importance and take very much to heart the slightest ridicule or mockery, the Greeks sanctioned ritual mockery and abuse, probably for cathartic purposes, at certain specified times and always under the auspices of a god. Like such scurrilous combats in other societies, ritual Greek abuse seems to have followed standardized canons of organization and language, and usually to have been carefully rehearsed or planned rather than spontaneous or free-form. In a society so sensitive to insults, the sanction of a holiday was demanded before public abuse (and obscenity) could take place. At no other time could it have been tolerated or deemed acceptable, although a man (an iambic poet, for example) might at any time wish to curse or slander another man for purely personal reasons. (See the lucid discussion of R. C. Elliott, *The Power of Satire: Magic, Ritual, Art* [Princeton, N. J., 1960], pp. 66 ff.) Our survey will not make use of the abundant evidence from many cultures regarding the abusive and combative nature of ritual obscenity. There is ample enough material from Greece itself. Those who are interested may consult J. G. Frazer, *The Golden Bough*³ (New York, 1935), 1: 287 ff. (rites including the hurling of filth), 267 f., 269, 284 n.; 3: 154 f.; 7: 62 f.; 8: 280. Additional material in T. Allen, W. Halliday, and E. Sikes, *The Homeric Hymns*² (Oxford, 1963) at *h.Cer.*, pp. 195 ff. See also W. Thomas, *Primitive Behavior* (New York, 1937) and the excellent account of E. Evans-Pritchard, "Some Collective Expressions of Obscenity In Africa," *Journal of the Royal Anthropological Institute of Great Britain and Ireland* 59 (1929): 311 ff.

35. Hsch. glosses τωθάζει with χλευάζει, λοιδορεῖ, καυχᾶται, ἐρεθίζει, κακολογεῖ. Cf. also Suda, Poll. 5.161.

drunken revellers, but a ceremonious duty."[36] The obscenity was well controlled and organized, and the vehicle for its use was some form of abuse.

In the Haloa festival of Demeter, closed to men, we hear that there was much playfulness and gibing (παιδιαὶ πολλαὶ καὶ σκώμματα), with the women saying the most shameless things to each other, perhaps even holding models of the genitals.[37] At the Stenia, in which women celebrated the ἄνοδος of Demeter, there was similar abuse (διασκώπτουσιν καὶ λοιδοροῦσιν, Hsch.);[38] likewise at the Thesmophoria,[39] where the ritual obscenity was thought to derive from the good-natured jesting of the maid, Iambe, which cheered up the grieving goddess (*h.Cer.* 202 ff.). Baubo, the "orphic Iambe," cheered up the goddess by actually exposing herself;[40] she may be connected with the ὄλισβος (dildo) of Herod. 6.19. We find companies (ὁμιλίαι) of obscenity-hurlers at the Syracusan Demeter cult;[41] groups of men and women reviling each other in the Demeter festival at Pellene.[42] The Demeter-Kore surrogates,[43] Damis and Auxesia, had cults on Aegina and at Epidaurus in which *choregoi* undertook the training of female choruses for ritual abuse (Hdt. 5.83). Compare Herodotus' account (2.60) of the Egyptian Isis cult, in which men and women sail riotously in a boat to certain towns where they disembark to let certain women shout abuse (τωθάζουσι) at the women of the town; some dance and hitch up their skirts lewdly.

The cults of Dionysus are even more important, for it is in them that we find many of the elements developed by early dramatists into what we know as Old Comedy.[44] A fixture of these celebrations was the freedom to say what one wanted, like those who jested from wagons (τὰ ἐξ ἁμαξῶν σκώμματα) mocking each other (σκώπτειν ἀλλήλους).[45] These wagons carrying special bands of jokesters seem to have been standard in Dionysiac

36. *Cults of the Greek States* (Oxford, 1896), 3: 104.

37. Schol. Luc. *d.meretr.* 7.4; full description in Deubner (n. 29, above), pp. 60 ff.

38. Cf. T 834 (with schol.), Eub. 148.

39. Apollodorus 1.5.1.

40. Fluck (n. 29, above), p. 28; Nilsson (n. 30, above), 1:657, n. 2.

41. Diodor. 5.4.6.

42. Paus. 8.27.9; similar is the Anaphaia with its male and female choruses of mockers: Apol. Rhod. 4.1719 ff.; Apollodorus 1.9.26; Conon 49.

43. Their names are transparently fertility titles; see Fluck (n. 29, above), pp. 21 f.

44. The most brilliant and (to my mind) most persuasive reconstruction is that of H. Herter, *Vom dionysischen Tanz zum komischen Spiel. Die Anfänge der attischen Komödie* (Iserlohn, 1947). A full discussion and literature in G. Giangrande, "The Origin of Attic Comedy," *Eranos* 61 (1963): 1 ff.; A. W. Pickard-Cambridge, *Dramatic Festivals of Athens*[2] (London, 1968).

45. Schol. Luc. *JTr* 44; see Suda, Phot. s.v. τὰ ἐξ ἁμαξῶν, Harpocration s.v. πομπείας, πομπεύειν.

festivals, a particular part of the spectacle,[46] at least in the Anthesteria and
the Lenaea, and probably in other less important festivals as well. They
traveled in the Dionysiac processions (πομπαί)[47] and made scurrilous attacks on people of the community whom they saw.[48] It is now generally
agreed that such songs were composed especially for the Dionysiac φαλλι-
κά(of which Dicaeopolis' procession in *Acharnians* is a humorous takeoff),[49]
and that there may even have been the germs of a dramatic performance
inherent in the central lyric hymn;[50] certainly the likely development of
the κῶμος (of which the φαλλικά were part) into the primitive κωμῳδία
suggests early dramatic activity which incorporated strife and, in keeping
with the occasion, obscenity.[51] The recent demonstration by Herter[52] that
Attica, as well as the Peloponnese, at an early date possessed indigenous
ithyphallic-steatopygic "actors" in addition to the masked chorus makes
such a supposition all the more attractive. We must return to these points
presently.

Although the Eleusinian mysteries included no obscenity or ritual a-
buse[53]—perhaps because they were so solemn—the faithful *were* subjected
to scurrilous abuse on their way to the holy place, in a strange custom
known as the γεφυρισμός.[54] It is not clear whether this practice had any
religious connection; as Deubner remarked (*Attische Feste* [Berlin, 1932],
p. 73), "Dergleichen Neckereien konnten sich bei enger Passage leicht
genug einstellen." The γεφυρισταί probably organized as a thiasos (cf. Plu.
Sulla 2), stood on a bridge (or bridges) to mock those in the procession. Al-

46. περίοπται, schol. Luc. *Eun.* 2. See Pickard-Cambridge (n. 44, above), pp. 5, 12, 17,
24, 34, 38; Farnell (n. 36, above), 5: 212.

47. Men. 396; Dem. *Cor.* 11 (with schol. which equates πομπεύειν with λοιδορεῖν at 124).

48. *AB* I.316; Lyd. *Mens.* 4.56.

49. Schol. Eq. 546; D. H. 7.27, in comparing the ceremonies surrounding the Roman
triumph with the processions of wagons in the Dionysiac cults, adds that in his own day
they sang improvised ποιήματα, perhaps implying that in earlier days the poems were
fixed (written?). Could the obscene abuse in R 372 ff. be a takeoff on such abusive songs?
It certainly is not an example of γεφυρισμός, as has been thought. See L. Radermacher,
Frogs, ad loc., p. 203.

50. Radermacher, *Frogs,* p. 12; M. Pohlenz, "Die Entstehung der attischen Komödie,"
NGG 1949, Phil.-Hist. Kl., pp. 38 ff. There is a good discussion in Giangrande (n. 44,
above), pp. 18 f.

51. Literature in Giangrande, op. cit., pp. 3 f.; L. Breitholz, *Die dorische Farce* (Uppsala,
1960), pp. 50 ff. Obscenity would be likely in company with the phallus itself. See H.
Herter, "Phallos," *RE* 38 (1938): 1681 ff.; Nilsson (n. 30, above), 1: 118 ff., 590 ff.

52. (N. 44, above), pp. 16 ff., 22 ff.

53. Nilsson, op. cit., 1: 658; Deubner (n. 29, above), pp. 73 f.

54. Hsch. s.v. γεφυρίς, γεφυρισταί; Ammon. *Diff.* 128 Valck.; Suda s.v. γεφυρίζων; Fluck
(n. 29, above), p. 54, n. 1.

though we do not know for certain whether this mockery included ὀνομαστὶ κωμῳδεῖν,[55] the likelihood that it did is great.

The prominence of obscenity in the Attic fertility cults does not automatically mean that Old Comedy derived its obscenity from that source.
The cults do seem, however, to have contributed to the growth of obscenity as a standard and accepted element in the comic performances: the
use of obscene language to expose individuals and thus to make them
comic was a standard feature of the cults as well as the comedies that were
eventually part of them, and there can be little doubt that the suspension
of the ordinary taboos and restrictions of society in cult prepared the way
for the same extraordinary freedom enjoyed by comedy as part of the
artistic side of the Dionysian festivals.

Again it must be stressed that it was not merely the uttering of obscene
language which appealed to the comic poets; it was the use of obscenity as
a means of abuse, criticism, and degradation which attracted them and
challenged their ingenuity. The cults, with their tradition of ritual abuse,
would have provided them with the general freedom to develop this
method of attack as an art. Perhaps there was direct influence from the
cults in obscene choral strife, as in the battle between the old men and old
women in *Lysistrata*; the epirrhematic parts of the agon, parabasis, and
other choral interludes doubtless reflect ritual structures, although their
artistic development in the middle of the fifth century was due more to the
influence of the law courts, sophists, word duels, historical ἀντιλογίαι, and
tragic debates. But surely freeform abusive songs such as R 392 ff. can still
be found that imitate the obscene satirical hymns of the φαλλικά. Nevertheless, it is the iambic part of Old Comedy which contains the richest
obscenities and most frequent attacks of all kinds. Thus the Ionic literary
tradition of obscene and abusive iambic poetry seems a more direct artistic
inspiration for the Attic playwrights than the cults.

Archaic iambic poetry, unlike poetry that treated heroic myth, was, to
use the phrase of G. Meyer, the "Poesie des gesteigerten persönlichen Af-
fektes,"[56] poetry that described the πάθη of the poet directly, without the
formalities and remoteness required by the conventional subjects of epic
or—later—tragedy. Unlike lyric poets, writers of iambic verse were aggressive, antagonistic, often coarse, vulgar, obscene, vituperative. Their
public attacks on individuals relied for their forcefulness not only upon
their victims' almost morbid sensitivity to public ridicule but also upon the
belief that words, especially words sung by a poet, had magical and even

55. Hsch. is confusing the Dionysus cult with the mysteries when he says that it did.
56. G. Meyer, *Die stilistische Verwendung der Nominalkomposition im Griechischen*, Philol.
Supplbd. 16 (1923): 106 ff.

lethal power. The malefic individual *will* of the iambic poet could, through his words, become sovereign over the powers of nature. The legend that Archilochus wrote iambics so insulting that his enemy, Lycambes, along with his entire family, hanged themselves from shame may be closer to truth than to fiction. It is easy to imagine, after what we have said about the power of obscene words in exposure and degradation, what effect obscenity must have had in the hands of an Archilochus.[57]

The origins of this kind of poetry are to be found in the abusive αἰσχρολογία of the cults; the figure of Iambe is merely the personification of iambic invective. To speak in iambs is virtually the same as "to revile and abuse."[58] It is therefore no coincidence that the literary perfection of iambic poetry took place in areas where the cults were important. Archilochus, the great pioneer writer of iambic verse, was personally involved in the cult songs of Paros (120, 322)[59] (once called Demetrias and boasting ancient cults of Demeter and Dionysus) and worked in part from the inspiration he received from them;[60] indeed, he seems to have sung his deadly attack on Lycambes at the Demeter festival (see n. 57). This literary development of the iamb coincided with the transition from oral to written verse composition,[61] and so we are not surprised at the strong *public* tone in the poetry: the poet's invective, gossip, ridicule, and personal opinions were communicated openly for all to hear.

Thus the origins, development, and social function of the Ionic iambos, of which Archilochus, Hipponax, and Semonides are the chief representatives, seem to run parallel to those of Old Comedy. All the elements are there:[62] personal invective (Archilochus vs. Lycambes, Semonides vs. Oroecidas [Luc. *Pseud.* 2], Hipponax vs. Athenis and Bupalus, even A-

57. G. L. Hendrickson, "Aristophanes and the Victims of His Iambics," *AJP* 46 (1925): 101 ff.; Elliott (n. 34, above), pp. 1–15.

58. Arist. *Poet.* 1448ᵇ 32; Apollodorus 1.5.1; Phot; *EM*; schol. Nic. *Alexiph.* 132; ἰαμβίζειν, ἰαμβιστής, etc. The word *iambos* seems to be cognate with other sacral terms like *dithyrambos, thriambos, triumphus.* See H. Frisk, *Griechisches etymologisches Wörterbuch* (Heidelberg, 1960–72) s.v. for full discussion and additional literature. In the following discussion, references to iambic poets are to the edition of M. L. West, *Iambi et Elegi Graeci* (Oxford, 1971–72): A = Archilochus, H = Hipponax, etc.

59. Cf. also the prominence of Dionysus in the Monumentum Archilocheum: text in M. Treu, *Archilochos* (Munich, 1959), pp. 40 ff.

60. A good discussion of the primitive song that was the background of Archilochus's poetry and of its social context is K. J. Dover, "The Poetry of Archilochus," *Archiloque,* Fondation Hardt, *Entretiens sur l'antiquité classique* 10 (Geneva, 1964): 183 ff.

61. See D. Page, "Archilochus and the Oral Tradition," in *Archiloque* (n. 60, above), pp. 119 ff.

62. There is a full review in F. Brecht, *Motiv- und Typengeschichte der griechischen Spottepigramms, Philol. Supplbd.* 22 (1930).

nacreon [16D³]), literary invective (Hipponax vs. Mimnermus [153], Xenophanes vs. Homer and Hesiod [D.L. 9.18]), parody,[63] obscene exposures, flights of fantasy. In fact, the numerous connections, already recognized in antiquity,[64] between the writers of Old Comedy and the iambic poets suggest that the development of the ἰαμβικὴ ἰδέα at Athens was heavily influenced by these Ionian models.[65] We note that Cratinus wrote an *Archilochoi* as well as directly echoing Archilochus,[66] as does Aristophanes.[67] Aristophanes also contains Hipponactean reminiscences (L 361, R 661); so does Eupolis in *Baptai* (74).[68] Alexis wrote an *Archilochus*, and the comic poet Hermippus was an iambographer in the style of Archilochus. We might even say that our surviving fragment of the legendary comic poet Susarion is a direct descendant of the stylized iambic misogyny of Semonides. Certainly the obscenity and abuse of Old Comedy and iambic poetry were thought of by ancient critics as virtually identical.[69]

An examination of the terminology, techniques, and motivation of obscenity in these iambic writers shows this remarkable similarity in our own area of inquiry quite vividly. The fundamental purpose of obscene language in both genres seems to be exposure, whether hostile or libidinous (or both), although the iambists are of course much more personal and vehement than is usual in Attic comedy.[70]

Slang terms for the genitalia abound:[71]

---

63. Hipponax; see Athen. 15.698B. Cf. also the mock-epic *Margites*, fragments of which are now in West (n. 58, above), 2: 69 ff.

64. See the important remarks of Aristotle *Poet.* 1448ᵇ 38–1449ᵃ 6; cf. Athen. 14.622A-B.

65. G. Gerhard, "Iambographen," *RE* 9 (1916): 659 ff.; Meyer (n. 56, above), pp. 110 ff.; L. Weber, "*ΣΥΚΑ ΕΦ' 'ΕΡΜΗΙ*," *Philol.* 74 (1917): 96 ff.; A. von Blumenthal, *Die Schätzung des Archilochos im Altertume* (Stuttgart, 1922).

66. Frag. 109 and Cratin. 198; Frag. 168 and Cratin. 10. Cf. Schmid (n. 28, above), p. 12, n. 2; Platonius in Kaibel, p. 6.

67. A 120, 279, P 603 (and schol.), 1148, Av 1764, L 1257, R 704.

68. Fr 74; see G. Gerhard, *Phoinix von Kolophon* (Leipzig, 1909), p. 202, n. 4.

69. E.g. Arist. *NE* 4.1128ᵃ 17 ff.; *Pol.* 7.1336ᵇ 20 f.; H. Reich, *Der Mimus* (Berlin, 1903), pp. 324 ff.

70. See the excellent treatment of this subject in V. Grassman, *Die erotischen Epoden des Horaz. Literarischer Hintergrund und sprachliche Tradition* (Munich, 1960 = *Zetemata* 39), pp. 1–17, and cp. the iambist's exposures of an enemy's private parts with those on *tabulae defixionum* (A. Audollent, *Defixionum Tabellae* [Paris, 1904]): αἰδοῖον (42B.5), βαίνεμεν (= fuck, 85A.3), πρωκτός (42B.5, 75B.2?), τύλον (= phallus, 74.17), ὑπογάστριον (74.14 f., 75B.3); none of these dates from before the first century A.D.

71. For parallels in Old Comedy, the reader may check the iambic terminology given here against the Index Verborum.

figs (as often in Old Comedy):[72] A 331, H 41, 124, 167

ἀηδονίς [nightingale] = cunt: A 263

ἀλλᾶς [sausage] = penis (?): H 84.17

ἄπυγος [assless] = lecherous (woman): Se 7.76

ἀσκός [bag] = cunt (?): A 119.1 (cf. *LSJ* 2, cp. σάκανδρος)

βορβορόπη = "dirty-holed": H 135b

γληχώ [pennyroyal] = pubic hair: H 84.4

δορίαλλον = cunt: H 174 (?)

ἐγχέλυς (τυφλάς) [eels] = penis: A 189 (Wilamowitz, n. 84, below)

ἔντερον = guts, reached via the vagina: A 302

θύμος = penis: H 10[73]

ἶνες μελέων [sinews] = penis: A 222

κέρας (ἀπαλόν) [tender horn] = penis: A 247

κέρκος (?) [tail] = penis: H 12.3 (κέρκον 15.3D[3], δαρτόν Masson, ἄρτον West)[74]

κήλων [beam-man] = having large penis: A 43

Κοραξικὸν λῶπος [mantle] = cunt: H 2

κορώνη [crow] = penis: A 331 (see G. Wills, "Phoenix of Colophon's *ΚΟΡΩΝΙΣΜΑ*," *CQ*, vol. 20 [1970], 112 ff.)

κοχώνη [butt] : H 151b

κύσθος [cunt] : H 174 (?)

κυσός = anus: ad ia 53; κυσοχήνη: H 82.2

κύστις = cunt: Ho 7.1

κωλῆ [meatbone] = penis: H 75.1

λειμών [meadow] = cunt (?): H 6[75]

μύκης [mushroom] = hard-on: A 252

μύρτον [myrtle] = cunt: H 174 (?)

μύσχον = genitals of men and women: A 309

ὄγμος [furrow] = cunt. A 188

τῆς ὄπισθεν ὀρθοθύρης = anus: Se 17; cp. Ar. *Eccl.* 316 f., Sotad. 1; parodying Homer *Od.* 22.126, 333?

ὄρχις [testicles] : H 92.3

πρωκτός [ass-hole] : H 104.32

πυγή: Ar 187 (cp. Πυγέλησι H 92.15, πυγεών H 92.2, πυγιστί H 92.2)

72. V. Buchheit, "Feigensymbolik im antiken Epigramm," *RhM* 103 (1960): 200 ff.

73. θύμῳ, "a warty excrescence" (*LSJ*), suggested by M. Schmidt, *Philol.* 16 (1860): 522; codd. θυμῷ.

74. See O. Masson, *Les Fragments du Poète Hipponax* (Paris, 1962), pp. 114 f.; O. Hoffmann, *Griechische Dialekte* (Göttingen, 1891–98), 3: 137 f.; Herod. 5.45.

75. See W. Madeiros, *Hipponactea* (Coimbra, 1969) on Frag. 27.1; D. Gerber in *Phoenix* 25 (1971): 166 f.

σάϑη: A 25.3, 43.1, 82.4.
Σινδικὸν διάσφαγμα [fissure] = cunt: H 2a
τράμις = anus: A 283, H 114a
τρίορχος [three-balled] : Se 9.2
ὕσσακος: A 48.8 (conj. Lasserre)
φάλης: H 21, 92.3
φῦμα ⟨μηρῶν μεταξύ⟩ [knob] : A 66
χοῖρος (?) [piggie] = cunt: H 174

Sexual acts, described with great realism, are also common, very often involving the poet and, as often in comedy, a prostitute: A 30, 31, 41, 48, 119, 189, 205–08, 246, 302, 331; H 104.34, 119, 135, 135 a-c, 160, 182; ad ia 5, 9 (?), 37, 61; Hermipp. 5, etc.
Fornication:

Love-scene between Hipponax and Arete: H 16
ἀνασυρτόλις: H 135a is a comic coinage from ἀνασύρεσϑαι (expose the genitals)[76], cf. Eub. 140 προανάσυρμα παρϑένου, illegitimate pregancy
ἀποσκολύπτειν: A 39 = draw back the prepuce in coitus
ἀσκαρίζειν: H 19.2 = fornicate (σκαρίζειν jump, throb, palpitate; cf. the images in Cratin. 26 and Ar. Fr. 495 ἀπασκαρίζειν ὡσπερεὶ πέρκην χαμαί)
βασαγικόρος: H 139 (βάσκ[ι κόρλαζε], 14A.1D³; see J. Whatmough, *Poetic, Scientific and other Forms of Discourse* [Berkeley and Los Angeles, 1956], p. 76)
βινεῖν: A 152.2, H 84.16, ad ia 37 (= CA 55)
δῆμος: A 207 = common whore
εἴλειν: Se 17 = penetrate sexually
ἐξορύττειν : H 104.35 = penetrate a woman sexually
ἐργάτις: A 208 = whore.
ἵνας δὲ μελέων ⟨τῶν μέσων⟩ ἀπέϑρισεν: A 222, "she peeled back the fig-leaves [prepuce] of my manhood."[77]
μισητή: A 206 = lecherous.
περὶ σφυρὸν παχεῖα: A 209 = prostitute (cp. ad ia 37 παχυσκελής).
συκοτραγίδης: H 167 = "son of Raunchy" (figs = genitals), a "kostlicher Witz" worthy of Old Comedy.[78]
τρώζειν: ad ia 53 = penetrate sexually.

76. Hdt. 2.60, with reference to the Isis cult; Thphr. *Ch.* 11.2.
77. As in Thphr. *HP* 3.12.7; ἵνες is difficult to interpret ("sinews"?).
78. Meyer (n. 56, above), pp. 115, 140 ff.

Incest: Hipponax describes how Bupalus "despoils his own mother's little urchin (cunt) while she sleeps" (70.7 f.) and is therefore a μητρο-κοίτης (12).[79]

Homosexuality: For Hipponax's curse that someone be buggered (114a ἐξάκις τίλλοι τις αὐτὸν τὴν τράμιν ϑ' ὑπεργάσαι), cp. H 41, where Bupalus threatens to widen the poet's anus,[80] καὶ νῦν ἀρειᾷ σύκινόν με ποι-ῆσαι, that is, "to make me as holey as fig-wood,"[81] and perhaps H 104.32 ν]ενυχμένῳ πρωκτῷ.[82]

εὐνοῦχος as a pejorative epithet: H 26.3, cp. ἡμίανδρος H 148

κατωμόχανος: H 28.1 = so debauched that his rear end gapes all the way to his shoulders

κίναιδος: A 294

πύγαργος: A 313 = coward (womanlike)

Masturbation: H 78.16 ἀποδέφομαι (*hapax*).

Fellatio: H 17 κύψασα (punning on κύπτω in this sense are Κυψοῦν H 129, Κ]υψοῦ H 77.1, referring to Homer's Calypso).[83] A 42: as a Thracian or a Phrygian sucks (ἔμυζε) must through a straw, so did the woman bend over (κύβδα) and work at the phallus.[84] Cp. μυσάχνη(A 209, H 105.10), κολάψαι H 21 (?).

Cunnilingus: H 124 μηδὲ μοιμύλλειν Λεβεδίην ἰσχάδ' ἐκ Καμανδωλοῦ, "nor suck / eat[85] a dried Lebedian fig (cunt) from Camandolus (puns on χαμάν)."

Exhibitionism: see on ἀνασυρτόλις, above.

Scatology: ἀνατιλᾶν: H 79.6, cf. 73.3, 82.2: ὤμειξε δ' αἷμα καὶ χολὴν ἐτίλησεν: H 73.3, cp. ἐνώμειξεν Ho 7.6; βόλβιτος: H 92.9, 144; latrines: ἀμίς Ho 7.4, κοπρών Hermipp. 6, λαύρη H 61, 92.10, 155.

One of the longest fragments of Hipponax (92) is the first-person account of a dreadful anal penetration suffered at the hands of two Lydian women: the entire passage is very similar to the trials of Encolpius in Petronius *Sat.* 138,[86] and shares with the Petronian account the same comic verve

79. See Masson (n. 74, above), pp. 114, 141, n. 2.

80. See A. Bartalucci, "Hipponacteae Interpretatiunculae," *Maia* 16 (1964): 249 ff.

81. For this quality of fig-wood, see schol. Pl 946, schol. Theoc. 10.45; cf. Hsch. s.v.

82. Cf. Athen. 12.546E, Epic. *Fr.* 413.

83. See Grassmann (n. 70, above), pp. 4 f.

84. R. Lattimore, "Notes on Greek Poetry," *AJP* 65 (1944): 172 f.; U. von Wilamo-witz, "Lesefrüchte," *Hermes* 59 (1924): 271.

85. See Hsch. s.v. ἔμυζεν; Bartalucci (n. 80, above), pp. 247 f., thinks it means "to work the lips."

86. Full discussion in K. Latte, "Hipponacteum," *Hermes* 64 (1929): 384 ff. For this particular cure for impotence, see the remarks of Hopfner (n. 7, above), p. 269, and perhaps Aristophanes Frr. 24 ff.

and delight in sexual sadism. There are several clever coinages in the passage: πυγεών for πυγή (1.2), πυγιστί "in the manner of pederasts [?]" (1.2), Πυγέλησι, a comic locative (1.15).[87] Hipponax uses such comic place-names elsewhere: Κοραξικὸν . . . λῶπος (2) and Σινδικὸν διάσφαγμα (2a) are both puns referring to the female member; Καμανδωλοῦ (124) puns on χαμάν; Κυφοῦν (129) and Κ]υφοῦ (77.1) are puns referring to fellatio and parodying Homer's Calypso. βῦσον (92.2), ὄρχιν (1.3), βολβίτῳ = βολίτῳ (1.9), and λαύρη (1.10) are all favorites in Old Comedy, and the picture of over fifty dung-beetles (κάνθαροι) swarming in a squadron toward the latrine where the perversion is taking place, sharpening their teeth for the attack, is quite Aristophanic in its grotesque exaggeration, and distinctly foreshadows the prologue to *Peace*.

We must consider one final point. The highly refined elegy attributed to Archilochus (331), συκῆ πετραίη πολλὰς βόσκουσα κορώνας/εὐήθης ξείνων δέκτρια Πασιφίλη, contains several Aristophanic touches: the obscene fig-symbolism, the phallic crows, the invented hetaera-name. These invented names appear frequently in Old Comedy (for example, Charixene at E 943 is similar). The instructive example of Alcman 95D[3] allows us to see the cult origins of such names: Πολλαλέγων ὄνυμ' ἀνδρί, γυναικὶ δὲ Πασιχάρηα, "the man is called Prattler, the woman Everybody's Girl." As T. Nissen has shown,[88] the context is a marriage hymn and the verse an answer to the question, What are the names of the bride and bridegroom? Here the fictitious *Necknamen* are meant to confuse and repel evil influences that might try to spoil the happy occasion. It was from such innocent obscenities in cult and in folk customs that the iambic poets developed their more abusive and more artistic verses. That the writers of Old Comedy also derived the idea independently from cults is possible, but the Ionian iambic poets seem a likelier intermediate step.[89]

Our discussion so far has centered around Ionian and Attic developments. But there was a tradition in antiquity,[90] and still is a certain feeling

87. Bartalucci (n. 80, above), p. 245, n. 10.

88. "Zu Alkman frgm. 95 Diehl," *Philol.* 91 (1936–37): 470 ff.

89. Not much has been said of the comparatively gentle poems of Semonides. Frag. 17, quoted above, shows that he did have close affinities with the ethos of his fellow iambographers; perhaps this would be more perceptible had more of his work survived. The satirical poem on women has many comic touches, however, and seems to back up the judgment of Schmid (n. 28, above), 1: 399, that despite this poet's un-Archilochean affinities with elegiac, epic, and fable literature, there is enough realism and colloquial bite in what we possess of his poetry to establish firmly his kinship to the Ionian iambic school. Cf. Grassmann (n. 70, above), pp. 12 f.

90. Arist. *Poet.* 1448[a] 28 ff.; 1449[a] 37–68. Discussion in Breitholz (n. 51, above), pp. 34 ff.

among some modern scholars,[91] that the Dorians had a role in the development of Attic Comedy, especially in the inclusion of obscenity therein.[92] Since A. Körte's revolutionary articles,[93] these notions have been hard to shake off. Körte and his followers have assembled an imposing array of circumstantial clues pointing to Dorian areas (especially Megara), and from these clues have hypothesized the existence of a developed farcical drama which they suppose had a decisive impact on Athenian drama in its formative stages. I have summarized their arguments, along with what I feel are decisive refutations by several recent researchers, in an appendix. For the present argument it suffices to say that not one element of the Körtians' hypothesis concerning the existence of a mainland Dorian drama that antedates the formative period of Attic Comedy can be proved on the evidence we now possess. The hypothesis is built upon a foundation of misinterpreted, unfounded, or fictional facts and assumptions, and its conclusions are consequently of no use to us in explaining the nature (or the existence) of obscene language in the extant works of Attic Comedy. Most importantly, we need no longer feel tempted to explain away this obscenity as merely an un-Attic holdover from less sophisticated early influences.

If evidence for the (mainland) Dorian origins of the obscenity in Attic Comedy cannot be found in Megara or any other Dorian area, are we on any firmer ground with Sicilian comedy? Certainly Epicharmus lived early enough to have been influential in the development of Attic Comedy: his period of activity extends from the late sixth century down to the time of Hiero. The extreme views of Zielinski,[94] that Epicharmus was unknown in Athens before Plato Comicus, and A. von Salis,[95] that Epicharmus' influence is to be seen everywhere in Old Comedy, have been in recent years abandoned for a cautious middle ground. Scholars such as Pickard-Cambridge, Weinreich, and Wüst tend to admit the possibility of a certain influence, if for no other reason than the close commercial, social, and artistic ties then flourishing between Athens and the West. After all, Aeschylus' first trip to Sicily took place a mere fifteen years before Chionides' comic victory of 487/86.[96]

91. Complete review in Breitholz, op. cit., pp. 9 ff., and Giangrande (n. 44, above), passim.

92. Schmid, op. cit., 1: 635 ff.; 4: 4 ff.

93. A. Körte, "Archäologische Studien zur alten Komödie," *Jhb. d.arch. Inst.* 8 (1893): 6 ff.; "Komödie," *RE* 21 (1921).

94. Th. Zielinski, *Die Gliederung der altattischen Komödie* (Leipzig, 1885).

95. A. von Salis, *De doriensium ludorum in Comoedia Attica vestigiis* (Basel, 1905), pp. 9 ff.

96. See Schmid (n. 28, above), 2: 189 ff.

But "a certain influence" does not mean a profound, formative role in the development of Attic Comedy. It may very well be that some of Epicharmus' famous apothegms found their way onto the Attic stage, or that his technique of comic debate (such as that in Λόγος καὶ Λογίνα) may have appealed to some of his eastern colleagues. But these are minor and external matters. The evidence seems to point in the other direction. Epicharmus' comedy apparently lacked the essential elements of Attic Old Comedy: it had no discernible admixture of personal invective, no chorus (certainly not a very developed one),[97] and no standard meter. In addition to the iambic trimeter, which is very unlike that of Old Comedy (e.g. in its substitution of dactyls in the first five places), there are tetrameters and anapests (this latter being the only meter used in *Choreuontes* and *Epinicius*). His plays are therefore referred to by Aristotle and other ancient critics[98] not as comedies but merely as δράματα. It is not even certain that may of these pieces involved actors at all. They may have been mere dialogues, skits, or "recitative ballet."[99] Admittedly, much of this is speculation ex silentio; on the other hand, there is even less on which to build more positive hypotheses.

The obscene language that we encounter in the fragments[100] of the Sicilian comic poets amounts to very little, and what there is has no direct analogues in Attic Comedy; contrast the close similarities we observed when discussing Ionian iambic poetry. Most are innocent double entendres[101] which can be expected in any comedy and, for all we know, may have been borrowed from Attica: τὸν ἄρχον (Epich. 6) is both "anus" and "leader" (*LSJ* II); ἄγκυρα (Epich. 182, Sophr. 52) is "anchor" and "phallus" (Hsch.). Puns: κυπτάζειν = fellate appears in Sophr. 41 and as a pun in 39: ἃ δ' ἀμφ' ἄλητα κυπτάζει, "she works hard over her meal," can also be read obscenely as ἃ δ' ἂμ φάλητα κυπτάζει, "she bends over to work at the phallus." Slang: σωλῆνες (Sophr. 24) is "pipes" and "dildoes" (the χηρᾶν γυναικῶν λίχνευμα); γέρρα Ναξία (Epich. 174) for "phallus," a usage probably taken from the cult of Aphrodite at Naxos. Or comic comparisons such as that involving some men more debauched than ἀλφησταί, "fishes that travel in pairs" (Sophr. 63, Epich. 44). There are a few references to sexual or scatological acts that do not involve joke-

97. On this question see Herter, *vom dion. Tanz*, pp. 57, 176.

98. References in Kaibel, Cantarella, vol. 1.

99. T. B. L. Webster, "Some Notes on the New Epicharmus," *Serta Philologica Aenipontana* (Innsbruck, 1961), pp. 85 ff.

100. Fragments in A. Olivieri, *Frammenti della Commedia Greca e del Mimo nella Sicilia e nella Magna Grecia*[2] (Naples, 1946–47).

101. See L. Berk, *Epicharmus* (Groningen, 1964), pp. 46 ff.

technique: Epich 181 γυναικάνδρεσσι ποθεινοί, 183 χαλιμάζειν, 193 σικε-
λίζειν (a vulgar dance? cf. Phot., Hsch., Athen 1.22C), Sophr 11 f.
βαλλίζοντες τὸν θάλαμον σκάτους ἐνέπλησαν.

Such gentle and casual obscenity fits in well with the general picture
we get of Sicilian comedy: brief skits on a wide variety of mythological
and mundane subjects, much wit, sententious wisdom, and intellectual
sophistocation, with close affinities to the mime. Absent are the fiery
abuse, invective, and satire of Attic Comedy, the wild flights of fantasy
and absurdity, the outrageous and indecent costuming—in a word, everything that gave Old Comedy's obscenity its raison d'être and its bite.
Nothing we have seen warrants the conclusion that Sicilian comedy had
anything to do with the inclusion of obscenity in Attic drama.

The muted and somewhat Plautine tone of the obscenities in Sicilian
comedy has an Attic analogue in the satyr drama, which derives, like Old
Comedy, from the Dionysus cult and its κῶμοι of Silenus, satyrs, and other
rustic creatures. The very infrequent obscenities that we find in the
fragments of satyr drama are, like those of Epicharmus and Sophron just
examined, casual, nonabusive double entendres, sly references or colorful
slang intended to elicit a smile. We never see an outright obscenity like
πέος, cock, or πρωκτός, ass-hole. What obscenities there are, moreover,
seem to be restricted without exception to the chorus of satyrs and their
leader, and never associated with the heroic personages involved, no
matter how ridiculous those personages may be. And unlike the obscenities in Old Comedy, those of satyr drama do not appear to be connected
with dramatic developments or thematic material (as far as one can tell),
but are delivered simply as incidental jokes, jokes such as drunken and
aroused satyrs would make.

Thus the lecherous nymphs and satyrs of Aeschylus' *Dictyulci* are described in very chaste language,[102] as is the defloration Aristophanes
borrowed (Fr 160; cf. Poll 6.80): ὀξυγλύκειάν τἄρα κοκκιεῖς ῥόαν. The same
is true of Sophocles' 'Αχιλλέως ἐρασταί (the satyrs as frustrated lovers of
Achilles) and 'Ελένης γάμος (the satyrs passionately aroused by Helen).
There is no obscenity at all in the substantial remains of *Ichneutai*. Despite
their humorous content, satyr plays were felt to be part of tragic performances. Their diction has much in common with tragic diction and bears
very little similarity to that of comedy.

Thus the obscenities amount to very few, almost all of them in Euripides, which may indicate an idiosyncratic loosening of standards of diction and propriety by that iconoclastic writer, not to mention a certain

102. 821 ff. (all citations from V. Steffen, *Satyrographorum graecorum fragmenta*[2] [Poznań,
1952]).

amount of borrowing from comedy itself. At any rate, Sophocles has οὐρά (162), a common slang term to which the German *Schwanz* is exactly analogous; ἀναστῦψαι (102), to be erect; ἀποσκόλυπτε (104); τρίψει (111), rape (spoken by a drunken satyr of his own violation); ἐνούρηθρα (113). In Euripides we find νύμφας βήσομαι (24), which amounts almost to a euphemism; νυμφόβας (38), a bit more comical; and βαυβῶμεν (34; cf. βαυβᾶν μεθ' αὐτῆς, Incert. poet. fr. 20), also something of an elegant word (see Hsch.).

In the extant *Cyclops*, Silenus points to his phallus (τουτί, 169) as he rhapsodizes on the delights of drinking and fornicating:

> μαστοῦ τε δραγμοὺς καὶ παρεσκευασμένου
> ψαῦσαι χεροῖν λειμῶνος ὀρχηστύς θ' ἅμα
> κακῶν τε λῆστις

[feeling tits, palpating ready love-plots with both hands, having a ball, and forgetting one's cares!]

Here λειμών is a double entendre for the female pubis, and ὀρχηστύς a pun on ὄρχεις. Later the aroused Coryphaeus queries Odysseus about the capture of Helen (ἐλάβετε Τροίαν τὴν Ἑλένην τε χειρίαν, you captured Troy and took Helen in hand 177): χειρίαν is another pun. There are several puns and double entendres in the Coryphaeus' denunciation of the traitress: ἅπαντες αὐτὴν διεκροτήσατ' ἐν μέρει, you all banged her in turn (180), for which cf. E 257 and Pl. *Lg.* 795e (μέρη); θυλάκους (182), cf. R 1203, *Hippiatr.* 50; μέσον αὐχένα (184), cf. L 680 f. Later the vulgar Cyclops confesses, πέπλον κρούω Διὸς βρονταῖσιν εἰς ἔριν κτυπῶν, "I bang my clothes, vying with Zeus' thunderbolts in my crashing" (372 f), a bit of rusticity reminiscent of Strepsiades and Xanthias. More double entendres follow in σίφων (440), phallus; θύραν (502), cunt; δροσερῶν ἔσωθεν ἄντρων (516), cunt; Silenus is ultimately dragged off and raped by the drunken Cyclops (581 ff.).

Again, the similarity of the obscene puns and jokes in Euripides to those in Old Comedy suggests borrowing by Euripides, selectively, of course: none of the above-quoted jokes falls far enough below accepted standards of diction for satyr drama to be ranked with comic obscenity, and none is connected with anyone other than satyrs. There is no trace of scurrility or abuse. And the lack of even this kind of off-color joke in the rest of the surviving pieces of satyr drama makes the likelihood very great that Euripides was the exception to a general rule.

To conclude, we must rule out the idea that Old Comedy and its obscenity derives from Dorian sources. There is no evidence at all from the

mainland to support such a theory, and what little we find in Sicily will
not support derivation theories any more than will the scanty bits of obscenity in Attic satyr drama itself. Attic Comedy was, like its chief function
of *öffentliche Rüge,* an Attic-Ionian phenomenon which shared nothing
with and received nothing from the Dorians. Its obscenity derives from
purely Attic and Ionian sources, through the opportunity for development afforded by the cults and with some inspiration from the iambic art
of abuse and exposure characteristic of writers like Archilochus and Hipponax.[103]

From its early, formless days,[104] Old Comedy developed under the
guidance of poets of the school of Cratinus, whose first victory came in
455.[105] It was Cratinus who, taking advantage of the freedom to satirize
and ridicule—freedom deriving from the cults and supported by prevailing public sentiment—developed comedy into a great and powerful vehicle for the open treatment of public and social affairs of all kinds, as
acceptable to the δεξιοί καί σοφοί, the clever and sophisticated, as to the
ordinary citizen. Cratinus introduced varied subjects for comic treatment:
in addition to the realm of politics, he wrote plays dealing with social
(*Plutus*), ethical (*Malthakoi*), religious (*Trophonius*), and poetic (*Archilochoi*) issues. His aim was to rid the state of bad influences (4 Dem.), a
rationale we have seen at work in Aristophanes with great regularity.
Cratinus' plays were longer[106] and better made[107] than anything done
previously, and his satire was strong and often bitter (αὐστηρὸς ταῖς
λοιδορίαις), with little of Aristophanes' χάρις in his jibes, but much
φορτικόν.[108] We may be sure that Cratinus' school, of which Aristophanes

---

103. The development of the tragic and satyric iambos seems to have been a special
legacy of Solon and Thespis, taking place outside the natural (i.e. comic-abusive) development of Ionian iambic poetry in Attic drama. As Else says (Appendix, n. 9), pp. 61 f.:
"In the ancient tradition iambic poetry figures as the invention of Archilochus, and it was
always considered to have a special *ethos* or character: sharp, vituperative, satirical. This
recognized *ethos* of iambic constitutes a problem. Why did tragedy, of all literary genres,
choose the particular verse form that was identified with satire, vilification, the uninhibited expression of personal hatreds and animosities? Thespis cannot have adopted it
for such a reason. We have to assume another use of iambic which was quite different
from that of Archilochus, yet so significant and impressive that Thespis felt impelled to
use it for his new purpose. Once the problem is put this way, the answer is clear. There is
only one possible model: those iambic and trochaic poems of Solon."

104. See Kaibel, 1.7.11 ff., 18.20. ff.

105. Schmid (n. 28, above), p. 69, n. 5.

106. Ibid., vol. 2, p. 531, n. 9.

107. Kaibel, I.18.24 ff.

108. Ibid., I.6.

was a member in good standing, joyfully developed and honed the art of Attic-Ionian obscenity along with all the rest.

The obscenity in Attic Comedy seems to have been an indispensable feature of the genre. Its importance as a potent vehicle for ridicule, abuse, satire, and comic exposure could not be equaled by any other weapon in the poet's arsenal. Unique in ancient literature both in character and in social context, it derived its license from the openness of the Periclean polis and the traditional freedoms allowed by the cults, from which its sole literary models, the Ionian iambic poets, also drew inspiration. To equate (and thus explain away) the obscenity of Old Comedy, which attained a level of sophistication and functionality equal to any other aspect of the comic poet's art, with the hypothetical buffooneries of Dorian farce or the genial indecencies of the Sicilian school, is to misunderstand or falsify the fundamental nature of Old Comedy itself. It will be the task of the following chapters to illustrate in detail that sophistication and functionality.

The decline of obscenity in comedy after the debacle of 404/403 goes hand in hand with the decline of the *Rügekomödie* as a genre and as a social event.[109] Without its function in the humor of abuse and exposure, obscenity becomes mere smut and disappears, never to reemerge save in the witless and pornographic imitations of the epigrammatists. The comedy that arose in the fourth century played to audiences with different sensibilities, with appetites not quite so hearty as those of their grandparents. It remained for the Socratic and sophistic schools, particularly the Isocratean, to ban on ethical and philosophical grounds a phenomenon which had already expired of old age and social uselessness.

109. For a thorough treatment, see Schmid, op. cit., 4: 441 ff.; F. Wehrli, *Motivstudien zur griechischen Komödie* (Basel, 1948), esp. pp. 27 ff.

2 Varieties of Obscene Expression:
An Overview

Before we attempt an examination of the dramatic and literary functions of obscene language in the extant plays of Aristophanes, it is necessary to make a preliminary analysis of the various kinds of obscenity that appear in the remains of Attic Comedy and are cataloged in the final chapters of this book. Our analysis will involve two inquiries: as far as our evidence allows, we must try to ascertain precisely (1) the aesthetic and psychological effects created by each type of obscene terminology, and (2) to reconstruct, as an aid to that end, the peculiar Athenian attitudes toward the sexual and scatological aspects of human life which are reflected in the language used by their comic playwrights. That is, our concern is primarily with the artistic uses of obscene language but will necessarily involve not only the attitudes and reactions of the Athenians toward the sexual and scatological areas of life as they are manifested in the various types of obscene language, but also relevant aspects of their experience in regard to those areas.

Obviously, we must keep in mind the limitations imposed upon us by the centuries that separate us from the Athenians of the fifth century B.C. There are very great differences between the Athenian and the modern attitudes toward sexuality, and these reflect not only different ways of interpreting sexual experience but also great differences in the character of the experience itself. Certain pieces of evidence from Greek literature and plastic art can help us to define and understand many Athenian attitudes in our area of inquiry, but since we are examining the intimate life of a long-dead society, we necessarily lack much of the information needed to control our evidence fully—namely, the kind of information we know as statistical, clinical, and sociological. The evidence with which we must work is primarily artistic rather than popular. This means that what we will be examining is more *homo Aristophaneus* than real Athenian men and women, an artist's view of his world and the ways in which his imagination operated on the raw material of his life.

Works of art have their own conventions, which are more or less autonomous and are accepted as such by their audience. In the absence of any real Athenians it is impossible to gauge *exactly* what the attitude of Aristophanes' audience was toward his art or to discover their feelings about the relation between what is presented by an artist and the experiences of their own lives. Even in our own society the problems posed to the analyst of human sexuality are open to wildly differing interpretations, and the only scientifically verifiable conclusions are those which rest upon exhaustive compilations of statistical, clinical, and sociological information. We should no more ask Aristophanes or Plato to speak for the sexual attitudes and experiences of every member of every social class and age-group in Athens than we would ask a comparable spokesman of our own day to speak for ours; indeed, it is rarely the artist who is asked for his opinion about sexual matters, and although artists frequently say more profound and illuminating things about their culture than statistics do, we cannot use one as a substitute for the other.

This also means that the greatest caution must be observed in the application of modern analytical principles to the evidence we possess: too often literary critics err by extrapolating modern attitudes into ancient times, a process that rests upon unproved and frequently illegitimate assumptions about the universality of social responses to human experience. We must resign ourselves both to the remoteness of the Athenians of the fifth century B.C. from our own experience and to our lack of certain crucial kinds of evidence about them.

Fortunately, however, Old Comedy was an art form whose language and subject matter were geared, more than any other Greek genre, to the tastes of the man in the street. It is through Old Comedy that we can perceive most readily the attitudes and style of life of the average (as opposed to the exceptional) fifth-century Athenian. And so, although we must acknowledge the limitations imposed on us by our lack of certain kinds of evidence, the evidence we do possess is extremely rich and revealing, springing as it does from the current popular language of the day and standing in vivid dramatic contexts. It is thus the comic poets' concentrated and artistic use of the popular idiom, in combination with other documentary evidence from Greek literature and applicable modern analytical principles, on which our discussion is based.

A few preliminary remarks must be made concerning the general nature of the obscenity in Old Comedy. We are struck immediately by the abundance of all types of sexual and scatological words and acts in the plays, from the coarsest and least subtle references to the most intricate and sophisticated kinds of joke-technique. We are struck also by the absence of anything like this kind of language elsewhere in Attic literature. Athens was a society in which women and girls of citizen status were rigorously segregated, where sexual and social mores were controlled by strict notions of etiquette and propriety, and where a very sharp distinction was drawn in respect to propriety of language between humorous and serious, proper and improper, expression. Obviously, comedy was the one public occasion in which the usual strict standards of decorum imposed by Athenian society on the language to be used at public and social events were relaxed in favor of a complete absence of inhibition. The freedom of language and action characteristic of Old Comedy was an astounding and unique exception to the rule that obscenity and the sexual or excretory acts to which it refers are appropriate, just as they are today, only to the most private contexts.

That obscene humor is also found in the fertility rites in which Old Comedy in part originated has nothing to do with its retention and artistic development by comic playwrights, other than the likelihood, discussed in chapter I, that the established ritual freedoms of the cults allowed the unrestricted development of even greater freedoms by the comic writers. Such a prominent and artistically developed aspect of Old Comedy would not have been retained merely in deference to an old tradition: artists are too eager to perfect their art and win over their audiences to be bothered with toting the burdens of traditions that are obsolete. From simple beginnings Old Comedy in all its aspects developed rapidly and majestically, and the playwrights chose to develop its obscene features also. Clearly, the public enjoyed and demanded the presentation of obscenity in comedy; when the public largely ceased to do so, toward the end of the fifth century, comedy largely ceased to offer it. The same cults, with their traditional ritual obscenity, continued throughout succeeding centuries when comedy no longer featured much obscene language and action.

As we saw in the previous chapter, the Athenians did not feel as we do about obscenity, which we defined as verbal references to areas of human activity or parts of the human body that are protected by certain taboos agreed upon by prevailing social custom and subject to emotional aversion and inhibition, these references being made by an explicit expression that is itself subject to the same inhibitions as what it describes. The use of obscene language is therefore tantamount to exposing what should be hidden. The crucial difference between the Athenians and ourselves is the reason why these things should be hidden. We abhor obscenity because the objects and acts it exposes are felt somehow to be dirty; we are embarrassed by the public exposure of our sexual organs and acts because we feel them to be somehow unclean or even unhealthy. In public we profess total ignorance of them unless we are in the presence of companions we trust, and even then there is often a feeling of dirtiness or embarrassment.

The Athenians evidently did not feel this way at all. For them sexuality, like the human body, was accepted as a healthy and important (and sometimes awesome: note early personal lyric poetry and such tragedies as Sophocles' *Trachiniae* and Euripides' *Medea* and *Hippolytus*) part of one's life, something to enjoy to the fullest and to talk about in the proper contexts without embarrassment. As was pointed out in the previous chapter, society imposed strict controls on the language used *publicly* to describe sexuality because this was an area, among others, which deserved respect and therefore demanded a certain linguistic decorum. It was considered shameful to expose intimate matters publicly, but out of respect and propriety and not from feelings of disgust, dirtiness, or embarrassment. The place to enjoy and discuss sexuality was the privacy of one's home, or the brothel, or the symposium, in the company of friends of the same sex. Through most of the fifth century one could routinely purchase paintings and pottery that depicted every imaginable kind of sexual activity, and during the same period one could attend fertility cults and the performances of ithyphallic songs, compositions by iambic poets, and comedy that featured the most uninhibited language and action. These were the allowed public outlets for the exposure of sexuality: note what Aristophanes says (R 358) of those who use "buffoonish language" at "the wrong time" (μὴ 'ν καιρῷ). Needless to say, there are no such universally sanctioned public outlets in our time: if we wish to enjoy verbal or pictorial obscenity we must do so more or less surreptitiously, and our sources for this kind of enjoyment are constantly under attack by authorities representing the community. When we say that obscene art is shameful, we mean something quite different from what the Athenians meant.

We concluded in the previous chapter that the primary effect of obscenity on the audience was to allow an unrestricted exposure of what was usually hidden, to allow the audience to participate vicariously (usually on the side of the hero) in the hostile or libidinous exposure of actual or invented persons. Such exposures in real life would have been considered unacceptable aggression, but placed on the stage they became permissible channels for the audience's sexual aggressiveness, a kind of catharsis of sexual feelings and a kind of wish fulfillment. It must be stressed that this presentation of uninhibited sexuality, frequent reference to excretion, and unfettered vulgarity of utterance is entirely consonant and of a piece with all the other forms of the comic hero's, and thus the audience's, self-assertion against authority: the playwrights were expected to debunk and retaliate against the heavy authority of gods, politicians, intellectuals, generals, poets, unpopular or risible citizens, and foreign bogeymen.

Comedy offered a vicarious victory of the individual against society and of the average man against superior authority. The use of obscenity in itself served to accomplish the former end, and obscenity in its particularly hostile manifestations (degradation as opposed to simple depiction of pleasurable acts that arouse the libido rather than satisfy hostility) helped to accomplish the latter. We recall that the use of obscenity in the cults and in iambic poetry, both of which, like comedy, satisfied the people's need for occasional irreverence, parallels that of Old Comedy in most of these respects: the element of hostility and aggression is prominent alongside the simple portrayal of otherwise private sexual acts.

A word should be said about the composition of the audience.[1] It is usually assumed that women did not attend performances of comedies, but only men and boys (for boys see N 538 f.). This assumption is based on the feeling that the uninhibited obscenity of Old Comedy would have been offensive to or inappropriate for women of citizen status, about whose modest and decorous behavior in public we hear so much (for example in Thucydides' Funeral Oration). But there is no evidence that women did not attend and some evidence that they did. Plato (*Lg.* 658a-d, 817c), writing in the middle of the fourth century at a time when obscenity was still present in many comedies, implies that women could attend any kind of drama, and there is no good reason to think that the same assumption cannot also be made about the fifth century. Women may be assumed to have had routine and unembarrassed contact with obscene pottery, which was after all intended for the household, were free to participate in the city's cults and phallic processions, and, as we have seen, had their own cults in which the speaking of obscenity and the handling of representations of the sexual organs of both sexes were quite unrestrained.

If human sexuality was not considered dirty and unhealthy by Greek men, it would not have been by Greek women either. It is, in fact, entirely plausible, as K. J. Dover says, that "when the adult male citizens had seated themselves women, children, foreigners and slaves saw as much as they could."[2] It would, of course, have been inappropriate for women to watch the plays in the presence of men, but we should not imagine that as spectators they would not have enjoyed themselves, as they certainly did

---

1. Citations in A. Willems, *Aristophane* (Paris-Brussels, 1919), 1: 425 ff.
2. *Aristophanic Comedy* (Berkeley and Los Angeles, 1972), p. 17.

in their own cults, in the presence of other women in their own section of the theater. That we do not have specific references to their presence at the comic performances is hardly surprising: rarely are real (non-mythical) women, and whatever viewpoints they might have had, mentioned at all in Attic literature.

Keeping in mind these fundamental points we may pass to a consideration of the varieties of obscene language itself.

Primary Obscenities

The natural starting point is the Greek version of what I will call primary obscenities, as opposed to metaphorical words, euphemisms, clinical terminology, double entendres, or slang. Like any language, Greek possessed a small number of these "pure" obscenities, words that refer directly, without any intermediary associations or distancing, to the sexual organs, excrement, and the acts which involve them, and which are always improper. These are: πέος, dick;[3] κύσθος, cunt; ψωλή, hard-on; στύεσθαι, have/get a hard-on; σκῶρ, shit; πρωκτός, ass-hole; πέρδεσθαι (πορδή), fart; βινεῖν, fuck; δέφεσθαι, jerk off. In addition, there are a few metaphorical words whose originally nonsexual meanings were still barely perceptible to the ear but which had come to be used as primary obscenities: κινεῖν (move, fuck), ληκᾶν and λαικάζειν (move a limb/fuck; cf. ληκώ, pecker), σπλεκοῦν (probably hypostasis from εἰς πλέκος, into the sack/fuck). Noteworthy is the absence of an equivalent for English *piss*, and the fact that there are hardly any references to pissing in comedy. One can probably conclude that the Greeks were more casual than we about urination.

What separates primary obscenities from proper words like φαλλός, penis, and χέζειν, move the bowels? Certainly φαλλός refers as directly to the penis as πέος, yet one has a proper tone and one does not. The difference lies simply in the quality of the mental picture awakened by each word. There are two ways, basically, to perceive the penis. One may think only of the existence or the presence of the penis as an organ, or one may think of it as charged with those strong emotional and libidinous feelings about which one is taught to be circumspect in all civilized and social contexts. φαλλός is simply the uncathected organ, while πέος is the embodiment of raw sexuality. When a doctor says, "Let me see your penis," we feel no particular emotion. But if he were to say, "Let me see your

3. I use *dick* here instead of *cock* because the latter still retains some of its metaphorical (nonprimary) tone.

cock," we should very probably feel that our privacy was being threatened. *Cock* is appropriate only to situations where the issue is sexuality, just as σκῶρ, shit, expresses definite affective feelings, while κόπρος, dung, refers simply to excrement.[4]

It will be illuminating for our entire discussion to outline briefly a general theory of the psychogenesis of the use of primary obscenities before we examine their particularly Greek manifestations.[5] S. Ferenczi, in describing the uniquely expressive power of what we have called primary obscenities, speaks of their *regressive* and *hallucinatory* qualities, their power to bring to life memory-images and thought-processes characteristic of an early stage of development. A very young child thinks primarily in preabstract (nonverbal) images and is unable to differentiate reality from wish-fantasy (Freud's *Wahrnehmungsidentität*); this process of thinking is essentially hallucinatory and concrete (*dinglich*). The growing child gradually abandons this egocentric "thingness" in favor of the designation of reality by words, and so becomes increasingly capable of abstraction and precision; that is, he accepts reality and seeks to define it.

A child's perception of sexual and excretory functions undergoes a similar development, completed in the period of true latency. But between the period of infantile satisfaction and latency, the "polymorphously perverse" period (as Freud at one time in his career called it), the child clings to his hallucinatory perceptions of sexuality and excretion and is especially

4. S. Ferenczi (n. 5, below) reports, however, that the *analyst* ought to use, and make his patients use, primary obscenities rather than euphemisms or clinical terms because of their direct and emotional power; they help to expose crucial areas of psychic difficulty, where less direct expressions allow the patient to avoid confronting them.

5. The formulations of Freud and Ferenczi, on which much of the present argument is based and upon which I develop new arguments, are generally accepted by the small number of responsible critics who have dealt with obscenity: see especially Freud's *Wit and Its Relation to the Unconscious*, part 2, and "The Antithetical Sense of Primal Words," in *Collected Papers*, vol. 4; Ferenczi, "Über obszöne Worte," in *Schriften zur Psychanalyse* (Frankfurt am Main, 1970), 1: 59 ff. (also in *Sex In Psychoanalysis*, trans. E. Jones (Boston, 1916]); E. Bergler, "Obscene Words," *Psychoan. Quart.* 5 (1936): 226 ff.; L. Stone, "On the Principal Obscene Word of the English Language," *IJP* 35 (1954): 30 ff.; H. Sperber, "Über die Einfluss sexueller Momente auf Entstehung und Entwicklung der Sprache," *Imago* 1 (1912): 405 ff.; brief discussion and up-to-date bibliography in M. Grotjahn, *Beyond Laughter: Humor and the Subconscious* (New York 1966), pp. 113 ff. There has been, surprisingly, almost no attention devoted to specific kinds of obscene terminology, as opposed to consideration of the experience of obscene language in general. It seems to me that the psychological and sociological theories of the critics who deal with this problem would be more penetrating and precise if each variety of obscene expression were analyzed before generalizations were made concerning what is erroneously thought to be the wholesale effect of obscenity. This I hope to do for Attic comedy and its obscenity in this chapter.

fascinated by primary obscenities as the one way to define them with "absolute and exclusive explicitness in a conscious sense."[6] That is why he wants to hear, say, and write primary obscenities. This tendency is of course gradually stifled by the pressures of his society, which teach the child to acknowledge society's moral standards and to feel varying degrees of inhibition, shame, and even disgust concerning both his sexual feelings and the words that most directly express them; the child learns to express himself by means of accepted, proper words as a component of his developing adult thought. Primary obscenities are repressed in the period of latency along with the infantile perceptions of sexuality they represent. These words thus retain their "hallucinatory" and affective elements at a time when the rest of a child's speech moves toward greater sophistication.

Other kinds of obscenity vary greatly, as we shall see, in their approach to or distance from the expressive character of primary obscenities: some are qualitatively very close to primary obscenities in affective power, for example, *fuck* and *screw*, where the latter is perceptibly metaphorical, or *cunt* and *pussy*, where the latter is still more obviously metaphorical. There is only a slight difference in tone between the primary and the metaphorical obscenities in these two pairs of synonyms, and yet the difference is remarkable. Expressions like *sleep with, make, muff*, and *pecker* are progressively more remote from the hallucinatory-regressive area of perception and can more readily be integrated into adult thinking. Primary obscenities are the words most incapable of development or of real integration into the adult's speech or perceptual patterns.

Throughout one's life there is a tendency toward regression to the infantile mode of perception: the most universal example is the dream, which is nonverbal and hallucinatory and which seeks not only to evade the repressions that separate infancy from adulthood but also to return to the period of active wish-fulfillment and egocentric perceptions of reality. The power of primary obscenities also lies to a certain extent in their ability to return us to that vivid mode of perception. Words that once stood for valued objects of childish pleasure now return, in a context of civilized repression, as means by which morality, inhibitions, and shame can be bypassed or overturned: they afford us, simultaneously, the pleasure that once was natural in us and a powerful weapon by which to defy civilization and the adult way of perceiving the world. We shall have occasion later on to examine the important relationship between the process of dreaming and the uses of obscenity.

6. See Stone (n. 5, above), p. 35.

Two examples will suffice to indicate the tendency toward this kind of hallucinatory regression as it appears in the sexual sphere, in waking life as opposed to the obvious sphere of dream sexuality. A common emphasis in obscene humor concerns the smallness and inadequacy of the penis or vagina, a fear which clinical study has shown to be most often a regressive and illogical fear. A child naturally feels that his organ is too small to function adequately, especially when he compares it to the organ of an adult, and may retain this fear even when his organ is fully mature. Similar is the frequent emphasis (e.g. in *Playboy* magazine) on unnaturally large breasts, a strong preference in many men that recalls the little boy's perception of his mother's (or any grown woman's) breasts. Such men often find any woman's breasts inadequate in comparison with their childhood idea of breast-size.

In these two common cases infantile hallucinatory thoughts persist alongside, and overpower, developed adult perceptions of reality. It is evident that most of our hallucinatory relics of childhood center around the sexual and excretory areas because these are the areas which have undergone the most severe social repression and are for that reason often arrested before they can be fully developed alongside the rest of our perceptions. The arrested nature of primary obscenities is a by-product of this process, and their unique power lies in their ability to recall to us a pleasurable and uninhibited time of life, regression to which is a function of our occasional need to rebel against the repressions enforced by adulthood.[7]

The uses of primary obscenities in Attic Comedy illustrate this process. Unlike other kinds of words that indicate sexual and excretory functions, they are incapable of nuance or multiple shades of meaning; they are simply equal-signs cutting through social barriers and pointing directly toward, and invoking in the listener, the basic emotions adhering to the organs and acts themselves. When the Sausage-Seller threatens Cleon (Eq 364), "I'll fuck your ass-hole like a sausage-case," or bids him "bite off his own cock," (1010), his use of primary obscenities is the nearest possible approach to actual violation; the power of the language to recall infantile directness of perception endows these threats against Cleon's private parts with unique force, and in vividly recalling to us our own anxieties makes our laughter all the heartier. Proper or figurative words (that is, words of the kind appropriate to more advanced stages of thinking) would be much less effective: "I'll bugger you" or "I'll violate you

7. The strong *psychomotor* power of primary obscenities may be observed by listening to the (often involuntary) exclamations of a man who hits his thumb with a hammer.

from the rear" are too sophisticated and remote in tone to effect the
primal vision of assault the poet desires.

This process is the same in the realm of libidinal aggressiveness as it is
in the just mentioned examples of hostile aggressiveness. The poet wishes
to make the most direct possible appeal to the audience's sexual feelings:
Dicaeopolis cries in triumph, "Take hold of my cock, dearies!" (A 1216),
and thus vivifies the explicit stage action. Compare Philocleon to the
flute-girl (V 1345 ff.): "You see how cleverly I rescued you from that
banquet just as you were about to have to blow everybody—so be nice to
this here cock," and Peisetaerus to the pesky Iris (combining Sausage-
Sellerlike violence with an arousing image of sexual intercourse): "If you
keep on bothering me I'll lift up both your legs high and stick it in right
between them, and you'll be surprised at the triple-decker hard-on this
old geezer can still get up" (Av 1253 ff.).

In scenes like these it is inevitably the primary obscenities which are
used; other types of obscenity are reserved for more complex effects. In
addition to their use in threats, insults, and scenes of direct sexuality, primary obscenities are also used as simple throwaway laughs, sure to amuse
and needing no context, no comic devices or joke-techniques to bolster
them: they are often used to cap nonsexual jokes or to climax a passage
before the introduction of a new action or subject. So Euripides and his
Relation arriving at Agathon's house (T 29 ff.): "*Eur.* This happens
to be Agathon's house, the tragic poet. *Rel.* What Agathon? Let me
see . . . not the strong, swarthy fellow? *Eur.* No, another Agathon. *Rel.*
Never seen him. Wait—the bushy-bearded man! *Eur.* You've really never
seen him? *Rel.* Never, as far as I know. *Eur.* Well, you've certainly fucked
him, though you may not remember. But let's get to one side, his servant's
coming out."

As an example of true climax, see the use of πέος at L 124, which
climaxes the whole prologue up to that point and introduces the actual
theme of the plot. For the use of primary obscenities as throwaway laughs,
consider the following exchange between Socrates and Strepsiades, whom
the teacher has set on a pallet to philosophize (N 731 ff.): "*Soc.* Let me
see how this fellow's getting on. Hey! are you asleep? *Str.* No indeed, by
Apollo! *Soc.* Well, have you got anything? *Str.* Nope, by Zeus, nothing
here. *Soc.* Nothing at all? *Str.* Nothing but a handful of cock! *Soc.* Well,
why don't you cover up quickly and think of something?"

These primary obscenities in Greek are more or less identical in usage
and form to our own. The one area of difference is the absence in Greek
of anything like our tendency to transfer them from the concrete sexual

and excremental contexts in which they actually belong to nonsexual and nonexcremental ones. For example, the Greeks did not seem to use, as we do, generalized expressions such as "Oh, fuck!" or "Oh, shit!" or "It's a fucking nice day" or "What the fuck do you mean?"[8] The explanation may be that in Greece the social sanctions leading to latency did not repress obscene words and infantile sexual feelings as strongly or in the same manner as our own society (more on this later). That is, we choose primary obscenities to emphasize and heighten the power of any forceful expression because these words and the organs and acts to which they refer are the most strongly censored areas of our thought: they are deeply tinged in latency by notions of guilt, filthiness, and disgust. The Greeks, as we have seen, were taught only to think of sexuality as private and worthy of strong feelings of shamefacedness (*aidōs*). Their primary obscenities are much less pejorative and hostile in tone; they recall infantile sexual and excremental feelings as primarily pleasurable and healthy, and so do not make use of primary obscenity in generalized curses or as all-purpose expletives, but only in relation to explicit sexuality and excrementality. A cursing Greek instead uses the names of gods and resorts to specific (and usually nonobscene) epithets to insult enemies.

Certain words that have the directness of primary obscenities seem to have developed a more or less innocuous tone: πόσθη, "wee-wee" (a small penis or a child's), σάθη, "waggler" (compare English "dingle"), and πυγή, "butt" (both sexes). These words, if used in sexual contexts, have at most a tone of affectionate lubricity; they stand at a distance from the affective primacy of πέος and its company. All have entered everyday speech: in cult, as medical terms (πόσθη can mean a stye on the eyelid), as hypocoristic household words (σάθων and πόσθων meaning little boy),[9] as figurative words (πυγή as fat, swelling land, or tail). Such usages indicate that these words have been allowed to develop with the rest of a child's language into the period of latency, unlike the arrested primary obscenities, and thus to take on nuance and a certain metaphorical flexibility (capacities of the developed mind). The amusement they occasion is the amusement of an adult mind looking back from a distance toward the directness of childhood sexuality; primary obscenities, on the other

8. The closest approach to these usages in Greek is the meaning "deceive" or "give a raw deal to" attached to certain words for fucking (e.g. βινεῖσθαι), just as we say "He got screwed" or "He really fucked me over," a meaning that is not really very far from the idea of hostility and aggressiveness inherent in the primary sexual meaning of these words.

9. Freud, *Works* (London, 1953–), 5: 357, points out the widespread tendency to equate children with the genitals and genitals with children.

hand, momentarily strip the adult mind of its distancing powers and create an actual regression.

Metaphorical (Figurative and Comparative) Expressions

The great majority of obscene words are those which, although they may be unmistakably direct in their reference, neither attain to the absolute and exclusive explicitness of primary obscenities nor possess their hallucinatory and regressive power, but which distance the listener in a greater or lesser degree from undistracted perceptual concentration on the organs and acts involved. They do this by creating secondary figures, comparisons, and images that color and refract the perceptions and emotions evoked directly by primary obscenities. They are products and components of the capacity for abstract and metaphorical thinking characteristic of latency. Unlike the primary obscenity, valuable only for its directness and primitive force, the value of metaphorical obscenity lies precisely in its flexibility and nuance. It does not penetrate to the cathected objects and act directly, but forces us first to imagine those aspects of them which resemble something else. While primary obscenities play upon essentially nonverbal and hallucinatory regions of the mind, these words depend on sophisticated verbal thinking for their very meaning.

The mechanics of metaphorical obscenities are similar to the mechanics of dreams, wit, and other more or less dissociated states of mind. In all these activities the mind manipulates comparisons, symbols, and verbal displacements to identify objects and acts subject to underlying feelings of hostility, anxiety, and desire, and to achieve pleasure in that expression.

For example, βάλανος, *acorn* or *bolt* (indicating the penis), is the Greek version of an almost universal symbol (cf. our medical term *glans penis*). Aristophanes uses it as a double entendre in highly sophisticated jokes about sexual intercourse, such as L 408 ff., where the Probulus illustrates the ways in which husbands play along with their adulterous wives' peccadillos. One husband says the following to a young goldsmith: "Goldsmith, about that necklace you made: while my wife was dancing (double entendre = fucking) last night the bolt fell out of its hole. I've got to sail to Salamis (double entendre = fuck), so if you have time by all means drop over some evening and shove it in for her."

Several levels of mental activity are at work here. As a joke, as wit, the poet's use of established symbolism is a product of focal consciousness, the capacity of the developed mind for *intellectual association*. Aristophanes wants to make the husband ridiculous by showing how he virtually asks to be cuckolded; his focal consciousness provides a solution—the husband will use ambivalent language which the audience readily perceives as being sexual but which the husband uses only in its innocent meanings. The situation is familiar comic irony. On a deeper level, the symbolism the poet uses is a product of his subconscious mind, his capacity for *affective association:* the bolt has become a viable symbol for the penis as a result of a subconscious tendency, shared by the audience, to associate bolt and penis—a tendency deriving from childhood patterns of thinking about which shall speak presently. And on a still deeper level, this symbolism derives from a primitive level of consciousness capable only of *serial association:* this-follows-thatness. It is this basic primitive capacity for serial association which feeds the subconscious and enables the mind to manufacture symbolisms by affective association. The focal consciousness then draws on, and in turn feeds back into, the subconscious level selectively for intellectual constructs like the joke just discussed.[10]

We saw in the previous chapter that obscene wit (like most wit) begins with some degree of hostility, an intention to injure, which society requires us to suppress. The expression of this inhibited aggression is connected in the case of wit with some form of associative mechanism, a play on words, for example. The original aggressive tendency is allowed to simmer for a time on the subconscious, affective level and is eventually served up by the operation of the focal consciousness symbolically disguised but still readily perceptible to the listener. The more clever the disguise the better the wit. The pleasure in a play on words serves to remove suppression and repressions and allows a relatively harmless release of hostility. We receive pleasure both from the release of inhibition or repression and from the purely intellectual enjoyment of the wordplay.

The mechanism of dreaming, as explained by the Freudians, is quite similar in its essentials. A residue of daytime thinking simmers in the subconscious, where it is connected associatively with a wish awaiting an opportunity for fulfillment on the conscious level, which has been denying that opportunity. The dream is formed on the subconscious level by means of disguise and symbolization and takes the form of a hallucinatory, pictorial sequence of images that are perceived by, but are often incomprehensible to, that part of the consciousness still functioning during sleep. The main difference between wit and dreams is that whereas dream associations function as asocial, nonverbal, and hallucinatory wish ful-

10. See the careful discussion, with bibliography, of this process as it relates to creative genius in A. Armstrong, *Shakespeare's Imagination* (Lincoln, Neb., 1963), especially chap. 19.

fillments, wit appears as consciously formulated thought whose subconsciously arranged associations are decipherable and communicable to others. The disguises of the dream are meant to hide what is struggling for escape; the disguises of wit function only to cast the original hostility and aggression in a form that will still be perceptible enough to stimulate the listener but will be humorous and oblique enough to remove any kind of guilt feelings. Of course, wit involves additional complexities of a purely verbal nature: delight in language for its own sake, the enjoyment that derives from playful manipulations of conscious thought, and the simple desire on the part of most people to lift their speech from the level of banality.[11]

The creation of metaphorical obscenities, whether current in the language as slang (we might say "frozen wit") or invented by an artist for a specific context, has much in common with these processes of dreaming and wit-making; indeed, the very same symbols are frequently found in all three areas.[12] Unlike primary obscenities, metaphorical obscenities are products of a conscious formulation occurring partially under pressure from inhibition (a reaction away from the affective focus of primary obscenities) and partially in pursuit of intellectual play. They are similitudes whose evocative power is derived from the associative subconscious (affective intellection) but whose meaning and effects are perceptible and enjoyable on the fully conscious intellectual level. Their formal qualities enable them better to survive the social suppression inflicted on the less tractable and less civilized primary obscenities, and also allow their creator great scope for inventiveness, nuance, and wit.

11. Dreams can be controlled by words in various ways and in this often resemble wit, although their inner connections can be perceived, if at all, only afterward by analysis. The frequency of puns and double meanings in dreams (especially prophetic dreams) was, of course, widely acknowledged in antiquity. Freud tells of the girl who dreamt of walking among ears of corn (*Ähren*) and finds that her dream was based upon a precept that was obviously a source of anxiety in the dreamer: "einen Kuss in *Ehren* kann niemand verwehren," no one can object to a kiss in honor. The hallucinatory dream-image of ears of corn had disguised the verbal expression of an anxiety-producing daytime thought. In dramatic terms, Aristophanes often accomplishes similar hallucinatory effects: much of the plot of *Birds* is built by taking figurative expressions literally and making the characters act them out in a landscape of fantasy, and it does not seem too farfetched to point also to such scenes as A 729 ff., in which a central pun—*choiros*, piggie = cunt—is taken literally and acted out much as it might be in an actual dream; or to P 1136 ff., where a vision of roasting acorns in the fire (double entendres for fucking) resembles the symbolic wish-fulfillment of a sexual dream.

12. See Freud, *The Complete Introductory Lectures on Psychoanalysis,* trans. J. Strachey (New York, 1966), pp. 158 f., 163, 165 ff.

We are now in a position to discuss the principal types of metaphorical obscenity found in the remains of Attic Comedy.

Metaphorical obscenities for the sexual organs make use of symbolisms frequently encountered also in dreams and springing from an affective, associative level of consciousness still possessing infantile and archaic processes of thought. The use of certain bodily parts to represent the penis is instructive: the foot (*104*) and the finger (*15*) are universal symbols in this regard, and undoubtedly have their origins in early infantile experience. A very young child's first pleasurable experience with parts of his own body centers around areas of curiosity, areas most like playthings: these are primarily the fingers and toes. The most acute pleasure in this period is oral, the contact of the lips with the nipple. Finger-sucking quickly becomes a pleasurable surrogate for this activity, and even into adulthood the cathexes surrounding these early objects of pleasure remain active somewhere beneath the level of full consciousness, and frequently emerge in dreams and other forms of unconscious ideation: folklore, popular myths and legends (the most notorious being Oedi-pous the swell-foot), linguistic idioms, and word-plays. One might say that idioms like foot = penis are dream symbols which have become fixed and current in the language rather than remaining private or idiosyncratic.

One of the most common varieties of metaphorical words for the penis are words for tools, always indicating the erect penis.[13] From very early childhood all men are fascinated by tools and tool-using,[14] and it is most natural to equate tool-using with intercourse, just as it is most natural to compare any elongated object with the erect penis. Only three of these words are static in meaning: *beam* (*54*), *peg* (*61*) and the *Spartan baton* (*66*) whose wrapping suggests the foreskin; all the rest are used kinetically to represent the characteristic of penetration into the body of the recipient of the penis and frequently of injuring as well: a bolt (*57*) fits into a lock, the spit (*59*) pierces meat, a boat-pole shoves (*55*), and so on for spears and swords (*47, 58, 65, 67*), rams (*48*), goads (*53*), axes (*62*), drills (*68, 71*).

All these objects are mechanical extensions of a man's strength and a means by which a man can exert his strength and will upon other (weaker) objects. These comparisons of tools with the erect and potent penis are not only natural but gratifying and attractive to a man's mind and self-image;

13. Nearly all the metaphorical obscenities for *penis* in comedy indicate the *erect* penis, the organ ready for intercourse. Only two point to the idea of a dangling penis, and these are used only of impotent men: *snake* (*90*) and *rope* (*105*). *Tail* (*92* ff.), common in many languages for *penis,* never carries the idea of dangling but is merely a natural comparison of man's only "caudal" appendage with that of animals.

14. See the remarks of Sperber (n. 5, above), pp. 412 ff.

they carry in them each a small wish fulfillment. We might also include here animals or parts of animals which express similar mechanical extensions of strength, for example, the horn (*91*) or the ram (*87*). We note in passing the familiar tendency in men (called to mind by this type of phallic metaphor) to talk of their penises as smaller versions of themselves, as representatives of their own libidinous drives, which are then personified in exciting and amusing metaphors. The penis is thought of as a rather randy and uncivilized being that accompanies us through life and must be catered to and appeased in its imperious whims; no ordinary terminology will suffice to describe its nature and its ways.

As in the case of many metaphorical expressions for sexual intercourse, these words carry in them a distinct aggressiveness, an impulse to injure, subjugate, and overcome the resistance of the object of desire in ways other than wooing. Like the mechanisms of wit and dreaming, the metaphorical obliquity of these expressions allows a pleasant and harmless bypass of social inhibitions against violence and aggressiveness and produces a much greater release of tension than is possible with the more direct and affectively charged primary obscenities. We may compare the many metaphorical obscenities for intercourse which are violent and hostile in tone: piercing on a spit (*298* f.), all varieties of striking (*301*), thrusting on or into (*303*), banging (*305* f.), beating (*307*), hitting (*309*), pounding (*313*), smacking (*314*), stabbing (*304, 312, 315, 316*), grating (*322*), twisting around (*329, 338*), pressing (*334*), wounding (*339*), and so forth.

The female genitals are of course represented by all such objects as share their characteristic of enclosing a hollow area or taking something into itself; naturally, these are perceived as static and passive but almost always contain the concomitant idea of entry by the phallic object. These can be natural features like holes, pits, hollows, or caves (*150–55*), cracks (*196*) or the pink cavity of seashells (*160*), or flowers (see below), or man-made enclosures like boxes (*108*), doors, gates, and passageways (*140–43*), which are entered by means of keys or locked by bolts, sheaths for weapons (*144*), shoes (*132*), rings or circles (*145–48*), vent-holes (*156*) or bored holes (*157*), as well as all kinds of dishes (*166–67*) and ovens (*163*). An inspection of the contexts in which these metaphorical expressions occur reveals a frequent feeling of darkness and secrecy. Boxes contain secret things, caves are dark (see *Eccl.*, prologue), gateways and doors are unlocked on the sly or closed against entry (as in *Lys.*, passim), seashells are unsealed to reveal the secret places within.

Many sexual metaphors are taken from nature, as one might expect in a society whose most important natural resources were agricultural. The comparison of the processes of fertility in the land with human sexuality is inevitable and took place very early in the Greek consciousness, as most Greek myths about mother earth and father sky will reveal. As we observed in the preceding chapter, the line that separates metaphorical obscenity in this class of comparisons from the many noble and exalted metaphors found in serious poetry (see *279*) is very often delicate and sometimes merely a matter of context.

As a rule, however, metaphorical obscenities from agriculture stress more concretely the physical similarities between the genitalia and natural features of the land than do the vaguer and more figurative metaphors of serious poetry. Passages in tragedy about wives whose husbands "till" them to produce a "crop" of offspring have the effect of euphemisms, in that they distract the listener's imagination away from the physical act of procreation onto a figurative plane whose language is exalted by centuries of poetic and religious usage. Metaphorical obscenities, on the other hand, ignore the *telos* of procreation and instead emphasize the physical act of intercourse by choosing natural features which illustrate it most vividly. Thus these metaphors are no different in intention and effect from all the others, despite their bastard status in an otherwise noble family.

Most natural are comparisons of the landscape to the female genitals: the bushy thicket (*134*) and gulley (*135*) call to mind most concretely the appearance of the genitalia, while the well-cropped plain (*136*), the garden (*130*), and the meadow (*133*) are gentler images of smooth areas bearing short foliage (pubic hair) like pennyroyal (*129*), celery (*137*), spurge-flax (*131*), and mint (*138*). Pubic hair is also compared with the downy fuzz on fruits (*139*), as it is also in the case of very young boys. Certain flowers that resemble the vaginal orifice in color and shape are common: the red rose (*126*), the juicy red fruit of the fig (*127*), the hyacinth (*132*). Some flowers, like certain nonagricultural objects mentioned earlier, contain secrets to be plucked out and taken away (cf. the universal image of "defloration"), such as the myrtle-berry (*125*), barley (*124*), and fruits with pits (*123*). Agricultural terminology for intercourse reflects this idea: one "removes the pit" in intercourse (*285* f.), a metaphor related to that of "pressing out grapes" (*327*) or "sweeping out" or "debugging" (*325*) the vagina. All agricultural metaphors for intercourse contain the idea of breaking into the land: breaking up clods (*283*), stirring up or hoeing (*293* f.), working the land (*284*), digging down into it (*292, 295*), or taking its fruit away (*287*).[15]

Closely connected with the land are birds, often used to indicate the

15. Similar agricultural metaphors for the breasts are discussed in sections *200* and *202*, below.

vagina: the central idea is always the bird as a small, chirping thing that hides in the foliage, a nightingale (*190*), a thrush (*101*), a *titis* (*194*), or a swallow (*195*). Thus Peisetaerus twice asks his bird-host to "go into the thicket" and bring out the nightingale which is hiding there (*190*). Mouse and bird nests are used similarly to suggest the vaginal area (*192* f.): the secret place itself hides in a spot concealed by nesting foliage. It need not be stressed that birds, like the products of the land, are caught and eaten by men (see Peisetaerus' vivid description at Av 524 ff., in which the preparation and consumption of bird-flesh is couched in sexual terms). As in all agricultural metaphors for the female genitals, a strong underlying idea is always the taming of the land and the consumption of its products by the males and their phallic tools: one word for intercourse is literally "to feed on" (*320*).

The male organ is also the subject of agricultural metaphors, but in a static way: various plants resemble and are therefore compared to the erect penis. The fig tree with its large, pendant fruit (*31*) suggests the penis and testicles, as the acorn suggests the erect penis; so do barley corns (*43, 40* f., *44*), the bushy chickpea and its pealike fruit (*42*), and the mallow-stalk (*39*), which is long and stiff and can be peeled back like a foreskin. Metaphorical obscenities for manipulation of the erect penis include terms meaning to peel back leaves (of the fig, for example, *37* f.,), to scutch (*288*) or to flay the skin (*289* ff.). Homosexual contrectation is spoken of as "fig-gathering" (*35*) or "fig-squeezing" (*36*).

The connection between eating and sex, which we shall have much occasion to discuss in the following chapter, is related to the early pleasure of taking in food which constitutes a child's first strong feelings of gratification and enjoyment. The female genitalia are often compared to meats that are cooked (sometimes on a phallic spit, *168*) and eaten: pork (*168*), boiled (labial?) sausages (*168*a), assorted dainties (*169, 171*), slices of fish (*170*). Pastries and cakes are frequent metaphors (*173* ff.). Dish-licking is a frequent metaphor for cunnilingus (*166* f.), and sauces, soups, and juices are used to indicate vaginal secretions (*180* ff.).

The penis also is "meat" (*99*), just as in our own slang, or the large thigh-bone with the meat on it (*100*), or phallic pastries (*101, 103*; compare our "loaf"), all emphasizing the erect, fleshy appendage. Unlike food metaphors for the female organs, which are cooked and consumed, these are static comparisons. The only usurpation by male organs of the idea of edibility appropriate to female organs is in fact a reversal of the sexual roles: the man is passive and the woman fellates him ("consumes his relish," *102*).

The vagina, as often in myth and legend, is perceived as an oven, hearth, or brazier in which the penis is "cooked" during intercourse:[16] a man cooks his penis in hot coals (*344*), roasts it (*346*), bakes it (*351* f.) or smelts it like a rod of hot metal (*357*). A man is thought to "inflame" the vagina by means of his hot organ (*345, 350, 353* ff.), a process dramatized in the parodos of *Lysistrata* when the chorus of men, armed with flaming rams, launch an attack on the women, who, having sworn off sex, "close the gates" of the Acropolis and try to douse the flames with water. Men in the grip of sexual passion are "aflame" (*347*) and can be "set afire" by the attractions of women (*349, 351*). At the root of all these fire metaphors, common to all languages, is, of course, the actual physical feeling of heat accompanying sexual arousal and intercourse, a feeling which in these metaphors is distributed equally between the men and the women.

Animals, which to the human mind often symbolize strong and unrestrained passion, are used to indicate the genitalia of both sexes. There can be some degree of physical comparison in these metaphors, as in the case of "piggie" (*110* f.), which emphasizes the warm, pink, hairless member of a young girl, or "sparrows" (*98*), which remind us of the aroused penis's hopping about. But primarily these metaphors emphasize sexual power and passion as localized in and embodied by the sexual organs, just as power and passion can be symbolized by and embodied in beasts: that is why the aggressive women at L 683 threaten the men with the power of their sexuality by saying "we'll loose our sows (cunts) on you."

The penis is thus a horse (*84*), a ram (*87*), a bull (*89*), or a dog (*88*), and the female member is a pig (*110* ff.) or sow (*113* ff.), a dog (*117* ff.), a bull (*120*), and perhaps a horse (*84*). The fish called *kallionymos*, the "marine member," could represent both sexes. It is clear that most animal metaphors are bisexual in use, a fact which is puzzling but is probably due to the fact that these metaphors emphasize the power and passion of animals rather than their physical resemblance to the organs themselves; the organs are personified by comparison with headstrong beasts. When these metaphors do emphasize physical resemblance they are not interchangeable: piggies and sows do not indicate the penis, nor do rams the vagina.[17] The case of the *kallionymos* is less clear inasmuch as the identity and characteristics of the fish are unknown.[18]

A large number of sexual metaphors are based on various kinds of

16. Compare the story of Periander of Corinth (Hdt. 5.92) who "pushed his loaf into a cold oven," according to the testimony of his wife Melissa.

17. Freud (n. 12, above), p. 157, remarks that in dreams, symbols for the genitals are often used bisexually, sometimes signifying genitals in general, irrespective of whether they are male or female, sometimes interchangeably, sometimes with only apparent ambiguity.

18. The usual identification with the fish known as *Uranoscopus saber* lacks plausibility;

motion that remind us of the excitement, release, and exhilaration we feel in the motions of sexual intercourse. Several words for intercourse mean simply to move or move against (*205* f., *212* f.), and the rapid rhythmic movements of dancing are often compared with those of intercourse (*75*, *359* f.).

In this area nautical metaphors are most prominent. The idea of tool-using and male domination plays a certain part in this kind of metaphor: the oar as penis (*51*, *63*) and the notion that a man during intercourse "mans" his woman and sails her like the captain of a ship at the rudder (*259* ff.).[19] The terminology reflects this idea: playing a scull (*259*), driving a ship through the water (*260*), getting aboard or being a passenger (*262*, *264–69*), sailing (*270*). Mutual aggressivenesss is expressed by the comparison of intercourse to a sea-battle (*263*). Swimming, referring primarily to coital motion, also appears (*271*). A certain female equality, however, is attained in this class of metaphors, since intercourse with the woman atop the man (woman in the active role) was popular in Greece. Thus a woman can be said to sail the man (*274* ff.).

Metaphors of horsemanship are closely connected with these nautical metaphors, both conceptually (riding and sailing are both compared with coital motions) and in terms of the language itself: the same words often mean both to sail and to ride (*276* f.). The fact that both men and women can do the sailing or riding accounts for the use of $\kappa\acute{\epsilon}\lambda\eta\varsigma$, small yacht or racehorse, for the genitals of both sexes: again, the ambiguity here is due to the fact that the comparison is based on particular motions and positions of intercourse and not on any physical similarity of horses or yachts to the sexual organs.

A word should be said here about flying, an idea that appears occasionally to be metaphorically connected with sex. Freud notes the sexual nature of the dream-symbolism of flying[20] and connects this with "the remarkable characteristic of the male organ which enables it to rise up in defiance of the laws of gravity, one of the phenomena of erection," noting that in dreams the penis is often symbolized by "balloons, flying-machines and . . . Zeppelin airships." A person who dreams he is flying (having intercourse) treats the sexual organ "as the essence of the dreamer's whole person." Probably we should, rather, consider the flying metaphor as akin to those based on other activities similar to the exhilaration of coital motion, such as sailing, riding, or swimming. The phallus is several times

---

why the *kallionymos* should have been identified with the genitals is mysterious. See D. Thompson, *A Glossary of Greek Fishes* (London, 1947), pp. 98 f.

19. Freud (n. 12, above), p. 162, points out that ships regularly stand for women in dream symbolism.

20. (N. 12, above), p. 155.

referred to as a wing (*95* ff.) or as winged (*97* f.), and is regularly represented in plastic art as winged. We note also the (phallic, *98*) sparrows
that draw Aphrodite's chariot in Greek art, Eros' wings, and so forth. The
sexually aroused women deserters of *Lysistrata* attempt to "fly away on
wings" or "on a sparrow," both metaphors for intercourse (*97* f.), and we
might very plausibly see some similar sexual element (albeit scatologically
tinged) in the flight of the erect (P 142) Trygaeus to Olympus on the back
of his winged dung-beetle.

Freud also draws attention to another symbol that appears in dreams
but has little in common with the others we have been examining, namely
the number three.[21] It is not certain that the magical character of this
number (and such lucky tripartite symbols as the cloverleaf, the fleur-de-
lis, and the *triskeles*) is based on its phallic connection (the stylized phallus,
penis, and two testicles, as a charm) or vice versa. At any rate, the connection of the number three with the phallus is frequent in comic metaphors and descriptions of the sex act (*49*): the phallus is often given a
tripartite character as a symbol of virility, and especially virile men who
have intercourse several times in succession always do it three times.

There is no specific terminology in comedy for ejaculation that corresponds to such English expressions as "come," "blow one's load,"
"shoot," and so on, nor is there any terminology covering male or female
orgasm,[22] although of course orgasm is *implied*.[23] The emphasis in all
terminology for intercourse lies, as we have observed, only on penetration
and motion. The one term that points to ejaculation, προσουρεῖν, to urinate upon (*336*), used contemptuously of minor poets in their nonpro-
creative (uncreative) relationships with Lady Tragedy, reflects a confusion of urine and semen common not only in dream symbolism[24] and
infantile thought[25] but also in Latin terminology (*urina* = semen, *meiere*,
mingere, and *commingere* = to ejaculate).[26]

21. (N. 12, above), pp. 163, 220.

22. Indeed, there is a curious absence in most languages of any slang expressions for the
clitoris: see A. Blau, "A Philological Note on a Defect in Sex Organ Nomenclature,"
Psychoan. Quart. 12 (1943): 481 ff.

23. Three euphemisms point a bit more directly to orgasm than obscenities: περαίν-
εσθαι, "finish off" (*244*) and two words meaning "fill up" (*335*).

24. *The Basic Writings of S. Freud,* trans. A. A. Brill (New York, 1938), p. 375.

25. See Freud's interesting essay, "The Acquisition of Fire," *Works,* 22: 187 ff., which
discusses the child's perception of the dual function of the penis (urination and ejaculation) and its significance in myths concerning fire and water. The parodos of *Lysistrata,*
in which the men attack the acropolis (closed by the women) with flaming rams only to be
doused from above, is revealing in this connection.

26. See *ThLL* 6.2.2322.36–47, 8.998.71 f.; R. Muth, "Urin," *RE Supplbd.* 11 (1968):
1301 ff.

Despite this lack of distinct terminology regarding the orgasm, obscene (and some nonobscene) language in comedy does allude, far more than in English, to the many ways in which sexual intercourse can be made more varied and stimulating. There are specific terms for foreplay: rubbing and chafing (*328, 340*), feeling (*319, 341, 341*a), arousing the woman (*318*), causing the woman's genitals to moisten (*273*), women inciting erection in men (*288* f.), women masturbating men (*252*), and numerous varieties of kisses (*366* ff.); terms for modes of intercourse: lifting up the woman's legs before and during intercourse (*317*), women's leg-motions during intercourse (*317*a), rough sex (*246, 249*), the woman on top (*274*), the woman with arched back and gyrating hips (*358* ff.), the woman bending over, holding onto something or on all fours while being penetrated from behind (*361* ff.); and frequent reference to fellatio and cunnilingus. All of this shows an unabashed enjoyment in the mechanics of sexuality and a desire on the part of both the woman and the man to heighten their partner's enjoyment of the sex act.[27]

The frequent allusions to fellatio and cunnilingus (citations in *380* ff.) are part of this process. The great emphasis placed upon these activities is evidence of a marked degree of orality in the sex life of the Greeks[28] (note also the stress laid on the techniques of kissing, *366* ff.), and shows that the Greeks valued, and considered entirely proper, other types of sexual intercourse than vaginal penetration (compare also the popularity of anal intercourse, both heterosexual and homosexual). References to fellatio indicate that the man was usually fellated to orgasm, and those to cunnilingus imply that this activity, too, was valued as a pleasure separate from vaginal intercourse.

The Greeks considered oral sex, like anal sex, as an enjoyable alternative to the usual modes of vaginal intercourse, and rightly allude to the oral activities of animals (*395*), which observation will be corroborated by anyone who has spent any time at the zoo. Fellatio is frequently depicted in vase-paintings, sometimes in scenes of group sex, and passages from comedy suggest that flute-girls (!) openly performed fellatio upon the men at symposia. No vase-painting that I have seen depicts cunnilingus, and there is no evidence that it was ever performed as a group activity, as was

27. We recall that one of Lysistrata's emphases in her sex-strike was that the wives, if forced to have intercourse, not do anything to make it enjoyable for the husbands; the oath taken by the women enumerates several such techniques (L 225 ff.).

28. See our remarks on this subject below, pp. 183 ff.

fellatio, but references in comedy indicate that the private practice of cunnilingus was not considered irregular.

References to fellatio and cunnilingus in comedy reflect no feelings of disgust or obloquy, except in the case of certain practitioners, Ariphrades the cunnilinctor and Aristyllus the fellator, who seem to have preferred these activities to the exclusion of others. Ariphrades is spoken of as frequenting brothels to perform cunnilingus (thus overdoing it in the poet's eyes) and Aristyllus, who habitually chooses to be the passive partner in a homosexual act, would have come under the general contempt expressed in comedy for all pathics (see sections *458* ff.).

The terminology for both acts is instructive. There are no metaphorical obscenities for fellatio (such as "blow" in English), but only obvious descriptive language: to lick (*382*), bend down over (*380*), work the mouth (*383, 383*a), or "do it Lesbian-style" (*381*: compare English "french" = fellate). Cunnilingus, usually called "licking" (*391*), does, however, boast some revealing metaphorical terms. We have seen that cunnilingus is often compared to licking soups and sauces from dishes, or as "having breakfast" (*392, 394*); the vagina is popularly called a "tongue-case" (*390*). These usages suggest that, apart from a desire on the part of the man to give his partner special pleasure, there was also a special pleasure for the man in smelling and tasting the woman's genitals and their secretions.

Freud's observation[29] that although the genitals most strongly arouse us, we do not consider them attractive has to be rejected in the case of the Greeks. That the female genitals were, in fact, considered especially attractive by the Greeks is indicated not only by the nature of this practice of cunnilingus but by the frequent references in comedy and in plastic art to the many styles of genital depilation practiced by Greek women and to the many kinds of perfumes used to enhance lovemaking. It may be that the absence of obscene language for ejaculation and orgasm in Greek can be explained in the same way as can the similar lack of such terms for urination: the Greeks were much more matter-of-fact than we about bodily secretions (other than excrement) and were not repelled, as we are, by them.

We will remark here, as we shall again in a later discussion of homosexuality, the pronounced tendency of the Greeks[30] to lay more stress on the sexual *instinct* itself than on the *object*; in glorifying the former they

---

29. *Three Essays on the Theory of Sexuality,* trans. J. Strachey (New York, 1962), p. 22.
30. Noted by Freud (n. 29, above), p. 15, n. 1.

were much freer than we are to vary sexual objects on their relative merits, whereas modern man tends to be limited in his choice of objects by outright taboos or by feelings of shame, disgust, or shyness which our culture has imposed upon certain kinds of objects. While we tend to consider the performance of certain sexual acts or a preference for certain objects as perversions per se, the only kinds of perversion remarked by the comic poets are cases in which sexual acts other than vaginal intercourse, otherwise perfectly proper, are carried to excess or practiced in an inappropriate setting.

This easy sliding from one sexual object to another is further illustrated by comic terminology for homosexual penetration and for the anus. It is a commonplace of psychology (and indeed common sense) that in anal intercourse the anus is perceived as an ersatz vagina;[31] anal intercourse is performed by analogy to vaginal intercourse. In addition, the Greeks seem to have retained into adulthood a strong cathexis of the anus, an area which is a source of great pleasure in children: the process of defecation, the sensation of the fecal column in the intestines[32] (note the joke about the column of feces which "buggers" Blepyrus, *437*, and the term κοπραγωγεῖν, *284*, gather shit = to bugger), and the excitement of observing one's excrement are all components of narcissistic infantile pleasure, of which our society disapproves and which is repressed in children very early in favor of what adults consider the "normal" genital development. Children are taught that excrement and the anus are dirty and nasty-smelling and so are broken of their attachment to them. The Greeks, on the other hand, encouraged through adolescence in their freedom of choice regarding sexual objects, retained the erotic significance of the anal zone alongside their developing genitality.[33] What in our society would be considered an inversion, a defiance of normal sexual behavior, was for the Greeks merely another sexual option, whether it be pathic sex as a young man or the occasional penetration of a male anus by a predominantly heterosexual adult.

Thus many obscenities for vaginal intercourse are used interchangeably for anal intercourse, not only the principal primary obscenities for fucking (*205* ff.), but also metaphorical obscenities: shoving bolts (*41*), goading (*359*), banging (*305*), pounding (*313*), chafing (*340*), words for motion (*337*), embarking on a ship (*262*), baking the penis (*351*), bending over (*363*)—all can mean penetration of a man or a woman. The same is true of words that mean both vagina and anus: κυσός (*109*), dried fig (*122*),

31. See, for example, Freud, *Works,* 16: 315 f.; 22 101.
32. See Freud, "Anal Erotism and Castration," *Works,* 17: 72 ff.
33. See below, pp. 205 ff.

gates and doorways (*140* f., *142, 437, 451* f.), isthmus (*143, 441*), sheath (*144*), bored hole (*157*), gulf (*151, 203*), bull (*453*).

This cathexis of the anus is clear also in comic language describing defecation, urination, and excrement. The abundant treatment of these subjects by the comic poets is fully discussed in chapter 6, but a few points apply here. Although defecation in comedy is used primarily in slapstick routines and as a way to degrade a character (by dramatizing his dependence upon, and frequently his lack of control over, his bodily needs), there is a marked curiosity about and an enjoyment of the excremental processes: its colors, shapes, sizes, and smells. Feces are long and vary in hue; farts are sudden and surprising, as loud as thunder, and occur especially when we are happy and well-fed, gleeful or contented or lazy. Farting and excreting are very often ways to signify joy, contentment, contempt, friskiness, displeasure, or strain, and as such they are an important component of the comic hero's "arsenal" of self-expression. By talking openly of (or acting out) farting, shitting, and pissing, a comic hero breaks free from and violates social inhibitions and the natural inhibitions of the adult, like a child who puts feces where adults do not want them.

Excrement, urine, and farts have strong smells which belong generically with the smells of rotting flesh and vegetation; they are death smells and as such are considered bad, as are all the activities involving the organs of excretion. A child is naturally ignorant of this kind of valuation and in fact feels a strong liking for his excreta, which give him physical pleasure both in the process of elimination and in the handling and smelling of his productions. This pleasurable feeling about one's own excretions never quite leaves us, even after we have been taught by adults that they are bad and smelly and to be kept out of sight and smell. Scatological language or the actual hurling of filth, for which it is a replacement, therefore become potent weapons against society's rules and produce old feelings of pleasure and release when they are employed or when we hear or see others employing them.

Euphemisms

A final word must be said about euphemistic terminology. Euphemisms, which are frequent in comedy, are of course not obscene but are nevertheless akin to metaphorical obscenities in that they indicate the identity of the organ or act to which they refer by comparing (or allying) it to something else; they differ in that the "something else" is vague in its nature and respectable in tone, and serves not to emphasize and highlight the physical characteristics of its reference but to give only the blurriest and remotest suggestion of it, to distract our attention from the realities that obscenities insist on by appealing to socially acceptable concepts instead. That is, we *know* what a euphemism is driving at, but the respectable images it calls to mind block the emotional force of the reference and make it impossible for the mind to focus on anything but vague impressions.

The euphemisms of comedy are natural and are found to be common in all languages: the penis is "nature" (*27*), joy (*28*), it (*17*), youth (*20*), thing (*24*), privates (*13*); intercourse is "manning" (*216*), enjoying one's youth (*217*), having or doing the work of Aphrodite (*218* ff.), having relations with (*223*), possessing (*231*), and so on. These words belong to the common vocabulary of the civilized adult and cannot cause hallucinatory regression, like primary obscenities, or affective imaging of sexual acts or organs, like metaphorical obscenities. They are society's way of referring to things that must be both physically and verbally hidden.

Euphemisms are used when no comic purpose would be served by using a primary or metaphorical obscenity. Often they are employed to build up to a climax in which more vivid language is used; sometimes they serve to differentiate a polite character from an uninhibited one (Just and Unjust Logic, for example); and sometimes they are used in lyric passages aiming for poetic beauty, such as the parabasis of *Birds*.

The one remarkable feature of this body of expressions, as they appear in comedy, is the absence of euphemistic expressions for the female genitals. The male organs are frequently alluded to euphemistically but the poets seem always to insist on obscene language for the female organs. The explanation is surely that no opportunity for euphemistic descriptions of women arises: the poets use women in the plays solely as objects of male desire, and in their presentation of women to their male audiences (the women in the audience do not count in determining a play's success) the poets lose no opportunity to call attention to the female genitals in the most direct and arousing manner possible.

With the points made in this brief overview in mind, we may proceed to a consideration of how Aristophanes, the author of our only surviving plays, employed the various kinds of obscene language in his artistic creations.

3   The Dramatic Function of Obscenity
in the Plays of Aristophanes

In the course of his career Aristophanes wrote comedies dealing with many different subjects in a variety of dramatic styles: comedies about peace, politics, social phenomena, and the sexes; lyrical fantasies; tragic parodies; satires on leading statesmen and the Athenian way of life. The eleven surviving plays constitute approximately one-fourth of his total output and represent very various periods of his creative life over a span of thirty-seven tumultuous years from 425 to 388. Of course, the nature of the characters, the plot, the themes, and the dramatization will vary from play to play, sometimes greatly, sometimes not so greatly, depending on factors ranging from simple differences in subject matter to major changes in the poet's style and method, some due to the rapidly changing social and political conditions in Athens toward the end of the fifth century, some because of conscious developments in Aristophanes' own technique.[1]

Yet in each of the surviving plays, from the earliest to the last, obscene language and themes related to it, as we have described it in the previous chapters, play an important role in the characterization of personae, in the development of themes and ideas, in the plot and the action we see on stage. Having treated obscenity historically and analytically, it is now our task to examine briefly the nature of the dramatic function of this one aspect of Aristophanic comedy: which characters use obscenities, when and how they use them, what kinds of obscenities appear in what contexts, how sexual and scatological themes contribute to the general thematic development of individual plays or groups of plays.

In the first part of this chapter we are concerned with the comedies that survive from the 420s. These five plays show a conspicuous unity of

1. See D. Grene, "The Comic Technique of Aristophanes," *Hermathena* 50 (1937): 114 ff.

tone, structure, and subject matter within the body of Aristophanes' extant work, a unity distinct enough from the later plays to warrant close comparison as well as individual scrutiny. The obscenity in these five plays is in many ways strikingly uniform in function, and possesses a richness and dramatic coherence to be found in none of the later extant plays save *Lysistrata*. Obscenity in these plays is a major ingredient in the grotesque humor, the wild lyrical flights, the free and abundant fantasy, and the savagery and abandon of personal and political invective that are all hallmarks of Aristophanes' early work.

Although a simple chronological treatment of these plays would be acceptable in view of their mutual similarities, it seems better to discuss as a group *Acharnians, Peace,* and *Knights,* which concern war, peace, and Cleon, followed by *Clouds* and *Wasps,* which concern primarily the questions of nature versus convention and the role of education therein.

Acharnians

The first scene of the play (1–203) establishes themes common to all the plays of the period of the Archidamian War: our hero, Dicaeopolis, is poor (497, 558, 578, 593 f.), old (600, 993 ff., 1228), and obviously out of place in the city, which he loathes but where he has been forced to live for the duration of the war. He longs for his rural deme (33) as do Demus, the Farmer (Frr. 100–11), Strepsiades, and later Trygaeus. When we first meet him he is sitting in lonely isolation from the city and its citizens; he is, in fact, as his name suggests, the only just citizen, the only one for whom the Assembly and the affairs of the city are a serious concern. What he sees in this first scene convinces him that no action is possible for one who is content to accept the conventional morality and work through the ordinary channels, because the entire city is corrupt and uninterested in the just things. The polis uses law and morality dishonestly, as masks for its injustice and greed.

The only course of action left to Dicaeopolis is to transcend the polis and its war by establishing in the countryside a private world in which all wishes are satisfied, all enemies are powerless, and all conventional laws and morality can be overturned by his own boundless self-assertion. That is, what the poet sees as dishonest and unnatural morality, allowing politicians and generals to foist war and destruction upon helpless little men like Dicaeopolis, is to be replaced in Dicaeopolis' new world by the healthy, natural drives toward food, sex, procreation, and general fertility. This devaluation and annihilation in fantasy of authority-figures—politicians, generals, nobles, gods, intellectuals, and other representatives of forces superior in power to the average citizen—is accomplished by heroes with whom the audience can identify and in that way retaliate vicariously against society.[2] All of the heroes of the plays of this period, Dicaeopolis, Demos and the Sausage-Seller, Strepsiades, Philocleon, and Trygaeus, in their own ways make use of the same outrageous mechanisms in accomplishing their overturning of society: these include violence, deception, the uninhibited indulgence of bodily drives (especially the sex drive), and the unrestrained use of obscene language, whether (*a*) positively, to celebrate sensual indulgence or (*b*) negatively, to expose enemies.

Midway through his opening monologue, Dicaeopolis breaks wind (30), a sign of boorishness and rusticity in Aristophanes; he also toys with himself, plucking pubic hairs from boredom (31). These are things no polite person would do, but which are done very frequently by Aristophanic heroes. Dicaeopolis is from the country, where (according to the comic poet) people are simple and uninhibited, and say what they mean. In other words, Dicaeopolis is already presented as living more or less in accordance with nature and not by the hypocritical conventions of the polis; he is not afraid to behave and speak accordingly.

In fact, Dicaeopolis is virtually the only character in the play who utters obscenities, that is, who feels free to expose what is usually hidden. All of the other characters (save the chorus of Acharnians, fellow-countrymen) are imposters with something to conceal. Later in the play, Dicaeopolis' obscenities will celebrate the freedom from restraints enjoyed by the hero; in this opening scene, Dicaeopolis' obscenities serve to cut through the disguises of the various corrupt envoys who appear before the Assembly and who represent the maddening depravity of wartime Athenian politics.

These exposures all involve references to unnatural sex, namely the *risible* varieties of homosexuality: here the reader is advised to consult chapter 7, where the delicate nuances of the Athenian attitude toward homosexuality are explored. It is a standard Aristophanic notion, which we will see again and again in the plays, that the only natural sex is the free heterosexual variety between husbands and wives or husbands and girls (and the occasional young boy). Sex with prostitutes as well as with older homosexual objects is nearly always frowned upon by the poet and is at best a poor substitute for normal sexual relations between man and woman. This is especially true of plays like *Acharnians,* where heterosexuality is so closely bound up with themes of general fertility and the idealized freedoms of rural life.

In 79 Dicaeopolis crudely but accurately maintains that only promiscu-

2. See K. J. Dover, *Aristophanic Comedy* (Berkeley and Los Angeles, 1972), pp. 31 ff.; C. H. Whitman, *Aristophanes and the Comic Hero* (Cambridge, Mass., 1964), passim.

ous pathics and pederasts are considered real men in Athens, and when the ambassador tells what he considers an amusing tale about the gourmandizing of the Persians (whom he admires and envies), Dicaeopolis interjects obscenely that the Persians are probably pathics too (83 f.). The ambassador affects not to believe this, however, nor does he believe Dicaeopolis' correct interpretation of Pseudartabas' garbled insult of 104, that all Athenians are pathics. The ambassador deliberately bowdlerizes the word χαυνόπρωκτος, gape-ass, into the innocent ἀχάνας (108), and this enrages Dicaeopolis: he is beginning to see through the whole hoax. Through his personal cross-examination of the envoys it soon becomes clear that the Assembly is dealing not with Persians but with the notorious Athenian pederasts, Cleisthenes and Straton, a discovery that leads to more derisive obscenities by Dicaeopolis (117–22). But the crier shouts him down. It is not long, however, before Dicaeopolis again breaks out with his obscene (and therefore impolitic) descriptions of the envoys: when he loudly complains about the hard-earned money of lowly citizens like himself going to degenerate Odomantians (158) he is pummeled and robbed, but gets no help from fellow Athenians. It is at this point that the fraudulent Assembly is dissolved and Dicaeopolis makes his private peace.

Dicaeopolis' obscenities in this first scene are all homosexual, that is, the honest and "natural" Dicaeopolis refers to unnatural sex as a way of exposing the unnaturalness and corruption of the polis. The same is true of obscene homosexual references later: Dicaeopolis' insult to Lamachus (592) and his pathic young soldiers (604), and the Acharnians' choric references to contemporary (and therefore debauched) youth (716) and to Cleon (664). In the city a man runs the risk of having Prepis or Cleonymus brush off their "wide-arsedness" onto him (842 ff.) or running into the adulterous Cratinus (848 ff.), or having Cleon "tongue him into submission" and "filthy him all over" (380–82). The war itself is seen by Dicaeopolis in terms of degraded sex, since it was caused (he contemptuously maintains) by the reciprocal rapes of "sluts and whores" (524 ff.).

The perversion and secretiveness which Dicaeopolis exposes in the first scene by means of his obscenities contrasts with the open honesty of the countryside. For it is only in the country (it would appear) that one can break wind, speak out plainly, and fornicate naturally. As Dicaeopolis says (271 ff.), it is far better to frolic and have sex out in the fields than to put up with troubles, fights, and Lamachuses in the city; playful sexual aggressiveness is better than planned political whore-snatching and incessant buggery. Dicaeopolis' small country Dionysia (241–79), with its uninhibited ritual obscenities and open glorification of the phallus, offers a refreshing contrast to the manifest depravity of the opening scene and pro-

vides a transition from the prologue to the dramatization of Dicaeopolis'
reestablishment of a rural style of life, which means an unlimited supply of
good food, wholesome sex, and general fertility, none of which can be had
or enjoyed amid the sterility of wartime Athens.

Food and sex, the rewards of peace, are in fact the controlling themes of
the second half of the play, whose action begins immediately after the
reconciliation between Dicaeopolis and his natural allies, the Acharnians.
This reconciliation consists of spirited fights, a visit to Euripides, and lively
masquerade sequences. There is hardly any obscenity between the close of
the country Dionysia and the opening of Dicaeopolis' marketplace (719).
Obscenity (other than for incidental swipes at the polis by the chorus and
at Lamachus by Dicaeopolis) is not needed during this agonistic portion of
the play: there is no one to denounce for degeneracy and, as yet, no sexual
pleasures to celebrate. But the obscenity begins again in earnest with the
arrival of Dicaeopolis' first customer, a Megarian.

This Megarian wants to sell his two small girls as piggies. His scheme is
Megarian (738) not only because it is deceitful but because χοῖρος was a
slang term for the youthful female member. Aristophanes bases the entire
scene around this play on words,[3] but he intended something more than
merely a series of vaudeville-style turns on an obscene double entendre.
The motifs of food and sex are to be introduced simultaneously by means of
this scene in the first moments of Dicaeopolis' private truce. Dicaeopolis
realizes at least as early as 781 that the Megarian's sack contains girls and
not piggies, but perseveres in a discussion of piggie-sacrifice, which in its
ambiguity could mean either eating or fornicating. The ambiguity is
continued as Dicaeopolis offers to feed the piggies, who will "eat anything
you give them": Dicaeopolis' offerings are double entendres referring to
the male member, which the girls will "eat" (797 ff.).

Interesting dramatically are the roles of the two characters in the obscenity: the deceitful Megarian never intentionally uses outright or even
indirect obscenity; he is the straight man for Dicaeopolis, whose growing
recognition of the Megarian's scheme provides ample opportunity for
double entendres and occasional outright obscenities (as in 781 f., 789).
Dicaeopolis thus reestablishes by the use of open and salty language his
identity as "natural man," his ability to acknowledge and enjoy bodily
drives and verbally to cut through all kinds of deceptions and disguises.
But the context of his exposures is changed: in the first scene Dicaeopolis,
as a member of the Assembly, exposed the deceivers for no reward and
only at the risk of bringing down upon himself wrath, physical violence,
and the loss of his food. In the country and on his own terms as a private

3. Dover, ibid., gives a lively description of the entire scene (pp. 63 ff.).

citizen, Dicaeopolis' sagacity and outspokenness bring him glory, food, and sex. In the prologue obscenity was unnatural in that it uncovered only ugliness and society's corruption; therefore it had to be suppressed by the forces of conventionality. In the countryside, obscenity exposes and celebrates what is joyful and fructifying, and is thus the natural, festive expression of healthy desires.

The mingling of motifs of food and sex through obscene language continues beyond the Megarian scene: the Theban's Copaic eels are apostrophized as "maidens" (883), and the pleasure of eating them is given in sexual language (883 ff.). The foods and processes in Dicaeopolis' description of the banquet (1005–07, 1014) are all double entendres for sexual organs and acts, referring probably to the "easy women" who will attend (1091). Both themes, gluttony and sexual abandon, rise to a crescendo as the play nears its climax.

Of course, the banquet with which the play ends is a grand marriage-feast celebrating the union of Dicaeopolis and the beautiful Diallage (989 ff.), who represents in her naked charms the sexual nature of Dicaeopolis' (and the poet's) conception of peacetime. Dicaeopolis' rhapsodic address to Diallage (989–99) contains a striking series of sexual double entendres based upon agricultural terminology; Dicaeopolis' reworking of the land after long years of wartime sterility is seen simultaneously as sexual rejuvenation and procreation.

Like Diallage and the countryside, the Truce itself is endowed with sexual powers, revealed obscenely by Dicaeopolis in a brief scene (1048–68) in which a groom's man asks Dicaeopolis for some of the Truce so that his friend will not have to fight but can spend all his time making love to his bride. In other words, like all the other "imposters" or intruders in this half of the play, he wants to benefit from Dicaeopolis' unique style of life without having earned the right to it. Like the others he is refused. But Dicaeopolis is only too happy to give some of the Truce to the bridesmaid, who he says had nothing to do with the war (1062). This girl is the only person so honored in the play, unless we include also the young girls with whom Dicaeopolis exits at the end. Dicaeopolis is otherwise quite selfish with the blessings of peace.

During the last scene the triumphant Dicaeopolis uses obscenity as a powerful means of contrasting his present state of blessedness with the wretchedness of the campaigning Lamachus, champion of the city. Lamachus asks his boy for some rotten fish rolled in a leaf ($\vartheta\rho\tilde{\iota}o\nu$), but Dicaeopolis tells his own boy to take hold of his foreskin ($\vartheta\rho\tilde{\iota}o\nu$), promising to "bake it" later (1101 f.); Lamachus tells his boy to grab hold of his spear, but Dicaeopolis tells his own boy to grab hold of his phallus (1121). A chorus sums up the extended stichomythy with a song contrasting Lamachus' cold guard duty with Dicaeopolis' warm sexual exploits with a "most luscious little girl" (1143–49). The contrast is further sharpened when Lamachus enters, wounded by a vine-pole (1190: fertility victorious over war), while Dicaeopolis enters with two naked courtesans, whose charms he describes obscenely (1198–1201): note the artful juxtaposition of Lamachus' "take hold of my broken leg" (1214) and Dicaeopolis' "take hold of my erect cock" (1216), Lamachus' σκοτοδινιῶ ("I swoon in the encroaching darkness") (1219) and Dicaeopolis' σκοτοβινιῶ ("I fuck the dark night through") (1221). Finally, as Lamachus is carried offstage groaning, Dicaeopolis exits toward the consummation of his marriage to triumphant cries of "τήνελλα καλλίνικος."

Peace

Peace returns to many of the ideas treated in *Acharnians*, although the methods of dramatizing them are different.[4] Since the play is a festive masque[5] celebrating the accomplished fact of peace and her blessings for all the Greeks, rather than the story of one aggressive man and his establishment of a selfish private peace, its action and its characters are simpler and more symbolic, its mood more joyous. Trygaeus is a nonviolent, less demonic Dicaeopolis, the chorus of farmers (603 ff.) more typically countrymen than the bellicose Acharnians, Polemos more a symbol of war than an execrable practitioner of martial arts like Lamachus, and the armament-makers are essentially straw men whose weapons Trygaeus turns magically into ploughshares. The names themselves reflect the less astringent and political character of the play when compared with their counterparts in *Acharnians*.

Since there is less intrigue and less conflict, less concentration on characters as individuals in *Peace* than *Acharnians*, the obscenity in *Peace* is benign and celebratory rather than aggressive and abusive, and more consistently symbolic than that of the earlier play. Although Trygaeus uses obscene language more often than anyone else, he is not, like Dicaeopolis, the only one who does. The obscenities in *Acharnians* were closely linked to the character and doings of Dicaeopolis in his fight to transcend the city, its politicians, generals, and personal enemies, in a quest for private blessedness. Obscenity in *Peace*, on the other hand, is used primarily to contribute to the universal themes of the play through more or less static

4. See Th. Geizer, *Aristophanes, RE Supplbd.* 12 (1971): 1456.53 ff.
5. Cf. Whitman (n. 2, above), p. 104.

images and symbols: the return of peace to the world and the blessings that result.

Like Dicaeopolis, the Trygaeus of the prologue wants somehow to be rid of the war and to enjoy once again the blessings of peace in his native countryside. In the earlier play the prologue put before us a picture of the corruption and unnaturalness of wartime Athens, which Dicaeopolis then exchanged for the gay life of sensual indulgence depicted in the later part of the play. The harsh and negative obscenities of the prologue contrasted in quality and function with the benign and celebratory obscenities of the later part of the play. In *Peace* the pattern is the same: the obscenities of the first part of the play (to 341) are scatological and serve to characterize the unnaturalness of wartime: they stand in sharp contrast to those of the second, which (like those of the second half of *Acharnians*) are uniformly sexual and serve to celebrate peacetime.

The world without peace presented to us in the prologue is visualized in images of excrement,[6] evil smells, and the total absence of heterosexual sex (sterility). If in *Acharnians* "perverse" homosexuality represents the opposite of healthy sexual release, in *Peace* the dung-beetle embodies a more complete reversal of the proper order of things: he eats rather than excretes excrement, his foul-smelling mouth is like an anus, he loves what we naturally abhor. Fully consonant with this disgusting state of affairs is the presence of Cleon amidst the excrement (43 ff.): Aristophanes makes an Ionian (i.e. a debauchee) guess that the dung-beetle actually represents Cleon, and Aristophanes does not deny it—like the dung-beetle, Cleon has become powerful by eating excrement (48); he is a τέρας that stinks like a seal, has unwashed private parts and the anus of a camel, and behaves like a degenerate (754 ff.). He is thus the ideal human symbol for the present disastrous state of the world.

Homosexuality, too, figures in the obscenity of this first section: the beetle is "dainty" in his own revolting way, and especially likes the excrement of pathics (11 f.), an Athenian specialty. The Athenians whom Trygaeus surveys on his flight upward are to be found in outhouses, around brothels, and are pathics all (101, 154–72). Yet the only subsequent references to homosexuality (that is, after the prologue) are Aristophanes' denial, in the parabasis, of improper homosexual inclinations (762 f.) and Hermes' fitting remark (724) that the dung-beetle will stay in heaven to "feed on Ganymedes' ambrosia" (= excrement), a remark

6. The only sexual references in the first part of the play are two incidental (and metaphorical) double entendres referring to Zeus' mistreatment of the (personified) cities, at 59 and 63.

that concludes the play's main exchange: the gods get the foul and sterile dung-beetle while humanity receives peace and fertility.

It is interesting to note that in *Peace* the gods are presented as unnatural in sexual terms: they have an affinity with the character of the dung-beetle. Zeus is σκαταιβάτης, the shitwalker or shitmounter (pederast, 42), Ganymedes is a pathic (724), Polemos makes men defecate in terror (241), the gods are pimps (849 f.) and rapists (59, 63) and make Theoria perform fellatio upon them (854)—not to mention their burial of Peace and the edict of death for anyone found "digging her up" (i.e. having intercourse with her, 37 f.). Thus Trygaeus' Bellerophon-like[7] journey to heaven on the dung-beetle accomplishes a return to the correct order of things: perverted sex is exchanged for natural sex, war for peace, the evil smells of excrement for the sweet smells of flowers, food, and girls, the execrable dung-cakes of the prologue for the wedding cakes of the climactic wedding feast.

There are few references to excrement in the second part of the play, and all are thematically connected with the first part: bad poets are called "droppings" by the chorus (790), and people who are connected with war are singled out for excremental humiliations: thus the fate of the sword-maker (547), the pike-maker (549), the taxiarch (1176), and the arms-merchant whose breastplate Trygaeus uses for a bedpan (1228, 1236 ff.). Like war itself, such creatures must be excluded from the new order of the world.

Once Eirene and her two companions, Opora and Theoria, have been returned to society, fertility and happiness burst forth in abundance. The resumption of normal sexual relations is closely connected with the return of peace (cf. 341, 439 f., 666, where Eirene bears a κίστη [box] of truces, a pun on κύσθος [cunt]), and specifically with a return to the fields: cf. 536, 707 f., 1329–31, and 867 ff., where Trygaeus says,

> ἔσωσα τοὺς ῞Ελληνας, ὥστ'
> ἐν τοῖς ἀγροῖς
> ἅπαντας ὄντας ἀσφαλῶς
> κινεῖν τε καὶ καθεύδειν.

[I saved all the Greeks so that they might safely take to the fields, to sleep and to fuck.]

The close connection between sex and the renewed fertility of the fields is captured in images like that of 706–08, Hermes' exhortation to Trygaeus:

7. See the schol. at 76, 135 f., 146 f., 154; *Arg. Pac.* 2; schol. at V 757.

ἴθι νῦν, ἐπὶ τούτοις τὴν Ὀπώραν λάμβανε
γυναῖκα σαυτῷ τήνδε· κᾆτ᾽ ἐν τοῖς ἀγροῖς
ταύτῃ ξυνοικῶν ἐκποιοῦ σαυτῷ βότρυς.

[Come now, on these conditions take to wife Opora here, live alongside her, and in your fields produce . . . grapes!]

(cp. A 994–99). Similarly Opora at 711 ff. represents both a sex partner and the fruit of the harvest, ·and the wedding hymn with which the play closes mingles sexual and agricultural terminology: double entendres for ·intercourse include τρυγᾶν (1339), which plays on Trygaeus' name, συκολογεῖν, fig-gathering (1348), and figs for the genitals of both bride and groom (1351 f.); all serve to allegorize and elevate the standard sexual byplay that was expected at the end of comedies.

As in *Acharnians*, eating and sex are closely connected: the pennyroyal tonic of 712 is vaginal fluid, simultaneously a cure for overconsumption of fruit and overindulgence in sex with Opora; at the banquet described at 868–70 the foods are double entendres for the female parts, and lack only the πέος for perfection; grain is both sustenance and the penis at 965–67; at the wedding feast (1353–59) food and sex are indistinguishable; compare 1136–39:

κἀνθρακίζων τοὐρεβίνθου
τήν τε φηγὸν ἐμπυρεύων,
χἄμα τὴν Θρᾷτταν κυνῶν
τῆς γυναικὸς λουμένης.

[and I'll toast my chickpeas and roast my acorn and kiss my Thracian slave-girl—all while the wife's away at her bath!]

Like Dicaeopolis, Trygaeus is rejuvenated sexually as part of the rewards for his heroic transcendence (859 ff.) and receives a beautiful wife symbolic of peace and fertility. In the earlier, more political play, the wife is Reconciliation; for Trygaeus she is Opora, symbol since the dawn of Greek literature of plenty, of ripe fruits and ripe bodies in the prime of life.[8] Trygaeus' name marks him allegorically as her "harvester" and sexual partner; this is explicit at 1339. After the wedding, we assume that he will return with his bride to Athmone to resume his vine-dressing. But Trygaeus, not as selfish and egocentric as Dicaeopolis, has provided the entire Council with a sex-partner, too. After all, everyone is sex-starved

8. A good survey and discussion of this traditional aspect of Greek poetry can be found in H. Fränkel, *Wege und Formen frühgriechischen Denkens* (Munich, 1955), pp. 45 ff.; see also *LSJ* s.v. Ὀπώρα II, III.

after thirteen long years (990) of sterile and sexless warfare (727 f., 964 ff.):
everyone in the city is "a lover" of Eirene (988). Theoria is to be the common sex-partner of the city.

We note that neither Eirene nor Opora, symbols of Peace and the
countryside respectively, is ever made the object of coarse sexual humor;
the sexual humor surrounding them is gentle and bound thematically to
noble motifs. But we get a different impression of Theoria's future in the
city, at the hands of the aroused Council. Aristophanes makes this thought
his excuse for a long series of violent and extravagant sexual jokes (871–
908) traded between Trygaeus and a slave, which emphasize the less lofty
aspects of coupling: here the images are of beating (874), anal penetration
(876), tent-pitching (880), gang-rape (882, 889 f.), cunnilingus (885),
roasting and scorching (891–93), and a culminating tour de force of
metaphors derived from the rousing and sweaty events of festal games
(894 ff.). Understandably, the prytanis takes hold of Theoria very eagerly
indeed (906).

Knights

Knights, like *Acharnians* and *Peace*, is concerned directly with the political
life of Athens, specifically the continuing war, the evilness of the leaders
(especially Cleon), and the desire of good men for peace. The conflict of
the play results in the reestablishment of peace and the good old days to
replace fear and warfare (although the new order following the fall of
Cleon is not dramatized as in the two preceding plays). Nevertheless,
Knights is quite different in tone and structure from its two sister plays. The
action consists almost entirely of a contest in roguery between two un-
savory characters, with the emphasis on ferocious scurrility more intense
than that found anywhere else in the extant plays. The hero, a sausage-
seller, is not, like Dicaeopolis and Trygaeus, morally superior to the city
and its leaders, but precisely the opposite: he is a product of the city's
lowest depths and knows nothing of the pure countryside. Demos, who
comes closest to the type of character we saw in Dicaeopolis and Trygaeus,
is hardly developed at all.

There is little fantasy. Where Dicaeopolis managed to create a utopian
state of blessedness which transcended the polis and bypassed the realities
of war, where Trygaeus in a state of heroic madness stormed Olympus and
brought Peace to transform the world, the Sausage-Seller accomplishes
nothing transcendent, establishes no new order of things. The focus from
first to last is on the immediacy of the city and its affairs. Nor does the play
ever show us the reality of the good things that are supposed to result from

the triumph of the Sausage-Seller over Cleon: the rejuvenation of Demos is not developed much beyond a plot-device, and the entrance of two naked Truces at the end seems to be a perfunctory gesture made to satisfy an almost obligatory tradition in Old Comedy of staging the good old days this way.[9] Moreover, even the actual political satire of this most political play contains very little specific criticism and no coherent program of reform, even on the trivial level of most other plays. The atmosphere of topicality and realism is only a mask; the real purpose of *Knights* is to attack and degrade Cleon in the most violent possible ways. It is essentially a vindictive work that grew out of the standing feud between the poet and the politician.

The obscenity in *Knights* is particularly savage and almost entirely of a homosexual and scatological nature. In *Acharnians* and *Peace* the negative dramatic function of such kinds of obscene language (used to expose and degrade corruption and wickedness) was confined to the opening (negative) scenes; the heroes then proceeded either to transcend or to transform the evilness they uncovered. The obscenities of the later parts of the plays were therefore primarily sexual, their dramatic function gay and positive: to celebrate peace and unfettered fertility. In *Knights* a part corresponding to this second section is lacking, and thus there is no place for heterosexual language. The play is wholly concerned with a contest of attack and exposure between two profligates, and the winner, far from transcending the corruption he exposes, wins because he is actually more scurrilous and corrupt than his opponent.

The only sexual obscenity to be found in the play is in fact the comic coinage κατατριακοντουτίσας, thrice shoving in the old pole, which follows the entrance of the Truces (1390 ff.) at the end of the play, where it is intimated that Demos, like Dicaeopolis and Trygaeus free of his troubles, will take his wenches and head for the countryside. Elsewhere we find only nasty references to cunnilingus (a practice not thought of, when taken to excess, as proper heterosexuality: see chap. 2, p. 52): Cleon's plundering of the islands is visualized by the Sausage-Seller in terms of forcible cunnilingus (1032 f.), and the chorus describes for the audience the unspeakable practices of Ariphrades the cunnilinctor (1280–89). The faint sexual overtones of the dialogue between the virgin trireme and her older companion, who express disgust at the thought of being manned by Hyperbolus (1300 ff.), or those of the chorus regarding Dame Comedy (517), are meant to be anything but obscene.

The two slaves, Nicias and Demosthenes,[10] initiate an important homo-

9. Cf. Cratin. 160 f., 238, 239; Telecl. 1; Eup. 90 f., 276 f; Pherecr. 10, 130.

10. Although the generals are not named in the text, it seems plausible that they are the

sexual characterization of Cleon which continues throughout the play: specifically, he is presented as both a pathic and a *paedicator,* the aggressor in homosexual contact. Demosthenes tells us that Cleon's anus lies ἐν Χάο-σιν, among the gapers, that is, among the pathics (78). The idea is picked up again by the chorus, who portray Cleon as violating his victims sexually (263), and once more by Demosthenes, who makes another joke on χάσ-κειν, gaping (380 f.) Naturally, the Sausage-Seller is quick to adopt this kind of scurrility in his abuse of Cleon: when Cleon righteously declares that he has benefited the city by curbing the activities of the homosexuals, particularly Gryttus (876 f.), the Sausage-Seller retorts that this was done not with virtuous intent but simply to prevent other pathics from becoming Cleon's political rivals.

Of course, the Sausage-Seller, too, is guilty of homosexual practices, but there is a difference: whereas Cleon never admits the vice of which the other characters accuse him, the Sausage-Seller proudly proclaims it; he does not wait for Cleon to bring up the subject (as he does only obliquely at 962 f.). But the Sausage-Seller is not an aggressor like Cleon; he is not a *paedicator.* The Sausage-Seller grew up in the marketplace where he was subjected to buggering (1242). One of the first signs of his future greatness was the episode of the "meat" which as a young man he was holding between his buttocks. A passerby prophesied that this was surely evidence of a great future in politics.

The anecdote runs like a minor leitmotif throughout the play (423–26, 483 f., 1263). The Sausage-Seller's reamed anus in fact makes him at one with the people in comic terms (as well as the most extreme case), as opposed to Cleon, who is an oppressor (bugger) of the people. As the Sausage-Seller says to Demos, "You will agree that you have never seen a man worthier than me in this city of Κεχηναῖοι" (that is, the Reamed as well as the Gullible, 1262 f.). Two insults reinforce the characterizations: Cleon tells Demos that if he listens to the Sausage-Seller he will become a μολγός, an old hide pouch (i.e. well-worn anally) like the Sausage-Seller (962 f.). The Sausage-Seller replies that if Demos listens to Cleon, he will become "ψωλός all the way to the pubis" (963 f.)—that is, a totally aggressive pederast, all hard-on.

We must understand the use of the ἐραστής, lover-theme, in the same light. Cleon proclaims himself to be Demos' ἐραστής; the Sausage-Seller calls himself a rival, ἀντεραστής, and goes on to explain that Demos is like a young ἐρώμενος, the beloved: the Sausage-Seller and other good men

---

men intended by the poet: see Gelzer (n. 4, above), 1427.58 ff. We shall therefore refer to slave A as Demosthenes and to slave B as Nicias.

have been waiting their chance to treat Demos as he deserves, but are blocked by Demos' fatal tendency to "give himself" to such scum as Cleon (733 ff.).[11] Here again is the motif of Cleon as violator of the people, expressed by means of homosexual obscenity. The joking portrayal of Demos as a young ἐρώμενος continues through to the last part of the play (946, 1163), when his rejuvenation entitles him to a παῖς ἐνόρχης, a well-hung boy "such as the nobles have" (1385–87), in addition to the Truces. Like Dicaeopolis and Trygaeus, Demos in his liberation from oppression earns a simultaneous liberation from the restrictions of age and sexual restraints.

Cleon uses only four obscenities, in comparison with the many used by his rival, and those he does use are comparatively mild: his threat to drag his opponent away by his πυγή, butt (a mild word, 365), his threat to rip out the Sausage-Seller's "tender parts" (he uses the euphemism, τἄντερα, 708), his boast about Gryttus (876 f.), and his reference to the Sausage-Seller as a μολγός (962 f.), use no harsh words. In a revealing interchange (896 ff.) Cleon even breaks off a series of crude jokes on flatulence with which the Sausage-Seller and the rustic (43 ff.) Demos are amusing themselves, complaining that they are the. rankest buffooneries (βωμολοχεύματα). The delighted Sausage-Seller replies that his destiny is to overpower Cleon in roguery.

If roguery includes the abundant use of obscenities, the Sausage-Seller certainly qualifies as a rogue. Nearly all of the obscene language in the play is his. If Cleon threatens to tear out the Sausage-Seller's "tender parts," the Sausage-Seller threatens to "drag Cleon into the Cerameicus by the testicles [ὀρχιπέδων] with a meathook" (772), and hopes that he "bites his own cock" when he bends over to consult his oracles (1010). Cleon threatens to "tear in pieces" his rival; the Sausage-Seller replies that he will "bugger" Cleon (κοπροφορήσω, 295); at 364, the Sausage-Seller vows to "fuck Cleon's ass-hole as if it were a sausage-case," a threat which Cleon's meager reply (365) cannot hope to match.

In addition to homosexual scurrility, the Sausage-Seller makes frequent use of excremental language: he calls Cleon βόλιτοι, bullshit (658), turns Cleon's political program into a crude joke on the powers of his own well-muscled anus (721), and often alludes to defecation as a means of trivializing Cleon's arguments (280 f., 888 f., 896–903, 1057), or twisting his off-hand statements in a vulgar way (997 f.). The Sausage-Seller's anecdotes, too, are full of gratuitous excremental coarseness: witness his account of the

11. For the meretriciousness of the post-Periclean demos, cf. Th. 2.65.10, Xen. *Ath.* 1.7. 2.19.

Assembly meeting at 638–42, and his continuous references to guts, stuffed or unstuffed.

Clouds

Clouds does not, like the plays we have been examining, deal with the grand problems of war, peace, political corruption, and Cleon. There is no transcendent hero, no fantastic liberation from the constraints of society, no grand causes of the compelling urgency that surrounded the questions of war and peace and politics debated in other plays. The play focuses entirely on the family of Strepsiades and their dealings with the new amorality and chicanery then (according to the comic poet) sweeping Athens and embodied in Socrates' school. Unlike such larger-than-life creatures as Dicaeopolis, Trygaeus, and the Sausage-Seller, the characters of *Clouds* (with the exception of the chorus of clouds itself, in which the poet invests most of the overarching intellectual dialectic of the play) are mere individuals with small and selfish concerns, without intellectual distinction or unusual strengths of character, and incapable of any grand or extraordinary achievement. Aristophanes treats within this all-too-human context the problems of pedagogy, belief in Zeus and the gods, the relationship between rationalism and morality, the conflict of generations, the nature of education, and the question of nature versus convention. The essential comedy is built around the *Begriffsstutzigkeit* of Strepsiades and the difficulties in which it involves him when he leaves the tolerant safety of his own home to try to hoodwink the city.[12] Socrates and his pupils, Pheidippides, the Logics, and the creditors are secondary characters who illuminate the various facets of Strepsiades' predicament, besides providing much opportunity for the satire of current ideas.

Strepsiades, like the other comic heroes, has a scheme: to cheat his creditors. But since this is a dishonest and unfair scheme, he is not allowed to get away with it. He must pay for his poor judgment and reckon with the consequences of his bungled attempt at fraud. If there was little fantasy in *Knights*, there is none at all in *Clouds*. In the absence of anything grand and fantastic with which to identify the characters, it is their personal idiosyncrasies and foibles which must provide the comedy and sustain our interest. The invincible and transcendent power of heroic self-assertion in the face of a corrupt society, which initiated the fantastic and superhuman successes of Dicaeopolis, Trygaeus, and the Sausage-Seller, is schematized in this play by means of the then current dichotomy be-

12. See W. Schmid, *Die attische Komödie* in Schmid-Stählin, *Geschichte der griechischen Literatur* ser. 1, vol. 4 (1946), pp. 261 f.

tween φύσις, the urgings of nature, and νόμος, the conventions of society.[13] But since Strepsiades' scheme and the disreputable men with whom he must conspire to achieve its success are viewed as stupid and dishonest, while society appears (for once) to be sane and honest, Strepsiades cannot, like other heroes, use the force of liberated φύσις to overturn the laws of society. Instead, the unrestrained exercise of φύσις appears in the speech of Unjust Logic, and the result of the play demonstrates that anyone who follows the advice of Unjust Logic must be defeated by the forces of civilized life and convention. For Strepsiades this means paying his debts and his damages at last, not to mention dealing with his now corrupted son; for Socrates it means dealing with the outraged Strepsiades.

Thus, the sensory indulgences that were part of the victory of the comic hero in other plays, as well as the obscene language which helped first to achieve that victory and then to celebrate it, appear in *Clouds* to be mere outlawry and hubris, intolerable to society and involving the transgressors in ruin. The role of obscenity in *Clouds* will therefore be different from what it has been hitherto.

Obscenity in *Clouds* is, in fact, used to flesh out and animate a character's personality. This use of obscenity to differentiate characters and add depth to their personalities is new, and demanded by the novel and more subtle nature of the play itself (cf. V 1044 ff.).[14] In the plays we have been examining, obscenity belonged primarily to one character but was for that character more a weapon of abuse and/or exposure than an integrated part of his personality. Moreover, the obscenity was very closely connected with the themes and fantasies in which the protagonist was involved rather than being a real aspect of the protagonist's personality. The obscenities of minor characters, like the slaves in *Peace*, were without distinctive characteristics and were intended merely to provide farcical amusement. In *Clouds* all of the major characters use obscenities (except for the elegant Pheidippides, who would not stoop to using coarse language), although, like all protagonists of this period, Strepsiades has by far the most.

Before we examine the obscenities of the major characters in detail we may note that *Clouds* has neither women nor references to the countryside

13. The fullest treatment of philosophical and cultural problems involved in this dichotomy is F. Heinimann, *Nomos und Physis* (Basel, 1965), especially pp. 101 ff., 121 ff.

14. The remarks of Grene (n. 1, above), pp. 117 f., are worth quoting: "Within its particular parts . . . *Clouds* shows a distinct move toward more effective dramatization, and also a kind of psychological humor which we find again only in the late and fully developed plays, *Lysistrata, Ecclesiazusae, Plutus*. . . . This subtler kind of humor, which consists in observation of a purely *human* personality and its contacts, is that which informs much of Aristophanes' later works."

(apart, of course, from the magnificent nature poetry of the parodos, which is nevertheless different in tone and context from that of descriptions of the countryside in, say, *Acharnians* and *Peace*), peace, or fertility—subjects which in *Acharnians* and *Peace* called for much heterosexual obscenity. The closest approach is in Strepsiades' monologue contrasting the simple sex life of bumpkins with the sophisticated lovemaking of city women (see below), a reference which is but a brief nod to themes that literally filled earlier plays. There is even less heterosexual obscenity in this play than there was in *Knights:* all we find here are Just Logic's moralistic references to fornication (996 f.), Unjust Logic's teasing replies thereto (1068–82), and Strepsiades' shocked reaction to the incest in Euripides' plays (1371 f.).

As in *Knights,* the obscenity is entirely homosexual and scatological, although there is very little obscene invective, which was the special realm of such obscenities in earlier plays. The obscenity of *Clouds* does not serve to establish the violent vulgarity of any one character, nor is it used by one character to expose another. It is almost totally benign, and the exposures it effects are self-exposures: a character's obscenities reveal aspects of his personality and motivations. The only suprapersonal, thematic use of obscenity—to underline the conceptual points Aristophanes wants to make about the new morality in Athens—occurs in the debate of the Logics, but here, too, the points are made through revealing self-characterizations and not through the exposure of someone else. Just Logic reveals his own unhealthy sexual interests, and Unjust Logic his own shamelessness, without each other's help.

We may begin with Strepsiades who, like Dicaeopolis and Trygaeus, is a countryman (43, 134, 138) forced by the war to take up residence in Athens. Unlike Dicaeopolis and Trygaeus, however, Strepsiades has little dynamism or strength of character. He is an ignoramus, puzzled and confused by the city and its ways but unable either to transcend or transform what dissatisfies him. The reason is simple: he is selfish and without the strongly developed sense of morality that characterized the other protagonists; he wants his share of the corruption. The obscene language of Dicaeopolis and Trygaeus served to expose corruption and liberate φύσις, then to celebrate the establishment of a new society. Without that kind of dynamic function, Strepsiades' many obscenities serve merely to emphasize his vulgarity, clownishness, and stupidity. Lacking a target for exposure or a subject for celebration, Strepsiades' obscenities turn inward and expose their speaker as a buffoon.

The pressure of the polis lies much heavier on Strepsiades than on

Dicaeopolis and Trygaeus. Strepsiades has a city wife whose inexplicable ways trouble him as much as those of their hippomaniac son. In a wonderfully vivid bit of characterization, Strepsiades soliloquizes about his unhappy life in terms of sexual incompatibility (41 ff.):

εἴθ' ὤφελ' ἡ προμνήστρι' ἀπολέσθαι κακῶς,
ἥτις με γῆμ' ἐπῆρε τὴν σὴν μητέρα.
ἐμοὶ γὰρ ἦν ἄγροικος ἥδιστος βίος
εὐρωτιῶν, ἀκόρητος, εἰκῇ κείμενος,
βρύων μελίτταις καὶ προβάτοις καὶ στεμφύλοις.
ἔπειτ' ἔγημα Μεγακλέους τοῦ Μεγακλέους
ἀδελφιδῆν ἄγροικος ὢν ἐξ ἄστεως,
σεμνήν, τρυφῶσαν, ἐγκεκοισυρωμένην.
ταύτην ὅτ' ἐγάμουν, συγκατεκλινόμην ἐγὼ
ὄζων τρυγός, τρασιᾶς, ἐρίων, περιουσίας,
ἡ δ' αὖ μύρου, κρόκου, καταγλωττισμάτων,
δαπάνης, λαφυγμοῦ, Κωλιάδος, Γενετυλλίδος.
οὐ μὴν ἐρῶ γ' ὡς ἀργὸς ἦν, ἀλλ' ἐσπάθα.
ἐγὼ δ' ἂν αὐτῇ θοἰμάτιον δεικνὺς τοδὶ
πρόφασιν ἔφασκον, ὦ γύναι, λίαν σπαθᾷς,

[Oh, how I wish that that matchmaker had perished cruelly before she persuaded me to marry your mother. I had a very sweet life as a countryman—lazing, unshaven, sleeping whenever I wished, abounding in bees and flocks and olives. And then I married the niece of Megacles, son of Megacles—I a farmer, and she a woman of society, elegant, grand. On our wedding day, reclining at her side, I smelled of new wine, cheeses, wool, abundance—she, of perfumes, saffron, tricky lascivious kisses, expenses, gluttony, Aphrodite of the Hard-on and Genetyllis. I shall not say that she was slothful; on the contrary, she banged at her loom constantly. But I would hold up this nightgown here between us and say, "Wife, if you keep banging like this you'll use it all up!"]

All of Strepsiades' suspicions about the city and his longings for the familiar, uncomplicated life of the countryside are encapsulated here in sexual terms: his perplexity about his wife's sophisticated (and thus "unnatural") odors and ways of making love is at one with his anxiety over the family's spendthrift ways: note the obscene double entendre in σπαθᾶν, which means both "to whack away [make love] continually" and "to squander wool/money." Kolias, whose name puns on κωλῆ, the male member, and Genetyllis, goddesses of sex and reproduction who were favorites with city women, puzzle Strepsiades as much as the newfangled deities of Socrates. Even the constant activity of city people puzzles him: like his wife in bed, everyone seems always to be doing something—or, rather, to be up to something.

The major function of Strepsiades' obscenity is to provide country-bumpkin farce. He uses πέρδεσθαι, fart, in the opening soliloquy as a synonym for "sleep" (9); we note, a few lines later, his suspicion of "long-hairs" (14), that is, nobles whom he suspects of pederastic debauchery, something he finds strange and about which he often makes jokes. Strep-siades' antics throughout his stay in the Phrontisterion demonstrate his fondness for simple kinds of rustic humor: he mightily enjoys the story of the lizard that defecates on Socrates (171–74); he is particularly amused by the odd posture of the disciples who are bent over to study "the things beneath the earth" and immediately makes crude and obscene fun of them (193, 196 f.). We note that later he continues to poke fun at homosexuals by personifying the bedbugs (κόρεις) who bite him like "Cor-inthian" pederasts (713 f.), by joking obscenely about Cleonymus (675 f.), and by calling his newly reeducated son a "cistern-ass" (1330). When he is sup-posed to be meditating ascetically, he is found instead to be masturbating (it is difficult to repress Strepsiades' raw naturalness, 734), a joke that Socrates does not find amusing. Socrates rebukes him as blasphemous and clownish for comparing his flatulence to the Clouds' thunder (293–96, although he later gives in on this point) and calls him vulgar and perverse for making an obscene gesture in answer to a serious question (649–55). All of this is, of course, the familiar situation in comedy of a serious teacher questioning an ignorant buffoon who reduces everything to his own base level. The same kind of comic routine reappears in *Wasps* the following year.

Strepsiades' own anecdotes are full of scatological references. The bladder that exploded at a country picnic he says "defecated" on him (411); his bathetic reminiscences about Pheidippides' childhood bowel troubles serve only to broaden the comedy of his own urgency (1384–90); his dialectic of the chicken-droppings is his notion of Socratic discourse (1430 ff.); the idea that rain is Zeus urinating through a sieve (372) betrays incredible naiveness; and his reference at the end of the play to the moon's backside (1507), at which he feels it is impious to peek, under-lines both his simple backwardness and his sexual conservatism (cf. 43–55, 1371–76), not to mention his newfound moral standards. When he is in an abusive mood he is apt to use violent obscenity, as in his threat to the creditor (1299 f.) or his insult to Pheidippides (1330).

Similar to Strepsiades in buffoonishness is the disciple who greets him at the Phrontisterion. This fellow, no less than Strepsiades, is fascinated (if not as hugely amused) by the gnat's proctal buzzing and the defecating lizard, as well as all the other ludicrous things he speaks of. The obscenities he uses are intended primarily to help establish Strepsiades' vulgar and credulous nature, but they also serve as a comment on the frivolous and farcical character of the subject matter taught by the Socratic school and of the people who go there to learn claptrap and dishonesty.

Socrates himself uses obscenity, too, but of a different kind. After his initial disgust with Strepsiades for comparing his own flatulence with the Clouds' thunder, Socrates gives in and a bit later lowers himself to Strepsiades' level by resurrecting the flatulence comparison, this time not as a joke with sound effects, but as an illustration of a scientific principle (385–94). Aside from being a good way to illustrate further the block-headedness of Strepsiades, Aristophanes uses this scene to poke fun at Socrates' notorious habit of illustrating his ideas by using lowly examples (although we may be sure that in real life Socrates never stooped quite this low), and also to ridicule what the poet feels is an idle game of vapors and a waste of time for a grown man like Socrates.

All of Socrates' other obscenities are contemptuous jokes about homo-sexuals and effeminates (348–50, 355, 673 ff., 687–92), which might be expected in the discussions of the protean quality of the Clouds or the peculiarities of verbal gender in which they occur. They seem, however, to be entirely in character for Socrates, given his ascetic life-style and rigid code of continence. Socrates' contempt for homosexuality is based upon his contempt for softness and anything that distracts men from contempla-tion. This indifference to the pleasures (and perversions) of sex is similar to that of Strepsiades. Both men are out of step with the "morality" of the city, Socrates by conscious choice, Strepsiades because of his rustic up-bringing, the accidents of war, and the frightening demands of his elegant wife.

Obscenity plays a crucial role in the debate of the two Logics (see also *478* ff.). Just Logic, who speaks first, complains that none of the young men want to follow his lead any longer (916 f.) because of the evil influ-ence of Unjust Logic, whom he calls "shameless and a pathic" (909) and the instigator of what he feels has been a disastrous decline in decency and morality. In his speech on the ἀρχαία παίδευσις, the old-fashioned educa-tion (961 ff.), he lauds the simple, upright pleasures of the good old days, namely, continual athletic training and the learning of wholesome knowl-edge, good manners, and strict continence under the tutelage of the nobles. From such a regimen emerged the stout warriors of Marathon days. Just Logic's throngs of clean young men, bronzed by the sun and well-muscled from constant exercise, stand in striking contrast to their

pale, flabby, and degenerate modern counterparts. The decline of chastity
has, in the view of Just Logic, led to a general decline in morality and civic
health.

There is nothing in all this of which the Acharnians, the Knights, or the
Aeschylus of *Frogs* would disapprove. But, unlike the usual *laudatio tem-
poris acti*, Just Logic's illustration of the theme of chastity of the good old
days is held up to comic ridicule and ultimately fails, not because chastity
on the part of young men and decorum on the part of their elders are
indefensible, but because Just Logic is a clumsy debater and a weak
personality, and therefore a poor spokesman for his theme: he makes
Unjust Logic's case for him.

In the struggle for Pheidippides' allegiance, Just Logic takes an entirely
negative position: he tells Pheidippides what he must *not* do, what he
should abstain from. The vices and unseemliness against which he rails are
described in such lurid detail and with such obvious longing that we must
feel there is something very attractive, not to say enjoyable, about them.
Just Logic manifestly counsels Pheidippides to deny what seem to be irrepressible urges. We might go even further: the sexual tastes of Just
Logic, although suppressed, do not really differ from the blatant tastes of
those he would call pathics (909, 1023), except that they are regulated not
by promiscuous whim but by the time-honored code of the upper class, a
code often ridiculed by Aristophanes' lowbrow heroes. Propriety and
etiquette appear to be mere masks for the lust that is in all of us. We note
that Just Logic does not prohibit pederasty itself: he prohibits only
wantonness, flirtatiousness, and promiscuity. The act itself is delicately
concealed but hardly invisible.

The language of Just Logic's speech is worth savoring: the long anapes-
tic section (961–1008) contains no outright obscenity but much suggestive
detail: note the piquant tone of ἀπηνές (974), the hot euphemisms ἥβης,
token of youth (976), and τοὐμφαλοῦ . . . ὑπένερθεν, the regions below the
navel (977), and the strikingly sensual ἴσχειν τὼ πόδ' ἐναλλάξ, keeping the
legs crossed (983), and τοῖς αἰδοίοισι δρόσος καὶ χνοῦς, the dewy down of
young privates (978), to mention but a few. Note also the affectionate
πόσθην μικράν, little dingle (1014), used of the good boy's member, in
delicate balance with the vulgar κωλῆν μεγάλην, big meat, of the bad boy's
(1018). The short lyrical section following the anapests (1009–23) shows
Just Logic in a more excited mood: hence his stronger, but still preciously
euphemistic, language.

Unjust Logic at once perceives his rival's unhealthy sexual inhibitions
and takes a positive approach. He makes no secret of his own sexual
desires, but maintains that they are perfectly natural impulses, an ac-

ceptable part of human nature. Sexual drives are to be seen as "nature's imperatives": τὰς τῆς φύσεως ἀνάγκας (1075, with a pun on φύσις = penis). We must, he says, "use our φύσις, jump, laugh, and consider nothing shameful" (1078). It is unnatural to oppose nature. Included in Unjust Logic' list of life's pleasures are the sexual enjoyment of both men and women (1073), and our only concern in satisfying these urges should be that, if caught, we be able to talk our way out of punishment (Strepsiades' aim from the beginning). Unjust Logic makes his cynical and blasphemous references to Thetis' grounds for divorce from Peleus (he was an unimaginative lover) to poke fun at his opponent's misogynistic feelings (more unnaturalness: cf. 996 f.) and to twit him for his old-fashioned, romantic notions about physical love. Moreover, this reference to the sexual life of the gods undermines Just Logic's assertion that "right" is with the gods, that is, that the gods must be chaste. We notice that Unjust Logic is quick to deny Just Logic's claims of divine support: if Zeus beats his father, if Heracles likes warm baths, and if Thetis likes to peform exotic variations on the sex act, perhaps the gods say one thing but do another (like Just Logic). Perhaps human beings should do what the gods do rather than what they tell us to do.

Just Logic's reply to all this is to maintain that without modesty and chastity we would all be εὐρύπρωκτοι, gape-asses (1084), which he assumes is an evil thing to be. But times have changed, as Unjust Logic proceeds to demonstrate, *more Socratico*: with a brief but triumphant cross-examination, Unjust Logic makes his opponent admit that the majority think εὐρυπρωκτία to be a fine condition. Everyone in the city—politicians, tragedians, and the man in the street—is an εὐρύπρωκτος. This point made, Just Logic, last spokesman for the good old days, deserts to the victor's camp: ἡττήμεϑ', ὦ κινούμενοι, "you win, buggers!" (1103).

The victory of Unjust Logic is necessary to the plot. We must have the abstract triumph of that sophistic and dishonest cleverness which is the heart and soul of Socratic teaching before we can be shown that in practice the lessons of Unjust Logic lead to disaster. Strepsiades' outraged burning of the Phrontisterion is the opposite of the usual comic hero's deed: it is the reflex of outraged νόμος striking back at its attackers and reestablishing its right to dominate and control the forces of φύσις. When Strepsiades comes to his senses, he turns to the position of Just Logic against that of Unjust Logic (and, we suppose, Dicaeopolis and Trygaeus). The moral of all this is wobbly but clear: νόμος may shield the εὐρυπρωκτία of the citizens and the secret lusts of Just Logic, but it is better than enduring the chaos of liberated φύσις.

In purely sexual terms, wider moralism aside, the city Strepsiades con-

fronts is the same that confronted Dicaeopolis, Trygaeus, and the Sausage-
Seller. It is characterized by total corruption, for which homosexual
promiscuity is the symbol. However we might challenge the other assumptions of Unjust Logic regarding human nature, he is (as the poet implies)
correct about that fact. But without fantasy, without the miracles of
transformation accomplished by more fantastic comic heroes, there is no
way to expose it successfully or exchange it for more admirable sexuality
(such as love in the fields with pretty maidens). As Unjust Logic says to
his rival when pelted by vile epithets, "You're just tossing rose-petals."
Abuse is powerless unless it is backed up by the power of fantasy.

It would seem that only rustics like Strepsiades any longer believe in the
old values, but Strepsiades is much too simple and too weak to change
things, even if he could become outraged about corruption (and he does
not: his reaction at the end of the play is personal, not civic-minded). The
absence of anything but degraded sex and buffoonish scatology in the play
means an absence of that gaiety and freedom which characterize Aristophanes' best and most characteristic work. Moralizing is no substitute for
gaiety and the fun of shattering morality. That is, in part, why Unjust
Logic could defeat Just Logic, why Dicaeopolis could defeat the Acharnians, and why Cratinus and Ameipsias were able to defeat Aristophanes at
the City Dionysia of 423.

Wasps

The dilemmas of *Clouds* appear again in *Wasps*: can Philocleon's style of
life be altered by education? What are we to make of the contrast between
the older and younger generations? Can and should φύσις be mastered by
νόμος? As in *Clouds*, the roles of the generations seem to be reversed: the
son, who as a young man ought to be championing the new ideas and
questioning all authority, is the spokesman for behavior according to
values and authority; his aims in the play are (1) to cure his father of the
"disease" of litigiousness that disrupts his notions of comfort and propriety,
and (2) to provide his father with a broader, more productive old age.
Philocleon, the father, lives as he wants, says what he feels, and does not
trouble himself about propriety or convention as long as he and his friends
are left alone to pursue their mania for litigation.

Wasps, however, is free of the moralizing and dispassionate analysis
that made *Clouds* so unsatisfying and ambivalent. Strepsiades, too, was an
old man who wanted to live as he pleased and say whatever he wanted with
impunity, but was frustrated by the poet in the name of law and convention. That is, Aristophanes in *Clouds* made the suppression of nature

Bdelycleon attempts in *Wasps* successful. But the ebullient nature of Philocleon is not to be stifled or corrected at the end of the play, even though it might be more dangerous to society than Strepsiades' fraud.[15] Philocleon retains his self-assertive idiosyncrasies despite all attempts to change him; the promptings of nature will not be ruled by convention this time.

> τὸ γὰρ ἀποστῆναι χαλεπὸν
> φύσεος, ἥν ἔχοι τις ἀεί, (1457–58).

[It is most difficult to escape the nature which a man carries with him always.]

Although Philocleon is thus much closer to the transcendent heroes Dicaeopolis and Trygaeus than he is to the dull and ineffectual Strepsiades, he is prevented from fully realizing his fantasies; for his own protection he must be controlled by the common sense of his son. He remains true to himself and achieves a heroic stature of sorts as "natural man" unbent by social conformity, but he must remain in the real world and submit to its laws. In short, Aristophanes returns in *Wasps* to the problems of *Clouds*, but this time he dramatizes them according to the comic principles that made heroes like Dicaeopolis so appealing, rather than trying to analyze too closely the hero's actual moral position.

Wasps has the least obscenity, whether functional or merely farcical, of any extant play of this period.[16] Philocleon, not being a buffoon like Strepsiades, provides less opportunity for the obscenity of low farce. Not having much invective or abuse, *Wasps* has little homosexual language, nor do we find the kind of thematic development which in the earlier plays called for obscenity: one cannot imagine a more anerotic environment than the law courts, the jury-box, and the genteel home of Philocleon and his son. Yet the obscenities we do encounter follow the patterns we have observed in other plays, particularly *Clouds*: as in that play, *Wasps* uses obscenity mostly as a characterizing device rather than as a component of broad thematic development. Even so, obscenity plays a very minor role in the development of themes and characters. Only in the scene with the flute-girl near the end is there a significant concentration of obscene language and action.

Naturally, most of the obscenities are associated with the protagonist. Philocleon's language, as befits a salty old man, runs to the colorful, and he is fond of using extravagant and vulgar expressions, especially scatological

---

15. See Dover's penetrating appraisal of Philocleon's character (n. 2, above, pp. 125 ff.).

16. Noteworthy in this connection is Aristophanes' programmatic statement at lines 54 ff.

ones. Thus he counters his son's irritatingly rational arguments by calling
him "an ass-hole that defies washing" (604) and urges his waspish friends
to sting their enemies "on the ass" (431).[17] Instead of simply threatening to
eat the poor canine defendant, Labes, the harsh and testy (604) old juror
concentrates on the other end of the digestive process in his threat (χεσεῖ-
σθαι, 941). A gurgling flagon of wine (ὄνος) suggests to him the contemptuous crepitations of a wide-breeched donkey (ὄνος, 618 f.). Philocleon
refers continually to his excretory incontinence: the statue of Lycus, placed
before the tribunal, apparently served as his usual convenience (394), and
to the delight of his cleaner he frequently soils his clothing (1127 f.). The
private trial arranged by Bdelycleon is interrupted frequently by jokes on
the piss-pot and its use (807 f., 858, 935, 940 f.).

The vigorous and excitable chorus of Philocleon's colleagues displays a
similar passion for strong invective: their savage description of Cleon
(1035) and of Ariphrades (1280 ff.) are particularly harsh for any chorus,
and their contemptuous preference of old age to the "ringlets and gape-
assedness" (1068 ff.) of youth places them squarely in the company of those
other stout Marathon fighters, the Acharnians (the Wasps are also farmers,
250 ff.).

Philocleon's obscenities play a significant role in the scene in which
Bdelycleon tries to dress his reluctant father in elegant clothes and school
him   in *Salonweltlichkeit.* Of course, Philocleon, like Strepsiades in his
similar scene with Socrates, manages to reduce the elegance and intellectual refinement of Bdelycleon's society to his own vulgar level through
bathos and crude jokes. Later, Philocleon will comically misuse what he
absorbs in this scene to his son's further mortification, just as Strepsiades
distorts and garbles what he has learned from Socrates. The point is that
natural man cannot be sweetened by or redeemed for the conventions of
polite society.

The difference between the two scenes is important. Strepsiades was
clownish and vulgar through stupid misunderstandings; Philocleon deliberately sabotages his son's efforts by feigning ignorance and poking fun
at what he is told to do and say. That is, whereas Strepsiades is a victim of
his own stupidity, Philocleon consciously fights against conformity; he rejects what he sees as restrictive and therefore unacceptable behavior. Thus
he imitates what he considers the mincing and effeminate gait of respectable people (1170 f.), and declares his desire to "waggle his ass" (σαυλο-
πρωκτιᾶν, 1173). He refuses to tell polite stories, preferring stories about
"how Lamia broke wind when caught" (1177) and how "Cardopion———

17. Compare the similar jokes at Av 438 ff. and Pl Com. 173.21.

his mother" (Bdelycleon breaks him off before he can supply the verb, 1178). When Bdelycleon orders him to recline, Philocleon does so in a crude manner: not εὐσχημόνως, elegantly (1210 ff.) but, we suppose, comfortably. Strepsiades was only an inadvertent, and thus ineffective, champion of φύσις against society's conventions; Philocleon knows what he is doing.

When the real test comes, Philocleon naturally reverts to his usual behavior, forgetting (or ignoring) the admonitions of his son: he makes a shambles of an elegant dinner party. As a messenger tells us, he was by far the most unrestrained of anyone there (ὑβριστότατος, 1303), behaving in fact very much in accordance with the exhortations of Unjust Logic:

> ἀνήλλετ', ἐσκίρτα, 'πεπόρδει, κατεγέλα,
> ὥσπερ καχρύων ὀνίδιον εὐωχημένον [1305 f.]

[He jumped, gamboled, farted, laughed, like a frisky overfed little donkey.]

When he enters he is clutching the naked flute-girl he has stolen, and is babbling drunkenly to her in a very obscene fashion (1335 ff.). Hitherto Philocleon has expressed a certain amount of sexual passion, but only in the limited context of the courtroom: there he is permitted to see naked boys at their δοκιμασία, the examination undergone upon reaching manhood (578), enjoy power over girls (χοῖρος, piggie, is a pun at 573), and "unseal heiresses" (more puns, 588 ff.). In the period of his jury duties he had been, as far as society was concerned, more or less innocuous; the potential of raw φύσις to disintegrate the functioning of society was contained by the self-imposed prison of the jury-box. The well-intentioned Bdelycleon mistakenly releases him from that safe enclosure and turns him loose on society; an abundance of wine and the confused politeness of his fellow banqueters now precipitate the vulgar and violent behavior which disrupts the party and finally erupts into the streets in an outpouring of uncontrollable libido and hubris.

In his long monologue to the flute-girl (1341–63) we learn that Philocleon feels younger than he ever has, more exhilarated; he acts the part of a wild and reckless youth in total disregard for society's laws. The flute-girl, whom he has rescued from the polite ritual of symposiac fellation (1345 f.),[18] becomes a kind of symbol of sexual abandonment, as had the sex partners of Dicaeopolis and Trygaeus. We must contrast Philocleon's self-centered lust, in its straightforward honesty, with the ritualized and

18. See chap. 5, n. 120, below.

conventional ceremony from which he has saved the flute-girl. His act compares in a way with the digging up of Eirene and the liberation of Theoria and Opora, who, we recall, also had to perform fellatio in their heavenly prison. The liberation of sex partners usually involves rejuvenation, and so it does here.

But unlike Dicaeopolis and Trygaeus, Philocleon has taken hold of no magical creature; she is merely a flute-girl who does not belong to him and does not care to minister to his lusts. Despite our amusement and sympathy, we must agree with Bdelycleon, cast in the role of stern father, who sees that this rejuvenation is not really a rejuvenation but simply the drunken reenactment of youthful exploits long past. Philocleon cannot be free of his old age just by wishing it so. Bdelycleon rightly calls his father a "dirty old man" ($\chi o \iota \rho \acute{o} \vartheta \lambda \iota \psi$, 1364) and warns him paternally of the danger of what he is doing (1366). "I am going to take the girl away from you," he says, "because you are decrepit and impotent" (1379 ff.). Bdelycleon uses the same word ($\sigma \alpha \pi \rho \acute{o} \varsigma$) used earlier by Philocleon himself to refer to his own phallus, which is like a rotten old rope (1343). That is, although Philocleon might boast of his rejuvenated sexual prowess and promise the flute-girl a great performance, his limp and withered phallus, visible to all, betrays the bitter reality of old age.[19]

We sympathize with Philocleon's yearning for liberation from the physical restraints of old age and the social restraints demanded by society's conventions, but we must agree with the failed educator, Bdelycleon, that home is the best place for the old man. Without the supernatural help of fantasy, $\varphi \acute{v} \sigma \iota \varsigma$ must bow to $\nu \acute{o} \mu o \varsigma$ if society is to survive. We realize that beyond the wild, reeling dance of life with which Philocleon ends the play, await a hangover, court appearances, and fines for damages. But we realize equally clearly that Philocleon will be as impenitent and manic as ever, and that his spirited, irrepressible nature will survive Bdelycleon's attempted cure.

Birds

The plot and structure of *Birds* reminds us in many ways of the plays of the 420s; in fact the play might be seen as the artistic culmination of Aristophanes' earlier technique:[20] two aging Athenians, Peisetaerus and Euelpides, have grown sick of life in Athens, with its constant litigations, business pressures, fines, and petty irritations (30 ff.). They are $\dot{\alpha} \pi \eta \lambda \iota$-

19. See J. Vaio, "Aristophanes' *Wasps*: The Final Scenes," *GRBS* 12 (1971): 333, n. 41, and Whitman (n. 2, above), pp. 157 f.

20. See Whitman (n. 2, above), p. 218.

αστά, tired of political duties (110), looking for a place free of πράγματα, city business (44, 120 ff.).[21] Like Timon they have been driven to misanthropy by Athens; and like the protagonists of Pherecrates' *Savages*, produced six years earlier, they have decided to leave Athens to search for a life of pastoral bliss and perfect ἀπραγμοσύνη, freedom from duty of any kind.[22] After having found such a world in the realm of the birds, they proceed to win over the birds and transform the bird kingdom into a kind of airy imperial polis. By intercepting the smoke of sacrifices rising heavenward, they ultimately force the gods themselves to parley and extort from Zeus his scepter and Princess Basileia, the personification of absolute supremacy. During the latter half of the play the hero must deal with newcomers and humbugs who wish to participate in the blessings of his new world.

Yet *Birds* is in important respects different from the preceding five plays. Since the action takes place far from Athens and literally up in the air, the play is almost completely free of political concerns; there are few topical allusions, no mention of the war and its current fortunes, no consistent satirical or abusive motifs. The comedy of *Birds* is almost entirely fantastic and has detached itself from the immediate topicality upon which the earlier plays relied so heavily for their impact and humor. Not even the traditional structural elements of the play are allowed to disrupt the illusion or interrupt the unusually tight dramatic unity: the parabasis integrates itself into the action by taking the form of an ornithogeny, and even the appeal for victory in the comic competition is delivered by a bird-Coryphaeus (445 ff.).

In the absence of abuse, topicality, and other undramatic intrusions, there is little need of obscene exposures; *Birds* has by far the least obscenity of any extant Aristophanic play. But what obscenity there is occurs in forms and contexts in which the plays of the 420s have accustomed us to expect it.

Much of the obscenity is standard buffoonery: the jokes on fear-inspired defecation, which Euelpides and Peisetaerus make upon first encountering a bird (65 f., 68), seem to be standard in situations where two characters meet frightening apparitions in an unfamiliar place: compare Dionysus and Xanthias in the underworld (R 308, 479 ff.). So also the incidental jokes on bird-droppings (1054, 1114 ff.), birds pecking the rear end of enemies (438 ff.: cp. V 431), pathics (829 ff.), and lascivious foreigners (504–07: cp. A 158 ff.).[23]

21. Cf. A 266 ff., N 43 ff., P 240, 350 ff.
22. See Pl. *Protag.* 327C.
23. Here Euelpides' vulgar remark is perfectly in character for the standard buffoon-figure.

All the rest of the obscenity is completely devoted to the motif of sexual freedom: freedom to gratify one's lusts with an impunity possible only in a world of utopian self-assertiveness outside the conventions of the polis. The fantasy empire of Peisetaerus affords him sexual license (and heroic rejuvenation) much like that of Dicaeopolis in his private country market-place, and Demos and Trygaeus in their new worlds of peace and fertility. The difference lies in the unusual tone and character of Peisetaerus' sexual freedoms.

Early in the play, the hoopoe asks the two wanderers what their ideal polis would be like. Euelpides answers (128 ff.) that he would like to be forced to go to wedding-feasts, but Peisetaerus says (137 ff.) that he would like to be encouraged by parents to take his pleasure with their young sons as they leave the palaestra fresh and rosy from exercise and bathing. That is, whereas Euelpides wishes for something not really very extraordinary or unlikely, Peisetaerus wishes for something that actually amounts to freedom from the strictures of convention, a license to satisfy bodily drives that are usually prohibited or severely circumscribed. Thus Peisetaerus' answer is not merely a random, comical wish but represents a pattern of fantasy which in Aristophanes is constantly connected with heroic self-assertion; it in fact foreshadows Peisetaerus' heroic triumph. In this play, heroic triumph means the freedom of the winged life Peisetaerus enjoys after his alliance with the birds.

Indeed, sexual self-aggrandizement is continually mentioned as a special privilege of birdhood. At 703 ff,. birds are said to be the descendants of Eros, since it is through their mediation (in the form of gifts) that lovers are able to win their favorites ($\delta\iota\varepsilon\mu\acute{\eta}\rho\iota\sigma\alpha\nu$, 706). Having wings means that one can fly out of the Assembly, fornicate with someone's wife ($\beta\iota\nu\acute{\eta}\sigma\alpha\varsigma$), and fly back again (793 ff.), or (like the birds) spend the winter in caves, "playing with mountain nymphs" and feeding on virginal foliage (puns for the pudenda) in the Garden of the Graces (1097 ff.). One of the most delightful attractions of the birds' society is Procne, who appears as a feathered flute-girl (665 ff.), available for the amusement of the chorus (660) and its human guests, who are immediately and strongly aroused at the sight of her and indulge in an obscene sexual commentary (667 ff.) reminiscent of the interchange between Trygaeus and his slave over Theoria, another symbol of unrestricted sexuality (P 871 ff.).

When Peisetaerus' victory comes, he is quick to insure the inviolability of his airy new polis by consolidating his power and establishing a rigidly disciplined and highly organized society. One of his first acts is to amass and regulate all sexual prerogatives: among other regulations, the "hard-ons" of the gods are to be infibulated to prevent them from prowling around, erect, in search of Alcmenes, Alopes, and Semeles with whom to fornicate (556–60).

The arrival of Iris, messenger-girl of Zeus (1202 ff)., provides Peisetaerus with an opportunity to demonstrate both his sexual superiority over the gods and his heroic rejuvenation. Where the gods had been free in the past to have their way with mortal women, Peisetaerus now turns the tables on them by capturing and hubristically mistreating their pretty envoy. From the first, Peisetaerus whittles away Iris' air of superiority by means of sexual double entendres (1204, 1206, 1214 ff.); he denies that the gods any longer have the power to punish him; on the contrary, he will do the punishing if the gods misbehave. As for Iris, Peisetaerus unceremoniously shoos her away, but not before he dresses her down in an obscene speech that amounts almost to verbal rape (1253–56, translated, p. 39):

> σὺ δ' εἰ με λυπήσεις τι, τῆς διακόνου
> πρώτης ἀνατείνας τὼ σκέλει διαμηριῶ
> τὴν Ἶριν αὐτήν, ὥστε θαυμάζειν ὅπως
> οὕτω γέρων ὢν στύομαι τριέμβολον.

The rise of Peisetaerus to heroic transcendence over gods and men is accompanied by the simultaneous rise of his rejuvenated phallus. As a final insult, Peisetaerus invites Iris to fly elsewhere and "burn to ashes" (καταιθαλώσεις) one of the younger men (1261 f.), using in an erotic sense a word Iris had used earlier (1242) in speaking of the terrible wrath of Zeus.

Of course, the triumph of Peisetaerus is complete with his assumption of Zeus' scepter, his marriage to Princess Basileia, and his actual apotheosis. Such a triumph, aside from its unusual grandeur, is not essentially unlike that of Dicaeopolis, Demos, or Trygaeus. One striking difference is the complete lack of any accompanying obscenity, even much erotic nuance. Indeed, there is no obscenity at all in the final 504 lines of the play after the mild double entendre καταιθαλώσεις in 1261.

The reason lies in the characterization of Peisetaerus himself. Unlike the earlier heroes, Peisetaerus is primarily concerned not with ego-gratifying indulgences—food, drink, sex, and uninhibited behavior—or even with his stated goal of ἀπραγμοσύνη, but with power and the establishment of an empire. Peisetaerus' triumph is not, like those of Dicaeopolis, Demos, and Trygaeus, tied in with themes of peace, fertility, and joyous abandon, but comes about through careful and often ruthless diplomacy, clever rhetoric, and wily intelligence—qualities that resemble (and echo) the slippery techniques of the Socratic school in *Clouds*.[24]

24. Av 430 f.; N 317 f., 412 ff., Av 462 ff.

Throughout the play, obscenity has been used to describe the sexual
privileges open to those who have wings; Peisetaerus' object has been to
get wings himself and then to take over the leadership of winged creatures,
with the ultimate goal being nothing less than absolute tyranny over birds,
gods, and men. Sensual indulgence is merely one of the benefits of supreme
power, but hardly an end in itself. In a sense, Peisetaerus' career moves in
a direction opposite to those of earlier heroes, who begin with troubles and
end by relaxing amid the joys of the senses. Peisetaerus begins *Birds* in a
peaceful thicket far from the hubbub of Athens and her empire, but by
play's end he has built (chiefly by means of typical Athenian techniques) a
far busier, far more extensive empire of his own. It is not surprising, then,
that the few obscenities present in *Birds* serve a more limited and subordinate function in the intrigue and thematic development of the play
than we observed in the works of the 420s.

Thesmophoriazusae

Thesmophoriazusae is one of the most benign and lighthearted plays of
Aristophanes. There is no harshness in the characterization of any of the
personae, virtually no allusion to politics or current affairs—the situation
in Athens in the early months of 411 was difficult and sensitive[25]—and no
political malice or invective. Instead, the action of the play, like that of
Frogs, is given entirely to literary parody and slapstick. Also as in *Frogs*,
the slapstick portion of the play, in which is included almost all of the
obscenity, is confined to the first half (1–654). Unlike *Frogs*, however, the
literary parody is not confined to the second half of the play but is present
from first to last. *Thesmophoriazusae*, to a greater degree than *Frogs*, uses
these two elements—slapstick and literary criticism—to complement one
another both structurally and thematically.

At the center of the plot is the lampooning of Euripides and Euripidean
tragedy. The tragedian, who is so adept at constructing clever words and
plots out of the merest claptrap, wishes to extricate himself from a death
sentence passed by the women of Athens at the Thesmophoria; they resent
his accurate but inconvenient exposure of their wicked ways. To do this
Euripides must rely on strategems taken from his own plays. Once applied
offstage, of course, all of his strategems fail, and he is forced in the end to
stoop to an earthy, quite untragic ploy in order to escape the consequences
of his ineffectuality. In addition to the major parodies of Euripidean tragedies (and minor parodies of Agathon's) upon which this main plot-
premise is constructed, the play contains much satire on effeminacy,

25. See Gelzer (n. 4, above), 1467.67 ff.; Dover (n. 2, above), pp. 168 ff.; van Daele's
preface to *Thesmophoriazusae* (Budé edition, pp. 9 f.).

adultery, the ways of women,[26] and the relations between the sexes, all unified and focused by the constant presence of the Relation, the most richly developed buffoon in Aristophanes.

Though not the hero, the buffoonish Relation, like the heroes of earlier comedies, holds a virtual monopoly on obscenity and general outspokenness, of which there is a great abundance in this play. The role of his obscenity and overall bluntness of speech is very varied: its major functions are to provide an earthy, masculine contrast to the effeminate posturings of Agathon and Cleisthenes; to cut through and expose humbug; to enliven and intensify the tragic parody; to add spice to the satire on women; and to underline the theme of the masculine versus the feminine, under which the decline of contemporary tragedy is broadly adumbrated.[27]

Compared with the Relation, the other characters (aside from the archer, another βωμολόχος, buffoon-figure) have almost no obscenity, a circumstance which might at first appear odd, given the nature of the play's subject matter. It will soon become apparent, however, that the distribution of obscenity is functional.

The women, in contrast to those of *Lysistrata*, do not utter a single obscenity in their opening of the meeting (295–330) or in their description of Euripides' slanders (331–465), although they admit their bibulousness and frequent adultery. The only obscenities spoken by women are (1) those of woman A, which are dramatically in character for the traditional comical old lady (cp. Cleonice in *Lysistrata*)[28] and serve to counterpoint the farcical behavior of the Relation (536–39, 640, 691); and (2) the mild double entendre of woman B (ἐξεκόρησε, deflower, 760).

Euripides uses obscenity only twice, both times unavoidably: (1) in 30–35, Euripides and the Relation are involved in a parody of a tragic cross-examination, in which the effeminacy of Agathon is gradually revealed to the Relation: Euripides' obscene remark at 35 is a necessary climax to this routine; (2) the slang reference to the κέρκος, tail, of the Relation in 239 is part of the general buffoonery of this scene and must be remarked by someone other than the Relation; it cannot be Agathon, whose delicate and lofty airs make it impossible for him to utter obscenities[29] or even acknowledge the provocations of the Relation (130 ff.).

26. Women in speaking roles appear for the first time in the year 411 (if we omit the goddess Iris in *Birds*). This development was probably connected with the influence of female heroines in tragedies: see Schmid (n. 12, above), p. 418.

27. See Whitman (n. 2, above), pp. 223 f.

28. See H. Oeri, *Der Typ der komischen Alten in der griechischen Komödie* (Basel, 1948), pp. 31 f.

29. The double entendre at 204 is a frigid conceit and not an obscenity, as is clear from the response of the Relation in 206.

Cleisthenes' obscenities also are delivered as "feeds" to the Relation: in 611 f. the Relation asks to go out to urinate, a request to which Cleisthenes reacts euphemistically at first (612), then obscenely when it becomes apparent that the Relation is merely trying to avoid examination (615). The farcical scene in which Cleisthenes is made to chase the Relation's phallus elicits from Cleisthenes only one obscene joke (on the Corinthian Isthmus, 647 f.).

The opening scenes are reminiscent of the technique of earlier plays. Agathon's position here is roughly analogous to that of Euripides in *Acharnians*. Euripides has decided to dress someone up as a woman and send him to the Thesmophoria to plead his case before the angry ladies; he considers the effeminate Agathon perfect for this real-life drama (cf. 189–92). Agathon must, of course, decline the offer, but agrees (like Euripides in the earlier play) to provide from his own store all the paraphernalia needed for the hoax.

The role of the Relation in the scenes with Agathon and his servant is that of the pure βωμολόχος, or stock buffoon. Like Dicaeopolis in *Acharnians*, he is the ordinary fellow who finds himself in the company of posturing ἀλαζών (charlatan) figures; he mirrors the amusement and hostility of the audience, whose allegiance he wins by deflating the humbugs and exposing them obscenely.

Thus, the Relation continually interrupts Agathon's servant (who enters singing a vacuous hymn in honor of his master, 39 ff.), first by cries of βομβάξ and βομβολοβομβάξ (45, 48), then by interjecting some vulgar words for fornication (50, 57), and finally (note the familiar *Steigerung*-technique) by constructing out of the servant's Agathonian diction his own stanza, in which each word is an obscene double entendre and which amounts to a threat of pederastic rape (cp. the similar threats by the Sausage-Seller and Strepsiades). But the servant is but a mild warm-up for Agathon himself, an apparition of androgynous decadence who is rolled out on the *eccyclema* (95) singing a song whose metrical and melodic intricacies seem to the Relation as involved and incoherent as ant-tracks (100), and whose air of effeminate softness, he says, actually makes his rear-end tickle (130–33).

The irreverent behavior and obscene remarks of the Relation during the Agathon scene, for all their broad slapstick, have a role in the development of important themes. Agathon, who has all the visible characteristics of the standard effeminate transvestite—he is pretty, clean-shaven, pale, delicate, and languid (191 f.)[30]—is also made the symbol of the emasculated art of contemporary tragedy, invented by Euripides (cf. 173 f.) and fur-

30. See sections 480 ff., below.

thered in its decline by successors like Agathon. According to Agathon's theory of tragic composition, the poet must imitate in his own dress and behavior the characters in his dramas—in this case, women (149–52). The nature of the poet determines the nature of his poetry; that is why Agathon's poetry is as weak, delicate, and impotent as Agathon himself. The Relation, on the other hand, is just the opposite: hairy, loud, swarthy, and outspoken; unlike any other character in the play except the archer, he wears the badge of masculinity, a large phallus. Throughout this scene he gives free rein to his masculinity by continuing the pathic-baiting he began with the servant: he jeers obscenely at Agathon's girlishness and εὐρυπρωκτία, wide-assedness (153, 174 f., 200 f.), offers to bugger him himself (157 f.), and mischievously substitutes vulgar terms for Agathon's euphemisms (206).

But it is quite a different role the Relation must play once he volunteers to help out Euripides: instead of the masculine buffoon he must now assume female characteristics. In accordance with the spirit of tragedy exemplified by Agathon, he must abandon his masculine identity and become a transvestite himself, a process that involves shaving his beard, singeing his private parts (215 f.), and dressing himself in women's clothes. The business of fitting out the Relation as a woman occupies a long scene (214–79) whose farcical character is accented by the victim's obscene jokes (235, 237, 242, 247, 248, 253 f., 263).

There is no further word from the Relation following his practice-run as a lady (279–94) until 466, where he delivers the speech he was sent to deliver. It is clear from the start, however, that he has no aptitude for role-playing and deception: far from soothing the women's tempers and explaining away their charges, he actually delivers a long account of female shamelessness which exceeds anything that Euripides ever said. To add to the pungency of his slanderous but undenied remarks, the Relation tactlessly uses a large number of obscene expressions, in pointed contrast to the speakers for the women, who used none (479, 480, 481, 484 f., 488 f., 491 f., 493 f., 515 f.).

These obscenities and clownish anecdotes demonstrate the inadequacy of Agathon's theories when applied in real life: a tragic poet may be able to write feminine verses by becoming effeminate, but a flesh-and-blood man like the Relation cannot be turned into a tragic heroine simply by depilation and a change of clothes (cf. Strepsiades and Philocleon, who also resist transformation). The women, of course, instantly grow suspicious and begin to question the Relation closely, but even as he courts exposure he finds it impossible to play the woman and continues his insulting remarks amid growing hostility (more obscene abuse in 570).

Cleisthenes, another effeminate transvestite (571, 574 ff.), diverts the women's attention from the Relation at this point by running onstage with the details of Euripides' plot. A search for the imposter is initiated at once. Even at this desperate point the Relation cannot resist a joke about effeminates (592 f.), and in his attempt to slip away (he asks permission to urinate) he only draws further attention to himself: urination proves to be a problem for a lady with a large phallus under her dress (611–17). After some futile questioning by Cleisthenes, woman A manages to unmask the Relation by asking him what the women did at the previous ceremony. "Drink" gets him by for two responses, but on the third his ignorance of women's slang for potties trips him up: "Xenylla demanded a σκάφιον," he says—so far so good—"because there was no ἀμίς" (633). The game is over: no woman would mention the ἀμίς: σκάφιον was the accepted euphemism.

The remainder of the scene (to 654) is occupied with the logical conclusion to the unmasking of the Relation and the destruction of Euripides' scheme: the actual badge of his masculinity must be rooted out and exposed to view. Thus the Relation is stripped, and Cleisthenes, after running from front to back several times, finally manages to isolate the πέος and complete the anagnorisis. In the naked Relation's futile attempts to hide his phallus the controlling themes of the first half of the play are neatly encapsulated.

Between the exit of Cleisthenes and 1114 (460 lines) there is no need for obscenity: this part of the play is taken up with the seizure and killing of a wineskin baby by the desperate Relation (the Telephos motif, as in A 335 ff.), the parabasis, and scenes in which the Relation tries to escape captivity by reenacting (with the help of Euripides) various roles from Euripidean tragedy, principally *Andromeda* and *Helen*. After all of these strategems fail, Euripides is forced to admit defeat, apologizes to the women, and promises to mend his ways. Tragic ruses having finally been abandoned, Euripides resorts (ironically) to an unsubtle and quite classically feminine ploy in order to rescue his long-suffering Relation. Disguising himself as an old female pander, Artemisia, Euripides brings on a girl piper and a dancing-girl who lures the aroused archer offstage just long enough for the two men to make their getaway.

The obscenity in this last section of the play belongs exclusively to the foreign (and therefore crude and lascivious) archer, who takes over from the Relation the role of βωμολόχος. During the *Andromeda* parody the archer's vulgar references to anal intercourse contrast sharply with Euripides' paratragic and euphemistic love-language (1114, 1119 f., 1123 f.). Later, the humor is provided by the gradual rousing of the archer's lust (and his phallus) by the dancing-girl, a process which elicits from him a series of obscene comments, made all the more comical for being delivered in pidgin Greek (1185, 1187 f., 1190, 1191 f, 1215).

Frogs

Frogs, like *Thesmophoriazusae*, deals mainly with tragic parody and the criticism of tragedians, but this time with a view toward examining the moral and political role of tragedians as teachers of the polis rather than merely exploiting their superficial literary pecularities. Euripides now comes under scrutiny as a possible corrupting influence on the very fiber of society, where in *Thesmophoriazusae* Aristophanes used only his literary personality, heavily laced with the characteristics of the traditional quack. This more serious moral focus involves a return for the last time in Old Comedy to the open voicing of political opinions[31] and advice,[32] absent in *Thesmophoriazusae*, although the seriousness of the situation in 405—*Frogs* was produced only six months after Arginusae and six before Aegospotami—still demanded caution.

Like *Thesmophoriazusae*, *Frogs* has two main kinds of humor: literary criticism and slapstick. But unlike the earlier play, the slapstick in *Frogs* is confined entirely to the first part of the action (1–673), the underworld journey of Dionysus and Xanthias. This first section is completely distinct from, and forgotten in, the second section (738 ff.), the tragic contest, and is not mentioned again until the very end of the play (1414 ff.). The two sections are sharply separated by a parabasis dealing with political and moral questions (674 ff.), and by a new slave-prologue (738–813) which helps introduce the contest to come (cf. the anticipations at 810 f., 830 ff., 871 ff., 895 ff.). Thus, the farcical Hades-journey of the first section amounts to a kind of extended prologue which does not introduce the main action of the play.

Virtually all of the obscenity in the play is contained in the first action; most of it is scatological; and all of it is the obscenity of the βωμολόχος, buffoon, a role Dionysus and Xanthias share. In no other play of Aristophanes does the obscenity remain on such a low and unessential level. What obscenities there are in the second section are comic relief provided by Dionysus in a continuation of his role as βωμολόχος. These are: (1) his vulgar and bathetic contribution to Aeschylus' description of the softness of modern men (1074 f.); (2) his ludicrous story of the crepitating fat man (1089–98), which relieves the tension of Aeschylus' serious remarks

31. Cf. on Cleophon, lines 678 ff., 1504, 1532 f.
32. Especially in the parabasis (674 ff.) and the discussion of Alcibiades (1420 ff.).

in 1078–88; (3) his remark about blows and buboes (1280) which comments on Euripides' parody of Aeschylean lyrics (1264 ff.); and (4) his aside about Euripides' Muse (1308). All of the other references to sex or scatology in the second section are made by the rough-spoken Aeschylus, but are euphemistic and used to illustrate the corrupting influence of Euripides' shameless creations (1044 f., 1069 ff., 1078 ff., 1325 ff.).

It is apparent from the first that Dionysus is meant to be a farcical figure: we recognize this not only by his outlandish costume but by his low interaction with the slave, Xanthias, another *Possenfigur*. That Dionysus was often so presented seems clear from Cratinus' *Dionysalexandros* and Eupolis' *Taxiarchoi,* not to mention the satyr plays. The two enter discussing a theatrical problem: Xanthias, who as a baggage carrier is literally φορτικός (cf. 12 ff.), wants permission to make the standard kind of jokes (φορτικά), which he considers witty (ἀστεῖον, 5) and at which the audience always laughs (2) but which make Dionysus angry (4), nauseated (11), and a year older (18). As god of the theater, Dionysus would naturally prefer fresh and inventive jokes to the stale crudities of Phyrnichus, Lycis, and Ameipsias (13 f.). But this does not prevent the appearance of a vulgar climax-joke about farting and shitting, standard in contexts involving exertion: πιέζομαι, I'm hard-pressed (3), θλίβομαι, I'm pinched (5), χεζητιᾷς, I'm about to shit (8). The irony is that it is not Xanthias but Dionysus, spokesman for taste and innovation, who makes the crude jokes.

Dionysus continues to provide the kind of humor he pretends to condemn in the opening scene. At 308 he soils his costume in childish fear of the Empusa described by Xanthias, and in 479–91, where Dionysus again soils himself (from fear of Aeacus), there is a series of hackneyed defecation jokes.[33] The frog chorus (209–67)—part agon, part parody of the Dionysus hymn—is a more creative but still completely farcical variation on the ancient motif of the πρωκτὸς λαλῶν, the babbling ass-hole.[34] Dionysus, fat and unaccustomed to exertion, answers the frogs' refrain by breaking wind. Like the similar crepitation routine in the opening scene, the κόαξ/πορδή takes the form of a climax joke: the progression is from proctal friction and discomfort (221 f.), to irritation (226 f.), to blisters (236) and oozing defecation (237), and finally to incipient "speech" (238), first drowned out by the frogs (239), then sounding forth in full antiphonal majesty (250, 255, 261, 264 ff.).

Depending on one's view of the unity or lack of unity of *Frogs,*[35] it is

33. See L. Radermacher's commentary (pp. 215 f.).
34. See O. Crusius at Herod. 2.44.
35. See Whitman (n. 2, above), pp. 230 ff., who bases much of his argument for unity on C. P. Segal's careful and imaginative article, "The Character and Cults of Dionysus

possible either to dismiss the frog-chorus as low burlesque with no further connection with the plot, or to see it as an aesthetic contest that foreshadows the greater agon to come, and thus as a definite stage in the *Bildungsreise* of Dionysus as he passes, in the course of the play, from confused buffoonishness to artistic redemption.[36] In any case, the frog-chorus has an undeniable connection with the major themes of the play in that it satirizes the poetic ranting of inferior poets;[37] frogs are a traditional symbol of puffed-up conceit that amounts to nothing but κόαξ.[38]

The rest of the obscenity in the first section consists entirely of isolated jokes and personal invective. There is standard pathic-baiting abuse of Cleisthenes (48, 57, 422–27), random jokes on excrement (145 ff., 153, 295, 366), and threats by Aeacus to rip out Dionysus' testicles (475 ff.). On the heterosexual side (not well-represented in *Frogs*) there is a reference to the impotence of modern tragedians (93 ff.), in which sexual potency is a metaphor for poetic creativity; an abusive stanza on the worthlessness of Callias as a fighter (his battles are seen in terms of nautical modes of sexual intercourse, 428-30); various allusions to the charms of dancing-girls (513 ff., 542–48), whose presence offstage provides part of the motivation for the farcical scenes of costume-changing between Dionysus and Xanthias; and a playful stanza in the chorus of Mystae about the "peeping tit" of one of the girls in the procession.

Lysistrata

Lysistrata, technically the most advanced play we have from Aristophanes,[39] treats the familiar themes of war, peace, and sex in a manner very different from that of *Acharnians* and *Peace*. The structure of the play is more dramatic in its steady building of suspense and in the brilliance and tight construction of its episodes; the characters are drawn with more subtlety; the humor is fresher and cleverer, less reliant on stock routines; and the focus of themes and imagery rests on areas not previously touched on in the earlier plays. As in *Peace,* the goal of the protagonist is panhellenic reconciliation, and as in *Acharnians* the realization of this goal requires

---

and the Unity of the *Frogs*," *HSCP* 65 (1961): 207 ff. For a more doctrinaire approach, see Gelzer (n. 4, above), 1486.44 ff.

36. This is the view of G. Wills, "Why are the Frogs in the *Frogs?*" *Hermes* 97 (1969): 316 f., rejected (too hastily, I feel) by Gelzer, ibid., 1489.6 ff.

37. See Radermacher (n. 33, above), pp. 171–73.

38. Cf. Arist. *Phgn.* 810[b] 14–16.

39. Gelzer (n. 4, above), 1475.37 ff., 1479.10 ff.; Schmid (n. 4, above), pp. 319 f.; Grene (n. 1, above), pp. 122 f.

battles and strategic manoeuvers, but the end result of the strife is visualized differently: peace no longer means the attainment in fantasy of hedonistic abandon, endless eating, and promiscuous sexual opportunism (mostly by the hero), and does not consist of abstract blessings that must be imaged in choral descriptions of festal games, flowering fields, and happy harvesting.

In *Lysistrata* the attainment of peace takes place in the polis rather than in an idealized countryside, and the focus is more immediate and concrete. Peace means the recovery and renewal of ordinary family life: cooking, making cloth, tending the children, going to the fountain, making love. The controlling images of the play are thus those of married life, domestic duties, sexual loyalty, and the sanctity and integrity of the home.[40] Sexual language, organs, and action are more in evidence in *Lysistrata* than in any other play; yet their use is more straightforward and less preposterous in that the reference is nearly always to themes of marriage[41] rather than fornication, rape, homosexual assault, or wholesale invective. The language of sex in *Lysistrata* bears no trace of the glamor, unreality, salaciousness and grotesquerie of earlier plays, and no harshness or depravity, either, in contrast with what we find in *Thesmophoriazusae* and *Ecclesiazusae*. The tone remains merry and ebullient throughout.

The plot itself is designed to emphasize the less fantastic and more domestic aspects of sex. The plan of Lysistrata is for a select group of older wives to seize the acropolis and hold it for the others (175 ff.), and then for the younger wives to drive their husbands mad with lust while withholding their bodies until the men agree to stop fighting (149 ff.). In order to believe this plan capable of success we must ignore certain facts and logical inconsistencies. The reason for the wives' strike is to secure the safe return of the men, who are away at war and thus unable to satisfy their wives' sexual needs (99 ff.). We must assume that the slaves and mule-drivers, not to mention the ordinary adulterers, with whom bored housewives entertain themselves in *Thesmophoriazusae* (491 f.), do not exist here.

As for the men, they are suddenly to be found at home after all, ready to be seduced and frustrated by their wives (on leave from duty on the acropolis?) and apparently unable even to masturbate, fornicate with slave-girls or prostitutes, or find a man or boy on whom to exercise their lusts.[42] If Cinesias is to have any sexual release he must come to the acropolis and

40. See Dover (n. 2, above), pp. 160 f. for a perceptive discussion, and Whitman (n. 2, above), pp. 205 ff.

41. Everyone in the play is assumed to be married.

42. Cf. 622, 1092, 1113.

petition for his wife. The assumption of the plot is that no sexual fulfillment is possible outside the context of traditional family life, and that
until family life returns to normal there is to be an unnatural state of
sexual warfare between husbands and wives.

The part of the plan that calls for seduction and frustration is illustrated
later in the play by Cinesias and Myrrhine (829–979). Meanwhile the
women capture and close off the acropolis. Lysistrata's defiant words at
the very end of the prologue, referring on the literal level to the gates of
the citadel, are also sexual double entendres that indicate the feminine
gates of love (247–51):

> Κλ. οὔκουν ἐφ᾽ ἡμᾶς ξυμβοηθήσειν οἴει
>   τοὺς ἄνδρας εὐθύς;
> Λυ.   ὀλίγον αὐτῶν μοι μέλει.
>   οὐ γὰρ τοσαύτας οὔτ᾽ ἀπειλὰς οὔτε πῦρ
>   ἥξουσ᾽ ἔχοντες ὥστ᾽ ἀνοῖξαι τὰς πύλας
>   ταύτας, ἐὰν μὴ 'φ᾽ οἶσιν ἡμεῖς εἴπομεν.

[*Cl.* Don't you think that the men will march against us straightway?
Ly. The men do not worry me, for they haven't enough threats or fire-
brands to open up these gates if we do not get acceptable terms.]

This ambiguity is surely designed to emphasize a symbolic connection
between the two parts of the plan: (1) to withhold sex from one's husband
is to rely on a woman's inherent and inimitable charms; and (2) to seize
and defend the acropolis is to supplant the act of love with an act of war. By
using sexual imagery Aristophanes makes the latter action analogous to
the former, and thus achieves a wonderful cohesion of action and theme.
The remarks of Cedric Whitman are worth quoting:[43]

> It should not be forgotten that the Acropolis was the shrine of virgin
> Athena, goddess of war, indeed, but one of the three who resist Aphro-
> dite. Athena and her rock thus become a complex motif, embodying
> generally the women's position; and it becomes a question, later in the
> play, whether they can maintain that position with Athena-like re-
> straint, or whether they will prove weaker than the men and yield to
> their own desires. Somehow, the total symbol of the Acropolis is felici-
> tously expressive of feminine sexual attitudes.

This symbolism is carried out dramatically in the parodos (254–386),

43. (N. 2, above), p. 203. J. Vaio, "The Manipulation of Theme and Action in *Lysistrata*," *GRBS* 14 (1973): 371 n. 8, objects sarcastically to Whitman's ideas here but offers
no arguments against them.

where the chorus of old men, decrepit old warmongers,[44] attack the closed
gates of the citadel with a battering ram. The language of the two half-
choruses is delicately ambiguous (265, 266–70, 286–90, 336 f.), and the
action is meant to symbolize the violent quality of male phallic thrusting
versus the woman's rooted steadfastness. These two images, bolstered by
those of fire and water, are suggestive, on the one hand, of belligerence,
stubbornness, and will to victory, and on the other, of the desire for security
and peace. This thematic antinomy continues with rising tension throughout the play.

The beginning of Lysistrata's scene with the Probulus employs on an
interpersonal level the symbolism of the phallic versus the female. After an
amusing speech on women's sexual untrustworthiness notable for its
double entendres (403 ff.), the Probulus orders that μοχλοί, rams, be
used against the women's "closed gates" (423–25, 428 ff.). But Lysistrata
descends the acropolis on her own; her remark deflates in a dignified
fashion the Probulus' bullheaded phallic diplomacy (430–32),

> μηδὲν ἐκμοχλεύσετε·
> ἐξέρχομαι γὰρ αὐτομάτη. τί δεῖ μοχλῶν;
> οὐ γὰρ μοχλῶν δεῖ μᾶλλον ἢ νοῦ καὶ φρενῶν.

[Cease your ramming! I'm coming down myself. Why do we need rams?
It seems that we need good sense and wisdom, not rams.]

Of course, the ubiquitous sexual language of the play does not always
keep to so lofty a level, although (unlike the case in earlier plays) it is
seldom simply gratuitous. In the prologue, for example (1–253), although
Lysistrata's goal is to rally support and proceed with her plan, much of the
time is spent creating indecent jokes that satirize the foibles of womankind.
As usual, women are presented as bibulous, adulterous, sexually shameless (women were considered to enjoy sex more than men;[45] this seems to
be the comic point behind the details of the women's oath of abstention
[211 ff.]), and possessing a low resistance to sexual temptation in contrast
with that of men.[46] This humor is integral to the plot, but it is for its own
sake that it is so richly developed.

Cleonice, who meets Lysistrata as the play opens, plays the βωμολόχος,
buffoon, to Lysistrata's heroine. She is an older woman (7), bibulous
(112 ff., 195 ff., 238 ff.), and especially lecherous (129, 133 ff., 159 ff.,

44. See Gelzer (n. 4, above), 1481.5 ff.
45. See Dover (n. 2, above), p. 159.
46. Cf. Agesilaus in Xen. *Ag.* 5.4, and Socrates in Alcibiades' encomium in Plato's
Symposium.

193)—in short, the typical comic old lady.[47] Her obscenities (and she delivers most of those in the prologue) are less functional than Lysistrata's and serve to provide comic relief from the high-mindedness of the heroine. Thus, she continually meets Lysistrata's philosophical and tactical concerns with jokes about sexual organs and acts (17, 23 f., 28, 59 f., 193), furnishes vivid sexual commentaries on the pretty young women (83 f., 89, 91 f.), and, like all buffoons, fails to see any aspect of sex other than the grossly physical (133–35, 159, 161 f., 215 f.).

The Spartan girl, Lampito, plays a role distantly analogous to that of comical foreigners in other plays: aside from furnishing a strapping body for admiring comments by the other women (78–84), she has three pert obscenities (82, 143, 155 f.) which are more humorous for being spoken in dialect.[48]

Of Lysistrata, although she is undeniably heroic and always serious-minded, we cannot say with Schmid that "sie macht keine Witze."[49] In fact she makes quite a large number of obscene jokes; they differ from those of the other women and the men in being more elaborate and always closely connected with the actual mechanisms of her master-plan (as befits a protagonist). Compare, for instance, the jokes of Cleonice in the prologue with those of Lysistrata: on the one hand there is stock buffoonery, on the other a speech on the absence of sexual outlets for women (107–12); the climax-joke at 122–24, in which the blunt reality of her appeal for sexual sacrifice is emphasized by the coarseness of her language; the description of the seductive techniques women should use to madden their husbands (149–51, 162–66); and the elaborately detailed oath of sexual abstention (212, 214, 217, 223, 225, 227, 229, 231).

The same patterns can be observed in Lysistrata's obscenities later in the play; with her mock oath we may compare her prayer for sexual charm (551–54) and her parodic oracle with its flagrant double entendres (770 ff.). The technique of the blunt word as a climax (124) is repeated at 715 ($\beta\iota\nu\eta\tau\iota\tilde{\omega}\mu\epsilon\nu$, we need to fuck) and 1119 ($\sigma\acute{\alpha}\vartheta\eta\varsigma$, prick). Her advice on seductiveness is put into practice in her "preface" to the Cinesias-Myrrhine scene (831–34, 839–41, 855). There are in addition several sexual double entendres in Lysistrata's pleas for peace and reconciliation (1121, 1135, 1184). The fears about the resolve of the women expressed by Lysistrata in the prologue (137 ff.) are realized in a scene where the women begin to desert from lechery (706–80). The excuses they give are thinly disguised double entendres for sexual intercourse (728–30, 732;

47. See Oeri (n. 28, above), pp. 30 f.
48. Myrrhine and the Corinthian girl utter no obscenities.
49. (N. 12, above), p. 330. It is true, however, that she is "nicht bewitzelt."

735 f., 739) and a crudely contrived pregnancy (742–61), all of which Lysistrata sees through immediately. Another stirring appeal for perseverence (762–68) and a sexually ambiguous oracle (770–76) are apparently enough to rally support anew.

The obscenities of the chorus of old women who defend the acropolis against assault by the chorus of old men are the familiar ones of invective and abuse. The parodos ends with a contest of insults exchanged by the two half-choruses (352 ff.), in which all the obscenities are spoken by the women and all refer to castration (363, 365, 367). We may compare the threat at 683–85, where the women promise to "loose their sows on the men" and "rake them over" (both refer to the cunt), or the series of violent verbal exposures of the pubic regions of both the men and the women at 800–04 (women exposing men) and 824–28 (men exposing women). The latter is preceded by a threat by the men in which the climactic word (λακτίσας, kicking, 799) is a surprise for a word meaning intercourse. It is tempting to read into these violent uses of sexual language a dramatization of the unnaturalness of warfare rather than love between the sexes. When the final reconciliation of the choruses arrives (1014–42), it is by means of a kiss, not a kick, that peace is made (1036): significantly, the trochaic tetrameters, which up to this point have been made jerky and irregular by resolution in the third foot, become regular again precisely at the moment of the kiss. Hereafter the sexual language of the now-united chorus emphasizes not abuse but healthy heterosexuality (cf. 1058–64).

The men in the play are characterized by their phalluses, from Lysistrata's first revelation of the plan by πέους (cock) in 124, to its glorious realization in the later spectacle of the men trying vainly to conceal their monstrous erections and psychic desperation. For the old men erection is a longed-for memory; it represents virility and the strength to fight (598, 661ff.) as well as victory over women (631 ff., 671–81). For the younger men erection is the outward manifestation of unsatisfied lust and inward yearning for domestic harmony. This is particularly clear in the *Exemplifikationszene* between Myrrhine and Cinesias (829–979), which demonstrates one facet of Lysistrata's plan (149 ff.). Alone after Lysistrata's amusing preface (829–64), the archetypal husband and wife (both have *redende Namen* signifying the genitals) act out the basic drama of the sexes, but without the usual climax: the husband's support of the war means that he cannot enjoy the benefits of peace. The pathos of Cinesias' frustration builds in a crescendo throughout the scene, until, hoodwinked and deserted, he sings a series of obscene and vehement songs with the sympathetic chorus, in which he fantasizes grotesquely about sexual fulfillment (954–58, 962–66, 972–79).

The other erection jokes are less poignant and more broadly farcical than those in the Cinesias-Myrrhine scene. In the following scene between the prytanis and the Spartan herald (982–1013), the prytanis furnishes the straight man to the herald's βωμολόχος, buffoon, but both make several obscene jests. Those of the prytanis comment on the condition of the herald (982, 985, 987 f., 989, 991–94); those of the herald are recherché allusions to the genitals that derive their humor from dialectal unfamiliarity (995 f., 1000 f., 1002–06). We may compare the interchange between the chorus, the Spartan, and the prytanis at 1076 ff., where the Spartan's condition is the source of much obscene commiseration (1076 ff., 1078 f., 1089, 1090–92).

During the final reconciliation, in which the women hold the men by their erections (1112 ff.), the prytanis and the Spartan use obscenity as comic relief for Lysistrata's serious oratory (1136, 1148, 1158, 1178–81). Included in this scene is some sly satire on the Spartan predilection for anal intercourse (1148, 1157, 1174).[50] The terms of the future territorial status quo are negotiated by means of obscene geographical place-names which become indistinguishable from the alluring bodies of the women (1162 f., 1163 f., 1166, 1169 f., 1172, 1173). These are of course delivered by the prytanis and the Spartan, not by Lysistrata, whose noble function in this part of the play must not decline into farce. That is, the characters who have been functioning farcically are employed in this climactic section of the play to fill in the thematic sexual images underlying the ideals of the victorious heroine, which can now be elaborated in full to a captive audience. It is noteworthy that the closing sections contain no obscenities —the last one in the play is in fact delivered by Lysistrata herself in a double entendre at 1184, just before she vanishes, her goals accomplished, into the general festivities.

Ecclesiazusae

Twenty cataclysmic years separate *Ecclesiazusae* from *Lysistrata*. The great war with Sparta had ended more than a decade earlier and a new war had taken its place. The Athenian navy was being revamped, and the Long Walls were being rebuilt once again. Politics and political personalities were very different and criticism of them seemed no longer to have been a desideratum of the audiences who watched comedies: *Ecclesiazusae* has only a few remarks about Agyrrhius (102, 184), and the poet speaks mostly about the corrupting influence on the polis of Persian gold and silver (173 ff., 183 ff., 197 ff., 205 ff.).

50. See van Daele (Budé edition), 3: 169, n. 1.

The nature of comedy was obviously changing, too. Although *Ecclesiazusae* retains many characteristics of fifth-century Old Comedy, its tone and structure show profound differences. The limited and perfunctory role of the chorus foreshadows its complete disappearance in Middle and New Comedy. Most of the older structural peculiarities of Old Comedy remain, but they are disintegrating; the parabasis has already vanished. Inner dramatic tightness and thematic unity are in full decay as the poet develops his interest (and, presumably, the audience's) in realistic character portrayal and social satire, which require not outlandish fantasy-figures but the episodic treatment of various genre-types (although these do not yet determine the plot, as in New Comedy). These innovations result in less cohesiveness between parts of the play: characters such as the two men in 746 ff. or the hags and lovers in 877 ff., whose intrinsic interest as types justify their presence, need have no connection with the protagonist; and the protagonist herself may disappear entirely not two-thirds through the play, without waiting to see the results of her initiative.

The emphasis on realism and social satire necessitates the disappearance of fantasy. Rather than forging a comic alteration of reality in which the comic hero proceeds to dismantle and transform society, Aristophanes now constructs a thoroughly ironic travesty of reality from which all fantasy has been excluded. Praxagora's scheme involves a restructuring of society complete with the Old Comic goals of sexual freedom, gluttony, laziness, and gaiety, but in the absence of fantasy her schemes clash with reality and prove to be failures. That is, a scheme like Praxagora's (or Lysistrata's, which was similar) can achieve success only if the poet carefully alters the causal necessities of the real world, as was the practice in the comedies of the fifth century. In *Ecclesiazusae* reforms that were designed to abolish misery and inequality end up by merely redistributing them. The plan to have all possessions in common (590 ff.) robs the haves and enriches the have-nots; the plan to share all women (613 ff.) ends in pleasure for the ugly and the old but misery for the young and the beautiful; and the planned communal feasting and merrymaking (675 ff.) turns out to be an illusion. The only characters in the play who are shown to profit from the new order of things are a drunken slave-girl and the oldest, ugliest hag. In short, the play is not a frontal attack on the various personages or institutions of Athenian democracy, as were earlier plays, but a satire on democracy itself in its most extreme form of egalitarianism. The play derives its ironic tone from the poet's pretending to accept Praxagora's egalitarian scheme while in fact rejecting it. By using the conventions and motifs of classic Old Comedy, Aristophanes carries Praxagora's plans through to their revolting conclusions, all the while pretending that their shocking failure deserves the kind of triumph which the worthy schemes of past heroes achieved.

This realism, irony, and harsh satire result in a play that teems with gross and unpleasant language. As Leo Strauss remarked, "It is not sufficient to say that the *Assembly of Women* is the ugliest comedy [of Aristophanes]; it is *the* ugly comedy."[51] The ugliness of the language and the plot situations of *Ecclesiazusae* is a functional component of the irony, in that it emphasizes the gap between reality and fantasy. Since much of the play deals with the sexual aspects of extreme democracy, there is an abundance of obscene language; the unique ugliness of the obscenity contributes to the play's general ironic view of society by emphasizing the sordidness of human sexuality.

The play's action falls into three parts: the women's assembly and seizure of power (1–519); the full revelation of their plans to the men (520–729); and episodes illustrating the results of the women's new laws (730 ff.). Our discussion of the obscenity in the play will follow this division, since the character of the obscene language differs according to its function in each of the three parts.

Praxagora's paratragic opening monologue apostrophizes a lamp, sole witness to the deceptions and secrets of women. Among these secrets are women's private parts and love affairs, described in lofty euphemistic language (7–13) under which the straining bodies and erotic acrobatics of fornication are easily discernable. In a sense these perfumed euphemisms, which attempt but fail to disguise the sweaty reality of illicit coupling, anticipate the ironies of the play as a whole. Just as Praxagora's euphemisms impose a linguistic artifice upon what is most accurately expressed by means of blunt language, so her fantastic ideas constitute an attempt to impose a noble and selfless social order upon what proves to be an ignoble and selfish society. Both impositions are manifest failures.

The palpable earthiness of human sexuality bursts through in the remainder of the prologue (14–284), in which the obscenity, like that of the similar prologue of *Lysistrata*, is devoted mainly to satirizing the sexual foibles of women; this time the satire has a derisive impact that recalls the damning speech of the Relation in T 466 ff. rather than the light-hearted indecencies of *Lysistrata*. Praxagora has almost all of the obscenity; woman A (256, 261) and woman B (38 f., 265) share a role exactly analogous to that of Cleonice in *Lysistrata*. In no case do the passages that recall the sexual motifs of the prologue of *Lysistrata* bear a trace of witty playfulness or joviality; they are instead vulgar and direct. In E 38 ff. the sexual joke

51. *Socrates and Aristophanes* (New York, 1966), p. 279.

on Salamis reappears (cf. L 58 ff.), but this time with a crude and explicit reference to intercourse (39) rather than mere innuendo. The litany of feminine faults in 221 ff. heavily underlines the more shocking (and therefore less titillating) deceits of women and culminates in a witless climax (228), "yes, and women still enjoy a good fuck, too."

Similarly, the passage in which woman A asks Praxagora what to do if the men attack her (254 ff.; cf. L 157 ff.) makes use of language that would have sounded discordantly violent and almost dirty in the earlier play. We can hardly imagine Lysistrata (or even Cleonice) uttering remarks like these, not to mention lines 78, 95–97, and 225. The smuttiness of the sexual vocabulary of the whole play—there is more coarse slang from hitting and piercing, for example, than in any other play—constantly emphasizes an unadorned and unlovely view of copulation. In earlier plays the fact of copulation was mostly concealed or glamorized by jokes, euphemisms, or double entendres. As mentioned above, the absence of these techniques in this play is a deliberate device in the service of irony.

It is not long before scatological motifs make their appearance. While Praxagora, dressed in her husband's clothes, is taking over the government, her husband Blepyrus is just getting out of bed, unaware of the revolution his wife is about to impose on the city. He has noticed the absence of his wife and his clothes because he is under urgent pressure from his bowels. Forced to don his wife's dress and slippers, he has come out in front of his house to ease himself. The entire scene (311–71) is taken up with Blepyrus' constipated groaning and the commiseration of his similarly attired neighbor. The abundant excremental vocabulary of the scene is limited (predictably) to χέζειν (shit), and ἀποπατεῖν, (relieve oneself), and the only attempts at joke-technique are several pederastic personifications of his excrement by Blepyrus (316 f., 361–68). Thus the humor is purely in the degraded spectacle and not in any verbal artifice. Excrement, like sexual congress, is usually disguised or altered by the comic poet's language: we rarely actually see excrement, although it is referred to often. Here we are forced to contemplate a man who is actually relieving himself (squatting and making noises). Although Blepyrus prays to Eileithyia that he not become a σκωραμὶς κωμῳδική (371), a "comical old shitpot," that is of course precisely what he is in this scene. While his wife has risen to the highest position possible in the city, Blepyrus has sunk to the lowest.[52] We are meant to understand Blepyrus' scene as taking place simultaneously with Praxagora's in the assembly, as is clear from the appearance of Chremes at 372.

52. "Nicht weniger symbolisch," remarks Gelzer (n. 4, above), 1501.32.

Upon her return (after a short and unmotivated scene [529–70] in which Blepyrus, the old husband, accuses Praxagora, the young wife, of adultery),[53] Praxagora undertakes to explain the laws of the new regime to her skeptical husband. The sexual part of the plan is explained by Praxagora by the use mostly of slang terms (613 f., 617 f., 628 f., 631–34), while Blepyrus, occupying the traditional function of βωμολόχος (buffoon), uses much coarse language (611 f., 615 f., 619 f., 624, 640). Chremes contributes a sly joke about the fellator, Aristyllus (647 ff.; see section 386 below). Throughout this scene, as in previous scenes, the obscenity has a repetitive and tiresome dullness. The humor relies on the shock of unrelieved smut rather than on wit and jokes.

Between this exchange and the scene with the hags and lovers (877 ff.), there are only a few scattered obscenities. Praxagora' song at 689–709 sums up the new sexual regulations by contrasting the happy lot of ugly men with the sad lot of handsome men.[54] Its comic technique is the use of tantalizing euphemisms for intercourse to pave the way for a foul and explicit climax (706–09). The man who scoffs at Chremes' obedience to the new laws concerning property (746–876) gives voice to his contempt by using blunt scatological jokes (806–08, 831 f.). The speech of the girl messenger who comes in to describe the communal festivities (834 ff.) is part of a tradition of such banquet descriptions (cp. A 1085–93); this one contains rather more explicit sexual nuances and double entendres than usual (842–45, 846 f., 847 f.).

The remaining obscenity of the play is contained in the long and complicated scene (877–1111) illustrating the effect of the new sexual regulations on typical character-types. The scene opens with an interchange between an old hag and a young girl who is waiting for a lover. Although prostitution and intercourse between slaves and citizens have been abolished (718–24) and these women are thus technically not prostitutes, we should think of them as prostitutes inasmuch as they speak and act the part. Certainly the hags correspond to the type of the battle-hardened whore (cf. 877–82).[55]

The hag and the girl open the scene with mutual mockery and a rivalry of love-songs, that of the hag emphasizing a "ripe" woman's practical skill at lovemaking, that of the girl emphasizing a young girl's suppleness of body (893–99, 900–05). The love-songs are strictly euphemistic, but are followed by abusive replies that are extremely obscene (906–10, 911–24).

---

53. Obscenely at 525.
54. Compare the similar opposition of Dicaeopolis and Lamachus in A 1145–49.
55. See n. 61, below.

The essence of the hag's curse is that the young girl be frustrated in her lovemaking; the girl's curses emphasize such stock motifs of *uetula-Skoptik* as the use of dildoes (916 f.)[56] and the practice of fellatio (920).

The young man for whom the girl has been longing finally arrives, complaining bitterly about the new sexual laws (938). The girl assures him that the hag has gone, and the couple sing a love-duet which seems to be a parody of a conventional genre.[57] The song of the girl is completely euphemistic (952–59), as is that of the young man (960–75), except for a hotly explicit couplet that seems to play on a conventional erotic *topos* (964 f.).[58]

But before the young man can enter the girl's house the old hag lays claim to him. The girl manages to drag him to safety, but is chased off by an even older and uglier hag, who is joined by yet a third, the most hideous of the lot. The rest of the scene is a struggle between the old hags for possession of the young man, who finally winds up in the home of hag B. During the scene the obscenity of the hags displays no joke-technique; it is routine, straightforward, and usually euphemistic, often echoing the terminology of the Praxagora-Blepyrus scene (581 ff.).[59] It is the young man who, as βωμολόχος, (buffoon), furnishes the inventive obscenity: thus his self-conscious joke on Anaphystius (979 f.; see section 490, below), and those on Procrustes (1021) and the decree of Cannonos (1089–91);[60] his clever innuendo at 1047 f.; the Relation-like ruse of asking to go to the bathroom (1059 ff.; cf. T 610); the testicle joke on ἐγγυητής at 1064 f.; colorful metaphors like those at 1082 and 1091; and his final outpouring of misery in the face of the inevitable (1098–111), with its vivid sexual language (1099, 1104, 1106, 1107, 1109).

These are the final obscenities of the play, the final explicit view we are allowed of the nauseating consequences of Praxagora's scheme. It is surely ironic in the extreme that the young man's metaphorical death at the hands of the monstrous old hags is followed immediately by the sham triumphs of the exodus, begun by the drunken cry of a slave-girl (1112), ὦ μακάριος μὲν δῆμος, εὐδαίμων δὲ γῆ ("Blessèd the city! Happy the earth!").

Plutus

The content and much of the dramatic form of *Plutus* mark a new depar-

56. See van Daele (Budé edition), 5: 57, n. 6.
57. See chap. 2, n. 171.
58. See section 151, below.
59. 990, 1008 f., 1015–20, 1049 f., 1062. So also the girl, 1038 ff.
60. Cf. the savage joke on δημοκρατεῖν, to be democratic, turned to degraded sexual uses at 944 f. (see van Daele [Budé edition], 5: 66, n. 1).

ture for Aristophanes. Not only are the choral parts drastically truncated—there are only a dozen lines to be sung by the chorus and thirty to be spoken by the Coryphaeus—but there is a further intensification of Aristophanes' interest (already apparent in *Ecclesiazusae*) in social satire, irony, generalized popular morality, and the realistic characterization of stock types. The "comic hero" has completely disappeared in *Plutus;* the pale remnants of his vivid personality have been inherited by the clever slave, Carion, forerunner of the prominent and dominating slaves of New Comedy. There is no interest in current politics or government: the names of a few leading individuals are mentioned with only lukewarm interest (170 ff., 550), and the sycophant, a mere type, is the only official representative of the polis itself (850 ff.).

The question of the unjust distribution of wealth and its blessings, which forms the substance of the plot, is not brought into relation with the life of the polis but is presented as an abstract moral problem, played out in the isolated and apolitical microcosm of a small group of *kleine Leute*. The treatment of the theme is thus quite different from what it might have been in the heyday of Old Comedy. We might contrast Cratinus' *Plutoi* of a half-century earlier, in which the chorus, composed of the *daimones* who distribute wealth, join forces with the enemies of the nouveau riche general, Hagnon, for an all-out critique of the current political scene.

The obscenity in *Plutus* shows a parallel change in character and function. The marvelous ingenuity and inventiveness once displayed by Aristophanes in the creation of sexual themes, obscene jokes, innuendoes, routines, and clever farces have now disappeared. There remain only two types of obscenity in *Plutus:* blunt and hackneyed crudities, and obscenity in the service of realistic character-portraiture. The former appears in standard contexts in the first section of the play (1–801), which consists of Chremylus' and Carion's capture and subsequent cure of Plutus, their victory over Penia, and their resulting enrichment; and the latter appears in the second section (802 ff.), a series of episodes illustrating the consequences for various character-types of the new distribution of wealth.

The obscenity in the first section is limited to three functions:

1. In personal invective: the rich Agyrrhius is said to break wind from (we assume) an overabundance of food and drink (176). Plutus is called ψωλός (all hard-on), by Carion (267) as a climax to a series of insulting epithets (266). Since ψωλός is an inappropriate word for an old man like Plutus, we must assume either that Carion is being facetious or that ψωλός had assumed a more general abusive tone. The intermezzo at 290–315 consists of strophic parodies of Philoxenus' dithyramb, *Polyphemus and Galateia,* and the theme of Circe and Odysseus (*Od.* 133–399). The second

of these (302–15) is an abusive allusion to the liaison between Philonides and the notorious courtesan Lais, and features tawdry and perverted sexual σκώμματα (scurrilities), unrelieved by wit.

2. Obscene language is used to vivify the rather heavy-handed moralizing of Chremylus and Carion regarding the influence of wealth on the price of prostitutes and the willingness of young boys to succumb to the advances of lovers (149–59).

3. In slapstick: Carion's experiences in the temple of Asclepius include the breaking of wind. First, an old lady whom Carion terrifies in the dark breaks wind "more pungent than a weasel's" (693). Then Carion himself, who considers crepitation "exceedingly funny" (697), follows suit. His own offering is powerful enough to repel the god's attendant female deities (701–03) but not the god himself; Carion takes this opportunity (difficult for a buffoon to resist) to call the god a shit-eater (706), a remark Carion's female companion finds shocking (706).

καταπαρδεῖν (fart) at 618 is meant only as a vulgar surprise at the end of Blepsidemus' song and has no further relevance to the action or the character.

The only sexual or scatological language in the second part is contained in the scene (959–1096) between the old hetaera and her youthful ex-lover, who (newly wealthy, thanks to Plutus' renewed sight [1004]) no longer needs her gifts and feels free to indulge the contempt he once had to dissimulate. It is a question whether this ungrateful young man ought to be considered just; perhaps Aristophanes is simply being inconsistent with the basic premise that in the new order of things only the just will be rich, and perhaps the cruel treatment of a comical old lady was felt by the Athenians to raise no moral issues. At any rate, the complaints of the old lady are not taken seriously, and the comedy of the scene relies entirely on jokes about her age and physical deterioration.

Despite certain similarities between this scene and the scene of strife between the old hags and the young girl in *Ecclesiazusae* (877–1111)—and it is mainly the element of mockery which is similar—the old lady in *Plutus* is essentially a different type from what we saw in the earlier play.[61] She is not a tough, lascivious, and foul-mouthed streetwalker but an aging hetaera who once charged dearly for her company (1029) and who must now purchase the affections of younger men. Vanity prevents her from acknowledging the signs of old age and she continues to behave like a young girl. The type of the love-sick old lady was apparently standard in

61. Oeri (n. 28, above), pp. 19 ff., misclassifies the old hags of E 877 ff. under "die liebestolle Alte;" they should be classified under "die alternde Hetäre" (pp. 47 ff.) as a subcategory.

Old Comedy: we may compare Cratinus' *Graes,* T 345, the wife of Lycon,[62] the mother of Hyperbolus,[63] and the Phaedra-like character in Fr 51.[64] The absence of this type in the fragments of Middle and New Comedy[65] suggests that the frequent references to it in the paroemiographers[66] refer to its appearance in Old Comedy.

In contrast to the crude streetwalkers of *Ecclesiazusae,* who have no illusions about their age and in fact consider it a professional asset (E 895 f.), this old lady behaves in a quite dignified manner. She says nothing unseemly or even remotely suggesting obscenity,[67] which was one of the notable elements of the prostitutes' speech in *Ecclesiazusae.* Instead, she plays straight man, as it were, ignoring the jests of the chorus, Chremylus, and the youth, and thus providing them with continuous opportunities for mockery. Some of Chremylus' mockery takes the form of slyly obscene double entendres (970 f., 1024); that of the young man is more straightforwardly obscene and not a little sadistic (1055–58, 1082 f., 1093).

62. Schol. L 270, Eup. 215.
63. Hermipp. 10.
64. See Kock, ad loc., Meineke, 2: 2.962; cf. Eur. *Hipp.* 219.
65. Oeri (n. 28, above), p. 47.
66. Cf. Diogenian. 3.74, 4.10.
67. With the possible exception of the double entendres in 995 ff. and 1015 (of which she is unaware).

4   The Sexual Organs

The Male Organs

1. πέος (*pes-os, cf. *penis* [*pes-n-is]) appears most frequently and seems to be the vulgar *vox propria*. Evidently its usefulness lay in its shock value, hence its use primarily in surprises, violent oaths, smut, and low slapstick. Lysistrata, gradually announcing her plan to bring home the men by stopping the war, comes climactically to the principal sacrifice required of her troops: they must give up the πέος (124); the word is meant to hit with blunt force after the paratragic language which precedes (and follows, cf. 134). The profane relation of Euripides uses πέος with similar climactic bathos in turning the high-flown poetry of Agathon's servant into a violent threat (T 59–62), with which we may compare the Sausage-Seller's oath, τὸ πέος οὑτοσὶ δάκοι, may be bite his own cock (Eq 1010), a surprise intended to outdo in savageness Cleon's boast in 1006.[1]

In heterosexual contexts we find only smut, that is, language whose sole purpose is to play up, with little or no attempt at wit and in the most direct manner, the purely physical aspects of sexuality: thus the servant at P 870, 880, and Trygaeus at 898 (where πέει is a comic substitution for σκέλει, leg) are engaged in a dialogue of extended and unadorned smut concerning the beauteous Theoria. πέος occurs in other such passages: V 1347 where Philocleon chatters filthily to the flute-girl; A 1216 (Dicaeopolis to the two courtesans); A 1060, 1066 (Dicaeopolis to the bridesmaid); L 415 (the Probulus' speech on female lechery), 928 (Cinesias' frustrated lust); V 739 (Bdelycleon must purchase a πόρνη, whore, for his father); E 620 (Blepyrus and Praxagora discuss the new sexual regulations). Finally, the

---

1. Blaydes' explanation is unnecessarily specific, "quia Cleon tunc curvato corpore et inclinato corpore intentus oraculis disponendis et investigandis esset." There is no need to assume any particular action on stage; this is merely a violent oath based on a standard expression: see N 1369, V 1083, R 43.

word gives flavor to the ludicrous game of hide-and-seek that Cleisthenes plays with the phallus of the Relation (T 643 ff.), or the latter's paratragic outburst of amazement at Agathon's androgynous appearance (124), or to Strepsiades' crude masturbation (N 734).[2]

2. πόσθη (probably—if the linguistic terminology may be excused—an o-grade of *pes- with expansion; cf. σά-θη, κύσ-θος; for other theories see Frisk s.v.) is a small member or a young boy's member, and seems to have had an affectionate and somewhat respectable tone, in contrast to the vulgar, almost violent tone of πέος. πόσθων means "boy" at P 1300, where the scholiast notes that this playful nickname was common in Attic households.[3] The pederast Agathon's clothes smell sweetly of ποσθίου (T 254, a surprise for μύρου, perfume, or the like) because of his predilection for small boys. One of the signs of a well-spent youth, according to the boy-loving Just Logic, is a πόσθην μικράν (N 1014): the tone here is definitely one of affectionate lubricity, in contrast to the comical vulgarity of the κωλῆν μεγάλην, big meat, the bad boy's member (1018). The joke made by the old woman at T 515 carries a more abusive tone: a man's new son resembles his father in every detail, including his πόσθιον, "limp and withered like a little shot pine-cone."[4] The woman's implication is that the husband's member is also small and useless (seedless like the κύτταρος ?), and that may account for the wife's reliance on the baby-market for her child.[5] The use of πόστιον by the archer at T 1188 is of course ironic: we may be sure that the barbarian's member was anything but boyish. The more or less respectable tone of πόσθη is reflected by its use in scientific prose to mean "foreskin"[6] or "stye on the eyelid,"[7] as well as in cult.[8]

3. σάθη is the normal-sized organ and seems to have had a tone similar to that of πόσθη;[9] Wilamowitz, *Lysistrata*, at L 1119, even thinks that it

2. The πέος as a visual and verbal symbol of lust and base drives appears in such comic coinages as πεοίδης (CA 1111 = AB 72.26 ὁ μέγα καὶ ἀπρεπὲς αἰδοῖον ἔχων, having a large, gross member) and πειώλης (= κίναιδος EM 668.36).

3. Cf. also Men 480, Phot., and Hsch., who note that πόσθων was also used of childish or foolish adults.

4. See Thphr. *HP* 3.3.8, 3.7.4; I follow van Leeuwen ad loc.

5. For jokes on small penises, often used in low comedy, see Th. Hopfner, *Das Sexualleben der Griechen und Römer* (Prague, 1938), pp. 39 f.

6. Hp. *Ulc.* 12, Dsc. 4.153, Ruf. *Onom.* 102, Orib. *Fr.* 84, Ph. 2.211.

7. Gal. 12.741, Aet. 7.84.

8. See J. Taillardat, "Ποσθαλίων et Ποσθαλίσκος (Ar. *Thesm.* 292)," *RPh* 35 (1961):249 f., and the inscription given by D. M. Robinson in *Hesp.* 27 (1958): 74. Dindorf's reading in T 291, καὶ ποσθαλίσκον, which Taillardat defends, is probably incorrect: see Coulon ad loc., A. Willems, *Aristophane* (Paris-Brussels, 1919), 2: 548 ff. πρὸς σάθωνα (Willems) or πρὸς σαθίσκον (Coulon) is wanted.

9. See H. Frisk, *Griechisches etymologisches Wörterbuch* (Heidelberg, 1960–72), s.v.

might have been an elegant and exotic word at Athens. Thus in a relatively high-minded passage Lysistrata prefers σάθη to a coarser word (L 1119).
Σάθων could, like πόσθων, be used as a term of endearment of young boys
(Telecl. 65).[10] Its use in cult is assured by the Priapus epithets ἀνδροσά-
θων[11] and ἀνδροσάθη.[12] Σάθη was, however, capable of abusive connotations despite its playful tone: it has an undeniable harshness in Archil.
43 and in the name Σάθων, used by Antisthenes of Plato in a scurrilous
dialogue attacking the Platonic school.[13]

   4. ψωλή, a penis ready for intercourse, was, like πέος, thoroughly vulgar. Lampito uses ψωλή to describe the indispensability of a husband's
ready cock (L 143); the lecherous gods at Av 560 and the Coryphaeus at
L 979 are quite upright and ready for intercourse. The verb ἀποψωλεῖν, to
draw back someone's prepuce by causing an erection, appears in uniformly
coarse contexts: thus the libidinous Thracians of A 161 are called τοῖς
ἀπεψωλημένοις, those with ready ψωλαί, as are the fornicators of P 903 and
Pl 295, and the distended prytanis at L 1136. Dicaeopolis' remark to Lamachus (A 592), τί μ' οὐκ ἀπεψώλησας; εὔοπλος γὰρ εἶ, is a double entendre
meaning (1) lop off my ψωλή and (2) use your charms to arouse me sexually (see ὅπλον).

   5. ψωλός is used of men who are "all phallus": thus the call of the
aroused Egyptians at Av 507, κόκκυ ψωλοὶ πεδίονδε, cuckoo! all cocks to
the plain (see πεδίον, plain),[14] and the efficacy of ψωλός as an insult:
Cario's ultimate insult is to call Plutus ψωλός (Pl 267), and the Sausage-
Seller's oracle predicts (Eq 964) that Demus, should he listen to Cleon,
must become ψωλός "all the way to his pubic bush," i.e. absolutely debauched. Diphilus 39 imitates and expands this violent image, substitut-
ing "gullet" for "pubic bush."[15] It is likely that ψωλός also refers to circumcision (n. 17, below).

   6. The state of erection was indicative in Old Comedy of high sexual
excitement and libidinous character.[16] As a dramatic device the depiction
of men in this condition, by means of huge artificial erections and byplay
on stage, could not fail to produce laughter. An audience enjoyed the
physical and verbal exposure of men in their manifest dependence upon

   10. Cf. Phot., *AB* 394.5, 27.
   11. Phot. p. 127R, Eust. 1968.43, *AB* 394, Suda.
   12. Hsch. = CA 932.
   13. Athen. 5.220D, 11.507A, D.L. 3.35.
   14. See the discussion of Willems (n. 8, above), 2: 304 f.
   15. Cf. also ψώλων (Hsch. s.v. πόσθων), ψωλήκυσθος (Hsch.), ἀκρόψωλος (Suda), all
indicating men of great profligacy.
   16. For the rich literature in antiquity concerning the humor of erections, see Hopfner
(n. 5, above), pp. 34 ff.

(base) bodily drives and relished the resulting feeling of superiority occasioned by their safe contemplation of the comic character's obvious pain and frustration. The ordinary comic phallus was of course not erect, but as described at N 538 f.: made of leather, pendant, red, uniformly thick;[17] compare Hor. *Sat.* 1.8.5 *obscenoque ruber porrectus ab inguine palus.* When the situation called for it, erections could be provided by using special phalli. Erect phalli were especially appropriate for depicting the triumph of rejuvenated comic heroes like Dicaeopolis (A 1121, 1216 f., 1220), Demus (Eq 1391), Trygaeus (P 856 ff.) and Peisetaerus (Av 1256), or for showing profligacy (A 158, T 1187 ff., etc.) or desperation (P 728, L passim) or some special comic effect (V 68 f., E 890).[18] The kind of farcical byplay to be expected in this kind of scene is abundantly illustrated in the latter half of *Lysistrata*, where the distended men wear the ὄρρος κατατεινόμενος, stretched-out member (965), and walk about doubled over like λυχνοφορίοντες, lamp-bearers (1003), to hide their condition. They resemble the priapic Konisalos[19] and must bunch their upper garments around their waists like wrestlers (L 1093, cf. 1093 f., 1096) to avoid the notice of any Hermocopidae who might be about.[20] Everyone complains of spasmodic pains (σπασμός 845, 1089; ἀντισπασμός 967) and indulges in much obscene language and byplay.

17. Depending on dramatic desiderata, it could be left to dangle, be tied back, covered, and so on; see the discussions of Webster and Beare (preface, n. 7). Dover maintains, discussing N 538 f., "Notes On Aristophanes' *Acharnians*," *Maia* 15 (1963): 12 f., that the phallus could be circumcized for humorous effect. The description of the comic phallus in *Clouds,* which makes the penis "red at the end," must refer to circumcision: the foreskin cannot be retracted (except by hand) when the penis is "hanging down." Vase-paintings frequently show slaves (presumably from Phoenicia or Egypt, where circumcision was universally practiced) with pendulous circumcised members of great size (e.g. V. Ehrenberg, *People of Aristophanes*, Pl. XIIIa), but paintings of *kaloi* tend to show very small, thin penises with elongated foreskins. The Greeks (who disapproved of circumcision: Hdt. 2.37.2) would have found this barbarian practice quite amusing: see, for instance, Athens red-figure pelike 9683. In a society like ancient Greece, where circumcision was not practiced, such a mutilation of the penis must have caused strong anxiety, and that anxiety is naturally manifested in the humor of comedy in the form of extraordinary skotomata. This gives Av 507 its point, and in Pl 267 ψωλός, circumcised and erect, is climactic after the list of defects in 266.

18. Philocleon at V 1343 is still limp: see J. Vaio, "Aristophanes' *Wasps:* The Final Scenes," *GRBS* 12 (1971): 333, n. 41; C. H. Whitman, *Aristophanes and the Comic Hero* (Cambridge, Mass, 1964), pp. 157 f. Presumably, old men who are to be "rejuvenated" wore pendant phalli at the beginning of the play and later changed the costuming to fit their new role as mighty lovers.

19. L 982, cf. H. Herter, *De dis atticis Priapi similibus* (Bonn, 1926), Chap. 3; Pl Com 174.13, *SIG* 1027.10, Str. 13.1.12.

20. Hermes jokes are frequent in comedy: Phryn. Com. 58.1 ff.; Fr 553, etc.

7. στύω/στύομαι was the standard improper word for getting an erection or being erect: improper probably because the idea of sexual aggressiveness is built right into the word, unlike such technical terms as ἔπαρσις (L 937 in double entendre) and τέτανος (L 553, 846), which express a physical state only and have a more proper tone.[21] Thus every appearance of the word in Aristophanes occurs in contexts where lovemaking or rape is imminent, and there is always an accompanying word meaning "fornicate": A 1220, P 728, Av 557, 1256, L 214, 598, T 157 f. At Pl Com 173.20 στύματα virtually = intercourse; the same implication undoubtedly lies behind Eubulus' play, "Αστυτοι, the limp ones, and the ἄστυτος ᾦκος, limp house, (surprise for ἄστυλος, without pillars) of Xenarch. 1.4;[22] cf. 'Αστυάναξ γέγονα at CA 744.

8. ἀναστῦψαι (ἀναστύφειν) = τὸ ἀνασπάσαι τὸ αἰδοῖον, to draw back the member (CA 81).

9. ἀσύντατος refers to "limp" members punningly at Xenarch. 1.2.

10. ὀρθός, upright, is common and perfectly proper in the meaning "erect;"[23] in Aristophanes it is the source of several puns: the names Orsilochus (L 725) and Orthagoras (E 916),[24] ὀρθὴν ὁδόν, the upright road (L 834), ὀρσὰ Λακεδαίμων πᾶα, all Sparta is straight (L 995); cf. also A 243, 259 f. (the processional φαλλὸς ὀρθός), Pl Com 173.10 δέμας ὀρθοῖ = cause an erection, CA 1096 ὀρθοσταδόν, Hsch. s.v. ἐξηνδρωμένος = ὀρθιάζων, ὀρθίας = ἱστὸς νεώς, ship's beam = penis.

Proper and Euphemistic Words

11. φαλλός was, of course, a proper word, and its use in Aristophanes is almost always technical, as in Dicaeopolis' miniature Rural Dionysia.[25] At A 260, however, ὁ φαλλὸς ἐξόπισθε τῆς κανηφόρου, behind the basket-girl, is a joke referring to the slave Xanthias' phallus as well as the processional one.[26] At L 771 φαλήτων is only semitechnical, being used for its high-sounding tone in Lysistrata's bawdy parody of a serious oracle. Cratinus (14) used ἰθύφαλλος to refer to the erect member.

12. There are many plays on the word: in the new kingdom of birds the φαληρίς will receive Aphrodite's old hegemony in sacrifice (Av 565);

21. See Arist. *HA* 572[b] 2, 604[b] 4.

22. Cf. 'Αστυάναξ (*AP* 12.11, Eust. 849.54), 'Αστυάγης (*AP* 12.174).

23. Pi. *P.* 10.36, Hdt. 2.51, *PLond.* 1821.166, etc.

24. See V. Coulon, "Beiträge zur Interpretation des Aristophanes," *RhM* 105 (1962): 26 f.

25. A 243, 261, 263, 271, 276; cf. Fr *954 Blaydes and compare D. Chr. 2.31, Hor. *Sat.* 1.8.1 ff.

26. For (ἐξ) ὄπισθεν in an obscene sense, cf. A 868, T 157 f., 1124, V 1376, L 1170, E 482, Eup. 334.

Hermes is τρικέφαλος (Fr 553); the swinish and illiterate sons of Hippo-crates are "procephalous" (Fr 557); and Alcibiades was supposedly born in the archonship of Phalenias (Fr 554), an allusion to that young man's dissolute habits.[27] In Fr 320, a list of women's paraphernalia, we find κεκρύφαλον (1. 6), both "girdle" and "secret phallus" (cf. the ὄλισβος in l. 13). The obscenity in A 835, where the Megarian bids his daughters παίειν ἐφ᾽ ἁλὶ τὴν μᾶδδαν, can be explained as a segmentation-pun on φαλλός (ἐφαλί); the passage reads "My little piggies, even without your father you must try: (1) to bang down some bread with your salt, if anyone should give you any; (2) to bang your cunt against the phallus, in case someone should give [it] to you"[28] (see παίειν and μᾶζα). This pun can be compared with that in Sophron 39 Olivieri, quoted above, p. 25. The un-usual use of ἐπί to refer to the condiment instead of the main dish, and of the singular ἅλς instead of the more usual ἅλες for salt, can be accounted for only if this obscene pun is acknowledged.[29] Finally, there may be a pun (similar to that in CA 243, quoted in section 13, below) at R 134, where Dionysus, urged by Heracles to jump off a tower in order to reach Hades quickly, fears he will destroy ἐγκεφάλου θρίω δύο: (1) the twin rissole-wrappers of his brain, and (2) the two bundles/wrappers of his phallus (i.e. testicles?).

Euphemisms

There are many euphemisms for the male member in comedy.

13. τὰ αἰδοῖα, "the private parts," is the standard one, at least in non-comic literature. In Aristophanes it appears at N 978, where the proper Just Logic avoids a coarse term in referring to young boys,[30] and at V 578 in almost the same context: Philocleon enumerates the rewards of jury duty, one of which is looking at naked boys at their δοκιμασία, inspection at puberty. Both uses are meant to be titillating. CA 243 ἐν τοῖσιν αἰδοίοις τὸν ἐγκέφαλον ἔχων, having his brain in his genitals (if from a comedy; see Kock ad loc.) seems to parody obscenely Demosthenes' famous rebuke to the Athenians (7.45).[31]

27. Kock translates "C. Peniculo L. Mentula consulibus."

28. I have defended this reading in detail in "A Note on Aristophanes' *Acharnians*, 834–35," *CP* 68 (1973): 289 f.

29. The supposed pun κυνοκεφάλλῳ at Eq 416 is doubtful for the traditional κυνοκεφ-άλῳ: Cleon would hardly invent such a scabrous epithet for himself. Coulon rightly rejects it, although Cantarella does not. Other phallus-puns are Φαληρὶς ἡ κόρη (or Φα-ληρικὴ κόρη) at Eub. 75.4, Φαληρικοί at Antiph. 206.7, ἐγκέφαλον at CA 243 (see section 13, below).

30. Cf. 977, τοὐμφαλοῦ . . . ὑπένερθεν.

31. ὅσοι δ᾽ Ἀθηναῖοι ὄντες μὴ τῇ πατρίδι, ἀλλὰ Φιλίππῳ εὔνοιαν ἐνδείκνυνται, προσήκει

14. ἀκμή: used punningly at E 720, τῶν νέων. . . τὰς ἀκμάς. The unusual use of the plural gives away the pun by disrupting the usual metaphorical connotation "youthful prime"[32] expressed by the singular, emphasizing instead the literal, and thus comical, image of "tip," "point" or "excrescence."[33]

15. αὐχήν seems certainly to be euphemistic for phallus at L 680 f.,

> ἀλλὰ τούτων χρῆν ἀπασῶν εἰς τετρημένον ξύλον
> ἐγκαθαρμόσαι λαβόντας τουτονὶ τὸν αὐχένα.

If the (ambiguous) genitive is taken with ξύλον (stocks), then ξύλον becomes a double entendre for *cunt* and αὐχήν a double entendre for *phallus*.[34] Thus (1) we should get hold of all these women and put their *necks* into the *wooden stocks;* and (2) we should get hold of this here *cock* and put it into the *cunts* of all these women.

16. There is good evidence that δάκτυλος (finger) could be used as a double entendre. The chorus of women dare the men to touch Stratyllis "even with the finger" at L 365; the surrounding threats and oaths all contain explicit references to the sexual organs, and thus it is highly probable that here, too, we are meant to take δάκτυλος in a double sense. At Eq 1168 f. Cleon announces that he brings Demus pastry-boats molded and gravied by the ivory hand of the goddess; the mischievous Demus remarks that the goddess must have had a big finger (μέγαν δάκτυλον; see on μέγας). The joke lies in the commonly acknowledged resemblance between the female member and various pastries (see below, sections 173–78), and there is a further reference to the female *secreta venerea,* often compared with soup and gravy (below, sections 180–81). Demus means to say that only a large phallus could have resulted in such a well-gravied cunt. For ἔχειν, meaning "to accommodate a penis in coitus," cf. A 787. Eubulus 75.10 ff. has a very similar but much extended joke in which the pastry is further personified as "Pluto's Spouse," and the finger compared to the ramming beak of a trireme (cf. below, section 48):[35]

αὐτοὺς ὑφ' ὑμῶν κακοὺς κακῶς ἀπολωλέναι, εἴπερ ὑμεῖς τὸν ἐγκέφαλον ἐν τοῖς κροτάφοις καὶ μὴ ἐν ταῖς πτέρναις καταπεπατημένον φορεῖτε:

[Those wretches who show their loyalty not to the fatherland but to Philip should perish wretchedly at our hands, and so they shall, if you carry your brains in your heads, not squashed under your feet.]

32. E.g. Th. 8.46, Xen. *Lac.* 1.6, S. *O T* 741.

33. See *LSJ* s.v. ἀκμή I, IV, *Suppl.* s.v. ἀκμαῖος.

34. Cf. Eur. *Cyc.* 184, and see C. L. Iungius, *De vocabulis antiquae comoediae atticae quae apud solos comicos aut omnino inveniuntur aut peculiari notione praedita occurrunt* (Amsterdam, 1897), p. 133.

35. μιμουμένην (codd. -η) must be read with φάραγγα. For πίεσμα see *AP* 12.41.3, πιέζειν (section 334, below).

> μεμαγμένη δὲ Δήμητρος κόρη
> κοίλην φάραγγα δακτύλου πιέσματι
> σύρει, τριήρους ἐμβολὰς μιμουμένην
> δείπνου πρόδρομον ἄριστον.

[Demeter's girl, when kneaded, has a hollow cleft—like the swath of a trireme—made in her by the *finger's* poking: the excellent precursor to a meal!]

17. τὸ δεῖνα appears at A 1149 for *phallus*. This expression is usually used in Greek (1) when one forgets something and must fill in with τὸ δεῖνα, much as we say "so-and-so," and (2) when one does not wish to say something unpleasant or offensive directly.[36] With this Aristophanic allusion (and possibly another at P 879) we may compare Antiph. 129.6 f., where τὸ δεῖνα means both "eel" and "phallus,"[37] and Eup. 244.1,[38] where it stands for some unidentified but undoubtedly phallic "Megarian jest."

18. δέμας, flesh,[39] at Pl Com 173.10 τὸ γὰρ δέμας ἀνέρος ὀρθοῖ(an aphrodisiac) straightens up a man's "meat."

19. δέρμα, skin, seems to mean "prepuce" at Eq 29, where a slave compares the skin on the backs of flayed slaves with that on the phalli of masturbators, τὸ δέρμα δεφομένων ἀπέρχεται (see the schol.). The word as used at Pl Com 174.18 probably means, more generally, the whole phallus.[40]

20. Just Logic speaks loftily but lubriciously of the imprint of a boy's burgeoning "youth" (εἴδωλον τῆς ἥβης N 976); the scholiast rightly glosses ἥβης as indicating the genitals.[41] This euphemism, common in technical writers,[42] appears elsewhere in comedy only at Theopomp. 37, where it refers to the sexual parts of both sexes.[43]

21. μέγας,[44] large, seems to be indicated in the sense of "erect" at V 68 f.,

36. See the remarks of Starkie, *Wasps*, at l. 524.

37. See Edmonds, 1: 222, n. *b*.

38. I follow Meineke's reading τὸ δεῖν' ἀκούεις; see Edmonds, 1: 399, n. *a*.

39. Cf. σάρξ (*LSJ* s.v. II.1).

40. Not the ὄλισβος, as supposed by Kock; we want an implement used in actual intercourse, not τὰ μεμιμημένα. See *LSJ* s.v. δέρμα 2, Frisk (n. 9, above) s.v. δέρω.

41. For the *Clouds* passage as a parody of Pythagoreanism, see J. Hewitt, "The Image in the Sand," *CP* 30 (1935): 10 ff.

42. Hp. *Epid.* 3.4, Arist *HA* 493b 3, etc.; with ἥβη we may compare the common euphemistic word for pubic hair, ἐφήβαιον.

43. Perhaps we may add Pherecr. 62, with Herwerden's emendation of ἤδη: ἥβης μὲν ᾤαν λούμενος προζώννυται, he put an apron over his "youth" while washing.

44. See W. M. Calder III, "An Unnoticed Obscenity in Aristophanes," *CP* 65 (1970): 257; see also Prof. Marcovich's amusing reply and Calder's rebuttal thereto in *CP* 66 (1971): 262.

where ὁ μέγας makes sense only if we visualize "the large phallus of the comic actor, easily visible to the audience, silhouetted against the sky;"[45] this would be one of the occasions where an erect phallus would be employed for a special humorous effect. Similar are ὁ μέγας Ζάν Av 570, where Euelpides jeers at Zeus' masculinity. ἄρχοντα μέγαν at Av 1733 may be an ithyphallic reference similar to that of Sappho in III.6 L-P;[46] the contexts of both passages are hymenaeal. μεγάλοις at E 628 means "well-endowed sexually" (the opposite of the ugly runts at line 629). μέγας (often with πηχύς) is often found as an adjective describing erect phalli: L 23 ff., P 927, 1351 f., E 1048, A 787, N 539, Fr 130.3.

22. μέγιστος may also be used with this meaning: N 549, μέγιστον ὄντα Κλέων᾽ ἔπαισ᾽ εἰς τὴν γαστέρα seems to be a double entendre: I struck into Cleon's belly (1) at the height of his power, i.e. in 424 (cf. Eq 180 ff.), and (2) when he was hugely erect, with reference to Aristophanes' figurative rape of Cleon (see παίειν). The μέγιστος/κριὸς ἐρέβινθος, chickpea ram, of Sophilus 8 refers without a doubt to the erect phallus (see κριός, ἐρέβινθος). Cf. also Eq 1168 f., quoted above, section 16.

23. νεῦρον, sinew, like Latin *nervus*,[47] was a technical term for the erect phallus.[48] Aristophanes constructs a humorous metaphor at L 1078, νενεύρωται μὲν ἥδε συμφορά:[49] the predicament of the men has gotten very "stiff." Cf. also Pl Com 173.19 f,

> τρίγλη δ᾽ οὐκ ἐθέλει νεύρων ἐπιήρανος εἶναι·
> παρθένου ᾽Αρτέμιδος γὰρ ἔφυ καὶ στύματα μισεῖ.

[The red mullet does not want to stiffen up "nerves": for it comes from virgin Artemis and hates hard-ons.]

24. πρᾶγμα, like English *thing*, appears at L 23, 26, 661, 994 in puns; at N 196 f. Strepsiades jokingly expresses a desire to share πραγμάτιόν τι, a certain little thing, with Socrates' (pathic) pupils. At T 581 the πρᾶγμα δεινὸν καὶ μέγα, large and remarkable thing, seems to refer to the Relation's phallus. The young man's joke at E 1089 may possibly contain a punning reference to this euphemism.[50]

45. Calder, p. 257.

46. See G. S. Kirk, "A Fragment of Sappho Reinterpreted," *CQ* 13 (1963): 51 f.; H. Lloyd-Johnes, "Sappho Fr. 111," *CQ* 17 (1967): 168, and now J.F. Killen, *CQ* 23 (1973): 198. Marcovich continues the debate in "Sappho Fr. 31: Anxiety Attack or Love Declaration?" *CQ* 22 (1972): 29 ff.

47. Hor. *Ep.* 12.19. *Priap.* 68, Petron. 131.46.

48. Gal. 8.442, Callim. 199 Pf. the proverb at Athen. 2.64B, οὐδέν σ᾽ ὀνήσει βολβός, ἂν μὴ νεῦρ᾽ ἔχῃς, the purse-tassel plant will do you no good unless you have "nerve."

49. See the schol. τὴν ἔντασιν τοῦ αἰδοίου λέγει.

50. For πρᾶγμα see further *PMag.* 7. 186.

25. σχῆμα, "equipment,"[51] appears in a punning sense at E 482, where the chorus of women bid one another to be on guard μή πού τις ἐκ τοὖπισθεν ὦν τὸ σχῆμα παραφυλάξῃ, lest someone from behind watch our equipage closely.

26. τύχη at Amphis 20.6 τὴν ἀναγκαίαν τύχην, necessary thing, Xenarch. 1.3 (pl.).

27. For φύσις see above, p. 5.

28. For χάρις see below, section 251.

29. The use of the demonstrative pronoun deictically or the complete omission of an off-color word are very common euphemistic devices and usually indicate comical byplay on stage. Thus, when Lamachus instructs his boy to take his weapon, Dicaeopolis tells his own boy to take hold of τοῦδε, indicating his erect member (A 1121; cf. 1216). Kinesias at L 863 and 937 uses τοῦτο thus, as does the aroused archer at T 1195. At L 956 ταυτηνί probably understands ψωλήν. See further τοδί (L 991), τούτου (L 1121), οὖ (L 146), τουτί (T 664), τούτῳ (V 1349).

30. The same device applies equally to areas other than the phallic. πρωκτός is understood at Av 442 f. (τόνδε) and R 308 (ὁδί). At E 890 τούτῳ is the middle finger, at L 418 τοῦτο is the cunt (below, section 146). Verbs denoting sexual intercourse lie behind P 370 (ἀγαθὸν τοσουτονί), L 1117 (τοῦτο), 841 (ὦν), 1175 (ταῦτα), E 114 (τοῦτο), T 1194 f. (τοῦτο = κατεύδει παρ' ἐμέ, 1193), Timocl. 23.4 (ἑκάστῳ = the individual act of coitus). πυγή, butt, is understood at Eq 785 τὴν ἐν Σαλαμῖνι; women's genitals at L 92 ταυταγὶ τἀντευθενί; crepitation at P 88 (τοῦτο); intercourse at L 923 (αἰσχρὸν γὰρ ἐπὶ τόνου γε, it's terrible on box-springs!), Timocl. 22.4 (πάνθ' ἕτοιμα). The dainty Cleisthenes shuns an outright indecency when the Relation asks to go to the bathroom, σὺ δ' οὖν ποίει τοῦθ' (T 611 f.), at least until he becomes annoyed later (615). Similarly, a coarse word for incest is tactfully omitted at V 1178, ἔπειτα δ' ὡς ὁ Καρδοπίων τὴν μητέρα, and then Cardopion—his mother. Compare the straightlaced Aeschylus at R 1194 τὴν ἑαυτοῦ μητέρα,—his own mother, and Sophocles himself in *O T* 1289 τὸν πατροκτόνον/τὸν μητρός.[52]

Agricultural Terminology[53]

31. A common source of double entendres for the organs of both sexes is the fig,[54] although such references to the female member far outnumber

---

51. See *Lxx. Is.* 3.17 καὶ Κύριος ἀνακαλύψει τὸ σχῆμα αὐτῶν.

52. Other instances: Antiph. 18.6, 129.4; Eur. *Cyc.* 169; Theocr. 1.104; *AP* 3.78.

53. See also the agricultural terminology in chap. 3.

54. Literature and citations in V. Buchheit, "Feigensymbolik im antiken Epigram," *RhM* 103 (1960): 200 ff. See also A. Bartalucci, "Hipponacteae Interpretatiunculae," *Maia* 16 (1964): 244, nn. 8, 9.

references to the male member. συκῆ, the fig-tree itself along with its pendant fruit, is used to indicate the male's whole sexual apparatus; σῦκον, the fruit itself, indicates the cunt. Naturally, the word συκῆ never appears alone for the phallus but always includes mention of the testicles: thus δίφορος συκῆ (E 708) means the branch from which the twin fruit hang; Antiphanes 198 τὴν δίφορον συκῆν κάτω and Pherecrates 97 σῦκα τῶν διφόρων have almost exactly the same phrase. Hesychius' σακκινόσυκοι (he-men) looks like a comic coinage; the image is of a man with large testicles, hence especially virile.

32. The νέα μοσχίδια συκίδων, the young shoots of fig-slips, of A 995, in a passage full of obscene agricultural puns, seem to refer to the erect member alone.

33. The use of σῦκον for both sexes at P 1351 f., τοῦ μὲν μέγα καὶ παχύ, τῆς δ' ἡδὺ τὸ σῦκον, his is fat and large, hers sweet, is a case of brachylogy for the sake of parallelism in which σῦκον is technically appropriate to the female in the second clause but not to the male in the first clause, in which συκῆ must be mentally supplied.

34. φιβαλέως ἰσχάδας, dried early figs, at A 802, despite ἐρεβίνθους a line earlier, cannot be a double entendre for phallus, as proposed (e.g.) by van Daele ad loc. ἰσχάς always indicates the female member. Dicaeopolis is merely preparing to bring out some dried figs to feed the girls, their father, and perhaps the audience too (805 ff.).

35. ψηνίζειν with a sexual connotation appears in CA 12, where it is maintained that every noble ψηνίζεται,—that is, gathers fruiting branches of the wild fig. This pederastic image is taken from the process of caprification (see *LSJ* s.v. ἐρινάζω).

36. Similar homosexual references to figs are ἀποσυκάζειν (to squeeze figs, Eq 259), used of Cleon's victims. Cleon is presented often in this play as a *paedicator*, or homosexual rapist (see below, section 479); and ἀποσεσύκασται in Ameipsias 33.

37. The petals of the fig (θρῖα) indicate the foreskin: A 1102, E 707 f. ἀποθριάζειν, to draw back the petals, is in meaning identical to ἀποψωλεῖν (q.v.): to draw back the prepuce in preparation for sexual activity or to be circumcised (n.17, above).[55] The Odomantian barbarians of A 158 are hugely erect (dissolute) and circumcised,[56] as is clear from line 160, where their savage sexual proclivities are obvious. They are "all too violently virile"[57] counterparts to the dissolute pathics, Cleisthenes and Straton, unmasked earlier by Dicaeopolis. For θρίω (dual) perhaps = testicles, see section 12, above.

55. For circumcision see n. 17, above.
56. τίς τῶν 'Οδομάντων τὸ πέος ἀποτεθρίακεν.
57. Whitman (n. 18, above), p. 61.

38. ἐντεθριῶσθαι at L 663, to be wrapped in a fig leaf, is a triple pun: (1) to be muffled up in our clothes; (2) to be hoodwinked; (3) to remain limp and unerect like codgers, that is, with foreskins unretracted. The attempted rejuvenation of the old men is one of the major themes of the agon of *Lysistrata,* which is full of such phallic allusions.

39. ἀμοργίς, mallow stalk, is the erect member at L 735: a sex-starved woman explains to Lysistrata that she left one at home ἄλοπον, unscutched (see λέπειν).

40. βάλανος, acorn, was apparently a standard name for the *glans penis,* to judge from its use in technical writers;[58] similarly motivated is its common meaning of "iron peg" or "bolt-pin" (*LSJ* II.4). These two images, the acornlike knob and the hard shaft, make βάλανος a vivid vehicle for double entendres on erect phalli like those in the Probulus' speech at L 410 ff.[59]

41. In verbal form the image appears to mean "penetrate sexually": at L 337 the old men run toward the women on the acropolis ὡς βαλανεύσοντες, and at E 361 the constipated Blepyrus personifies a stubborn prickly pear: νῦν μὲν γὰρ οὗτος βεβαλάνωκε τὴν θύραν, now he's banging at my back gate (= τὸν πρωκτόν, ass-hole).[60] Cf. Timocl. 2 καὶ τὸ γλωττοκομεῖον(q.v.) βαλανεύεται, and the tongue-case is penetrated too.

42. ἐρέβινθος, chickpea, is the erect member: A 801, P 1136, R 545, E 45. We have already noticed the κριὸς ἐρέβινθος of Sophilus 8 (section 22).[61] This usage certainly derives from the appearance of the plant itself: the *cicer arietenum* is bushy with rather large, pealike fruit.[62]

43. κριθή, barley-corn. Like πόσθη, the small, elongated κριθή is used by medical writers to mean styes on the eyelid.[63] The bearded appearance of barley stalks may add a further point of comparison. Certainly ἡ ἀμφίκαυστις(= ἡ ὡρίμη κριθή, early barley), used by Cratinus 381 for the loins

58. E.g. Arist. *HA* 493ᵃ 27, Gal. 10.381, Poll. 2.171.

59. For (τὴν βάλανον) ἐνάρμοσον (L 413), cf. the phrase τὸ μέλαν τῷ μέλανι συναρμόσῃ *PMag.* 4. 405.

60. Cf. ἐπιβλής, socket-bolt (*AP* 5.241.6); τύλος, knobbed bolt, in Poll. 2.176, Hsch., Zon., *EM* 125.24 (for a possible pun on φίλοις/τύλοις in Xenarch. 1.5, see Kock ad loc.); μεσσοτύλαρον (Hsch.); ἀποτυλοῦν, which at Pherecr. 204 means ἀναφλᾶν (cf. *AP* 4. 271.11, *AB* 423, Poll. 2.176, Hsch. s.v. ἀπετύλουν. Th. de Wit-Tak, *Lysistrata: Vrede, Vrouw, en Obsceniteit bij Aristophanes* (Groningen, 1967), p. 119, n. 92, mistakenly attempts to describe a double sense of βαλλάντια at L 1054 which does not exist; see van Leeuwen ad loc. With βάλανος compare Lat. *balanus,* as at Pers. 4.37 f., and κορύνη, mace or knobby bud, used as a technical term (Nic. *Al.* 409) and a comic one (*AP* 5.128).

61. Cf. also Juv. 6.373 *circerisque relicti.*

62. "Peascod" at Shakespeare *As You Like It* 2.4.52, quoted by Starkie, *Acharnians,* at line 801, derives from a different image.

63. Hp. *Epid.* 2.2.5, Gal. 12.742.

(ὀσφῦν), suggests the pubic hair.[64] κριθή as phallus indicates erection and lechery: P 965 ff., Av 506, 565. The notion of sexual potency also appears in the verb κριθᾶν, to wax wanton, used of both beasts[65] and men,[66] and in the comic name Κρίθων (Hsch.).

44. φηγός, acorn, is the *glans penis* at P 1137, in a description of the playful rape of a Thracian girl.[67] Cf. 'Eub. 137 (?).

Phallic Implements

Weapons and other hard elongated objects form an important category of double entendres.

45. The slender, cylindrical alabastos, a vessel approximately four to eight inches long[68] and used exclusively by women, usually to hold perfumes, forms the basis for several phallic jokes.[69] L 947, *Mu.* λαβὲ τόνδε τὸν ἀλάβαστον. *Ki.* ἀλλ' ἕτερον ἔχω, *My.* Take this alabastos. *Ki.* But I've already got one! In this scene Myrrhine has fetched an alabastos and there is much byplay on stage.[70] Similarly, in *Acharnians* Dicaeopolis consents to give a bridesmaid some of his treaty, and accompanies his libation with instructions on how to anoint the groom's phallus, a process Dicaeopolis vividly demonstrates on the alabastos.[71] In addition, a line from the *Triphales* (548), ἀλαβαστοθήκας τρεῖς ἔχουσαν ἐκ μιᾶς, having three alabastos-cases in one . . . is unquestionably phallic (note the feminine participle): it seems to refer to a woman who has been the object of Triphales' trimentulate attentions.

46. For βάλανος see above, section 40.

47. δόρυ, a spear shaft or long pole, is presumed by the prytanis at L 985 to be the cause of the peculiar bulge in the Spartan herald's costume, a condition of course caused by his huge erection. Cf. Latin *hasta*.[72]

48. ἔμβολος, a peg, ram, or bar, suggests the notion of sexual penetra-

---

64. See Hsch. s.v. καῦστις; *EM* 90.33, τὸ αἰδοῖον ἀπὸ τοῦ περικεκαῦσθαι. Eust. 1446.29 indicates that this word also indicated the female organs.

65. A. *Ag.* 1641, S. *Fr.* 876.

66. Cleanth. *Stoic.* 1.132, Cerc. 17.16, Babr. 62.2, Poll. 7.24.

67. For φηγός in the sense of "knobbed bolt" (compare βάλανος) cf. *IG* 2².1534.103, φηγοειδὲς ῥαβδίον.

68. The same size as the ὄλισβος (L 109).

69. For the intimate connection between alabastoi and lovemaking, see L 941 f., E 525 f.

70. Full discussion and citations in J. Henderson, "The Lekythos and *Frogs* 1200–1248," *HSCP* 76 (1972): 136 f. Recent notions that the lekythos in this scene, or anywhere else, can mean "phallus" are incorrect.

71. τοὐξάλειπτρον of line 1063 is the alabastos of ten lines earlier.

72. *Priap.* 43.1; Apul. *Met.* 10.21 (cod. Laurent. 54.24, etc.); Auson. 359.17 (= Verg. *Aen.* 9.744).

tion expressed by verbs in –βάλλειν (q.v.): the ἔμβολος of Fr 317 is a phallus swollen by lust and wine (see Hsch.), and Peisetaerus' phallus, menacing Iris, is similarly swollen by the effects of his heroic rejuvenation, στύομαι τριέμβολον, "I've got a triple-decker hard-on" (Av 1256). This comical image of a three-pronged ship need not imply the actual existence of such ships but signifies in its exaggeration the superhuman triumph of the rejuvenated hero. The obscene use of the phrase τριήρους ἐμβολάς, rammings of the trireme, at Eub. 75.10 ff. may be an imitation of this passage.

49. The number three has a special significance in ancient comic writings, one that clarifies the metaphor in Peisetaerus' boast. The ability to perform the sex act thrice in succession was apparently considered proof of great virility.[73] "To win the pancration" meant τὸ τρὶς πλησιάζειν, to screw three times.[74] In Aristophanes we find allusions to this idea often: the newly "rejuvenated" chorus at A 994 promises to make love (προσβαλεῖν) to Diallage thrice; so also the newly rejuvenated Demus at Eq 1391 (κατατριακοντουτίσαι, q.v.). A particularly virile guardian bird at Av 1205 f. is the τρίορχος, which was supposed to grab Iris on her flight into Nephelococcygia. We may compare Aristophanes' *Triphales*,[75] which had to do with an extremely satyric and debauched person (not, as has been thought, Alcibiades);[76] Hermes τρικέφαλος (Fr 553); and the base barbarian, Triballus, of Av 1529 ff.[77] Outside Aristophanes note Cratin. 183.3.[78]

50. ἐπιβολή at V 769 is a double entendre: "fine"/"assault" and "rape" (entering); see ἐπιβάλλειν.

51. ἐρετμόν, oar, at Pl Com 3.4, ἡ μὲν ἐλαυνομένη λαθρίοις ἐρετμοῖς, ὁ δ' ἐλαύνων (see Hsch.).

52. For ἐτνήρυσις, soup-ladle, at A 245 see below, section 181.

73. See Hopfner (n. 5, above), pp. 260 f. for citations.

74. Hsch. s.v. παγκρατιάζειν.

75. See Plb. 12.15.2.

76. Süvern's suggestion is based upon a misreading of Fr 544: see Th. Gelzer, "Aristophanes," *RE Supplbd.* 12 (1971); 1410.37 ff. For virility expressed in terms of the number three in this play, cf. Frs 548, 549, 553, 556 (a geographical pun?).

77. For Triballus see *LSJ* s.v., Eub. 75.3: τριβαλλοποπανόθρεπτα μειρακύλλια: all barbarians are lustful and perpetually erect (read -ποπανο- with Causabon; the MS τριβαλλοπανόθρεπτα, referring to Pan, which Kock defends, is not satisfactory, nor is Meineke's -μαμμο-. The obscene meaning of πόπανον [section 178, below], not to mention the bouncy metrical resolution, make Causabon's reading attractive). See the remarks of J. G. Griffith, "Ληκύθιον ἀπώλεσεν: A Postscript," *HSCP* 74 (1970): 44.

78. See Edmonds, 1: 86, n. *a*. In Latin note Hor. *Ep.* 12.15 and the charming graffito in *CIL* 4.4816, *Chryseros cum successo hic terna futuimus*, Chryseros and his pal fucked here three times each.

53. κέντρον, any point or goad, was common for phallus. In Aristophanes this term seems to be involved in puns surrounding the wasps' stingers (V 225 f., 408, 1115, 1121), and to be the basis for the pejorative epithet κέντρων, used to describe the products of Socrates' school at N 450.[79]

54. κῆλον, shaft or beam, forms the comic term κήλων (cf. πόσθων, etc.), one who is especially lecherous (ὁ θερμὸς εἰς συνουσίαν EM 510.51, Suda; ἀνὴρ κήλων· καὶ λάγνης ἢ λάγνος διὰ τοῦ ō Eust. 1957. 28). The usage seems originally to pertain to male animals (Archilochus 43.3; Hsch.s.v. = ὀχευτής; cf. κηλώνειον, as in Fr 679), hence its appropriateness to Pan at Cratin. 321.

55. κοντός, boat-pole, from κεντεῖν (below, section 359) is used in a series of nautical puns by Epicr. 10.4 (quoted below, section 258). See also κατατριακοντουτίσαι. κόντιλος (a variety of κοντός [EM 529.8]?) appears to have a phallic meaning at Eup. 334. Perhaps we should read κοντίλος here, which Hsch. (s.v.) says is a kind of bird or snake.

56. λαβή, haft or handle: an ad hoc double entendre at L 671 suggesting λαβεῖν in its common sexual sense.

57. μοχλός, bolt or bar for a doorway, crowbar, appears to have sexual overtones (though perhaps not a specific punning meaning) in the bolt and lock imagery of *Lysistrata*: the women's closed gates must be forced open by crowbars in the hands of men at 424 (cf. 428 ff., 246, 264): that is, the resistance of the women must be overcome by phallic aggressiveness, the characteristic of males. Note also the phallic battering ram at 255 (κορμός). See the remarks of C. H. Whitman, *Aristophanes and the Comic Hero* (Cambridge, Mass., 1964), p. 203.

58. ξίφος appears several times: L 632 φορήσω τὸ ξίφος τὸ λοιπὸν ἐν μύρτου κλαδί, I'll carry my sword henceforth in a branch of myrtle (see μύρτον), is an obscene parody of the famous Attic scolion concerning Harmodius and Aristogeiton.[80] At L 156, Lampito, in a paratragic double entendre, tells how Menelaus dropped his ξίφος at the sight of Helen's bare breasts (μᾶλα).[81]

---

79. The only other occurrence of the word is S. *Fr.* 306N (= 329P), μαστιγίαι, κέντρωνες, ἀλλοτριοφάγοι, where it refers to disreputable persons of some sort. The two explanations of the scholiast, that these were (1) people of the harsh and slippery disposition of those who drive animals with goads, and (2) like thieves who had to undergo beatings in the torture, are patent guesses which cannot be substantiated. If κέντρων is indeed based on κέντρον = phallus, then it is of the type σάθων, πόσθων, κήλων, etc. For κέντρον see Sotad. 1, Eust. 413.7, 1308.59, 1564.63.

80. Athen. 15.695A.

81. For ξίφος outside comedy, cf. *AP* 5.237.1, 9.361.5, Hsch. s.v. σκίφος, Lat. *machaera* (Plaut. *Pseud.* 1185).

59. ὀβελός, the long spit used to roast meat, appears as a pun in the Megarian scene of *Acharnians* (796), piercing "piggie meat" (the cunt).[82]

60. ὅπλον is used by Dicaeopolis to insult Lamachus at A 592.[83]

61. πάτταλος, peg, appears outside comedy in medical prose[84] and epigram[85] to indicate the erect phallus; that it had a slangy and vulgar tone is clear at E 1020, where its position at the end of a rather formal decree is meant to be bathetic. At E 284 τοῖς . . . ἔχουσι μηδὲ πάτταλον is an obscene double entendre based on an expression meaning "to be empty-handed" (literally, without even a clothes-peg); see Ussher, *Eccl.*, ad loc. In the joke at V 808, where a chamber pot is said to hang ἐπὶ τοῦ παττάλου, (1) on its peg and (2) near the phallus, Bedlycleon must be making a sarcastic joke about his old father's manifestly limp member. διαπατταλεύειν, to peg someone in a spread-eagle position, seems at Eq 371 to mean "bugger." προσπεπατταλευμένον at Timocl. 2.2 Dem. *may* have an obscene meaning.

62. πελεκᾶν, to hew with an axe (πέλεκυς): Arar. 5, ἡ σὴ θυγάτηρ ὅτ' ἐκεῖνος αὐτὴν ἐπελέκα, and your daughter, when that fellow put his axe to her . . . (see *AB* 112.18).

63. πηδάλιον, oar, occurs with a phallic meaning as early as Theognis 458. At P 142 Trygaeus asserts that, should he make a wet landing upon his return to earth from Olympus, his sturdy "oar" will stand him in good stead.[86] See also Theophil. 6.3.

64. ῥοπαλισμός, a comic pseudo-technical term for priapism at L 553, derives from the use of ῥόπαλον, club, for phallus, attested outside of comedy.[87]

65. καταπελτάζειν at A 160 uses πέλτη, spearshaft, for both cavalry and phallus: the erect and lecherous Odomantians will work over with their "shafts" all of Boeotia, here spoken of not only as a country to be overrun but also as the personified victim of rape.

66. σκυτάλα, the Dorian baton wrapped in a special leather strip (the prepuce) for recording messages, is used by the embarrassed Laconian herald at L 991 in an attempt to explain away his manifest priapism.

67. σαυνίον? (Cratinus 443): Poll. 10.143 = καὶ πάλτα καὶ σαρίσσας; Hsch. = ἀκόντιον βαρβαρικὸν καὶ σαθρόν, χαῦνον, ἀσθενές, παρὰ Κρα-

82. See now K. J. Dover, *Aristophanic Comedy* (Berkeley and Los Angeles, 1972), pp. 63 ff.

83. See also V 27, Hsch., Athen. 15.683E, *AP* 4.242.11.

84. *Hippiatr.* 115 = ἵππος ὀρθόκωλος.

85. *AP* 5.129.5.

86. This pun was first recognized by Meineke; see W. Süss, "Zur Komposition der altattischen Komödie," *RhM* 63 (1908): 19.

87. *AP* 4.261. Hsch. s.v. ῥόπτρον.

τίνῳ. Meineke (2, pp. 213 f.) seems to be correct in asserting that Cratinus' usage refers to the limp phallus.

68. For στρόβιλος, whirling top or shaft, at Pherecr. 145.14, see below, section 301.

69. σύμβολον, token, at Av 1214 f., depends for its double meaning on ἐπιβάλλειν (q.v.) in 1215, 1216.[88]

70. σφραγίς, seal, appears to mean that which fills up or closes, or which one stamps upon something, as well as merely authorization, at Av 1213,[89] and this is clearly a double entendre for phallus. σφραγῖδες are also part of a suspicious cargo of women's items (Fr 320.12); they may well refer here to ὄλισβοι as well as "gem-rings."[90]

71. τόρος, drill, at Phillyl. 18 (see n. 179, below).

72. φλεβὸς τροπωτήρ, the vein's (= prick's) thong, at Xenarch. 1.8. is explained by Meineke (3, p. 615), "cum τροπωτήρ proprie sit lorum quo remi ad scalmos alligati impelluntur et reducuntur, non male φλεβὸς τροπωτήρ explices venae alligatorem, quo nervus tamquam remus muliebri parti quasi paxillo ita inseritur et illigatur ut et impelli possit et reduci." [Since τροπωτήρ is properly a thong by which the oars, bound to the thole-pins, are pushed and pulled, we may interpret φλεβὸς τροπωτήρ as the vein's thong, by which the penis is so inserted into and bound to the female member that it may be pushed in and pulled back.][91]

Testicles

References to testicles in Aristophanes almost always occur in threats (to rip out someone's testicles) or violent erotic advances (seizing the testicles in preparation for sexual contact).

73. The *vox propria* for testicles was, of course, ὄρχεις, and in Aristophanes ὀρχίπεδα.[92] Most of the contexts have to do with violent seizure: the Sausage-Seller (Eq 772) threatens to drag Cleon away with a meathook by his ὀρχιπέδων; at L 363 the seizure is by a "bitch" (= cunt); at Pl 955 f. by a bath-man (both fearsome creatures). At N 713 and Av 442 testicle-grabbing is a homosexual advance to be followed by buggery (expressed by double entendres on ὀρύττειν, digging, q.v.); presumably buggery also follows the amorous testicle-seizure at Av 142.[93] Another abusive use of ὄρχεις is the description of Cleon's unspeakable private parts at P 758.

88. σύμβολον at Luc. *Asin.* 56 is not the same kind of term: the woman there means "that great, visible token of asshood" (i.e. the large phallus Lucius once had).

89. *LSJ* s.v. σφραγίς II.1–3, σφραγίζω II.

90. *LSJ* s.v. σφραγίς I.

91. Cf. γονίμη φλέψ (*AP* 6.218, *PLitLond.* 77 Fr. 2.7, *AP* 4.261 [absol.]); Lat. *vena* (Hor. *Sat.* 1.2.3, Pers. 6.72).

92. Cf. λακκόπεδον, scrotum (see chap.5, n. 4); Frisk (n. 9, above) s.v. ὄρχεις.

93. Compare the action at *AP* 10.20.

74. The testicles are important as proof of sexual potency. The τρίορχος (Av 1206) is a particularly well-endowed bird; cf. the παῖδες τρίορχοι of V 1534, and CA 592. The παῖς ἐνόρχης of Eq 1385 means a well-hung boy to minister to Demus' rejuvenated lusts (cf. ἐνόρχην λαόν, ballsy folk = τὸν ἐπὶ ἥβης, youths, CA 90). The ὀρχίλος ὄρνις, new King of Birds, deserves the sacrifice of a σέρφον ἐνόρχην, ballsy gnat (Av 568 f.), just as his supervirile predecessor, Zeus himself, always received a ram. The chorus of codgers in L 661 exhort one another to be ἐνόρχης, strong and sprightly enough to overcome the resistance of the women.[94]

75. In addition to these straightforward uses of ὄρχεις, there are several puns. The series of agricultural double entendres in A 995, 997 contains puns on ὄρχος/ὄρχις (vine-row/testicles), ὄσχον/ὄσχη (vine-shoots/scrotum).[95] We have already noticed the ὀρχίλος ὄρνις (crested wren/ballsy bird) of Av 569 (section 74, above). The pun at L 409, ὀρχουμένης μου τῆς γυναικὸς ἑσπέρας (dancing/fornicating), is similar to the current slang term for fornication, "to ball."

76. νεφροί, kidneys, is a common euphemism for testicles in Greek.[96] In comedy, νεφροί are explicitly called ὄρχεις in the testicle-seizing and eating scene in Philippid. 5. νεφρώ, twin kidneys, is certainly euphemistic for testicles at R 475 ff., where the Gorgons threaten to rip them out of Dionysus, and at R 1280 where Dionysus complains, τὼ νεφρὼ βουβωνιῶ. Such fatigue or battering, leading to swollen testicles (βουβωνιᾶν), is a favorite excuse for testicle humor in Aristophanes: the amused and mocking prytanis finds occasion for it at L 987, as does the chorus at V 277; see also R 1278 ff., Call. Com. 26.[97] At Pherecr. 23.3 βουβῶνες indicates testicles (cf. Luc. *Tim.* 56).

77. Similarly euphemistic is ἔντερα, innards, which at Eq 708 Cleon threatens to tear out of the Sausage-Seller, and at L 367 the women threaten to tear out of the men.[98]

78. The pun made by the witty young man about to enter the hags'

94. If large, or extra, testicles were a sign of virility, the absence of testicles meant the opposite: thus the seedless cucumber at Pl Com 64.4 is called εὐνούχιος, opposed to the σπερματίας at Cratin. 136; this also explains the abusive name Σικύας (Athen. 6.257A). The cucumber (σίκυος) means the phallus at *AP* 12.197.3; see P. G. Maxwell-Stuart, "Strato and the Musa Puerilis," *Hermes* 100 (1972): 216.

95. For the confusion of ὄσχη with ὄσχος, cf. Nic. *Al.* 109, Hsch. λακκοσχέας, with hanging scrotum, is a comic coinage: see chap.7, n. 4.

96. Athen 9.384E; Eust. 1231.41; Paulus-Festus 157.12 ff. Lindsay; Lxx. *Ps.* 15(16).7.

97. For this condition see Athen. 9.384E and Arist. *Pr.* 1.39, who recommends a bath for relief—just what Dionysus wants at R 1279. MacDowell, *Wasps*, at line 277 suggests that blood poisoning or swollen lymph nodes, resulting from stubbed toes (like Philocleon's) or dirt, is the probable cause for the swollen groins so popular in comedy. See also van Leeuwen at V 276 ff.

98. For this term see also M. Ant. 6.13.

den for sexual mistreatment (E 1064 f.), ἀλλ᾽ ἐγγυητάς σοι καταστήσω
δύο ἀξιόχρεως, "I will put down two worthy pledges," plays upon the
word ἐγγυητής in its root sense of "something put into the hands,"[99]
which then becomes "surety." Blaydes fittingly translates, "testiculos
duos."[100]

79. κάρυα, nuts, seems to have been a common slang term: at Pl 1056
nut-seizing seems to involve a joke on fellatio. The guests entertained by
the lecherous women at L 1059 and 1181 are "Karystians," that is, well-
endowed men (cf. Eub. 137 where the collocation κάρυα Καρύστια
appears with φηγούς [q.v.]).

80. παραστάταιν δυοῖν, twin companions, at Pl Com 174.13 involves
a euphemism common in medical writers.[101]

81. πεττός, which indicates any oval-shaped object, seems to be used
punningly for testicles at E 987 f. by the old woman and her young flame.

82. There is an amusing riddle involving the testicles at Eub 108:

> ἐν θαλάμῳ μαλακῶς κατακείμενον, ἐν δὲ κύκλῳ νιν
> παρθενικὰ τρυφερὰ χλανίσιν μαλακαῖς καταθρύπτω,
> τὸν πόδ᾽ ἀμαρακίνοισι μύροις τρίβουσι τὸν ἀμόν.

[Lying softly in their chamber, virginal, dainty, and affected in their
soft coverlets, they rub my *foot* (= cock) in spicy oils.]

For the double entendres on πούς and τρίβειν, see below, sections 104 and
340.

83. ᾠά for testicles is implied in the threat at L 695, αἰετὸν τίκτοντα
κανθαρός σε μαιεύσομαι, I'll midwife you like the beetle delivering the
"pregnant" eagle! The allusion is to the Aesopic story[102] of a beetle that
rolls the eagle's eggs out of her nest, perhaps with reference to punishments for adultery. Here the meaning is unmistakable.[103] In CA 5.10
Dem., dildoes are compared to eggs in which there are no yolks/chicks
(νεοττία), a reference to the testicles.

Animals

84. ἵππος, horse, is mentioned by Hesychius as indicating the genitals
of both sexes, although its applicability to the female member is difficult

99. See Frisk (n. 9, above) s.v. ἐγγύης.
100. The pun at Plaut. *MG* 1420, *salvis testibus*, is very similar.
101. Ph. 1.45, Athen. 9.395F; also = the epididymis: Hp. *Oss.* 14, Gal. 19.128; cf.
Herophil. ap. Gal. *UP* 14.11, Ruf. *Onom.* 185, Gal. 4.643; also = seminal vesicles: Poll.
2.174. Compare ἥλικες and γείτονες (Hsch. s.v. γίτονας).
102. See further J. Trencsenyi-Waldapfel, "Eine äsopische Fabel und ihre orientalischen
Parallelen," *Acta Antiqua Acad. Scient. Hung.* 7 (1959): 317.
103. See Aesop. 7 Halm, P 133 and schol.

to imagine. Probably Hesychius misunderstood ἵππος in its common meaning "lecherous woman" (as Arist. *HA* 18.572ᵃ 10, Aelian *NA* 4.11). References to the horse in Old Comedy refer only to the phallus. The λευκὸς ἵππος, white horse, of L 191 f., is an appropriate sacrificial victim for the lecherous and, at this point, less than serious, women conspirators (note Lysistrata's annoyance in the following line). There is perhaps an additional reference here to the equestrian mode of intercourse. The name Rhodippe, one of Lysistrata's friends, is a similar pun, combining ῥόδον (q.v.) and ἵππος; compare the similar phallic-vaginal pun at Pherecr. 131.4 ἱπποσέλινον (see below, section 137).[104]

85. For καλλιώνυμος, see section 159, below.

86. For κέλης, see chap. 3, n. 61.

87. κριός, ram, at Sophil. 8 (quoted in section 22, above); cf. *LSJ*, Hsch. καὶ τὸ προβάτων ἄρσεν. Cp. κριηδόν L 309.

88. κύων, dog, usually stands for the male member (Hsch.).[105] In Pl Com 174.16 κυνί τε καὶ κυνηγέταιν, dog and dog-drivers,[106] refer to the phallus and the testicles, and the *vox* κυνέπασαν (κύν' ἀνέσπασαν?) = ἀναστῦψαι, cause to be erect (Poll. 2.176), at CA 1057 is a pun glossed by Hsch. as meaning ἐξέδειραν, that is, excite oneself into having an erection.

89. The ταῦρος, bull, which the strapping Lampito could easily throttle at L 81 is the phallus (see Suda). There may be a further play on this meaning in ἀταυρώτη, unmarried/unmanned, at L 217: interfering with the normally paratragic tone of this word (cf. A. *Ag.* 245) is the unusual feminine ending, the presence of a phallic pun, and the obscene context.[107]

90. ὄφις, snake, usually means limp phallus, as in the curse at E 908[108] directed at a young girl by her older rival, "May you find a snake in your bed." The joke at L 759 concerning the "snake" on the acropolis is made by an overimaginative and oversexed woman who does not specify the exact tensile state of the phallus she has in mind.[109]

91. κέρας, horn, appears in comedy only in double entendres at Pl Com 210 (ἀσελγόκερως, randy-horned) and Eub. 67.4 (ἐπὶ κέρως).[110]

---

104. See also Hippocleides (section 198, below).

105. *EM* 549.27 κύων· τὸ κάτω τῆς πόσθης συμπεφυκὸς τῷ δέρματι, that is, the *frenulum praeputii* (Antyll. ap. Orib. 50.3.1; see Hopfner [n. 5, above], p. 27). Phot. κυνοδέσμη = a fibula for the prepuce (ἀκροποσθία); pl. in Phryn. *PS* p. 85B; compare κυνοδέσμιον in Poll. 2.171.

106. See Kock's note ad loc.

107. See further, Poll. 2.173 on ἀταύρωτος; Wilamowitz, *Lysistrate,* ad loc.; J. Taillardat, *Les Images d' Aristophane* (Paris, 1962), pp. 71 f., both deny a pun here.

108. See Ussher, *Ecclesiazusae,* ad loc.

109. See schol. at E 908, ὄφιν ἢ τὸ ζῷον ἢ ἐπὶ τοῦ αἰδοίου, *AP* 11.22.2. Compare σαύρα, lizard = πόσθη, at *AP* 11. 21.1, 12.3.5. Lat. *anguis* is similar (*Priap.* 83.33).

110. For the meaning cf. Archil. 247; *PLitLond.* 77 *Fr.* 2.19; Eur. *Fr.* 278; *AP* 12.95.6.

92. κέρκος, tail, appears as early as Hipponax 12.3 (?) and often in comedy as slang for phallus: the offhand tone of Euripides' remark at T 239 and the puns at A 785 and 787[111] suggest that the term was a common slang usage. Cf. Eub. 130, Strattis 66.4 Herod. 5.45, and compare Ger. *Schwanz*, Lat. *cauda*.

93. ὄρρος, usually tail or rump, is known to have meant phallus (Ammonius *Diff.* p. 27, cf. Poll. 2.173); that is indeed its meaning at L 964.[112]

94. οὐρά, tail, at Antiph. 129.4:[113] cf. (ἀπο)μυζουρίς = *fellatrix* at CA 1352, νώθουρος at CA 1367, μυλουρίς (Hsch.).

95. πτέρων, wing-man, and στρουθίας, sparrow-man (CA 592) are, as Kock and Meineke observed, names referring to lecherous men. Presumably they will have been based on slang terms for the phallus:

96. πτέρων is said by Hesychius to be a kind of bird; if he is correct, this bird would be a slang term for phallus. πτέρων might, however, refer to the phallus as a "wing" and thus would be analogous to such words as πόσθων, ψώλων, etc. πτερόν = phallus is nowhere explicitly attested, but Plato *Phaedr.* 252b. 4 ff, is very suggestive: λέγουσι δέ, οἷμαί, τινες Ὁμηριδῶν ἐκ τῶν ἀποθέντων δύο ἔπη εἰς τὸν ῎Ερωτα, ὧν τὸ ἕτερον ὑβριστικὸν πάνυ καὶ οὐ σφόδρα τι ἔμμετρον. ὑμνοῦσι δὲ ὧδε· τὸν δ' ἤτοι θνητοὶ μὲν ῎Ερωτα καλοῦσι ποτηνόν/ἀθάνατοι δὲ Πτέρωτα, διὰ πτεροφύτορ' ἀνάγκην: I believe some Homeric scholars quote two lines from the unpublished works, and they are about love. The second line is remarkably bold and a little unmetrical. They run as follows: "Mortals call him Eros, cleaver of the air; immortals call him Pteros because he must grow wings." πτερόν in some indecent sense must be the explanation of ὑβριστικόν in reference to the second line.[114] Winged representations of ithyphallic subjects are frequent in Greek plastic art; πτερόν in a phallic sense would be entirely natural, even though we have no other specific literary attestation.

97. πτέρυξ, wing, *does*, however, seem to indicate the phallus at L 774:

> Λυ. ἢν δὲ διαστῶσιν καὶ ἀνάπτωνται πτερύγεσσιν
> ἐξ ἱεροῦ ναοῖο χελιδόνες οὐκέτι δόξει
> ὄρνεον οὐδ' ὁτιοῦν καταπυγωνέστερον εἶναι.

If the swallows (= cunts) start fighting and fly off on wings/grab hold of cocks from the temple, no bird of any kind will appear nearly so shameless.

111. With this line compare N 538, P 927, 1351, L 1062, E 1048.
112. Cf. also Suda s.v. ταῦρος. In Ruf. *Onom.* 101 ὄρρος = τράμις.
113. Hsch. s.v. σαννίον (with Kock's note at Antiph. 129), S. *Fr.* 1078, Phot.
114. I would like to thank Prof. William Arrowsmith of Boston University for this reference; see the further discussion by Arrowsmith in *Arion*, n.s. 1/1 (1973): 164 ff.

There is probably a pun here on ἀναπέτομαι (fly off) and ἀνάπτομαι (grab hold of; cf. Pl 1067 f. ἐφάπτεσθαι); χελιδών (q.v.) = cunt.

98. στρουθίας (section 95, above) derives from στρουθός, sparrow, meaning phallus: Paulus-Festus 411.4 f. Lindsay, "Strutheum membrum virile a salacitate passeris, qui Graece στρουθός dicitur, a mimis praecipue appellatur." Cf. Hsch. s.v. The sparrow was always associated with Aphrodite and was thought to be especially lecherous (see Eust. 1681.40; cf. the hetaera-name Strouthion, schol. Luc. *Cat.* 12). In Aristophanes στρουθός appears in a pun at L 723, where a young deserter from the women's ranks wants to fly off to a brothel ἐπὶ στρούθου, on sparrow-back.

Miscellaneous

99. κρέας, meat, appears only in homosexual contexts, as in the running joke concerning the youthful depravity of the Sausage-Seller (Eq 428 and schol., 484) and in the remark in Fr. 130.3 concerning Euripides' καταπυγοσύνη, pathic debauchery.

100. κωλῆ, the thighbone with the meat still on it, is used to mean the members of debauched young men at N 989 (with schol.) and 1018.[115] In addition, Kolias, the epithet of Aphrodite (compare in form στρουθίας, section 98, above), probably contains a phallic double entendre on this *vox*. Aristophanes mentions this goddess only in contexts ridiculing feminine lechery: at N 52 it is with reference to Strepsiades' sexually oversophisticated wife, and at L 2 with reference to the irresponsible habits of women. Both times it appears in collocation with Genetyllis, a birthgoddess who is used, among other references, by the Relation to revile Agathon for his effeminacy (T 130).

101. ὀλισβοκόλλιξ, CA 1094, is a cake in the shape of a phallus (see ὄλισβος).

102. ὄψον, a relish, is an ad hoc double entendre involving fellatio at a banquet at Alex. 49.1 (see section 290, below).

103. For πλακοῦς, flat cake, at Pl Com 174.8, see n. 193, below.

104. πούς, foot, indicates the phallus at Eub. 108.3 (see the schol. to Eur. *Med.* 697, where πούς is the "foot of a wineskin" or phallus; Kock's emendation of τὸν πόδα to τὼ πόδε is due to his ignorance of this double en-

115. Line 989, τὴν ἀσίπδα τῆς κωλῆς προέχων, "tiennent leur bouclier devant leur sexe" (van Daele). See P. Thielscher, "Zu κωλῆ bei Aristophanes *Nub.* 989 und 1018," *PhW* 57 (1937): 255 f., "Die Scham vor der Göttin ihn eigentlich daran abhalten sollte, das Glied sich aufrichten zu lassen. Das geschiet aber trotz der Göttin, und dann muss er das Glied mit dem Schilde verdecken, den er eigentlich so tief nicht halten sollte" [Modesty should, of course, have restrained him from allowing his member to rise. But this happens despite the presence of the goddess, and so he must cover his member with his shield, which he naturally should not have been holding so low].

tendre). At Epicr. 10.5 πόδα indicates phallus in a nautical pun (see below, section 258).[116] For πούς = phallus in double entendre at L 416, see section 146, below. λευκόποδες, white-footed, at L 664 may possibly contain a pun on this usage; the old men would thus be celebrating their newfound eagerness for sexual battle.

105. σχοίνιον, rope, indicates the aged Philocleon's limp phallus at V 1343:[117] it is as old and rotten as Philocleon himself (σαπρόν 1343, 1380).[118] Jokes on limp members are of course in the grand tradition of comic scurrility and appear often: T 409 f. (old men), 515 (the duped husband), E 619 f. (ugly and impotent men), N 1068 ff. (the hapless Peleus), Fr 600 (old men), Cratinus 443, etc.

106. τύλη (shoulder-) pad or lump, at Fr 949 is glossed by Photius as τὸ ἐπὶ τενόντων φῦμα, the excrescence on those who are erect; perhaps there is a similar double entendre at A 860, with reference to τὸ βουβων-ιᾶν (see section 76, above). Compare Telecl. 50, which *may* be an imitation (cf. schol. A 860).

The Female Organs

107. The most common vulgar term is κύσθος, whose etymology is unclear but is probably connected with κεύθειν (see Frisk s.v.); κύσθος would then have a root meaning of a hidden place (cf. Lat. *custos, cunnus*).[119] Its tone is analogous in harshness and indecency to that of πέος. Predictably, its use in Aristophanes occurs in especially indecent scenes: the Megarian scene in A 781 f., 789; the abusive chorus of R 430; the sex-starved men's ogling at L 1158; the barbarian archer's lewd lustfulness at T 1114. Compare its tone in the description of debauchery in Eup. 233.4. κύσθος seems to have been a popular component of obscene hetaera-names in comedy: κυσθονεφέλη (a reference to pubic hair),[120] κυσθοκορ-ώνη = νύμφη(CA 1060; see Archil. 331, p. 20, above), ληναιόκυσθος (Athen. 13.583E), ξενοκυσταπάτη (*AP* 11.7.4).

108. Aristophanes twice puns on κίστη, box, and κύσθος: P 666 (with reference to Eirene) and L 1184 (where Lysistrata bids the city's women to share what they have ἐν ταῖσι κίσταις).[121]

116. See Kock, ad loc.
117. K. J. Dover, "Aristophanic Scholarship," *Lustrum* 2 (1957): 56 f.; P. Arnott, *Greek Scenic Conventions* (London, 1962), pp. 33 f.
118. For this use of σαπρός see E 1098 ,Pl 1086, Machon 185 Gow.
119. See under "Holes, Pits, and Hollows," below.
120. CA 1059 (following Meineke); cf. *EM* 548.40.
121. For a religious (and not very humorous) interpretation of these words, see G. W.

109. Euelpides' remark about the beauteous (and probably naked or seminaked) Procne at Av 670, ὅσον δ' ἔχει τὸν χρυσόν, ὥσπερ παρθένος, what marvelous *gold* she has, just like a young girl!, contains a pun on κυσός, the female member (Hsch.),[122] a word whose root notion seems simply to be an opening or hole. In comedy it was widely used to mean both cunt and anus (in homosexual contexts). Although there is no trace of the word in Aristophanes, apart from this pun (and a possible pun at L 408), elsewhere we find κυσιᾶν, to be lecherous (CA 1061), κυσσοβά-κχαρις (CA 1062), κυσολέσχης (CA 1066), κυσοδόχη (Alciphr. 3.72).[123]

110. χοῖρος, piggie, is the land animal to which the cunt is most frequently compared in double entendres; this word seems to have been a most popular slang expression. The entire Megarian scene of *Acharnians* is built around its double meaning.[124] Like Lat. *porcus* or *porcellus*,[125] χοῖρος indicates the pink, hairless cunt of young girls as opposed to that of mature women: thus Dicaeopolis' remark at A 781 f., νῦν γε χοῖρος φαίνεται, ἀτὰρ ἐκτραφείς γε κύσθος ἔσται, she may look a piggie now, but when she's grown she'll be a real cunt! This fact explains the use of χοῖρος as slang for "young girl" in obscene conceits involving piggies following their mother, as at T 289 and Pl 308.

111. A pink, hairless state could, however, also be achieved even for grown-up cunts by depilation, a practice especially associated with hetaerae and other female sex-objects (seductive housewives, for example, as at L 151). Thus χοῖρος often appears in jokes about depilated slave-girls (E 724), flute-girls (as in Philocleon's synecdochic reference to the flute-girl at V 1353), or any cunt to be shaven, even that of the Relation at T 538. Prostitutes, for whom a depilated femininity was a professional necessity, were called χοιροπῶλαι, piggie-merchants (Fr 578);[126] hence also

---

Elderkin, *CP* 35 (1940): 395. The Relation's remark to the Thracian slave at T 284 f. may also involve such a pun.

122. First noticed by J. G. Fernandez, "Parerga II,2," *Emerita* 31 (1963): 135 f.

123. κυσός = anus (Hsch.) is used by comic poets only of the male anus and only in the abuse of pederasts: κυσονίπται = πόρνοι (CA 1064), κυσοχήνη = εὐρυπρωκτία (CA 1065, cf. Hipponax 82. 2), ἐγκυσίχωλος or ἐγκυσόχωλος (CA 6 Dem.), κυσολαμπίς (Hsch.), ἰωνόκυσος (Cratin. 419), κυσολάκων (CA 1063), διακυσοσαλεύων, to waggle the ass, Strattis *POxy.*, 2743, *Fr.* 8, col. ii, 1. 3. The respectable word κύσσαρος, anus (Hp. *Nat. Puer.* 17, Gal. 19.176), might simply be an expansion of κυσός = anus, or a figurative word, the true Ionian form of the Attic κύτταρος, cell (of a honeycomb), cone, pit in the receptacle of the *Nelumbium speciosum*. κύσσαρος does not occur in this obscene meaning in comedy.

124. See n. 82, above.

125. Varro *RR* 2.4.10; J. Andre, "Sur certains noms de plantes latins," *Latomus* 15 (1956): 299 ff.

126. Cf.χοιροπωλεῖν Plu. *Cent.* 1. 92.

the appropriateness of χοιροπώλης as an epithet for the Megarian at A 818: pandering was an especially "Megarian" calling.[127] A man who resort to prostitutes, like Philocleon at V 1364, deserves the name χοιρόθλιφ, piggie-squeezer.[128]

112. Hesychius notes that a certain feminine garment was known as the χοιροκομεῖον, a word that might possibly carry an obscene meaning at L 1073, although the joke there is very obscure.[129]

113. δέλφαξ, pig, and its diminutive, δελφάκιον, suckling pig, do not indicate the young, hairless cunt but the mature one (Hsch.); cf. Cratin. 3 ἤδη δέλφακες, χοῖροι δὲ τοῖσιν ἄλλοις: the women referred to are mature according to some, young according to others. δελφακεῖσθαι, to grow up to pighood, is an obscene comic invention of the Megarian at A 786. The chorus of women in *Lysistrata* speak of their δελφάκιον (L 1061) and the κηδεστής, about to be shaven below, exclaims (T 237) οἴμοι κακοδαίμων, δελφάκιον γενήσομαι, "Oh, my bad luck, I'm to be turned into a piglet!"

114. ὗς, sow, is identical in meaning to δέλφαξ: thus the Megarian's χοῖροι were born ἐξ ἀγαθᾶς ὑός, from a noble *sow* (A 741), and the older women at L 683 threaten the men with the power of their cunts:[130] λύσω τὴν ἐμαυτῆς ὗν ἐγώ, "I'll loose my *sow*!"

115. ὕσσακος, an obscure but unquestionably vulgar term for cunt at L 1001, is best explained as ὗς augmented by the suffix -αξ denoting bodily features: compare such words as βύσταξ and μάσταξ.[131] The genitive of the original *ὕσσαξ will then have become generalized as the nominative, as in the case of θυλακός, λιθακός, etc. On the whole this explanation is more plausible on linguistic grounds than Wilamowitz's contention (at L 1001) that the word is a compound made up of ὗς plus σάκος. That we are dealing here simply with a comic invention and not with a current word does not seem likely in the context, and is out of the question if Lasserre's conjecture at Archil. 48.8 is indeed correct.[132]

127. Cf. Μεγαρικαὶ σφίγγες (Call. Com. 23). For this image cf. σφίγξ = πόρνη at Anaxil. 22.22, Alexis 167.6; σφίγκτας = κιναίδους at Cratin. 446.

128. Compare the χοιρότριψ (?) of Hdn. 1.246.26, and the obscene epithet of Dionysus, χοιροφάλας (Polem. Hist. 72).

129. For suggestions see Blaydes, ad loc.

130. The scholiast remarks that ὗν = τὴν φύσιν, τὴν ὀργήν; probably these are meant as alternatives to φύσιν, indicating the cunt. Note that ὗς means cunt at Athen. 13.581A (Machon), as does σῦς at *AP* 12.197.4: see Maxwell-Stuart (n. 94, above, p. 216). πεκτούμενον in line 684 may also be a double entendre. Although unexampled elsewhere in an obscene meaning, πεκτεῖν is related to κτείς (as an augmented form of πέκειν; compare Lat. *pecto, pecten*) which does mean cunt (*AP* 5.132.2, Ruf. *Onom.* 109, Sor. 2.18).

131. See A. Ernout in *BSL* 41 (1940): 121, n. 1.

132. The glosses in *EM* 785.7 and Phot., which equate ὕσσακος with πάσσαλος, and

116. The Wilamowitz etymology for ὕσσακος probably owes its inspiration to another obscene but unrelated word, σάκανδρος, attested only at L 824 and glossed by the schol. as indicating the cunt. Two similar words with the same meaning, σάκας (Hsch., *AP* 12.174.3) and σάκτας (CA 1135), may help explain the root notion. σάκας is clearly related to σάκος, anything made of hairy cloth, expecially sacks; σάκτας means sack also but derives from σάττειν, to stuff full. Furthermore, σάκος, due to its hairy appearance, could mean beard.[133] The point of comparison common to these three obscene words is of the cunt to sacks made of coarse, hairy cloth: σάκτας may have a further indecent connotation in its connection with σάττειν.[134] As was the case with ὕσσακος, the context of σάκανδρος seems to rule out the possibility that we are dealing with an invented word.

117. κύων, dog, usually indicating the phallus, could also stand for cunt (Eust. 1821.53). At L 158 the phrase κύνα δέρειν δεδαρμένην, to flay the flayed dog, seems to refer to female masturbation (note the humorous use of the feminine participle), not, with the schol., to use the ὄλισβος (see lines 108 ff.). The phrase parodies a saying attributed to Pherecrates (179), meaning to engage in a hopeless task.[135]

118. Κύννη, an hetaera name (Hsch., Phot.), found at V 1032, P 755, Eq 765, may a reference to κύων as cunt.

119. κύνειρα, dog-leash, at CA 1056 seems to be a pun on κύων = cunt: Eust. 1822.15 ὡς δὲ κύων καὶ τῇ κωμῳδίᾳ ἐνέτηξε σκῶμμα γυναικεῖον τὴν εἰρημένην κύνειραν ἤγουν τὴν τὸν κύνα εἰρύουσαν, ὅπερ ἐστὶν ἐφελκομένην, ὃν δὴ κύνα χοῖρον ἄλλη κωμῳδία φησί (a reference to L 158?), παλαιὰ χρῆσις δηλοῖ, ἐμφαίνουσα πρὸς ὁμοιότητα τοῦ κυνόσουρα εἰρῆσθαι καὶ τὸ κύνειρα; cf. also 528.1 ἡ δ' αὐτὴ (κωμῳδία) καὶ παρὰ τὸν κύνα παίζει τὴν κύνειραν.

120. ταῦρος = cunt is mentioned by Phot. (s.v. σάραβον) as a frequent slang term in comedy; cf. also Hsch. In Aristophanes a probable pun is Lysistrata's oath at L 447, νὴ τὴν Ταυροπόλον. The comic term Κένταυρος (= τὸ γυναικεῖον μόριον, Theopomp. Com. 89; see glosses at CA 635) is a combination of ταῦρος and κεντεῖν (q.v.).

Euphemistic Terminology

121. Unlike the male member, the female parts have no euphemistic

---

Hesychius' gloss = ὕστακος (= πάσσαλος, Theognost. *Can.* 24) or πάσσαλος κεράτινος (s.v. ὕσταξ), must be confusions with ὑσσός, javelin, and have nothing to do with our subject.

133. Cf. E 502, Pl Com 122, Plu. *Pel.* 30.

134. Cf. σακτός, crammed full, at Antiph. 132.3, Eup. 439.

135. See the discussion by Willems (n. 8, above), 2: 426 f., who believes that Pherecrates' line is also obscene.

names in comedy, save πράγματα, things, in Fr 63 and perhaps τὸ γῆρας, agedness, at L 364.[136] Neither appears elsewhere in this meaning.

Agricultural Terminology

122. ἰσχάς, the dried fig, was used by Hipponax (124) to indicate the cunt; the elongated shape and wrinkled appearance of the dried fig naturally suggest the female organs. But this usage does not appear in Old Comedy; we must wait until Axionicus (1.4) for a prostitute called Ischas. Cf. also Men. 295, and compare Συκᾶς at Alciphr. 13.2.[137]

123. κόκκος, (pomegranate) seed, is said by Hesychius to have indicated the cunt. In Aristophanes only verbal puns attest this usage: ἐκκοκκίζειν, de-pit (deflower), indicates rape at P 63 (metaphorically Zeus' rape of the cities) and at L 364 where the men threaten to "de-pit" the women's γῆρας (see above, section 121). Fr 610, ὀξυγλύκειάν τἄρα κοκκιεῖς ῥόαν, you'll de-kernel the bitter-sweet flow, seems to be an off-color twist on a line of Aeschylus.[138]

124. Perhaps εὖστρα, roasted barley, can be compared with κόκκος. It is attested for the comic poets in an obscene sense by Eust. 1446.30, but the image may be different: it may refer to depilation, deriving from the root sense of singe (εὕειν) as in εὖστρα, pit for singeing swine, at Eq 1236. According to Eust. 1446.29 and Hsch. ἀμφίκαυστις, roasted barley, was used by the comic poets in the same sense.

125. μύρτον, myrtle-berry, was a common slang term.[139] In comedy see L 1004, CA 1416, Pl Com 174.14 (depilated myrtle-berries). μύρτον was also much used as a double entendre: the gay choral rhapsody of the winged Coryphaeus at Av 1100 (ἠρινὰ παρθένια λευκότροφα μύρτα) parodies the theme of the Garden of the Graces (cf. Pi. *Ol.* 9.40), and the Coryphaeus at L 632 makes an obscene parody of the old-fashioned political slogan about Harmodius and Aristogeiton. The hetaera-names Myrrhine (L 69, Eup. 44, Timocl. 25.3; at Eq 964 = the pubic bush of the male) and Myrtia (V 1396)[140] also play on the obscene meaning of the word. There may be a further pun in T 448, a joke on the lechery of women: "Since my husband died (ἐν Κύπρῳ—pun?), says Lady B, "I have had to

136. See A. von Blumenthal, "Beobachtungen zu griechischen Texten," *Hermes* 74 (1939): 97.

137. ἰσχάς could also mean "anus": AP 4.240.8, 241.5, ἰσχάδα τὴν ὀπίσω (AP 12.239); cf. συκόπρωκτος (Hsch. s.v. συκιδιαφόρος).

138. According to Poll. 6.80 Fr 610 = A. *Fr.* 363.

139. See Suda, Hsch., schol. Eq 964, AP 7.406.4, Luc. *Lex.* 12 (Myrton the debauchee).

140. This lowly saleslady's name contrasts comically with the pretentious and grandiloquent manner in which she gives her pedigree: see J. Truesdale, *A Comic Prosopographia Graeca* (Menasha, Wis., 1940), p. 25.

support my family (στεφανηπλοκοῦσ᾽ . . . ἐν ταῖς μυρρίναις), by plying
wreaths in the myrtle market." That μύρτον = cunt may have been used
in technical prose is indicated by terms like μυρτοχελίδες (Poll. 2.174) and
μυρτοχείλια (Ruf. *Onom.* 111 f.), both signifying the labia maiora.

126. ῥόδον, rose, is used exactly like μύρτον as a slang term; the plant's
soft, fleshy red petals are the obvious point of comparison.[141] Thus maidens
in Pherecr. 108.29 are ἡβυλλιῶσαι τὰ ῥόδα καὶ κεκαρμέναι, blooming in
their roses and freshly cut/depilated. The ῥόδιον μύρον, rose-scent, which
Myrrhine fetches her husband (L 944) puns on this *vox*, as do the girl's
name Rhodippe (L 370)[142] and Cratinus' rose-garden (ῥοδωνιά, 109.2).[143]

127. σῦκον, the fruit of the fig, appears for cunt in the wedding-hymn at
P 1351 f.[144] Puns on this usage are συκολογεῖν (P 1348), συκάζειν (= βινεῖν, Strattis 3), συκοφάντρια (Pl 970), the latter deriving from what
appears to be a common use of συκοφαντεῖν to mean κνίζειν ἐρωτικῶς
(Pl Com 255, Men. 1071). Cf. also συκάστρια, CA 1158.

128. Many comic double entendres involve comparisons with fields,
either smooth or bearing some kind of short foliage. Indeed, pubic hair is
almost always conceived of in agricultural terms as a flowering growth.[145]

129. βλήχων (or βληχώ), pennyroyal, is used jokingly by Lysistrata (89)
to refer to the Boeotian girl's neatly depilated *campus muliebris*, with a
clever reference to the smooth, fertile plains of that region:[146] κομψότατα
τὴν βληχώ γε παρατετιλμένη, with neatly trimmed pennyroyal plots. The
pennyroyal posset (κυκεῶνα βληχωνίαν) recommended as a remedy for
too much fruit (P 712) contains an obscene allusion to Opora's sexual
attractiveness (and perhaps cunnilingus, cf. 854 f.).

130. κῆπος, garden, seems to have been very common in comedy and
elsewhere,[147] although in Aristophanes only κηπεύματα appears (in the

141. See Shakespeare, *As You Like It* 3.2.112 f.

142. Compare Rhodope and Rhodocleia (*AP* 5.36), and Rhodia, the shameless wife of
Lycon, often pilloried in Old Comedy: L 270 and schol., Eup. 215. See van Daele at L
270.

143. See schol. Theoc. 11.10.

144. Cf. *AP* 12.185.3, *APl* 240.8, etc.

145. For the traditional and often banal nature of some of these terms, see Taillardat
(n. 107, above), p. 74.

146. The *Mentha pulegium* is short and bears small, hairy leaves: Dsc. 3.31, etc.

147. Archippus 2 Dem., 44; schol. A 995; *CA* 1352, 1366 (μανιόκηπος = nymphoma-
niac; also at Anacreon 164 Gentili); D.L. 2.116, Eust. 1921.53. See H. Erbse, "Zu Aristophanes," *Eranos* 52 (1954): 82 f., "Merkmal dieses κῆπος ist die durch sorgsame Pflege
erreichte Glätte." Compare Lat. *hortus* (*ThLL* 6.3.3018.71 ff.). For the connection between
Aphrodite and flowers, see Roscher, *Myth. Lex.* I.1.397 f. (s.v. Aphrodite); B. O. Foster in
HSCP 10 (1899): 39 ff.; E. Langlotz, *Aphrodite in den Gärten* (Heidelberg, 1954), esp. pp. 52
ff.; B. Gentili, *Anacreon* (Rome, 1958), pp. 183 ff.

Garden of the Graces parody at Av 1100; for χαρίτων here, see section 251, below).

131. κνέωρον, spurge-flax, at CA 1040 (Hsch., Phot).

132. κοσμοσάνδαλον, the *Delphinium Ajacis* (a kind of hyacinth), is *der Venuspantoffel* (Billerbeck, cited by Kock) at Pherecr. 131.4, κοσμοσάνδαλα βαίνων, in a series of obscene puns on flowers: see on βαίνειν (walk on/mount).

133. λειμών, meadow (cf. Eur. *Cyc.* 171, Aristaenet. 2.1), may derive from comedy, but does not appear.

134. λόχμη, thicket, used by the chorus of women to call attention to the pubic region of the men at L 800, also appears as a pun at Av 207 f., εἰς τὴν λόχμην εἰσβαινε κἀνέγειρε τὴν ἀηδόνα, go into the *thicket* and rouse the *bird* (see ἀηδών, βαίνειν).[148]

135. νάπος, grove or gulley, is mentioned by Hesychius but is not attested in comedy.

136. πεδίον, plain: the Boeotian girl's native plains provide the humor in L 89, καλόν γ᾽ ἔχουσα πεδίον, (a girl) having a beautiful plain. That this peculiar Boeotian landscape was commonly used to suggest the female pubic region is further indicated by A 160, where the lecherous Odomantians promise that they will καταπελτάσονται τὴν Βοιωτίαν ὅλην, that is, rape it (see πέλτη). Similar are the intentions of the lecherous Egyptians whose cry is ψωλοὶ πεδίονδε (Av 506 f.).[149]

137. σέλινον, celery, appears frequently: Phot. s.v. σάραβον, Pherecr. 131.3, 4 (γελῶν ἱπποσέλινα = γελῶν ἱπποπορνικῶς, Meineke), Pl Com 174.10 (see section 169, below), Cratin. 109.3, CA 1138. Cf. *Carm. Pop.* 6P.

138. σισύμβριον, a kind of mint, at Cratin. 109.3 (note the surrounding obscene puns); cf. the hetaera-name Sisymbrion in Theophil. Com. 11.2 and the remarks of Poll. 5.101, who lists this word among several terms for women's cosmetics used punningly by comic poets.

139. χνοῦς, down or fuzz on fruits, when used to indicate pubic growth always appears with a form of the verb ἀνθεῖν; the image seems to have had a loftier tone than is usual in such images: N 978 (Just Logic's hot speech on pubescent boys), E 13 (Praxagora's mock-tragic opening monologue). Even the lowly Megarian waxes poetic when he uses this image (A 790 ff.), the meaning being cleverly shifted from the fattening, bristling growth of a piggie to that of the maturing cunt.[150]

148. A pun recognized by Hopfner (n. 5, above), p. 157; compare E 60 f., τὰς μασχάλας/λόχμης δασυτέρας.
149. See A. Rapp, "*Aves* 507," *RhM* 88 (1939): 191.
150. See also Metag. 4.3, Theoc. 27.50, Callim. *Ap.* 37, *AP* 12. 36.2, Luc. *Amor.* 53.

Gates and Passageways

140. Of several words used to indicate the cunt whose basic notion is that of an opening or passageway, θύρα is the most popular. Understandably, this double entendre usually appears in contexts that involve actual gateways or doorways, as in paraclausithyra (E 962 f., 990; cf. 709 ἐν τοῖς προθύροισι δέφεσθαι = masturbate "outside the doorway"/outside the cunt),[151] or simple domestic activities, as at V 768 f. where a servant girl is punished sexually because she "opened the/her doorway on the sly," or at T 424 f. where a wife's opening the door (note the prefix of ὑποῖξαι) becomes through double entendres a metaphor for clandestine intercourse with a lover; the latter passage is discussed in section 145, below. See also σκαλαθύρειν.

141. The most notable use of θύρα occurs in *Lysistrata*, to mean both the gates of the acropolis and the gates of love; the women's closing of the acropolis against the crowbars and battering rams of the men is made analogous to their decision to forbid access to their cunts: e.g. L 309, where the men cry εἰς τὴν θύραν κριηδὸν ἐμπέσοιμεν, "let's rush the gates like rams!" (see κριός).

142. Also used in this kind of symbolism is πύλη: L 265 τὰ προπύλαια πακτοῦν (cf. πρόθυρα),[152] L 250 where Lysistrata swears not to ἀνοῖξαι τὰς πύλας ταύτας, open these gates, and L 423 where the men say ὑπὸ τῶν γυναικῶν ἀποκέκλεισμαι τῶν πυλῶν, "we've been closed out from the gates by these women!" Cf. δημίαισι πύλαις = common whores (CA 805) and see section 57, above.[153] We may note a less lofty appearance later in *Lysistrata*, τὰν Πύλον (1163), in a passage of geographical puns on the sexual organs.

143. ἰσθμός, a ridge or any narrow strip of land connecting larger land masses, is used in obscene jokes about men to refer to the perineum (located between the genitals and the anus) and in references to women to refer to the cunt. This obscene anatomical use of the word corresponds to such proper medical references as the neck[154] or the gullet.[155] In Old Comedy the specific reference is to the Isthmus of Corinth: thus the crude jokes at T 647 comparing the antics of the Relation's phallus to Corinthian shipping routes, and those at P 879 f. about the Isthmian games (i.e. sexual intercourse with Theoria). That this pun was common in Old Comedy is

151. For πρόθυρον cf. *AP* 5.56.2: cf. Martial 11.104.13.
152. Cf. Fr 721; both passages are discussed by Poll. 10.27.
153. See the remarks of Whitman (n. 18, above), p. 203 and the comments thereon by K. J. Dover in *CR* 16 (1966): 160.
154. Eup. 100.19, Pl. *Ti.* 69e.
155. Gal. 18(2).961, Aret. *SA* 1.6, Nic. *Al.* 80.508.

indicated by the hetaera-name Isthmias (Philetaer. 9.5) and the probable joke on cunnilingus at Canthar. 8.

144. κολεόν, sheath, is found in such comic inventions as κολεάζοντες, κολεασμός, Κολέαρχος (CA 1045–47).[156]

Rings and Circles

145. θύρα, δακτύλιον: the complaint of the woman at T 424 f., that Euripides has made it impossible any longer to hoodwink husbands, contains two double entendres intended to satirize the lechery and shamelessness of women: πρὸ τοῦ μὲν οὖν ἦν ἀλλ᾽ ὑποῖξαι τὴν θύραν/ποησαμέναισι δακτύλιον τριώβολον. Not only θύρα but also δακτύλιον means cunt: opening the pantry doors by using a three-obol ring becomes "opening our 'gates' by rendering our 'ringlets' for three obols," the latter reference probably being to the three-obol fee commonly demanded by cheap prostitutes.[157] Compare V 768 f. (above, section 140). A related image, found in technical writers,[158] is δακτύλιον = anus.

146. δακτυλίδιον at L 417 operates on a very similar pun: The Probulus, in a speech made up entirely of obscene double entendres, jeers at cuckolded husbands:

> ἕτερος δέ τις πρὸς σκυτοτόμον ταδὶ λέγει
> νεανίαν καὶ πέος ἔχοντ᾽ οὐ παιδικόν·
> ὦ σκυτοτόμε, μου τῆς γυναικὸς τοῦ ποδὸς
> τὸ δακτυλίδιον πιέζει τὸ ζυγόν,
> ἅθ᾽ ἁπαλὸν ὄν· τοῦθ᾽ οὖν σὺ τῆς μεσημβρίας
> ἐλθὼν χάλασον, ὅπως ἂν εὐρυτέρως ἔχῃ.

[Someone else says this to a young man, whose cock is hardly immature: Shoemaker, the sandal's cross-strap presses on the little toe of my wife's foot—it's so tender. Come round, then, some afternoon and loosen it up so that it will be more supple.]

On one level, the husband complains that the cross-strap of the sandal is pressing the little toe of his wife's foot; on the other, the yoke (bulk) of his phallus (see πούς) is ramming (see πιέζειν) her little cunt. This double sense is accomplished by ambiguous genitives and the ambiguous use of τοῦτο in 418 to refer both to τὸ ζυγόν and to τὸ δακτυλίδιον.[159] Note that

---

156. Cf. Aristaenet. 2.6, Plaut. *Pseud.* 1181 (*vagina*).

157. See Antiph. 300, Epicr. 2, 3, 18. Full discussion in H. Herter, "Die Soziologie der antiken Prostitution," *JbAC* 3 (1960): 81, n. 180.

158. Dsc. 1.70, Luc. *Demon.* 17, *PRyl.* 28.68 (IV AD); cf. δακτυλικὸς ἔμπλαστρος = anus at Orib. Fr. 83, Cass. Fel. 74.

159. Wit-Tak (n. 60, above), p. 120, n. 95, wrongly suggests that τὸ δακτυλίδιον is the

these lines parallel and compliment the other joke in the Probulus' speech: lines 408–13 deal with a wife whose cunt is too large for her husband, and lines 416–19 with a wife whose cunt is too small.

147. ἔγκυκλον, anything circular or which surrounds, is the name of a woman's garment used in the same sense as κύκλος (following section). At L 1162 the Spartans' ambiguous demand for τοῦγκυκλον turns out to be for τὰν Πύλον (see section 142, above), 1163.[160] Similarly, at L 113 Cleonice swears that she will go along with Lysistrata no matter what, κἂν εἴ με χρείη τοῦγκυκλον/τουτὶ καταθεῖσαν ἐκπιεῖν αὐθημερόν. This pun, pawn my shawl/lay down my cunt, constitutes another joke on female lechery. We must suspect also that the deictic demonstrative pronoun indicates byplay on stage.[161]

148. κύκλος, anything circular, is used obscenely, though in the service of noble imagery, in the series of double entendres that describe in agricultural language sexual relations with Diallage (A 998); it appears in the same sense at L 267, where the men propose attacking the closed gates of the acropolis with phallic tree-stumps which they intend to burn αὐταῖς ἐν κύκλῳ θέντες τὰ πρέμνα ταυτί, having put them in a circle/into a cunt. One of the intended victims of this figurative rape is the shameless Rhodia, wife of Lycon (n. 142, above).

149. For ξύλον, hole in stocks, see section 15, above.

Holes, Pits, and Hollows

150. A comparison of the female member to pits or great caves appears several times. βάραθρον is unquestionably obscene in the catalogue at Fr 320.8,[162] and at Pl 431 Chremes twits Penia, who is worried about being exiled, οὔκουν ὑπόλοιπον τὸ βάραθρόν σοι γίγνεται; that is, (1) there is always the pit for criminal execution and (2) you can always rely on your cunt. The common use of βάραθρον in this meaning is clear from the hetaera-name in Theophil. Com. 11.3 and from the similar use of barathrum in Latin (cf. Mart. 3.81.1).

---

same as Lat. *ligula* (Plaut. *Poen.* 1309), quoting Hopfner (n. 5, above), p. 104. But Hopfner in fact says nothing of τὸ δακτυλίδιον, and rightly points out that *ligula* means "den schlaffen, impotenten Penis," which of course is inappropriate here.

160. Possibly we should assume, with Willems (n. 8, above), 2: 446, that ἔγκυκλον here is, by a humorous reversal, the πρωκτός, given the anal predilections of the Spartans even in regard to women (see the remarks of van Daele, 3: 169 n. 1).

161. ἔγκυκλον in Fr 320.8 may possibly be another reference to the cunt, considering the numerous other double entendres in this passage.

162. See Edmonds, 1: 663, n. *d*, and compare ὄλεθρον τὸν βαθύν = cunt in 320.3. For both terms see Poll. 5.101.

151. κόλπος indicates the cunt at E 964 f.,[163]

$$\grave{\alpha}\lambda\lambda' \ \grave{\epsilon}\nu \ \sigma\tilde{\omega} \ \beta o\acute{\upsilon}\lambda o\mu' \ \grave{\epsilon}\gamma\grave{\omega} \ \kappa\acute{o}\lambda\pi\omega$$
$$\pi\lambda\eta\kappa\tau\acute{\iota}\zeta\epsilon\sigma\vartheta\alpha\iota \ \mu\epsilon\tau\grave{\alpha} \ \sigma\tilde{\eta}\varsigma \ \pi\upsilon\gamma\tilde{\eta}\varsigma\cdot$$

The trouble with traditional readings of this couplet (e.g. van Daele ad loc., "Mais je veux appuyé sur ton sein jouer avec ta croupe") are (1) that πληκτίζεσθαι, when it is used in ordinary erotic contexts (*AP* 12.209.4, Herod. 5.29, Dio Cass. 46.18.4, 51.12, Strabo 11.8.5), refers either to flirtatious sparring or slapping or, more figuratively, to resistance to the on-slaught of erotic passion, but never in a literal sense to coitus; and (2) πληκτίζεσθαι always is used with the dative, absolutely, or with the prepositions πρός or εἰς, but never, as here, with μετά, expressive of accompanying action or cooperation. It would seem that the Aristophanic couplet cannot be figurative, "to spar or flirt with," but must mean literally "to trade blows with the πυγή."

We must therefore consider a secondary meaning of κόλπος other than the usual "bosom." It seems that κόλπος could also indicate the vagina, a meaning explicitly attested in later medical writers such as Rufus,[164] Soranus,[165] and Sextus Empiricus,[166] all of whom derived their terminology and definitions from much earlier writings; Pollux[167] identifies these earlier writings as those of Hippocrates himself. We may therefore presume a fifth-century use of κόλπος in this sense. Such a genital usage, like the more common meanings "bosom," "folds in a garment," or "gulf," de-rives from the word's root notion of any hollow place, and corresponds to its use in describing other bodily cavities as well: not only the womb,[168] but also the ventricles of the heart[169] and the abdominal cavities.[170] The difficulties of E 964 f. disappear if we understand κόλπος to be a double entendre meaning "within the cunt" (and by implication over against the πυγή): there will thus be a literal trading of blows between the young man's thrusting member and the girl's πυγή. Our common erotic metaphor will

163. I have defended this interpretation in detail in "Sparring Partners: A Note on Aristophanes, *Ecclesiazusae* 964–965," *AJP* 96 (1975) forthcoming.

164. *Onom.* 196 εἶτα τὸ κοίλωμα τὸ ἐφεξῆς, γυναικεῖος κόλπος, καὶ αἰδοῖον τὸ σύμπαν σὺν τοῖς ἐπιφανέσιν.

165. 1.16. τὸ δὲ γυναικεῖον αἰδοῖον καὶ κόλπος ὠνόμασται γυναικεῖος.

166. *Adv. Math.* 5.62. τοὺς γυναικείους κόλπους.

167. 2.222, in his discussion of the term μήτρα, in which he quotes all the Hippocratic terminology (compare e.g. Hp. *Steril.* 222): οὗ στόμα ὁ πρῶτος πόρος, τὸ δ' ἐφεξῆς κοίλωμα γυναικεῖος κόλπος.

168. Pl.: Ar. *Birds* 694, Eur. *Hel.* 1145, Call. *Jov.* 15; sg.: Id. *Del.* 214.

169. Poll. 2.216.

170. Arist. *HA* 530b27.

thus have been debased not merely by inclusion in a highly undignified context,[171] but by actual *literalization* as well. This literalization is accomplished by clever, original, and unexpected variations in the usual terminology—namely, the obscene sense of κόλπος and the use of μετά with πληκτίζεσθαι.

152. κύτος, any hollow,[172] is used in a double sense by Xenarch. 1.9 f.: the πουλύπους (pun on πούς [q.v.] ?) is personified (ll. 4 ff.) and is said τῆς τροχηλάτου κόρης/πίμπλησι λοπάδος στερροσώματον κύτος, the polyp "fills up" the firm-bodied *hollow* of the *dish*, that maiden formed on the potter's wheel (see λοπάς, πίμπλημι).

153. In the paratragic prologue of *Ecclesiazusae*, a grandiose double entendre is used to describe depilation by lamp; the image is from scenes of the sudden illumination of cavernous underworld regions (12 f.),[173] μόνος δὲ μηρῶν εἰς ἀπορρήτους μυχοὺς/λάμπεις ἀφεύων τὴν ἐπανθοῦσαν τρίχα, lamp, you alone shine into the ineffable secret places between the thighs when you burn off the hair growing there.

154. For ὄλεθρον = cunt in Fr 320.3 see n. 162, above.

155. Holes on a smaller scale are to be expected in obscene double entendres. ὀπή, mouse-hole, appears at L 720, where Lysistrata catches a deserter διαλέγουσαν τὴν ὀπήν: picking open or enlarging (1) an escape route near the grotto of Pan and (2) her cunt.[174] ὀπή in this meaning is found as early as Hipponax.[175]

156. σαλάμβη, vent-hole, is common for cunt[176] and may lie behind the name of one of Aristophanes' favorite prostitutes, Salabaccho (Eq 765, T 805).[177]

157. Bored holes are natural in double entendres. τρῆμα, any bored hole (τετραίνειν), appears twice in an obscene sense: at L 410, ἡ βάλανος ἐκπέπτωκεν ἐκ τοῦ τρήματος, the bolt has fallen out of its hole, is clearly a double entendre, while in the curse at E 906, ἐκπέσοι σοι τὸ τρῆμα, may your hole fall out, it seems to be a genuine slang term.[178] We may compare the verbal uses of this image, τετρημένον ξύλον at L 680, and τρήσας at T

171. See C. M. Bowra, "A Love-Duet," *AJP* 79 (1958): 376 ff., 387.
172. Of bodily cavities: see *LSJ* s.v. 3.
173. μυχός is a common tragic word; see Ussher, *Ecclesiazusae*, at ll. 12 f.
174. Schol. ad loc.; see διαλέγειν.
175. 135b βορβορόπη; compare *AP* 11.338.2.
176. S. *Fr.* 1093, Lyc. 98; cf. Phot. and Hsch. s.v. Σαλαμβώ, who gloss the name as "the Babylonian Aphrodite."
177. See Frisk (n. 9, above) s.v. σαλάμβη for further discussion, and compare εὐδίαιος, bilge-hole (Hsch).
178. Willems (n. 8, above), 3:196, n. 1, thinks that this phrase is intended to vulgarize medical terminology (ἐκπίπτειν) referring to a "chute de l'uterus," ὑστερικὴ πρόπτευσις.

1124. The title of a play of Eupolis, *Eutresios* (56), may contain a pederastic pun of this kind.[179]

158. τρύπημα, any bored hole or the bolt-hole in gate-fastenings (Aen.
Tact. 18.3), is common.[180] The expression at E 623 f., προβεβούλευται
γάρ,ὅπως ἄν μηδεμιᾶς ᾖ τρύπημα κενόν, it's been voted : no woman's hole
is to be empty, may be proverbial, to judge from Eup. 354 οὐδὲν κενὸν
τρύπημα, every hole its bolt/every cunt its phallus, and *POxy.* 2741, *Fr.*
IA, col. ii, 12 (from Eup. *Marikas*). The series of obscene double entendres
in the women's catalogue at Fr 320 includes τρύφημα (line 7), a garment/
cunt.

Sea Animals

159. καλλιώνυμος, the fish called τὸ θαλάσσιον αἰδοῖον, was used to
indicate the genitals of both sexes (CA 1023) : see chap. 2, n. 18.

160. κόγχη, the cavity (pink or red) of a seashell, used in technical
writers for many bodily cavities,[181] is a double entendre meaning "vagina"
in the joke at V 583–89 concerning the seal on the young heiress's will :
Bdelycleon rebukes his father thus, τῆς δ᾽ ἐπικλήρου τὴν διαθήκην ἀδικεῖς
ἀνακογχυλιάζων. That is, you are wrong (1) to uncap the seal on her will
and (2) to unseal her virginity.[182] κόγχη is common in this obscene meaning :[183] compare κογχυλαγόνες = nymphs (Hsch.).

161. Other sea-animal double entendres are those involving urchins :
Ἐχινοῦς at L 1169 is a pun on ἐχῖνος, sea urchin. The image probably
derives from the prickly appearance of this creature, but may possibly
allude to another use of the word to mean hole, cavity, or vase (see *LSJ*,
Frisk s.v.).

162. Compare σπατάγγης, another form of sea urchin, at Fr. 409, an
obvious reference to cunnilingus, διαλείχοντά μου τὸν κάτω σπατάγγην.[184]

Cookery

163. Many double entendres are based on kitchen implements. In an

179. Cf. Sotad. 2D ὃ δ᾽ ὑποστεγάσας τὸ τρῆμα τῆς ὄπισθε λαύρας. τόρος is "phallus" at
Phillyl. 18, and Pan's epithet, τρύπανον, the drill, is phallic at Callim. *Fr.* 412.

180. Hermog. *Id.* 2.3, Theoc. 5.42 (ἐτρύπη : see *LSJ* s.v. τρυπάω 2), Procop. *Arc.* 9. An
epithet of Aphrodite (CA 1169) is τρυμαλῖτις : compare τρυμαλία in Sotad. I (= Athen.
14.621A) : εἰς τρυμαλίαν τὸ κέντρον ὠθεῖς.

181. Ears : Ruf. *Onom.* 44, Poll. 2.86 ; knee-pan : ibid., 188 ; cranium : Lyc. 1105 ; eye-
socket : Poll. 2.71.

182. For διαθήκη as a physical state, cf. Democr. 9.

183. Sophr. 25, 26 Olivieri ; Plaut. *Rud.* 704 (*concha*).

184. We have already mentioned Hipponax's βρύσσον (70.8) ; cp. also the many fish-
puns in the fragments of Antiphanes, especially 26.

obscene passage on the physical charms of Theoria, Trygaeus points to her "oven," P 891, to which the servant replies, διὰ ταῦτα καὶ κεκάπνικεν ἄρ᾽· ἐνταῦθα γὰρ/πρὸ τοῦ πολέμου τὰ λάσανα τῇ βουλῇ ποτ᾽ ἦν: "she is blackened down below [pubic hair] because the council used to put their pots [phalli] there for cooking before the war." λάσανα were trivets in which vessels were placed for cooking.[185]

163a. This black spot from smoke, indicating pubic hair, is τὸ μέλαν at V 1374, and may have been a common slang term, to judge from its appearance in *PMag.* IV.405, XVIIa, 23.

164. With blackened pots and ovens, compare hearths and braziers: κυκῶν τὰς ἐσχάρας, stirring up the coals, at Eq 1286 refers to cunnilingus; the schol. glosses τὰ χείλη τῶν γυναικείων αἰδοίων. An alternate interpretation of this image would be to derive the comparison from ἐσχάρα in its meaning of "scab" or "eschar" (as at Pl Com 184.4); this would thus be either simply a disgusting image or an actual reference to venereal disease,[186] both not inappropriate for this description of the unspeakable Ariphrades. Whichever derivation we choose, ἐσχάρα as labia seems to have been a common term.[187] Perhaps the cleverest use of the word is T 912, during the "recognition" scene between the Relation (Helen) and Euripides (Menelaus). Aristophanes seems to have made a pun out of a climactic line from Euripides' *Helen* (566): ὦ χρόνιος ἐλθὼν σῆς δάμαρτος ἐς χέρας, O timely arrived to the arms of your wife!, for the last two words of which Aristophanes has substituted ἐσχάρας. The original reading is preserved by R.[188]

165. ἄνθραξ, hot coals, twice indicates the cunt inflamed by coitus and poked by a (phallic) stoker: in the picture of the blissful man sitting in front of a fireplace with a young girl, κἀνθρακίζων τοὐρεβίνθου (P 1136), baking his chickpea in the glowing coals, and ἔχονθ᾽ ἑταῖραν καὶ σκαλεύοντ᾽ ἄνθρακας, having a young girl and stoking the/her coals (P 440).

166. Bowls and dishes tend to appear in descriptions of cunnilingus, probably because one commonly licks them clean after preparing sauces and the like. τρύβλιον, bowl, appears in a passage describing cunnilingus, τὰ τῶν γυναικῶν διακαθαίρει τρύβλια, he cleans out the women's bowls (E 847); note the presence at this banquet of the notorious cunnilinctor, Smoeus.

---

185. For the image see Diocl. Com. 8 ἀπὸ λασάνων θερμὴν ἀφαιρήσω χύτραν. For details see Willems (n. 8, above), 2:112 ff.

186. See J. Rosenbaum, *Geschichte der Lustseuche im Altertume* (Halle, 1882), p. 320 n.

187. Eust. 1523.28, 1539.33.

188. See W. Mitsdörffer, *Die Parodie euripideischer Szenen bei Aristophanes* (diss., Berlin, 1943), pp. 82 f.

167. λοπάς, a shallow pan or dish, seems to be common in this sense: at Eq 1034 the Sausage-Seller compares Cleon to a dog at work on the personified cities in an obscene fashion while Demus sleeps, νύκτωρ τὰς λοπάδας καὶ τὰς νήσους διαλείχων, licking at the bowls and the islands at night. Eupolis uses the same scurrilous image, ὦ πολλῶν ἤδη λοπάδων τοὺς ἄμβωνας περιλείξας, you who have licked around the rims of many a dish (52);[189] cf. Xenarch. 1.10 (above, section 152). Lopadion is the name of a courtesan in Timocl. 25.4.

Foods

168. As with the male genitalia, meat appears as a slang term for the female parts: piggie-κρῆς spitted on an ὀβελός at A 795; the κρέα . . . ἀπαλὰ καὶ καλά which form part of the feast of reconciliation at L 1062;[190] and the κρέας used in a coarse image of cunnilingus at P 717.

168a. The latter passage also involves χόλικας ἑφθάς, boiled sausages (the labia, one supposes).

169. τὰ λαγῷα, assorted dainties, is a double entendre for cunts in the sexual banquets of A 1006, E 843, Alexis 163.5. Pl Com 174.10 couples reference to σέλινον (q.v.) with this word, perhaps emphasizing the pubic hair, λαγῷα ἐπισέλινα.[191]

170. Similar are the slices of fish-meat (τεμάχη) which are "fanned into flame" at the banquet at E 842.

171. Compare τραγήματα, various foods for munching, in the banquets at E 844 and Alexis 163.2 f.

172. παροψίδες, hors-d'oeuvre, refers to love-play that leads up to intercourse: Pl Com 43, Fr 187.[192]

173. ἄμης, milk-cake, at Alexis 163.5 is one of various kinds of pastries used to refer to the cunt (see also above, section 16).

174. ἐλατήρ, a broad, flat cake (Hsch.) at A 246.

175. μᾶζα, barley-cake, at A 835 (cf. Eub. 75.10).

176. μυστίλη, pastry gravy-boat, at Eq 1168 (see section 16, above).

177. πλακοῦς, flat-cake, at P 869, 1359, E 223, Pl 995, Fr 202.[193] The verb used is usually πέσσειν, to bake a cake (in coitus).

178. πόπανα, round-cake, at E 843.

189. ἄμβων = cunt at Eust. 1539.33.

190. For the collocation see Av 668, Nausicr. 1.1, Luc. *dd* 2.2.

191. Not ἐπισέληνα: see Kock (who reads ἐπὶ σελίνοις), F. Blaydes, *Adversaria in Comicorum Graecorum Fragmenta* (Halle, 1890), p. 79.

192. See Taillardat (n. 107, above), p. 104, n. 1.

193. The πλακοῦς ἐνόρχης of Pl Com 174.8 is the phallus.

Secreta Muliebria

179. δρόσος appears in a description of cunnilingus at Eq 1285, ἐν κασωρείοισι λείχων τὴν ἀπόπτυστον δρόσον, licking the detestable dew in whore-houses. That this may have been a proper euphemism seems assured by its use in Aristotle.[194]

180. A less respectable play on the female secreta is ζωμός, soup or sauce, used in the joke on cunnilingus surrounding Theoria's adoption as sex partner of the Council, P 716, 885.

181. Similar is the double entendre on ἔτνος, soup, at A 245 f., ὦ μῆτερ ἀνάδος δεῦρο τὴν ἐτνήρυσιν/ἵν' ἔτνος καταχέω τοὐλατῆρος τουτουί, "Mother, hand me the ladle so I can pour the *sauce* over this flatcake/cunt." Here ἐτνήρυσις is the phallus. ἔτνος appears elsewhere in obscene banquet catalogues: L 1061, E 845, Alexis 163.7 (pl.).

182. ὄψα κεκαρυκεύματα (Alexis 163.6 f.) are morsels dressed in sauce (cunts).

183. πίττα, pitch or resin, indicates the female secreta at V 1375, where the flute-girl is visualized as a burning torch, that is, burning with sexual passion: ἡ πίττα δήπου καομένης ἐξέρχεται, presumably the pitch flows from her as she burns. καταπισσόω, to smear with pitch, indicates sexual

---

194. *HA* 727b34 ff., 739a37 ff.; cf. = semen at Callim. 260, with Pfeiffer's note. The δρόσος καὶ χνοῦς of N 978 (Just Logic referring to the "dewy" genitals of boys) has caused difficulties of interpretation. Dover (*Clouds*, ad loc.) gives a detailed physiological excursus in which he concludes that the dew refers to Cowper's secretion, a transparent mucus emitted in small amounts when the penis is fully erect for some minutes and its owner in a high state of sexual excitement (for ancient material on Cowper's secretion, see Hopfner, n. 5, above, pp. 33 f.). But this idea seems to be mistaken dramatically. There is no mention of erection in this passage and no hint that the boys in question are sexually excited—it is rather the grown men looking at the boys' genitals who are excited. Cowper's secretion is an obscure image in any case and simply will not fit this particular context.

Fortunately, a more natural explanation will account for the passage's two desiderata, namely (1) that δρόσος must be something *wet*, and (2) that the δρόσος καὶ χνοῦς appears when anointing oil is *not* used below the navel. I think that the expression must be an elegant hendiadys for δροσόεις χνοῦς, dewy down: see Willems, n. 8, above, 3:112, who rightly lists N 978 among numerous other such cases of hendiadys. The pubic down of boys is not artificially oiled but *naturally* dewy, like the surface of fruits (μήλοισιν), probably because of the boys' athletic sweat. For dew associated with sweat, see e.g. Herod. Med. in *RhM* 58.99, Plu. 2.695C. Moreover, dewiness is frequently associated by the Greeks with freshness and innocence, which are clearly wanted in our passage. (The comparison of N 978 with the δρόσοις . . . λεόντων of A. *Ag.* 141, which is sometimes made, is not relevant: for "young lions" Aeschylus uses δρόσος in the sense of semen = progeny: cp. γόνος and γονή).

aggressiveness, to render wet through intercourse, as at E 1108 f., Cratin. 189. At Pl 1093 a young man remarks of his aged flame, ἱκανὸν γὰρ αὐτὴν πρότερον ὑπεπίττουν χρόνον, "I've pitched her down below quite enough in the past". This verb, meaning to "smear below" (note the prefix), combines the image of secreta with that of tarring a leaky old vessel.

Miscellaneous

184. δέλτα (see Eust. 1539.34) at L 151 has caused difficulties, mainly because of a strange and grotesque idea of Wilamowitz, ad loc. The schol. glosses ἀντὶ τοῦ τὸ αἰδοῖον τὸ γυναικεῖον τοιοῦτον γὰρ τὸ σχῆμα. That is, the pubic region is naturally delta-shaped (V). This would appear to be the reasonable and correct explanation.[195] But Wilamowitz, basing his argument on the absence of an article, maintained that the delta referred to a specific styling of the pubic hair, and compared (irrelevantly) Av 806, σκάφιον ἀποτετιλμένος. But an article is not necessary (cf. E 624),[196] and it is difficult to imagine what the purpose of such a styling would have been, not to mention its inappropriateness to the context of L 151. Surely the scholiast was correct. It may be worthwhile to add that *delta* is used elsewhere in literature for its shape as the female pubis (e.g. Auson. *Epigr.* 120.4), and in cults in the form of triangular clay votive-offerings shaped to resemble the female parts.[197]

185. δορίαλλος = cunt at Fr 367; cf. *EM* 283.45, *Et. Gud.* 150.49 (δορύαλος), Hsch. (δορύαλλος), schol. R 516 (δορίαλος). See section 198, below.

186. For κέλης (CA 1033) see section 275, n. 61.

187. The strange term σάβυττα (CA 1134) seems to be an image akin to the delta (section 184, above), probably deriving from a hair-style which resembled the female pubis (see Hsch., Phot., s.v. σάβυττον).

188. σάραβον (CA 1137) should perhaps be placed here, although Meineke (IV, p. 660) derives the term from the name of a Plataean baker (see Kock at Posidipp. 29.1). If this is true, σάραβον would be related to the entries classified under *Proper Names,* p. 147, below. Cf. also σαραβίχιν = cunt at Telecl. 64; Phot. s.v. σάραβον, σαραβίχη.

---

195. See Taillardat (n. 107, above), p. 77, and the interesting material collected by M. Meyer, "Delta Praehistoricum," *PhW* 49 (1929): 91 ff.

196. Willems (n. 8, above), 2:421 ff., gives a long list of bodily parts named without an article.

197. See Hopfner (n. 5, above), p. 110, H. Licht, *Sittengeschichte Griechenlands* (Zürich, 1927–28), 2:76. Willems (n. 8, above), 2:422, n. 1, prefers to see in the delta an etymological relationship to such words as Skt. *jartush* (vulva), Goth. *kilthei* (womb), δελφύς (womb), δέλφαξ (section 113, above), δολφός (ἡ μήτρα, Hsch.). This is most farfetched.

Birds

189. ἀηδονίς (Archil. 263, *IG* 14.1942.6) and ἀηδόνιον (Hsch.) are not attested in comedy but seem to have been well known for cunt.

190. ἀηδών, nightingale, in *Birds* seems to be an obscene pun on the bird-name of the hoopoe's wife (represented onstage by a flute-girl): at 207 Peisetaerus mischievously says εἰς τὴν λόχμην εἴσβαινε κἀνέγειρε τὴν ἀηδόνα, "*Go into* the *thicket* and *rouse* the *bird*" (see λόχμη, βαίνειν), and at 664 repeats the joke in slightly different form: ἐκβίβασον αὐτοῦ, πρὸς θεῶν, αὐτήν, ἵνα καὶ νὼ θεασώμεσθα τὴν ἀηδόνα, "Call her out here, by heaven, so we can see the *bird*!"

191. κίχλαι, thrushes, = cunt at Alex. 163.5.

192. μυωνία, mouse-hole/nest, = cunt at Epicr. 9.4 f.: ἡ δ' ἄρ' ἦν μυωνία ὅλη means "all cunt."

193. νεοττίς, bird's nest, probably has a genital meaning as a hetaera-name, as in the plays by that title of Antiphanes, Eubulus, and Anaxilas; cf. *AP* 9.567.2 Παφίης νοσσίς, and νεοττός, describing the youthful Lais at Epicr. 2/3.15; see also Archil. 263.

194. τιτίς, small chirping bird, attested only in Photius.

195. χελιδών, swallow, at L 770, 775 is confirmed by Poll. 2.174, Suda. Cf. in Latin Juv. 6. 0. 6.

Split or Crack

196. The notion of the cunt as a split or crack, as in English slang, is present in the joke about the flute-girl being ἐσχισμένην at V 1373.[198] σχιστὰς ἐνεργεῖν at Eup. 266 is a similar joke: the phrase is a surprise for σχιστὰς ἕλκειν, to wear σχισταί (a kind of shoe)[199] in a dance which called for leg-crossing;[200] here σχιστὰς means "cloven" and is cognate accusative emphasizing a σχῆμα συνουσίας.[201]

Proper Names

The names of actual persons were sometimes used by comic poets as slang terms for cunt.

197. In Aristophanes the name of Phormisius is so used on account of his hairiness:[202] E 95 ff.,

198. Compare τεμνομένην *AP* 11.262.2.
199. Hsch., Poll. 7.85.
200. Poll. 4.105, Hsch. s.v. σχίσμα.
201. See Edmonds, 1:407, n. *f*.
202. Cf. schol. E 97. Perhaps he was also a profligate, as is implied at Philetaer. 6. See also schol. R 965, Pl Com 119.

οὐκοῦν καλά γ᾽ ἂν πάθοιμεν, εἰ πλήρης τύχοι
ὁ δῆμος ὢν κἄπειθ᾽ ὑπερβαίνουσά τις
ἀναβαλλομένη δείξειε τὸν Φορμίσιον.

[Wouldn't it be a fine thing if the Assembly happened to be full and one of us, pulling up her clothes to get over those already seated, should flash her . . . Phormisius!]

198. Other unfortunates so insulted by Aristophanes were Dorilaos (?, see section 185, above), an obscure tragic poet contemporary with Euripides,[203] in Fr 367;[204] and Hippocleides (παρὰ τὸ ἱππεύειν, according to Phot.) in Fr 703.[205]

Other Erogenous Bodily Parts

199. Aside from the phallus and the anus, no part of the male anatomy is much referred to in Old and Middle Comedy; male heterosexuality and pederasty are the chief subjects of humor and scurrility. The female body, on the other hand, was much exposed, both physically and verbally. Each of the extant plays, except for *Clouds* and *Frogs,* contains more or less extended scenes of sexual byplay involving the comic exposure of women, whether actual female "actresses" or men wearing female costumes and padding (see preface, n. 8).[206] These physical acts of inspection and palpitation are usually accompanied by obscene verbal commentaries that make use of highly colored terminology intended to spice the humor of exposure and/or degradation. Aside from the genitals, the breasts and the hindquarters are the main objects of attention.

200. τιτθός is a standard proper term for the female breast, whether animal or human.[207] It is used only once in Aristophanes, by a woman in an innocent context (T 640). The other proper words (such as θηλαί,[208] μαστοί, στέρνα, στήθη) do not appear at all. The vulgar τιτθίον appears to be the exclusive *vox propria* in comedy, and is always used as a symbol of female beauty and male sexual pleasure, rather than, say, to express any kind of female biological function apart from sexuality. Firmness (and

203. *POxy.* IX.1176, *Fr.* 39, col. XVI.
204. See Taillardat (n. 107, above), pp. 74 f.
205. For other victims see Hsch. s.v. Ἀριστόδημος, who lists Phormisius, Basilidas, Lacharas. Sarabus in CA 1137 (see Meineke, 4:638) might be a person: see section 188, above. The name of the victim of Eupolis, ἐξυρημένος σαβύττους, who wore his hair in the shape of a cunt, is unknown: *POxy.* 1803.59 (see *LSJ* s.v. I.1; Hsch. s.v. σάβυττος).
206. See Alexis 98.13, for example.
207. Hp. *Aph.* 5.40, Lys. 1.10, Gal. 6.673, 684, etc.
208. But θήλη in a proper sense in ἄθηλος (L 881).

thus youthfulness) is the usual attribute: breasts are "hard and quincelike" (A 1199), "as firm as young turnips" (T 1185), "as fresh as apples or strawberries" (Crat. 40), "as firm and virginal as salted olives" (young girls as compared with δρυπετεῖς ἑταίρας, over-ripe professionals, Fr 141; cf. Timocl. 22.3 for the same contrast, and cf. Fr 54 Dem.). That the costuming of naked women took these characteristics into account is clear from L 83, where Cleonice (an older and probably saggier woman) fondles and admires the firm breasts of Lampito; compare the joke at T 638 ff., where the women strip the Relation and initially feel jealous about what seem to be firm, youthful breasts: "She certainly hasn't got titties like ours," a woman says. We must suppose that the assembly of housewives had saggy breasts that were clearly differentiated by the costuming from those of younger, more enticing female characters.

201. We hear also of holding on to the τιτθία in intercourse: P 863, where the expectant Trygaeus savors his coming pleasures in the arms of Opora; Pl 1067 f., where fondling the breasts is a prelude to intercourse. For the term ὑπομηλαφῆσαι ("feel up the breasts") see section 341a, below. The captivating pleasures of looking at a young girl's breasts through torn clothing or diaphanous gowns appears frequently.[209]

202. The other comic metaphors for the breasts all derive from the above-mentioned desideratum of youth and firmness: κάρυα, nuts (Fr 647); κόκκος (Hermipp. 36); κύαμοι, beans (Fr 582);[210] μῆλα, apples (L 155 f., E 904, Fr 924, Cratin. 109.3, Canthar. 6). This latter seems to have been a standard image throughout Greek erotic literature.[211]

203. The buttocks and anus are mentioned in comedy almost exclusively with reference to men. However, there are occasional references to women; usually these are special cases in which puns or extravagant imagery are involved. For example, the "Melian Gulf" of L 1170 is a recherché reference to the anus in a series of geographical puns on several bodily parts: "Melian" refers to applelike buttocks and "Gulf" (κόλπος) to the anus.[212] The mention of πυγή at P 868, where the servant is speaking of Trygaeus' bride, ἡ παῖς λέλουται καὶ τὰ τῆς πυγῆς καλά, the child is washed, and favorable are the auspices of . . . her butt, is a surprise for a sacral formula such as τὰ τῆς τύχης καλά,[213] or τὰ τοῦ θεοῦ καλά.[214]

209. E.g. L 48, 931, T 638, R 409 ff., Frs 8, 325, 647, Xenarch. 4.5, Men. 727, Philem. 81, Chaeremon 14.

210. Cf. Ruf. *Onom.* 92, Poll. 2.163, Eustathius 749.21.

211. See Willems's comprehensive discussion (n. 8, above), 1: 403 ff. On Μηλιᾶ at L 1169 f., see Willems, 2: 447, n. 2. *LSJ* s.v. μῆλον (B) II.2 gives additional material.

212. See n. 211, above and Henderson, art. cit. (n. 163, above).

213. Eur. *IA.* 1403, *Alc.* 789.

214. Phryn. Com. 9.1, Eur. *Tr.* 27, *IT* 467, *Ph.* 1202, Xen. *An.* 3.2.9.

204. It is noteworthy that the semirespectable tone of the word πυγή (see section 450, below) makes it fitting for piquant references to women (as at P 868, L 82, T 1187, E 964, Pl Com 174.16). When we hear of well-rumped or well-padded women[215] it is invariably the word πυγή which is used. The thoroughly vulgar word πρωκτός is used to refer to women only three times in Aristophanes, each instance being a special case: at P 876 as part of a comic compound (πρωκτοπεντετηρίδα);[216] at L 1148 in the mouth of a Spartan, whom the audience would suppose to be not only ignorant of proper (i.e. Attic) Greek, but a habitual pederast who could think only of backsides;[217] and Pl 152, where πρωκτός, describing the seductive twitchings of Corinthian prostitutes, is used merely to set up the joke on pederasty which follows. Indeed, πρωκτός is very common in the humor of homosexuality: see section 449, below.

215. Full description in Alexis 98; see also Hes. *Op.* 373, Semon. 7.76, Athen. 12.554C, Cerc. 14, Stob. 1.45.45, Poll. 2.184.

216. "Une croupe comme on en voit peu, tous les quatres ans . . . -πεντετηρίς implique l' idée de fête renouvelée tous les quatres ans" (Taillardat [n. 107, above], p. 71).

217. See van Daele at L 1105.

5   Sexual Congress

205. The vulgar *vox propria* for sexual intercourse in comedy is βινεῖν, which seems to have had the same force and flexibility in Greek as *fuck* does in English. The connotation is always of violent and/or illicit intercourse.[1] κινεῖν, whose sexual meaning was originally a specialized, and perhaps euphemistic, use of the verb's basic meaning "move," came to be identical in usage to the straightforwardly obscene βινεῖν, a phenomenon that arose probably because of their similarity in sound and sense. Moreover, the two are often further confused in the manuscript tradition because of the similarity of κ and β in certain hands. Since there is no difference between the two in actual usage, we may treat them as equivalent terms.[2]

206. A glimpse into the original metaphor behind κινεῖν can be obtained by examining προσκινεῖσθαι, to move along with/against in coitus, as at E 256 f., προσκινήσομαι/ἄτ' οὐκ ἄπειρος οὖσα πολλῶν κρουμάτων, "I'll move against [my partner], since I am not unskilled at many strokes". The harsh and sensual tone of this passage is present in all other contexts in which προσκινεῖσθαι appears; it has much of the violent nuance of βινεῖν itself: L 227 (women's kinetic cooperation with their husbands' sexual motions), P 901 f. (the tumbling chariots[3] are metaphorical for mutually heaving bodies in coitus), Pherecr. 131.3 (προσκινῶν σέλινα, in which a word meaning "cunt" is the direct object). In Xenarch. 4.23, προσκινεῖσθαι is identical to βινεῖν:[4]

---

1. βινεῖν may be connected etymologically with βία: cf. Hsch. s.v. = παρὰ Σόλωνι τὸ βίᾳ μίγνυσθαι, s.v. ζάει = βινεῖ, and the Attic legal term βία = rape (schol. Pl. *Rep.* 464e, Lys. 1.32). Sanskrit *jināti*, overpower or oppress violently, although tantalizingly similar, cannot be connected as a true cognate with βινεῖν: see H. Frisk, *Griechisches etymologisches Wörterbuch* (Heidelberg, 1960–72) for, and P. Chantraine, *Dictionnaire étymologique de la langue grecque* (Paris, 1968–70) against this connection.

2. See G. Pascucci, "KINHTIAN," *Atene e Roma* n.s. 4 (1959): 102 ff.

3. For the expression, cf. R 543 ἀνατετραμμένος κυνῶν τὴν ὀρχηστρίδα, turned all topsyturvy and kissing the dancing-girl.

4. Compare κινεῖν (Herod. 5.2), ἐπικινεῖσθαι (Luc. *Asin.* 6), ἐπικινεῖ (Eup. 77.3).

ἆς πῶς ποτ', ὦ δέσποινα πότνια Κύπρι,
βινεῖν δύνανται, τῶν Δρακοντείων νόμων
ὁπόταν ἀναμνησθῶσι προσκινούμενοι;

[How ever can they fuck these girls, Queen Kypris, whenever they remember Draco's laws as they're thrusting away?]

We note also κἀπικινεῖν ταῖς κοχώναις (wiggle the buttocks lasciviously)
at Eup. 77.3.

207. At any rate, βινεῖν is used in the active voice of the male, in the
passive of the female; we also find a middle and an absolute usage.

208. In the active with no direct object, βινεῖν, like sleeping, loafing, and
breaking wind, often stands for the easy and responsibility-free hedonism
that is the goal of many Aristophanic heroes. Collocations like πίνειν καὶ
βινεῖν, drink and fuck (R 740) and πλεῖν μένειν βινεῖν καθεύδειν, sail,
laze, fuck, sleep (P 341) are common in descriptions of the easy life: A
1052, 1220 f., P 867, L 966, E 470, Philetaer. 6.2 (ἀποθανεῖν βινοῦντα, die
fucking; compare ibid., 9.4 ἀπέθανεν βινουμένη, she died while fucking).
In *POxy.*, 2806, *Fr.* 1, col. i, 1. 10 βινήσουσιν appears in the same absolute
meaning: when young men are of age "they will start fucking."

209. The other intransitive sense of the active is, more specifically, to
fornicate: Av 796 (adulterous fornication), L 715 (the desiderative βινητιῶ-
μεν),[5] 934, 1179 f., E 706, 1090. The middle voice often has the same sense:
T 15 (in an obscene play on the scientific use of κινεῖσθαι), E 228, 525,
Philetaer. 9.4. Compare Eupolis' κινητήριον, a place for fornication (8.5
Dem.). The middle voice can be used for pederastic fornication as well:
Eq 877, 879, N 1103, T 50, Fr 377.

210. With a direct object or in the passive voice, βινεῖν always connotes
force or violence: N 1371 (incest), Av 560 (the gods, who are ψωλοί,
raping mortal girls), L 954, 1166, E 468, 706, 1099 (enforced fornication).
Similarly, of pederastic rape: Eq 364, ἐγὼ δὲ κινήσω γέ σου τὸν πρωκτὸν
ἀντὶ φύσκης, "I'll fuck your ass-hole like a sausage-case," Eq 1242, N 1301
(the threatened rape of the second creditor), L 1092 (the threatened rape
of Cleisthenes), T 35, R 148, CA 25.1 Dem. Related to these violent connotations are instances in which βινεῖν, like English *screw*, can mean hoodwink or deceive, as at T 1215, where the hoodwinked archer exclaims to
his quiver, ὀρτῶς δὲ σὺ συβίνη· καταβεβίνησο γάρ, an artfully obscene bit of
paratragic word play: Rightly art thou called quiver (*sybine*), for you've
been thoroughly fucked over (*katabebineso*).[6] Compare the use of ἐπιτρίβεσθ-
αι at P 369.

5. Cf. Macho ap. Athen. 13.583C; of men in Pl Com 174.21, Men. *Dysc.* 462, Luc.
Pseudol. 27.

6. Cf. A. *Sept.* (passim), Eur. *Tr.* 990, S. *Fr.* 408, Ar. *Eq.* 1257 ff.

211. διαμηρίζειν, to spread and penetrate the thighs, seems to have been a common vulgar term.[7] In Aristophanes it is used of both heterosexual (Av 669, 1254) and homosexual (Av 706) rape.

212. ληκᾶν, like κινεῖν, seems originally to have indicated rapid body-movement such as dancing[8] or moving the limbs in some way.[9] Lat. *lacertus* and *locusta* may be etymologically connected.[10] Thus the sexual meaning of this word is, like that of κινεῖν, originally euphemistic and secondary. As descriptive of sexual intercourse, ληκᾶν is analogous to βινεῖν and has a similar, unmistakably violent tone. Its range, however, is somewhat broader than of βινεῖν since it seems to indicate not only fornication but also the unseemly behavior that accompanies constant wenching and debauchery. In the active it is used of the male (Pherecr. 177), in the passive of the female: T 493 f. ὑπό του ληκούμεϑα/τὴν νύκτα parallels Pherecr. 177 ληκούμεϑ' ὅλην τὴν νύκτα. These passages suggest continuous fornication, and indeed the substantive ληκήματα, found in Epicurus (414), seems to imply wenching and carousing, with all their concomitant shamelessness.

213. λαικάζειν, whether or not etymologically connected with ληκᾶν, shows little difference in meaning and usage. While with its intransitive use we find fornication as pure hedonistic indulgence, as with the analogous use of βινεῖν, at Eq 167 ἐν πρυτανείῳ λαικάσεις, in the Prytaneum you'll . . . fuck (a surprise for σιτήσει, you'll be fed), most often the connotation is pejorative: λαικάζει at T 57 is meant to be an insulting reference to pederastic fornication, as is the curse οὐχὶ λαικάσει at Strato Com. 1.36 (cf. Men. *Dysc.* 892) and the oath λαικάσομ' ἄρα at Cephisodor. 3. λαικάζειν can also, like βινεῖν, mean hoodwink or deceive.[11] The agent-nouns derived from λαικάζειν indicate continuous and/or professional fornication: λαικασταί are πόρνοι at A 79[12] and λαικάστριαι are the feminine equivalents thereof: A 529, 537, Pherecr. 149, Men. *Pk.* 235.

7. Zeno *Stoic.* 1.59 has both the verb and the substantive.

8. Hsch. ληκᾶν· τὸ πρὸς ᾠδὰν ὀρχεῖσϑαι.

9. ληκίνδα παίζει means "drum with the fingers" (Luc. *Lex.* 8, A.D. *Adv.* 152.11). Cf. λάξ, "with the feet." Perhaps ληκώ, the male member (Hsch., Phot.), originally indicated a "moving limb."

10. See Frick (n. 1, above) s.v. ληκάω, λάξ. Compare Lith. *lakstùs, lekiù, lekti,* all of which indicate bodily movements.

11. Suda, *EM* 555.15.

12. See the schol. There is no reason to understand λαικάζειν to mean fellatio, as do W. Heraeus, "Προπεῖν," *RhM* 70 (1915): 38, n. 1 and A. E. Housman, "Praefanda," *Hermes* 66 (1931): 408, n. 2. Housman goes even further than Heraeus and denies that the word even meant *scortari,* although all testimony suggests that it did. All of the citations Heraeus gives in support of fellatio (Housman gives none) are questionable: the scholiast at E 920 has been beguiled by the λ of λάβδα in the text and glosses λαικάζει,

214. σπλεκοῦν has a similarly violent and vulgar tone;[13] L 152 στύοιντο δ' ἄνδρες κἀπιθυμοῖεν σπλεκοῦν, if the men have hard-ons and want to fuck, Pl 1082 (of an old lady) διασπλεκουμένη ὑπὸ μυρίων τε τῶνδε καὶ τρισχιλίων, having been fucked over by these three thousand men (see Hsch. s.v.). Frisk s.v., following E. Schwyzer, *Griechische Grammatik* (Munich, 1934–53), Vol. 1, p. 413, suggests that the word derives by hypostasis from a curse, εἰς πλέκος (compare σκορακίζω from εἰς κόρακας). The alternative form, πλεκοῦν,[14] will then be secondary, with the loss of sigma by a familiar process,[15] or perhaps by conscious etymologizing.

Euphemistic Expressions

215. There are a large number of euphemistic words and phrases for sexual congress in Aristophanes and the other writers of comedy. They occur when a coarse term would serve no comic purpose, that is, when there is no farce, ridicule, threatening, bathos, or insulting. Frequently euphemisms appear in paratragic passages or passages parodying the language and tone of other serious genres. For example, the paratragic prologue to *Ecclesiazusae* or the old hag's wheedling (and therefore euphemistic) *melos* at E 893 ff., contrasted with the foul and abusive language she hurls at her younger rival at 906 ff., in a scene that parodies serious amoebean love-duets.[16]

216. ἀνδροῦσθαι, of women: to lie with a man,[17] Fr 744, Cratin. 287.

217. τῆς ἥβης ἀπολαῦσαι, to partake of sex, take pleasure in a woman's bloom, L 591.

218. ἀφροδισιάζειν, very common in Greek for sexual congress, appears in comedy only at Philetaer. 18.3.

219. ἀφροδίσια ποιῶν, having a debauch, Diphil. 43.22. Compare Crates 2.2 f. Dem., ἀφροδισίοις ἀθύρμασιν, erotic pastimes (cf. Eup. 3 Dem., ἀνδρογύνων ἄθυρμα, transvestites' play).

---

but here this means "behave like a prostitute" and not necessarily "perform fellatio." The gloss by Hsch. s.v. σκερόλιγγες, λαικασταὶ ἢ ὠπισταί, simply means that *fellatrices* are prostitutes. Ibid., s.v. λαί = ἐπὶ τῆς αἰσχρουργίας need not even refer to λαικάζειν at all (as Heraeus himself admits). The appearances in Latin of λαικάζειν (Mart. 11. 58.12. Petr. 42.2) are simply curses like that in Strato Com. 1.36 and certainly need not imply fellatio. One must take care with late glosses: in this case, a word that in classical times meant "do what a prostitute does" (fornicate) has been used to gloss words like λάβδα and σκερόλιγγες, which have the more specialized connotation of fellatio.

13. Hsch. glosses κατελάσαι.

14. Hsch., Poll. 5.93.

15. See Schwyzer, op. cit., p. 334.

16. See C. M. Bowra, "A Love-Duet," *AJP* 79 (1958): 376 ff.

17. Cf. *AB* 394.28, D.C. *Fr.* 67.3, 87.3.

220. τὰ τῆς Ἀφροδίτης ἱέρ᾽ ἀνοργίαστά σοι/χρόνον τοσοῦτόν ἐστιν, for some time you've let the holy rites of Aphrodite go unperformed, L 898 f., a comically inflated phrase meant to contrast with the rampant desperation of the speaker, Kinesias.

221. τὸ τῆς Ἀφροδίτης τυγχάνειν, partaking of Aphrodite, Alex. 271.4. For τυγχάνειν meaning to "take" a girl, see CA 16.15 Dem., εἰ δυνατόν ἐστι τῆς κόρης αὐτῷ τυχεῖν.

221a. ἀμφηγαπάζειν at Canthar. 2 Dem.: καὶ πρότερον οὖσα παρθένος/ ἀμφηγάπαζες αὐτόν appears to mean, "And when you were yet a maiden you made love to him."

222. βιάζειν, to rape, Pl 1092 (see schol.), in Chremes' promise to the young man that he will not be attacked by the hag, is a humorous reversal of the usual sexual roles.

223. διαλέγεσθαι can mean "have sexual relations with" in Attic Greek;[18] in Aristophanes it occurs at least twice,[19] both times with a rather harsh tone: Pl 1082 (schol. = ὁμιλήσαιμι) and E 890, where the hag's curse to the young woman (τούτῳ διαλέγου) is equivalent to English, "screw yourself" (τούτῳ refers to the middle finger).[20]

224. διαπαρθενεύειν, deflower a maiden, Diocl. Com. 16, Antiph. 75, Alex. 314; compare διαπαρθένια δῶρα, Amphis 49.

225. διαπράττεσθαι, finish an act of intercourse, at E 634; see *LSJ* s.v. πράσσω 3.

226. At Eq 263 the Sausage-Seller invents the word ἐγκολῃβάζειν, which means ἐπὶ κόλοις βαίνειν (bugger).[21]

227. βαίνειν, in the sense of "mounting," appears at Fr 329, ἀναβῆναι τὴν γυναῖκα βούλομαι, and at Pherecr. 131.4 (see section 137, above). This usage is usually limited to animal copulation.[22] εἰσβαίνειν, go into, at Av 208, is an ad hoc double entendre with λόχμη (see section 134, above).

228. Compare βιβάζειν at Alc. Com. 18 (= ὀχεύειν AB 85.6).

229. In the charming dialogue of the personified triremes (Eq 1306), the virgin trireme is described piquantly as ἥτις ἀνδρῶν ἆσσον οὐκ ἐληλύθει, a boat which hasn't gone near men; this use of ἔρχεσθαι is a common euphemism, like "go with" or "go (in) unto" in English.[23]

18. Suda, Hyp. *Fr.* 171, Plu. *Sol.* 20, Hierocl. p. 64A.

19. Fr 343 (= Poll. 2.125) may refer to other instances.

20. See V. Coulon, "Beiträge zur Interpretation des Aristophanes," *RhM* 105 (1962): 20.

21. Suda s.v. ἐγκολοβήσας, κολῃβάζειν (προσκρούειν) and cf. κολετρᾶν at N 552, κολεάζειν (*Ath. Mitt.* 59.66 [Syrus 5 BC]), which contain the same double meaning.

22. Hdt. 1.92 and the discussion at Zon. 195. Also Theopomp. Hist. 2, Xen *Eq.* 1.3.4, *LSJ* II.7.

23. Hdt. 2.115, 6.68, Sex. *Oecon.* 7.5, etc.

230. εὐφραίνεσθαι, to take pleasure with sexually, of men at L 165 and of women at L 591.

231. ἔχειν (see *LSJ* s.v. A.I.4) : τὰς ἑταίρας ἡδέως πάσας ἔχω, "I take on all the whores gladly" (Antiph. 102.2). At A 787, ἔχειν means "accommodate a penis (in coitus)."

232. κλέπτειν ὑφαρπάζειν τε θήλειαν Κύπριν, to steal and pilfer female Aphrodite (T 205) is a tragic parody given to Agathon[24] and sets up the vulgar bathos of the following line, spoken by the Relation: ἰδού γε κλέπτειν· νὴ Δία, βινεῖσθαι μὲν οὖν, pilfer my foot! By God, you mean fuck! Similar is ὑφαρπάζειν Κύπριν at E 722, which sets up the bathetic vulgarity of line 724. ὑφαρπάσαιο at E 921 is literally "steal from under me," with a play perhaps on the erotic sense (note the prefix). Similar is Eub. 67.8 f, λαθραίαν Κύπριν διώκειν, to pursue hidden Aphrodite.

233. κοινωνία (intercourse: *LSJ* I.2,II) appears at Amphis 20.3 γυναικὸς λαμβάνοι κοινωνίαν, to take a woman's "fellowship."

234. τῆς νυκτὸς λόγος, night's argument, at Ephipp. 20.3 refers to the nocturnal sexual activities of a young debauchee. Cf. Pl Com 2 Dem.

235. For μείγνυσθαι, to have relations with, see *LSJ* s.v. B.4. In comedy: Av 698 (Ἔρως) μιγείς, 701 ξυμμειγνυμένων δ' ἑτέρων ἑτέροις, T 890 f. βιάζομαι/γάμοισι Πρωτέως παιδὶ συμμεῖξαι λέχος, R 1081 μειγνυμένας τοῖσιν ἀδελφοῖς, Theopomp. 5 ὄνῳ μιγείσης μητρός . . . .

236. To grab someone μέσος, in the middle, was a term probably borrowed from wrestling[25] and very common in amatory literature. The genitals are of course thought to be "in the middle": cf. τοῦ πέους μέσου (A 1216). In Aristophanes it refers to rape: μέσην λαβεῖν, take her middle, of a thieving Thracian girl (A 274), ξυναρπάσει μέσην, seize her middle, of Lysistrata (L 437) μέση . . . ληφθήσομαι, I'll be seized in the middle, of Praxagora (E 260). μέσην ἔρειδε, drive at her middle, in Fr 74 means βινεῖν. At P 882 μέσους (pl.) is a double entendre emphasizing the phalli of the aroused councilmen.

237. μολεῖν, go/come, appears at Strattis 41 in an idiomatic phrase that seems to mean "have sexual congress with" (see Meineke II, p. 779): ἦ μήποτ', ὦ παῖ Ζηνός, εἰς ταὐτὸν μόλῃς,/ἀλλὰ παραδοὺς τοῖς Λεσβίοις χαίρειν ἔα, "Son of Zeus, don't go into her again—give her to the Lesbians and be done with her!" See section 381, below.

---

24. Compare συνεκκλέπτει γάμους (Eur. *El.* 364), S. *El.* 114, Eur. *Ba.* 459, 687.

25. See *LSJ* s.v. μέσος I.1.6; A 571, N 1047. Grabbing or holding onto someone (with physical byplay on stage) is often done preparatory to sexual congress. Certain stylized euphemisms appear in comedy to describe this sexual aggressiveness: προσάγειν (L 893, 1115, 1121), λαβεῖν (L 1115, 1121, V 1342, E 1020), ἐφάπτεσθαι (Pl 1067 f.; for the pun ἀν–at L 774 see section 97), ἔχεσθαι (P 863), ἕλκειν (E 1087), προσέλκεσθαι (E 909).

238. οἴφειν (or -εῖν), a Doric word meaning "to mount" (only of human beings), in CA 36 ἄριστα χωλὸς οἴφεῖ (cf. Mimn. 15D³, Diogenian. 2.2).

239. ὀπύειν, to marry, seems respectable enough in Homer and the early poets, although its apparently obscene use later[26] may indicate that it had a vulgar tone in the common language.[27] Thus it is difficult to determine precisely the tone of Dicaeopolis' remark at A 254 f. to his daughter, ὡς μακάριος/ὅστις σ᾽ ὀπύσει κἀκποήσεται γαλᾶς, "lucky the man who marries you and begets on you . . . weasels," although we may guess that Dicaeopolis is setting up the crudity of line 256 with some language taken from stilted blessing-formulas. In Fr 222.4, ὀπύειν (cj. Dobree and Dindorf; Bergk and Kock contra), if that is the reading, would refer to fornication (cf. Plu. *Sol.* 20).

240. παίζειν, to dally amorously, was a common euphemism in Greek love poetry and romantic prose.[28] This word appears several times in Aristophanes: Av 660, where the Coryphaeus wants to "play with" Procne while the hoopoe entertains his human guests; Av 1098, where the chorus wishes to spend the winter in a cave "playing with the mountain nymphs." In *Frogs* (414 f.) Xanthias wants to play with a young girl in the procession (she is called συμπαίστρια at 411; cf. our euphemism for a female sex partner, playmate). These expressions all appear in choral passages; the following, from dialogue, are somewhat harsher in tone: the young man at Pl 1055 asks his old flame whether she wants to play with him (πρός με παῖσαι; there is a pun here on παίειν, q.v.); she asks him what παιδιά (*schema*/game) he has in mind; from what follows it looks as if he was referring to fellatio, a stock insult thrown at old ladies.[29] τί ποτε παίσομαι at E 911 means "with whom shall I play?" (sexually).[30] παῖζε at Amphis 8.1 means "make love!"; παίγνια at E 922 has the same meaning as "tricks" in English, namely, a prostitute's clients (play-partners). At CA 5.6 Dem., παίζειν refers to female masturbation.

241. παννυχίζειν, to stay awake all night doing something (in this case, making love), appears twice in very similar contexts: at N 1069 Peleus is criticized for being a poor lover: οὐδ᾽ ἡδὺς ἐν τοῖς στρώμασιν τὴν νύκτα παννυχίζειν, nor can he perform sweetly in the bedclothes all night, and at Fr 695, where the subject presumably knows how to keep his mistress

26. Cerc. 17.41, Luc. *Eun*, 12, *Merc. Cond.* 41, etc.

27. Cf. Hsch. s.v. βινεῖν.

28. See *LSJ* s.v. I.5, Anacreon 14.4 Gentili (Eros and the Nymphs) and the many instances in the *AP* (e.g. 5.157.1). Compare Lat. *illudere* (*ThLL* 7.1.389.76 ff.).

29. See V. Grassmann (chap. 1, n. 70, above), pp. 18 ff. On this passage see V. Coulon (n. 20, above), p. 27.

30. See F. L. Agar, "Notes on the *Ecclesiazusae* of Aristophanes," *CQ* 13 (1919): 19.

satisfied: ὅστις ἐν ἡδυόσμοις/στρώμασι παννυχίζων τὴν δέσποιναν ἐρε-
ίδεις, you who stay up all night screwing your mistress in the sweet bedclothes.

242. πάσχειν, to have something done to one, appears in the old hag's
song at E 893 f. in the meaning "to have a good time sexually," and later
in the young man's speech at 1105, but elsewhere only of pathic homosexuality.[31]

243. πειρᾶν very often means (to cite Photius) τὸ πειράζειν ἐπὶ φϑορᾷ καὶ
συνουσίᾳ.[32] In Aristophanes it means actual rape only once (Pl 1067 f.),
where the young man jokingly suggests that Chremes, if left alone with the
old lady, might try to rape her. More commonly the meaning is "to force
one's attentions upon" as at V 1025 (the seduction of young boys at the
palaestra; cf. also P 763), Eq 517 (Comedy visualized as an hetaera at
whom poets make passes),[33] and Pl 150 (propositioned prostitutes; cf.
Artemidor. 1.80). At L 1113 (see schol.), ἀλλήλων ἐκπειρωμένοις almost
means "try each other out" as sex partners, but perhaps the idea of rape is
present here as well (see l. 1092).

244. περαίνεσϑαι, to bring something to a conclusion, is very common in
Greek for sexual congress.[34] Its two appearances in Aristophanes are both
double entendres: at L 1135 Lysistrata's quotation from Euripides'
Erechtheus gives an obscene twist to περαίνεται (to judge from the prytanis's
reaction in l. 1136), while περαντικός at Eq 1378, used of a debauched
orator, means both "conclusive" and εὐρύπρωκτος.[35]

245. ποιεῖν, like English "do" or "make," can mean βινεῖν. Thus the
Relation at T 174 f. deliberately misunderstands Euripides, who intended
ποιεῖν in the sense of "compose poetry," and turns the term into a joke on
pederasty. The same joke was used a few lines earlier (ll. 157 f.): ὅταν
σατύρους τοίνυν ποῇς, καλεῖν ἐμέ,/ἵνα συμποιῶ σούπισϑεν ἐστυκὼς ἐγώ,
"Well, whenever you make satyrs, call me, and I'll get right behind you
with my hard-on and make [it] with you." ἐστυκώς, erect, is a surprise
for ἑστηκώς, standing. Note also παιδοποιεῖν, (E 615) and ἐκποιεῖν (A
255, P 708).

246. σιναμωρεῖν, to ravage wantonly or violently,[36] has an amatory

31. Cf. the Relation's derisive joke on Agathon's effeminacy at T 201. Compare Lat.
pathicus.

32. Lys. 1.12, Eur. *Cyc.* 581. Pl. *Phaedr.* 337a, Plu. *Luc.* 18, *Mar.* 14, *Thes.* 26, *Cim.* 1.

33. For the personification see R 92 ff., Pherecr. 145.

34. Artem. 1.80, D.L. 2.127; pass.: CA 14 (pederasty), *AP* 11.339.2, D.L. 2.127.

35. Compare περάντης = buggerer at schol. Theoc. 13 (Pap.) and the other obscene
puns in the description (συνερτικός, κρουστικός).

36. Hdt. 1.152, 8.35, Paus. 2.32.3 σιναμωρία is joined with ὕβρις at Arist. *EN* 1149ᵇ 33.

meaning that seems to imply the degradation (or the cooperation in degradation) of the woman in some way, either by the man's treating her roughly or by making her perform specialized sexual acts. Thus Peleus is divorced by Thetis, according to Unjust Logic, for not being an ὑβριστής (q.v.): γυνὴ δὲ σιναμωρωμένη χαίρει (N 1070),"a woman likes to be used wantonly." There is some indication that σιναμωρεῖν implied, among other amatory acts, fellatio. Attic writers apparently used σιναμώρευμα to mean τὸ λιχνεύειν (*EM* 713.29), and σιναμωρεύματα at Pherecr. 230 is glossed as meaning τὰ τοιαῦτα κλέμματα, "that kind of *schema*," referring to fellatio.[37] σινάμωρος in a wider sense means "libidinous" at Anacr. 53 and in Plu. *de educ.* 4, and at Achilles Tatius 2.38.5 it modifies ἀπάτη, practiced amatory arts (compare κλέμματα). In short, this word implies the treating of lovemaking as a meretricious art rather than simply as pleasure or amusement; thus the connotations of wantonness, shamelessness, and perhaps even sadism or masochism, are always present.

247. συγγίγνεσθαι appears in a pederastic punch-line at R 57 and perhaps also at Eq 467; its use of both men and women is well-attested (*LSJ* s.v. II.3).

248. συνεῖναι, which often has the high tone "live with,"[38] was also a standard euphemism for intercourse itself.[39] It is in this latter sense, of course, that the word appears in comedy: Eq 1287, V 475, E 38, 619, 898, *POxy.*, 2741, *Fr.* IB, col. ii(iii), 20 f. (Eupolis' *Marikas*); at P 863 and Av 704 (the ornithogeny), the word is used in an almost technical way. See also Eup. 337, Anaxil. 22.12, 24. The common *vox propria* for sexual congress, συνουσία, does not appear in comedy before Theopompus (38) and Anaxandrides (33.9), unless συνουσία at E 110 f. is a pun (see Ussher, *Ecclesiazusae*, ad loc.).

249. ὑβρίζειν, like βιάζειν (cf. Alc. Com. 29), meant "rape" in the legal jargon of Athens (*LSJ* s.v. II.3); in comedy it means "to treat roughly during the sex act" or "be virile": thus the hapless Peleus is supposedly deserted by Thetis for not being more of an ὑβριστής (see section 246, above); similarly, the servant at T 63 teases the Relation, who has been making crude sexual remarks about Agathon, ἦ που νέος γ' οὖν ἦσθ' ὑβριστής, ὦ γέρον, "I suppose you were quite the ravisher when you were young, old man."[40] ὕβρις at Eub. 67.9 means "crude lust."

At Anacreon 27 Gentili, σινάμωροι brawl with a doorkeeper: see L. Weber, *Anacreontea* (diss. Göttingen, 1892), pp. 96 f.

37. For κλέμμα as an amatory *schema*, cf. Ael. *NA* 1.2, *AP* 5.17.2. See section 232, above.

38. Hdt. 4.9, S. *El.* 276.

39. Arist. *Pol.* 1262ᵃ33, of animal copulation in Arist. *HA* 540ᵃ13.

40. Cf. also V 1303 and compare Hdt. 4.129, Xen. *Mem.* 2.1.30. The ὕβριν ὀρθίαν κνωδάλων of Pi. *P.* 10.36 is the erect phallus.

250. χαρίζεσθαι, meaning to grant favors sexually (*LSJ* s.v. I.3), appears frequently in comedy: A 883 f., where the Theban paratragically bids the "mistress" of his Copaic eels to be nice (κήπιχάριτται) to Dicaeopolis; Eq 1368, punningly in a pederastic sense (compare Theopomp. 29); Eq 517, of Lady Comedy's favors; T 1194 f., E 629, Alex. 165, Timocl. 1.3 Dem.(?).

251. χάρις is common (and rather high-toned) in Greek for sexual charms or favors; in comedy the reference is always made more concrete by the chosen context and therefore more obscene than the usual euphemistic vagueness found elsewhere: in the young man's promise to his girlfriend at E 1047 f., εἰς ἑσπέραν/μεγάλην ἀποδώσω καὶ παχεῖάν σοι χάριν, "toward evening I'll give you a big, fat favor," χάρις is made to stand for phallus; similarly in Fr 202, where πλακοῦντα χαρίσιον probably means phallus.[41] At Av 1100 the χαρίτων κηπεύματα indicate cunts.[42] χάρις in the common sense of "favor" appears only at V 1347, where Philocleon orders a flute-girl: ἀπόδος τῷ πέει τῳδὶ χάριν, be nice to my cock. For the pun in ἀχάριστος (V 451) see section 289, below.

252. χειρουργία, handiwork, occurs at L 672 in a series of puns on various *schemata*. The Coryphaeus obviously meant "mischief," but λαβή a line earlier gives away the obscene double meaning of women masturbating men.

253. Compare ὑπουργία, services rendered, at Amphis 20.5 (meaning sexual intercourse; note the prefix); compare Hipponax 114a, quoted above, p. 22.

254. Euphemisms involving the idea "to lie with/beside" are very common: L 773 (an obscene parody of oracular language) and P 1330 f. (part of the hymenaeal song with which the play ends) both use κατάκειμαι in a semiserious sense. συγκατακλίνομαι (N 49) also appears in the context of the marriage-bed, where it is virtually a technical term.[43] κατάκειμαι in the scene between Kinesias and Myrrhine (L 920, 948) is used of the preparation for sexual congress rather than the act itself; the other main euphemistic term in this scene is κατακλίνειν (904, 906, 910, 918). This prominence of κατα- is easily understood when the stage action is considered: Kinesias keeps trying to get his wife to lie down. συγκαταδαρθεῖν and συγκατάκειμαι are used like a refrain in the anapests of *Ecclesiazusae*

---

41. If the reading δ᾽ ἰὼν πέμψω in line 1 is correct, as is likely. If we should read δὲ νῷν πέψω, a woman is the speaker and πλακοῦς χαρίσιος indicates the cunt, as at Pl 995–98.

42. ὃς χαρίτων μὲν ὄζει in Eup. 163 may also be a double entendre of this kind: the reference seems to be to a pathic (Callias?). Compare T 254 of Agathon's clothing, ἡδύ γ᾽ ὄζει ποσθίου, it smells sweetly of . . . cock!

43. See Dover, *Clouds*, ad loc., Hdt. 2.181.2.

(613, 614, 622, 628); συγκαθεύδουσ' ἥδομαι(E 1009) is more whorish wheedling by the old hag; compare the delicacy of the description of incest at Cratin. 279, συγκαθεύδειν τῷ πατρί. καθεύδειν παρά appears in a tone of mock-propriety in the speech of the Relation to the women (T 479) and with humorous incongruity in the mouth of the barbarian archer (T 1193). The phrase is one of the standard ones used to describe the new sexual status quo in *Ecclesiazusae* (700,894, 938,1039, 1051). With μετά it appears in a chorus at the close of *Acharnians* (1147), where it is used to set up an obscene punch-line (1149); so also κοιμᾶσθαι παρά at E 723 f., κοιμᾶσθαι μετά at Timocl. 22.1 f.[44]

255. To lie side by side with a woman: Antiph. 192. 4 f.: βράττειν[45] τε γεννικῶς παρασκευάζεται πλευρὰν μετ' αὐτῶν, he gets ready manfully to shake sides with them.

256. Bodily cooperation between sex partners in *Lysistrata* is indicated by such euphemisms as προσεῖναι (L 153, 214), συμφέρειν (L 166), πείθεσθαι (L 223), παρέχειν (L 162, 227, 362), ὑπέχειν (L 841).

257. The common Aristophanic term for refusing one's favors is ἀπόμνυμι (Eq 424, N 1232, Av 705, L 903). We find also θρύπτεσθαι (facetiously) at Eq 1163, ἀπέχομαι (L 153), ἀπεῖπον (L 165), ἀποκαθεύδειν(Eup. 399), and ἀναίνεσθαι (Pl Com 181). Understandably enough, there is not much refusal in comedy.

Nautical Terminology

258. Nautical metaphors for sexual congress, very popular in comedy, appear as early as Alcman,[46] Sicilian comedy,[47] and Theognis.[48] To illustrate the intricacy with which these metaphors could be contrived, consider the following effort by Epicrates (10):

> κατάβαλλε τἀκάτια, τὰ κυμβία,
> αἴρου τὰ μείζω, κεὐθὺ τοῦ καρχησίου
> ἄνελκε τὴν γραῦν, τὴν νέαν δ' ἐπουρίσας
> πλήρωσον, εὐτρεπῆ τε τὸν κοντὸν ποιοῦ
> καὶ τοὺς κάλως ἔκλυε καὶ χάλα πόδα.[49]

44. Cf. also μονοκοιτοῦμεν (of unmarried women) at L 592; συγκοίτας at Fr 862 (cf. CA 1203.7, *AP* 5.151, 190, 195); σύνευνος at E 953, The opposite notion appears at Eup. 399, ἀποκαθεύδειν.

45. βράττειν Kock; τάττειν AC.

46. *Fr.* 109D, *POxy.* 2307, *Fr.* 14II.13 f.

47. Cf. ἄγκυρα (Epich. 182, Sophr. 52 Olivieri).

48. 457 ff., imitated closely by Theophil. 6.

49. τἀκάτια = wine-cups/skiffs (Athen. 15.782F); likewise καρχησίου (*LSJ* s.v. I). γραῦν = old lady/scum on wine (Arist. *GA* 743b7; compare the wretched puns at Pl

1. τὰ κύμβια Kaibel/Meineke: καὶ κυλίκια CE
3. δ᾽ Causabon: τ᾽ CE

In our survey it will be convenient to treat first those metaphors which involve men sailing women (or other men: sections 259–73), then those which involve women sailing men (sections 274–78).

259. δικωπεῖν ἀμφοτέρας (E 1091), to ply two sculls at once (with the phallic oar), is used of a young man who must service two hags simultaneously; the metaphor seems to be an Aristophanic invention.

260. Similar is ἐλαύνειν, to drive a ship, as at E 37 ff.,

> ὁ γὰρ ἀνήρ, ὦ φιλτάτη,
> Σαλαμίνιος γάρ ἐστιν ᾧ ξύνειμ᾽ ἐγώ,
> τὴν νύχθ᾽ ὅλην ἤλαυνέ μ᾽ ἐν τοῖς στρώμασιν.

[My husband, dear girl—for I'm married to a Salaminian—sailed me all night long in the bedclothes.]

Compare Pl Com 3.4 on Aphrodite and Dionysus, ἡ μὲν ἐλαυνομένη λαθρίοις ἐρετμοῖς, ὁ δ᾽ ἐλαύνων, she's driven by secret oar-thrusts; he's doing the thrusting.[50] The image is obviously from sexual movements conceived as rowing motions. E 109, where the women proclaim that they neither run nor row ships (ἐλαύνομεν), *may* contain another such double entendre.

261. κατελαύνειν, on the other hand, is probably not nautical, although Taillardat (chap. 2, n. 107, above), p. 101, lists it as equivalent to ἐλαύνειν. Its use at P 711 and E 1082 betrays no specific nautical coloration, nor does it at Theocr. 5.116, where only the idea of penetration is prominent. In fact, it is driving and pushing down which lies behind the metaphor (cf. Fr 205, the pushing of a spatula into a jar). The double entendre ὄρχον ἐλάσαι at A 995 (section 75, above) is agricultural and based on the notion of driving down into. ἐξελαύνειν, an obscene metaphor at Antiphanes 300, probably derives from metallurgy (see *LSJ* s.v. III).

262. ἐπιβατεύειν, to serve as a marine or embark on a ship (Hdt. 7.96, Th. 3.95), is used in a pederastic joke at R 48, where Dionysus says that he was "in service with Cleisthenes" (ἐπεβάτευον Κλεισθένει).[51]

1205 f.). With ἐπουρίσας compare R 95. πλήρωσον plays on the meaning "fill up (sexually)" (*LSJ* s.v. III.2, πίμπλημι at Xenarch. 1.10, καταμεστοῦν at Pherecr. 145.28). For κοντός see section 55, above. For τοὺς κάλως ἔκλυε compare Eq 756 and schol., Eur. *Med.* 278. For χάλα πόδα cf. *LSJ* s.v. χαλάω I.6 and section 104, above, section 342, below.

50. For λάθριος cf. *AP* 6.300.1, and compare ἐρέσσειν at *AP* 5.54.4, 204.2, and ἐρετμόν in Hsch.

51. See the schol. and compare ἀναβαίνειν and ἐγκολ ηβάζειν (sections 226 f., above),

263. ναυμαχεῖν appears in the abusive chorus on Callias in R 430; he is said to have κύσθου λεοντῆν ναυμαχεῖν ἐνημμένον. This is the reading of the MSS, translated by van Daele, "Callias . . . s'est mis une vulve en guise de peau de lion pour livrer un combat naval." But better sense and more humor can be achieved by reading κύσθῳ with Bothe and Radermacher.[52] κύσθῳ ναυμαχεῖν would then mean βινεῖν as an image like δικωπεῖν and ἐλαύνειν,[53] although more fantastic, with its suggestion of mighty vessels circling and colliding. The lionskin further suggests the traditional role of Heracles, trivialized by contrast with the sexual "combats" the debauched Callias wages.[54] ναυμαχεῖν καὶ πλεῖν at L 675 is probably another double entendre.

264. The image appears in slightly tamer form in ναύκληρος, a whore's customer at Anaxil. 22.19. Cf. ναύαρχος, referring to the famous amateur erotologist Cydias (Pl. *Charm.* 155d), at Eub. 67.11.

265. We may compare the hetaera-name Nausimache (T 804 and schol.), who battered Charminus the sea-fighter (Th. 8.42).

266. ἀργοναύτης in Fr 544.2 makes the same joke, in what is probably a pederastic context: τίς δ' ἐστιν οὑγγὺς κατακλινεὶς τῆς ὀσφύος/ἐπὶ τῶν κοχωνῶν, ἀργοναύτης οὑτοσί. The corrupt state of these lines makes it difficult to tell exactly what the "argonaut" is doing or having done to him; presumably he is the active partner, sailing the ship's "stern" (κοχ-ῶναι): "Who is this pale sailor, hard by your loins, reclining against your stern?" The clearly anal nature of the act described would seem to rule out a heterosexual context.[55] There is a pun on ἀργός, white/pale: paleness is a notorious characteristic of homosexuals (see section 465, below).[56]

267. Artemisia is a sea-fighter at L 675 and T 1200, where Euripides playfully calls himself Artemisia as a joke on the archer.

268. The female triremes who talk together at Eq 1300 ff. use suggestive sexual imagery to express their fear that Hyperbolus will soon, 'board" them, an act of sexual aggression often associated in this play with Cleon.[57]

269. πλωτήρ, passenger (on a sexual voyage), at E 1087 ἕλκοντε τοὺς

ἐπιβαίνειν (Arist. *HA* 539ᵇ26, 547ᵃ20, Luc. *Asin.* 27, Horap. 1.46, 2.78), ἐπιβήτωρ (*Od.* 11.131; of animals, Theoc. 25.128).

52. See L. Radermacher in *SB* (Vienna) 198 (1923): 205, n. 4 and Taillardat (chap 4, n. 107, above), p. 102.

53. See section 48, above.

54. Compare Nicostratus as described by D. S. 16.44.

55. Kock's incorrect belief that Triballus is actually Alcibiades led him to suppose that the pale sailor rides the courtesan, Theodote (Athen. 12. 534D, 535C).

56. Compare Martial's similar pun on ἀργός (lazy): non nautas puto vos, sed Argonautas (3.67.10).

57. See the extended comparison of a hetaera to a ship in *AP* 9.416.

πλωτῆρας ἄν ἀπεκναίετε, by tugging your passengers about, you would grind them up thoroughly, derives its obscene meaning from its context in a passage made up primarily of nautical puns on the sex act: for ἕλκω see n. 25, above; for ἀποκναίειν see sections 322 f., below.

270. πλεῖν, to sail, usually = βινεῖν and thus is used of the male sailing the female: P 341, L 411, 675, E 1087 (see section 269, above), 1106 (ἐμπλέων). ἀποπλευστέα (Fr 142), however, seems to be used of the bride's imminent sailing of the bridegroom (see section 274, below).

271. συννήχεσθαι, to swim along with, refers to coital motion and appears to be an Aristophanic invention: the cry of a handsome young man doomed to suffer while servicing ugly women (E 1104), τοιούτοις θηρίοις συννήξομαι; appears in a passage whose dominant sexual imagery is nautical.

272. στύομαι τριέμβολον, to stand as gigantically erect as three ships' beaks (or a three-beaked ship), is primarily a nautical metaphor at Av 1256 (section 48, above), but as the schol. indicates in the gloss (πολλάκις ἐμβαλεῖν δυνάμενον), there is also a strong feeling of "ramming [it] in."

273. ὑποπιττοῦν, to smear underneath with pitch (Pl 1093; see section 183, above), is a metaphor from shipbuilding; the prefix gives this term its particularly obscene tone. The reference is to the female secreta.[58] Cf. E 1109, Cratin. 189 (καταπισσοῦν).

274. The *schema* in which the woman bestrides the man as if riding or sailing him forms the basis for many jokes in comedy. The great popularity of this humor may derive from the adventuresome and somewhat naughty character which this mode of sexual congress seems to have possessed. It seems to be associated only with shameless housewives and professional sex partners (whether prostitutes or figures of sexual fun like Theoria in *Peace;* for a possible exception, see section 270, above). We note the angry reaction the servant in *Wasps* gets when he asks a prostitute to perform this act (500 ff.), and its attribution to Phaedra, the very type of the *devergondée*.[59]

275. The most popular image in this kind of joke is that of the κέλης, a small, fast yacht run by a single bank of oars,[60] or a fast riding-horse (*LSJ* s.v. I). The image is particularly clear in the passage where Lysistrata complains that no women from the seaboard or from Salamis have come to her meeting, and Cleonice replies, ἀλλ᾽ ἐκεῖναί γ᾽ οἶδ᾽ ὅτι/ἐπὶ τῶν κελή-

---

58. For πιττοῦν, meaning to smear gummy substances on the body, see Theopomp. Hist. 195, Luc. *Demon.* 50. καταπιττοῦν at E 1109 and Cratin. 189 is used without specific nautical coloration.

59. T 153; cf. T 497, 547, R 1043.

60. Hdt. 8.94, Th. 4.9.8.

των διαβεβήκασ' ὄρθριαι, "I know that these women came early, *mounted on their yachts*" (59 f). The obscenity here is emphasized by the use for the normal βεβήκασιν of διαβεβήκασιν, to mount or bestride with the legs apart.[61] References to Salamis often appear in the context of *mulier superior* (the woman on top): Av 1204, L 411, E 38 (a wife complains that her Salaminian husband sails her all night).[62]

276. References to horsemanship frequently merge with the κέλης-image: at P 900 the sex act takes the metaphor of the ἱπποδραμία:[63] ἵνα δὴ κέλης κέλητα παρακελητιεῖ. Compare the lust-god ἥρως Κέλης at Pl Com 174.18.

277. Horse references by themselves invariably indicate this mode: as the men's chorus remarks at L 676 f., ἢν δ' ἐφ' ἱππικὴν τράπωνται, διαγράφω τοὺς ἱππέας·/ἱππικώτατον γάρ ἐστι χρῆμα κἄποχον γυνή, but if they turn to horsemanship, I'll enlist the Knights: for a woman is a very horsey creature and knows well how to mount.[64] Note the λευκὸς ἵππος, white horse, (phallus) at L 191 f.,[65] the libertine Smoeus' ἱππικὴ στολή at E 846 (with schol.), the "tyranny of Hippias," which the prostitute at V 502 accuses her client of trying to establish (this joke reappears at L 619), Pherecrates' ἱπποσέλινα (131.4), Eupolis' τὴν ἱππικήν (268), and the visitor to a whorehouse who is called an ἱππεύς, horseman (Anaxil. 22.10). The same joke lies behind the *redende Namen* Hippe (Athen. 13.583AB), Hippobinus (R 429),[66] Hippocleides (Fr 703), and Hippopornos.[67] The pathic sons of Teisamenus and Phaenippus at A 603 are called πανουργιππαρχίδαι, those who engage in shameless mounting and riding.

278. At L 139, οὐδὲν γάρ ἐσμεν πλὴν Ποσειδῶν καὶ σκάφη, looks like a

61. Cf. Eq 77, Xen. *Eq.* 7.5. Apart from the position implied, κέλης may here be a double entendre for the phallus itself: cf. Hsch. s.v. = τὸ μέρος. For κέλης meaning cunt see section 186, above.

62. Intercourse at night was the usual reference in comedy: N 1069, P 966, L 409, T 204, E 1047, Pl 998, 1031, 1201, Frs 13, 202, Xenarch. Com. 4.17. But frequently we hear of intercourse at noon (V 500, P 290, L 418) and in the morning (A 256, V 1055, L 17, 60, 966, 1089, E 20, 312, 469 ff.).

63. Cf. Hdt. 7.86, Pl. *Lys.* 205.

64. Compare Macho at Athen. 13.581D, καθιππάσθαι ὑπ' αὐτῆς πεντάκις, to be ridden by her five times.

65. Cf. Herod, 7.113, Luc. *Scyth.* 2, Arist. *HA* 6.18, Ael *NA* 4.11, and ἀργοναύτης (Fr 544.2: see n. 61, above).

66. The scholiast maintains that ἱππο- here means "large" or "excessive" and that the name is equivalent to ἱππόπορνος and πορνομανής.

67. For this *schema* elsewhere see Anacreon 88D³, Macho at Athen. 13.577D, AP 5.55, 202, 203. In Latin cf. Hor. *Sat.* 2.7.49, Ov. *AAm.* 3.777 ff., Mart. 11.104.13 f. For *natare* see Housman (n. 12, above), pp. 411 f., and compare συννήχεσθαι (section 271, above). See also the double entendre at L 773.

proverbial expression (cf. l. 138) given an obscene twist. On the first level the reference is to Poseidon and Tyro, who exposed her children by that union in a skiff (Apollod. 1.9.8); obscenely it means, we are good for nothing but childbearing and τὸ κελητίζειν.

Agricultural Terminology

279. Sexual metaphors from agriculture are extremely common in Greek in both comic and serious writing; in chapter 1 we discussed the fine but firm line that separates the obscene from the noble in this class. The reader may wish to examine the brief list compiled by Taillardat (chap. 4, n. 107, above), p. 101 nn. 1–2, of some of the most common serious agricultural metaphors, for comparison with the comic ones in this category.[68]

280. ἀλοᾶν, to thresh, is usually taken to mean "smite" or "thrash" at R 149, where among the sinners swimming in the infernal dung-river is a man who μητέρ' ἠλόησεν. But a reference to the sin of mother-beating would virtually duplicate the sin of father-beating mentioned in the same line. In this enumeration of six heinous offenses we might expect more variation. It is therefore probable that ἠλόησεν here might mean ἐβίνησεν, although that usage is not attested elsewhere. We note that Aeschylus later in the play (l. 1194) specifically condemns incest with one's mother.

283. βωλοκοπεῖν, to break up clods before the sowing,[69] appears in Fr 57 Dem., καλῶς με βεβωλοκόπησεν, he broke up my clods well. The same metaphor is found in an epigram from Tyrrheum dedicated to Pan.[70]

284. γεωργεῖν at L 1173, ἤδη γεωργεῖν γυμνὸς ἀποδὺς βούλομαι, I'm all prepared to strip down and do the ploughing, is given its sexual meaning by the surrounding geographical double entendres; it is also intended to set up the pederastic pun on κοπραγωγεῖν (bugger), which follows in the next line and satirizes the comic predilections of the Spartans.

285. καταγιγαρτίζειν appears in a choral fantasy of rape in the fields (A 275) and surely means "de-pit,"[71] hence deflower. The scholiast's alternative gloss, καταθλῖψαι ("pressurer le raison pour en faire du marc"),[72] seems implausible.

286. Compare κοκκίζειν (Fr 610), which has the same image: Kock

---

68. The reader is referred to the sections on agricultural terminology in chap. 4.

69. Schol. P 566, 1148.

70. Ἀρχ. Δελτ. 2 *App.* 47. See now Men. *Dysc.* 541f.

71. γίγαρτον, grape-stone (of unripe grapes), refers to virginity (and youthfulness), as in *PLond. ined.* 1821.

72. See Taillardat (n. 52, above), p. 100.

translates, "nondum maturae puellae vim paras."[73]

287. τρυγᾶν, to gather fruit and crops, appears of Trygaeus and Opora, fittingly enough, in the hymenaeal song at P 1339; τρυγήσομεν αὐτήν, a marvelous example of the thematic and symbolic use of obscene double entendre.

288. λέπειν, to peel off rind or husk, means to cause the foreskin to recede after inciting erection. Thus an aroused woman at L 736 mentions that her mallow-stalk (section 39, above) lies at home "unscutched" (ἄλοπον), that is, she wishes to go home and entice her husband into sexual congress by arousing him.

289. Compare the similar verb ἀποδέρειν, to flay or skin, used obscenely at L 739 and 953, where Kinesias complains "My wife enticed me and aroused me and departed leaving me erect (ἀποδείρασ')." The verb ἐκδέρειν at V 450 (see the imitation by Theocr. 5.116 f.) has the same meaning with reference to homosexual rape:[74]

> οὐδ᾿ ἀναμνησθεὶς ὅθ᾿ εὑρὼν τοὺς βότρυς κλέπτοντά σε
> προσαγαγὼν πρὸς τὴν ἐλάαν ἐξέδειρ᾿ εὖ κἀνδρικῶς,
> ὥστε σε ζηλωτὸν εἶναι; σὺ δ᾿ ἀχάριστος ἦσθ᾿ ἄρα.

[And don't you remember when I caught you stealing grapes and led you over to the olive tree where I *flayed* you right manfully, so that you were truly enviable? But of course you weren't at all charming about it!]

(ἀχάριστος is a further pun: see section 251, above.) For δέρειν simplex see L 158, Fr 320.5, Timocl. 2. 1 Dem. (?).

290. There is reason to suppose that this enticed erection and peeling back the foreskin, when accomplished by prostitutes or flute-girls, is done preparatory to fellatio. λέπει at Eup. 427 is glossed by Photius as meaning κατεσθίει (cf. Eup. 255), and λέπεσθε at Alex. 49.3 clearly means "get the penis ready for fellatio":[75]

> τοὖφον[76] λαβοῦσαι τοῦτο τἀπεσταλμένον
> σκευάζετ᾿, εὐωχεῖσθε, προπόσεις πίνετε,
> λέπεσθε, ματτυάζετε.

73. Compare Hor. C. 2.5.10, appositely cited by Kock. For κόκκος meaning cunt, see section 123, above.

74. See Willems (chap. 4, n. 8, above), 1: 90.

75. See ματτυολοιχός at N 451 (fellator: cf. Amm. Marc. 15.5.4). The image is of eating dessert, the last course at a banquet (Nicostr. 8, 17). Compare κωμῳδολοιχεῖν at V 1318 (scurriliter suppalpare diviti cuique, Blaydes); see Iungius (chap. 4, n. 34. above), pp. 208 f.

76. See section 102 and compare section 182, above.

[Get hold of these dainties, girls—you know how you must do it—and feast away, drink off to us, peel us back, eat your treat!]

The Lat. *glubere* (= λέπειν) seems to imply the same act: in Catullus 58.4, Lesbia would clearly be doing some specific sexual act in the alleyways, not merely "fleecing" her customers or fiddling with their prepuces; that she is in fact performing fellatio is argued cogently by F. Lenz.[77] Compare also Aus. *Epigr.* 71.7 *deglubit fellat molitur per utramque cavernam*: the sequence here is the same as in the passage from Alexis. See further section 385, below.

291. Someone who is in the state of erection publicly is considered indecent: at Mnesim. 4.18, λέπεται κόρδαξ implies an obscene dance in which masturbation (note middle voice) is featured.[78] As Athenaeus remarks,[79] τῷ δὲ λέπεσθαι χρῶνται οἱ Ἀθηναῖοι ἐπ' ἀσελγοῦς καὶ φορτικῆς δι' ἀφροδισίων ἡδονῆς, the Athenians used λέπεσθαι for wanton and vulgar sexual pleasures.

292. Words for "digging" are a popular source of double entendres.[80] ὀρύττειν seems to have been much used in this sense: at P 372 ταύτην ἀνορύττων is a pun on the proper sense, "dig up"; the opposite, κατορώρυχεν, to dig into the earth, is used autobiographically by the ravished Lady Music at Pherecr. 145.19. At P 898 ὀρύττειν is actually a wrestling metaphor meaning to "gouge" a tender area;[81] it is used again in a pederastic joke at Av 442 and at N 714, where διορύττουσιν refers to Corinthian bedbugs (κόρεις) digging a trench in Strepsiades' πρωκτός (see *LSJ* s.v. I.1): in the Phrontisterion even the bedbugs are shameless.

293. σκαλεύειν, to stir up or poke,[82] appears at P 440, ἔχονθ' ἑταίραν καὶ σκαλεύοντ' ἄνθρακας, having a party-girl and poking her hot coals. At A 1014 τὸ πῦρ ὑποσκάλευε adds an additional obscene touch by the use of the prefix; the word is found nowhere else.

294. σκαλαθύρειν at E 611 is surely an Aristophanic invention made up of σκάλλειν and θύρα, to poke/hoe the cunt.

295. διαλέγειν, in addition to its usual meanings, seems also to have meant "dig open" or "pick open" in a sexual, though not specifically agricultural, sense.[83] At L 720 Lysistrata remarks of a would-be escapee from her ranks, τὴν μέν γε πρώτην διαλέγουσαν τὴν ὀπὴν κατέλαβον, "I

77. In "Catulliana," *RCCM* 5 (1963): 62 ff.
78. Compare ἀποσκολύπτειν in Archil. 39, S. *Fr.* 423, Hsch.
79. 15.663B. Cf. also Eust. 1752.2.
80. Compare Latin *fodere* (Mart. 7.102, *Priap.* 53), *effodere* (Arn. 4.131).
81. Antiph. 119, Philostr. *VA* 8.25.
82. See Frisk (n. 1, above), s.v. σκάλλω.
83. Compare ὀπὴ . . . διαλέξαι at V 350 (with no sexual meaning).

caught the first woman digging at a/her hole." The schol. rightly glosses, διορύττουσαν· κακεμφάτως, as does Hsch. s.v. διαλέξαι· διορύξαι. The basic notion lies in the root *leg- with its sense of selection or discrimination; English "pick" still has something of the ambiguity of λέγειν and the Lat. *lego*. Wilamowitz, *Lysistrate*, ad loc., objects to all this: "es ist 'auseinander-lesen'; sie erweitert also das Loch, indem sie die Steinbrocken herausliest, die es verstopfen." But by ignoring Hesychius' διορύξαι for the alternative gloss ἀνακαθαίρειν, he serves only to leach all the humor from the joke (and there *must* be a joke here) without offering either a reasonable defense of his explanation or an alternative source of humor.

Metaphors from Sport

296. Wrestling and fighting imagery naturally suits itself to descriptions of sexual congress; there is a rich literature of such erotic combats in the classical authors, especially the Greeks, since the Romans preferred the battlefield to the palaestra as a source of comparisons. Thus we find sexual imagery from single combat everywhere in the pages of the Greek epigrammatists, elegiac poets, novelists, and erotic epistolographers. For one good example, compare Lucius and Palaestra in Luc. *Asin.* 11 ff. with the same scene as described by Apuleius, *Met.* 2.16 ff., where the wrestling metaphors of the Greek have been changed to those of the battlefield.[84]

297. Nevertheless, Aristophanes hardly ever uses this kind of metaphor. In fact, there is only one instance of an erotic image from the palaestra (E 965 f.), unless we admit P 899 as a borderline case. All of Aristophanes' other sport-images are contained in Trygaeus' speech at P 894 ff., a wild mélange of metaphors behind which it is impossible to discern the actual act of love. Aristophanes was hardly interested in depicting the kind of amatory clichés so popular in later poetry and erotic prose. As in this speech from *Peace* (894 ff.) he strove in his obscenity for full-blooded and extravagant humor, not suggestive appeals to sexual fantasy:

> ἔπειτ' ἀγῶνά γ' εὐθὺς ἐξέσται ποεῖν
> ταύτην ἔχουσιν αὔριον καλὸν πάνυ,
> ἐπὶ γῆς παλαίειν, τετραποδηδὸν ἑστάναι,
> πλαγίαν καταβάλλειν, εἰς γόνατα κύβδ' ἱστάναι,
> καὶ παγκράτιόν γ' ὑπαλειψαμένοις νεανικῶς
> παίειν, ὀρύττειν, πὺξ ὁμοῦ καὶ τῷ πέει·
> τρίτῃ δὲ μετὰ ταῦθ' ἱπποδρομίαν ἄξετε,

84. See further K. Preston, *Studies in the Diction of the Sermo Amatorius in Roman Comedy* (University of Chicago Libraries, 1916), pp. 51 ff.

ἵνα δὴ κέλης κέλητα παρακελητιεῖ,
ἅρματα δ' ἐπ' ἀλλήλοισιν ἀνατετραμμένα
φυσῶντα καὶ πνέοντα προσκινήσεται·
ἕτεροι δὲ κείσονταί γ' ἀπεψωλημένοι
περὶ ταῖσι καμπαῖς ἡνίοχοι πεπτωκότες.[85]

[Then tomorrow you can all straightaway celebrate a very pretty athletic contest, now that you have her: *wrestle* her on the ground, *get on all fours, throw her down on the flank,* push her *to her knees, bent over,* then, *oiled up* for the pancration, *strike* at her manfully and *dig* her with fist and—*cock*! On the third day, you shall have a *horse-race,* and *horse* will *ride side-by-side* with *horse,* and the *chariots,* all overturned in a heap, will *mingle together* puffing and panting. Others will *lie down,* their *foreskins pulled back:* the drivers, having *fallen* about the *turning-posts.*]

Hitting and Piercing

Many comic metaphors for sexual congress are quite violent and draw on language usually reserved for physical assault and abuse. In this respect Greek sexual slang is similar to English slang, which boasts such popular terms for intercourse as *bang, poke,* and *screw.*

298. ἀναπείρειν (A 1007) is used in the meaning "to pierce on a spit"; the prefix adds a further obscene feeling, "upwards."

299. ἀναπηγνύναι, to fix on a spit, appears to mean penetrate sexually at E 843 λαγῷ' (q.v.) ἀναπηγνύασι.

300. For βαλανεύειν see section 41, above.

301. Verbs in –βάλλειν are favorites of Aristophanes. ἐπιβάλλειν, to thrust something upon someone or affix (to), appears in the sense of "rape" at V 768 f. and Av 1215 ff. Compare στρόβιλον ἐμβαλών τινα at Pherecr. 145.14 (the whirling top/shaft = "musical term" = phallus); for the pun cf. Pl Com 254. καταβάλλειν, which can mean "ejaculate" in technical prose,[86] is used by Aristophanes to mean "strike downwards on a supine woman": πλαγίαν καταβάλλειν (P 896). At A 275 καταβαλόντα seems to mean "throw the girl to the ground preparatory to rape." At A 994 προσβαλεῖν, to assault violently, is used of the predicted gang-rape of Diallage.[87]

85. For the precise meaning of the various obscene words and phrases (underlined) in this passage, the reader may consult the index verborum.

86. Men. *Georg.* 37, Epicur. *Nat.* 908, Sor. 1.33.

87. See section 48, above, and compare the nickname of Pythodelus (an ἄσωτος), ὁ Βαλλίων (Axionic. 1); βαλλίον means phallus at Hdt. 6.69.

302. For διαπατταλεύειν see section 61, above.

303. ἐρείδειν, to push hard/thrust against, occurs, in the active, of men (E 616, Fr 74, 695; the latter is quoted above, section 241) and, in the passive, of women (T 488). There is an obscene pun on this term at T 204, ἔργα νυκτερείσια(*hapax legomenon*), a surprise for νυκτερήσια, nightly.

304. For κεντεῖν, see section 359, below.

305. κρούειν, bang or beat: when the young man at E 989 announces that he must knock (κρουστέον) at the young girl's door, the old hag replies, ὅταν γε κρούσῃς τὴν ἐμὴν πρῶτον θύραν, "You mean, when you've knocked at *my* door first," punning on θύρα = cunt. The same joke with reference to pederasty is made by Blepyrus at E 316 f., when he personifies his constipated feces as an ἀνὴρ Κόπρειος who "bangs at my doorway" (τὴν θύραν κρούων). Similarly, the speaker discussed by the two effeminate boys at Eq 1379 is κρουστικός, "striking," that is, a buggerer. At E 257 κρούματα means modes of sexual congress. κρούειν in its obscene sense was apparently common elsewhere in comedy.[88]

306. Aristophanes uses κρούειν in compounds for additional comic effect: at E 1017 f. προκρούειν means "bang in advance," a pseudo-technical obscenity designed to fit the peculiar sexual regulations put into effect by the women. The name of the fabled robber, Procrustes, who stretched (προκρούειν, cf. D.S. 59.57) his victims on a bed, puns on the obscene meaning in the joke made by the desperate young man at E 1021: he is about to suffer, at the hands of the three hags, a "procrustean" torture in both senses of the word. ὑποκρούειν, usually "interrupt," is made to mean "bang below" at E 618.

307. κυκᾶν, to stir up/churn, appears in the description of cunnilingus at Eq 1286 (see section 164, above).

308. παίειν, smite, appears at A 835, P 874, 898.

309. πατάσσειν, strike, seems to indicate "hitting the mark" or, to use a current expression, "scoring" sexually at CA 798 αὐτὸ ἐπάταξεν.

310. ῥιπτάζειν, to toss something about, is undoubtedly an ad hoc pun at L 26 ff.: the double sense is given it, with help from the dirty-minded βωμολόχος-figure, Cleonice, by the context of sleepless nights with much tossing about in bed over a πρᾶγμα (q.v.).

311. σπαθᾶν is an ad hoc pun at N 53–55, at the end of the rustic Strepsiades' agonized speech about the sexual differences between his city-bred and sophisticated wife and himself:

οὐ μὴν ἐρῶ γ' ὡς ἀργὸς ἦν, ἀλλ' ἐσπάθα.

88. Eup. 184, *AP* 5.99, 242, *AB* 101.26. Compare διακροτεῖν at Eur. *Cyc.* 180 and the inscription from Amorgos (*IG* 12[7].414) Ἐρασίς μ' ἐκρότει.

ἐγὼ δ' ἂν αὐτῇ θοἰμάτιον δεικνὺς τοδί
πρόφασιν ἔφασκον, ὦ γύναι, λίαν σπαθᾷς.

(see p. 73) σπαθᾶν is a term from weaving which properly means to strike
the woof with a σπάθη, a broad wooden blade; its figurative meaning is to
squander money, as at D. 19.43. Here Strepsiades' pun means (1) "holding up my shirt, I took occasion to reprimand my wife on her spendthrift
ways," and (2) "Holding up my nightshirt as a defense, I said, woman,
you hit too hard [in coitus] or, you are squandering my reserve of sexual
energy."[89]

312. For πελεκᾶν see section 62, above.

313. σποδεῖν, pound or crush, appears to have been common in comedy.[90] We find it in the passive voice at T 492, in the crude and offensive
speech of the Relation on the vices of women, to refer to women who are
habitually "pounded over" by slaves and mule-drivers. All the other occurrences are from *Ecclesiazusae* and appear to have an equally coarse tone:
at 908, 942, and 1016 the word appears in curses made by the old hag in
reviling her younger rival. At 939 διασποδῆσαι[91] is used to contrast the
ugly job of making love to an old woman with the pleasure of doing so with
a young girl, expressed by the gentle phrase, παρὰ τῇ νέᾳ καθεύδειν (938).
The sentiment expressed at E 112 f., where σποδεῖσθαι is used in a pederastic sense, is one with which the Sausage-Seller of *Knights* would
have agreed: λέγουσι γὰρ καὶ τῶν νεανίσκων ὅσοι/πλεῖστα σποδοῦνται,
δεινοτάτους εἶναι λέγειν, for they say that those young men who are
most frequently banged turn out to be the cleverest speakers.

314. τύπτειν certainly seems to have had a similar double sense (strike/
rape) at L 162, where Lysistrata addresses the women on how to handle
their husbands during the sex-strike: Κλ. ἐὰν δὲ τύπτωσιν; Λυ. παρέχειν
χρὴ κακὰ κακῶς, [*Cl:* And if they sock it to us? *Ly:* Then we must submit
in the way least pleasing to them]. Probably we should consider Pl 1015 a
similar joke: the old lady complains that whenever her jealous boyfriend
saw someone looking at her in public, ἐτυπτόμην διὰ τοῦθ' ὅλην τὴν
ἡμέραν, "I was banged for that the whole day through." At any rate,
such comic coinages as μοιχοτύπη (CA 1081), χαμαιτυπεῖν (D. Chrys.
33.60), χαμαιτυπεῖον,[92] χαμαιτύπη,[93] and χαμαιτυπία (Alciphr. 3.64)
attest to the popular slang meaning of this term.

89. Dover, *Clouds,* ad loc., misses the joke by assuming that ἐσπάθα in line 53 must be
the obscenity if any obscenity is present. He is correct in taking ἐσπάθα as a "lead" for the
joke in 55.

90. Cf. Hsch. s.v., Apollod. Car. 5.13, Luc. *Catapl.* 12, *CA* 1352 (σποδησιλαύρα =
πόρνη).

91. See Hsch. s.v. διεσποδημένη.

92. Phld. *Rh.* 2.281S, *Ph.* 2.228, Luc. *DMort.* 10.11.

93. Timocl. 22.2, Men 879, *Sam.* 133.

315. For κατατριακοντουτίσαι (Eq 1391), a play on the τριακοντούτιδες σπονδαί (personified by courtesans), see sections 49 and 55, above. The word puns on τρία and κοντός.[94]

316. Compare καταπελτάζειν: (1) to attack with infantry and (2) to thrust down upon with the πέλτη (phallus: see section 65, above). This double entendre is used at A 160 of the lecherous Odomantian army, which is about to attack/ravish the "Boeotian Plain" (see section 136, above).[95]

Miscellaneous

317. αἴρειν τὰ σκέλη refers to a common mode of sexual intercourse that seems to be almost de rigueur for women in lovemaking: L 229, part of the women's oath of abstention, includes the promise that one must never stretch the sandals toward the roof. Compare the joke at E 265, where a woman says εἰθισμέναι γάρ ἐσμεν αἴρειν τὰ σκέλη: "We women must remember that when one votes in Council one holds up the hand, not the legs." αἴρειν used of men indicates the male's readying the female for penetration: cf. Av 1254, ἀνατείνας τὼ σκέλει διαμηριῶ, and L 797/799,[96] βούλομαί σε γραῦ κύσαι—/κἀνατείνας λακτίσαι. P 889 f. is similar,[97] ὥστ' εὐθέως ἄραντας ὑμᾶς τὼ σκέλει/ταύτης μετεώρω κᾆτ' ἀγαγεῖν ἀνάρρυσιν. Cf also A 274, E 261. For other comic uses of the theme of raised legs, see Eup. 47, 50, 77.4.[98]

317a. A variant on this theme is the joke of Eup. 161.3, who speaks of γυναῖκες εἰλίποδες, girls with twining legs, playing on the Homeric phrase. See Suda. s.v. μυσάχνη· ἐκ τῆς εἰλήσεως τῶν ποδῶν κατὰ τὴν μῖξιν (see also Hsch. s.v.).

318. ἀνεγείρειν at Av 208 means "rouse (the cunt) sexually" (see section 190, above).

319. βλιμάζειν is equivalent to English "feel up"; that is, to make sexual advances preparatory to intercourse.[99] This meaning is standard in

94. Not on ἀκοντίζειν, as is maintained by *LSJ*: this word is never found with an obscene meaning.

95. For πέλτη see Hsch., Suda, Xen. *An.* 1.10.12; for πεδίον see section 136, above.

96. λακτίσαι here is a surprise for some word meaning βινεῖν. Blaydes, ad loc., thinks λακτίζειν is used obscenely, citing T 509, but no case can be made for that interpretation. The old men are in an assaultive, not an amorous mood.

97. In the last line there is a play on the celebration of the Anarrhysis (the second day of Apaturia) and ἀνάρρυσις, used of genital *secreta*.

98. Note also the οἰκία . . . τὰ σκέλη ἠρκυῖα (brothel) at Thphr. *Ch.* 28.3, and the Latin phrase *pedem tollere* (Cic *Att.* 2.1.5, Mart. 10.81.4).

99. *EM* 200.37 τὸ τιτθολαβεῖν, ἤγουν ψηλαφᾶν τὰ στήθη καὶ τοὺς μαστοὺς καταλαμβάνειν τῇ ἀφῇ, καὶ ἅπτεσθαι τῶν ἀπορρήτων μελῶν τῶν γυναικείων καὶ διεγείρειν τὰς ἐπιθυμίας, τιτθολαβεῖν was used of palpating the breasts or grabbing at them, also of taking hold

comedy: Cratin. 302, CA 766; cf. Hp. *Epid.* 5.1, S. *Fr.* 484. *LSJ*'s definition, which follows the schol. at Av 530, "to feel hens to see if they are fat," is a misunderstanding. Peisetaerus is cataloguing the sins of mortals who abuse birds; among these examples of mistreatment are men who "feel up" birds when they sell them. Here Peisetaerus makes use of a word usually reserved for sexual encounters in order to arouse pathos in his bird audience. The point is that men degrade birds and defile them; the image is of sexual violation. The Spartan uses βλιμάδδομες, to grope/long for, at L 1164 to emphasize the double entendre τὰν Πύλον.

320. βόσκεσθαι, feed on, is used at Av 1099 in conjunction with several agricultural puns on the female organs to mean "enjoy sexually." For a possible early parallel, cf. Anacreon 60.6 ff. and 78.5 Gentili (with Gentili's notes and discussion on pp. 182 ff.).

321. δευτεριάζειν (*hapax*) is used at E 634 in the crude sense "go seconds with" a girl. The metaphor is from wine-processing: δευτέρας is the poorer wine (*Ev. Jo.* 2.10) produced by a second pressing (Poll. 6.17). Compare Chremylus' advice to the young man who has discarded his old lover (Pl 1084 f.): ὅμως δ' ἐπειδὴ καὶ τὸν οἶνον ἠξίους/πίνειν, συνεκποτέ' ἐστί σοι καὶ τὴν τρύγα, "Since you saw fit to drink the wine in its prime, you must now drink its dregs also."

322. διακναίειν, grate, is used of the notorious Ariphrades in a double entendre referring to cunnilingus in Fr 63, and in Pherecr. 145.20 of Timotheus' rape of Lady Music.[100]

323. ἀποκναίειν πλωτῆρας (see section 269, above), of the hags at E 1087, seems to mean "to wear out sexual passengers by their insatiable appetites" (for this sense of the verb, see e.g. Pl. *R.* 406a).

324. διακορεῖν appears in its proper sense of "deflower" a maiden at T 480.[101]

325. In addition, there are several double entendres based on κόρη, girl: ἐκκορεῖν, sweep out, obscenely at P 59, T 760, Alex. 98.3 (ἐκκορηθῶσιν, to be exhausted by wenching); ἐκκορίζειν, to clear of bugs (κόρεις), appears in an amusing conceit in Fr 266, τί μ', ὦ πονηρέ, μ' ἐκκορίζεις ὡσπερεὶ κλιντήριον, "Why, wicked man, do you de-bug/deflower me like an old mattress?" The same verb in Eup. 233.4 τὸν κύσθον ἐκκορίζειν

---

of women's secret places and so arousing desire. Compare Harpocr. s.v. and schol. Av 530.

100. The word is specifically condemned in *Et. Gud.* 330.52. Compare the related terms μύλλειν (Theoc. 4.58, Eust. 1885. 22) and ἀλήθειν (Herod. 2.20). Compare also Latin *permolere* (Hor. *Sat.* 1.2.35).

101. See Ephor. 164, Sor. 1.8, Luc. *DMeretr.* 11.2, *Tox.* 25, Artem. 2.65, Ael. *NH* 11.16. Compare διακόρευσις (Sor. 1.25) and διακόρησις (Sor. 1.33, schol. *Il.* 18.493).

appears to be merely a play on κόρη. That puns on κόρη might also have been used to denote homosexual penetration appears at Anacreon 3.1 f. Gentili: τρὶς κεκορημένε/Σμερδίη, "thrice deflowered Smerdias!"

326. διαπετάννύναι, to spread (out), has a double meaning in the interchange at L 729 ff. between Lysistrata and a would-be deserter, whose excuse is that she must return home to "spread out her fleece on the bed."[102]

327. ἐκμιαίνεσθαι is literally "self-pollution" as used by the slaves at R 753, who mean "ejaculate happily" (schol. ἥδομαι ὡσανεὶ ἀποσπερμ-ατίζων).

328. θλίβειν, rub or chafe (compare τρίβειν, section 340, below), is used to mean chafe sexually in a series of double entendres at V 1289, where Cleon seems not only to be giving Aristophanes a hard time but buggering him as well.[103] We may compare χοιρόθλιψ, cunt-chafer, used by Bdely-cleon at V 1364 to insult his amorous old father, and πορνότριψ.[104]

329. κάμπτειν, bend or twist (in lovemaking), of forceful rape in Pherecr. 145.15, 28. Compare καμπή, any twisting or turning, used of a mode of sexual congress at P 904 (cf. Lat. *metae*) and Pherecr. 145.9 (musical "turns").

330. κορινθιάζεσθαι is synonymous in comedy with fornication because of the reputation of Corinth for wantonness and luxuriousness:[105] the saying attributed to Aristophanes (Fr 902), οὐ παντὸς ἀνδρὸς εἰς Κόρινθόν ἐσθ' ὁ πλοῦς, not every man gets to sail to Corinth, may allude to the "sailing" mode of intercourse as well as to Corinthian luxury.

331. νεβλάρεται (cod. νεβλάρετοι) at Fr 241; Phot. νεβλάραι (-ᾱ-?) = ἄσημος φωνὴ ἐπὶ τοῦ περαίνειν. Etymology unknown.

332. μολύνειν, sully/defile, was common with an abstract sexual meaning;[106] in Aristophanes it has a more literal and concrete meaning, "make filthy." At Pl 310 μολύνουσαν. . . τοὺς ἑταίρους is used of Lais' physical and moral effect on Philonides' men, and at Eq 1286 μολύνων τὴν ὑπήνην means "to besmirch with secreta" in cunnilingus. Compare in this same passage λυμαίνεσθαι, to injure/degrade (his tongue).

333. ὀρθοσταδόν means τὸ ὀρθὸν ἀφροδισιάζειν at CA 1096.

---

102. For the image see N 343 ἐρίοισιν πεταμένοισιν.

103. On the violent erotic language of this passage, see M. van der Valk in *KOMO-IDOTRAGEMATA. Studies in Honor of W. J. W. Koster* (Amsterdam, 1967), pp. 128 f.

104. Phryn. 389, Thom. Mag. p. 291R. Compare παιδότριψ and χοιρότριψ at Hdn. 1.246.26.

105. Steph. Byz. glosses, τὸ ἑταιρεῖν ἀπὸ τῶν ἐν Κορίνθῳ ἑταιρῶν. Compare Pl 149 ἑταίρας . . . Κορινθίας, Crat 273.4 τῷ Κορινθίῳ πέει (a substitution for Euripides' ξένῳ, according to Hsch. See T 404).

106. Theoc. 5.87, Isoc. 5.81, Apoc. 14.4.

334. πιέζειν, to press, is used to mean "penetrate sexually" (in a rough fashion). Thus at L 417 (see section 146, above) the word is used of the effects of a large phallus on a tender cunt, and at Eq 259 of pederastic rape, κἀποσυκάζεις πιέζων (see section 36, above). For πίεσμα at Eub. 75.11, see section 16, above.

335. For πληροῦν and πιμπλάναι, to fill up (sexually), used of the male in coitus, see n. 49, above.

336. προσουρεῖν, to urinate upon, is used at R 95 to describe the impotence and sterility of poets who are unable to produce healthy offspring (good tragedies) in their relations with Lady Tragedy; these are the opposite of the γόνιμοι ποιηταί whom Dionysus is seeking.[107]

337. The related terms σκινδακίσαι, σκινδαρεύεσθαι, σκινθαρίσαι, σκιν-θίζεσθαι (CA 1145) indicate illicit nocturnal intercourse with either sex. The etymology is uncertain but probably derives from a word implying movement: Phot. s.v. σκίνδαρον glosses προσκίνημα, s.v. σκινδάρειος glosses "a dance." Perhaps the name of the fish σκινδάριον (Alexandr. 27) is related.

338. στρέφειν, to turn about (in coitus) occurs at L 839, Pherecr. 145.15, Amphis 20.4 (στρέφοισθ' ὅλην τὴν νύκτα). See Hsch. s.v. στρέφει· διώκει, φιλοῖ, ἀποσείεται, and compare ἀπόσεισις at Poll. 4.101 (cf. Athen. 14. 629C), Hsch. s.v. φιλοῦν, AB 1.429.29, and POxy. 8.39 (Cercidas), where ἔρως Ζακωνικός is spoken of as στρέφειν ἄνω κάτω. Cf. στροφή (a musical strophe and a mode of intercourse) at Pherecr. 145.9. For διασ-τρέφειν and ἀποστρέφειν, see section 364, below. This double sense of στρέφειν appears earlier, in lyric poetry, at Anacreon 78.4 Gentili, where the poet equates horsemanship metaphorically with sexual intercourse. Anacreon's poem deserves comparison with P 894 ff. (above, p. 168).

339. τιτρώσκειν/τρώζειν, wound/penetrate sexually (Hsch. s.v. τρώζω; iamb. adesp. 53 W; A. Fr. 44), appears in a series of pederastic riddles about the anus in Eub. 107.4, 8. In the passage, τρωτός refers to the pathic, ἄτρωτος to the active pederast.

340. τρίβειν, to rub/chafe (an organ in preparation for sexual inter-course), appears in simplex and with a variety of prefixes. Simplex: V 739, 1344, P 12 (supply μάζης = anus), Eub. 108.3. With ἀνά-: A 1149, E 904. With διά-: L 943 (μύρον διατριπτικόν). With ἐν-: R 1070 (peder-astic). With ἐκ-: Eub. 96.2. With ἐπί-: P 369 (see van Daele, ad loc; Willems [n. 74, above], chap. 2, p. 28 n. 2; section 210, above), L 876, 952, 1090.[108]

---

107. For the sexual meaning of γόνιμος see J. D. Denniston, "Technical Terms In Aristophanes," *CQ* 21 (1927): 113.

108. Triballus, the type of the barbarian lecher, may be related to this meaning of

341. ὑποφαλάσσεσθαι, to feel below (L 84), is simply φαλάσσειν amplified by an obscenifying prefix. There is no specific justification for Taillardat's judgment (n. 52, above), p. 105, that this is an "image unique, mais qu'on ne peut guere croire inventée par Aristophane: elle a un air proverbial." Compare ἀφάλακτος, L 275.

341a. Compare Anaxil. 44 φηλαφίζει; CA 1182 ὑπομηλαφῆσαι, to feel the breasts covertly (see sections 201 f., above). Lat. *palpari* might be etymologically connected.

342. χαλάζειν, to loosen up by introducing the penis, is used punningly at L 419 and Epicr. 10.5. χαλαρά at T 263 is a pederastic reference to Agathon's εὐρυπρωκτία. χαλαρωτέραν, used of the defiled Lady Music at Pherecr. 145.5, is a sexual pun on the meaning "unstrung," used of musical instruments. ἀνῆκε, slacken, in the preceding line, contributes to the obscene double entendre (see *LSJ* s.v. II.7).

343. ψαθάλλειν, rub or scratch, seems to indicate self-induced erection preparatory to sexual congress: Pl Com 59 ⟨τὸ πέος⟩ ἐψάθαλλε λεῖος ὤν, being smooth (effeminate) he scratched his cock; cf. Phryn. *PS* p. 12B ἀναψαθάλλειν τὸ πέος· ἀνατρίβειν καὶ ἀνακνᾶν οἷον πρὸς τὸ πλησιάζειν to scratch the penis: that is, to rub it or chafe it as for sexual intercourse. Cf. διεψάθαλλε at CA 982.

Burning

Words for burning, used to describe the effects of erotic passion and to indicate sexual intercourse, are common in all languages.

344. ἀνθρακίζειν at P 1136 means "bake my penis in coitus." See section 42, above.

345. ἐμπιμπράναι, to burn up, *may* be a double entendre at L 269 referring to rape: note the special object of the Male Chorus' attention, the notorious wife of Lycon (line 270).

346. ἐμπυρεύειν at P 1137 means "to roast my phallus in coitus." See section 44, above.

347. ἐπιτύφεσθαι, to be inflamed by passion, at L 221.

348. θύειν, along with the whole area of sacrificial language and customs, forms the basis for numerous obscene jokes in comedy. This verb appears at A 792 (a χοῖρος for Aphrodite), Av 565 (κριθαί for the phal-eris bird), 568 (a σέρφος ἐνόρχης to the ballsy bird), L 191 f. (a "white horse" to swear by: see section 84, above), Eub. 130 (κέρκος and μηρός, as if to

---

τρίβειν: see J. G. Griffith, "*Ληκύθιον Ἀπώλεσεν*: A Postscript," *HSCP* 74 (1970): 44; J. E. Sandys and F. A. Paley, *Select Private Speeches of Demosthenes* (Cambridge, 1896), 2: 242.

pederasts). The tour de force of all extant sacrifice humor is the long parody from *Phaon* by Plato Comicus (174).

349. Iris, prim object of Peisetaerus' sexual aggressiveness, uses καται-θαλοῦν in its usual meaning, to burn to ashes, at Av 1242 to try to intimidate her antagonist. But Peisetaerus turns the word back on Iris by using it in an unusual erotic meaning (ll. 1260 f.), οὔκουν ἑτέρωσε πετομένη / καταιθαλώσεις τῶν νεωτέρων τινά;, "Why don't you fly off somewhere and burn up one of the young men?"

350. καταπισσοῦν, to cover with hot pitch: see section 183, above.

351. ὀπτᾶν, to heat up and thus excite, was a very popular term in serious literature for sexual incendiarism.[109] In Aristophanes see A 1105, L 839. But ὀπτήσω at A 1102, used by Dicaeopolis of his penis (he promises to "bake" it in the servant-boy), has an obscene tone, like ὀπτάνιον at P 891 (see section 163, above). The image in these two places is of the cunt or anus as an oven in which to bake the penis in coitus. It is worth noting that the heat of the phallus, too, was said to be desirable: in CA 5.16 Dem., a woman remarks that dildoes lack the heat (θάλπει δ' οὐδαμῶς) of a real penis.

352. πέσσειν, bake (the phallus in coitus): see section 177, above.

353. πυρπολεῖν, to assail with burning missiles, is used humorously of the effects on men of a hetaera at Anaxil. 22.9 (cf. Men. *Mon.* 195).

354. ῥιπίζεσθαι, to fan into flame, is used with τεμάχη (q.v.) at E 842. ἀνὴρ ἀναρριπίζεται, Pherecr. 4 Dem. (cf. Hsch. s.v. ἀνερριπίσθη· ἀνεκινήθη; Zon. 206 ἀναρριπίζειν· κινεῖν, ἀνεγείρειν).

355. ὑποπισσοῦν, smear underneath with hot pitch: see section 177, above.

356. φρύγεσθαι, to be roasted, is used with τραγήματα (q.v.) at E 844.

357. χοανεύειν, to smelt metal, is used humorously of the Relation's phallus at T 59 ff.: he threatens to "smelt" τὸ πέος in the anuses of Agathon and his servant.

Λορδοῦν and *Κύπτειν*

358. These two terms refer to two popular modes of sexual intercourse; they are personified in tandem by a pair of made-up coital gods, *Λόρδων* and *Κύβδασος*, at Pl Com 174.17.

359. λορδοῦν refers to a position in which the woman bends backwards and thrusts her hips forward.[110] As a sexual term this word always includes rapid pelvic motions, whether as part of a seductive dance or actually in

109. Sop. 6.9, Theoc. 7.55, 23.34, Call. *Epigr.* 43.5, *AP* 12.92.7.
110. Cf. Hp. *Art.* 46, 48, *Fract.* 16, Arist. *IA* 707[b] 18.

coitus. Thus Fr 140, λορδοῦ κιγκλοβάτην ῥυθμόν, strain your body backwards and move your rear end like a wagtail (κίγκλος), refers to an erotic dance; we may compare Mnesim. 4.55, σκιρτᾷ λορδοῖ κεντεῖ (= βινεῖ) and Procopius' description of the Empress Theodora (*Arc.* 9), εἰστήκει λορδουμένη τε καὶ τὰ ὀπίσω ἀποκοντῶσα, she stood there bent backwards and poking her hindquarters out. In coitus the term indicates bodies writhing and moving against one another, as in the phrase at E 10, λορδουμένων σωμάτων.

360. The wagtail of Fr 140 appears often in descriptions of women's pelvic motions in coitus. This was a bird that twitched its tailfeathers so seductively that it earned the nickname σεισοπυγίς (Phot.). The gyrations of the Lydian girl in Autocrates' *Tympanistae* are illustrative (1.7 ff.),

> τοῖν ἰσχίοιν
> τὸ μὲν κάτω τὸ δ' αὖ
> εἰς ἄνω ἐξαίρουσα
> οἷα κίγκλος ἄλλεται.

[She moves her buttocks up and down, jumping around like a wagtail bird.]

A woman in Fr 29 seems to be using all her technique to arouse an old man's passion,[111] ὀσφῦν δ' ἐξ ἄκρων διακίγκλισον ἠύτε κίγκλου/ἀνδρὶ πρεσβύτῃ, wiggle your ass like a wagtail against the old man. Compare Theocr. 5.117 (and schol.), εὖ ποτικιγκλίζευ καὶ τᾶς δρυὸς εἴχεο τήνας: here a boy is bent forward, holding onto a tree, and moving his hips rapidly back against his lover. A homosexual play on this use of κίγκλος appears in the pun at Eq 640 f., where the debauched Sausage-Seller bangs open the κιγκλίς (gate) of the Council Chamber with his πρωκτός (for κιγκλίς, meaning quick movements, cf. Hp. *Art.* 71).

361. The boy in the Theocritus passage above is engaged in the mode of congress opposite λορδοῦν, namely κύπτειν, to bend forward for penetration (whether vaginal or anal) from behind. The adulterous housewife of T 488 f. is penetrated by her lover in exactly the same manner, εἶτ' ἠρειδόμην/παρὰ τὸν Ἀγυιᾶ κῦβδ', ἐχομένη τῆς δάφνης, "Then, holding onto a laurel tree as I bent over, I was banged beside Apollo's sidewalk pillar." There is also a double meaning at L 161, where Lysistrata advises her confederates, if their husbands try to force them, "to hold onto the doorposts." This reference, like the women's oath at L 231,[112] οὐ στήσομαι/

---

111. Codd. ἀνδρὸς πρεσβύτου: I read with Taillardat (n. 52, above), pp. 106 f., who argues cogently for the change.

112. See Taillardat (n. 52, above), p. 107.

λέαιν' ἐπὶ τυροκνήστιδος, "I will not assume the position of a lioness on a cheese-grater," is designed as a joke on the shamelessness of Athenian housewives. In actuality κύπτειν, like the other special modes of intercourse we have discussed, may have been a σχῆμα ἀκόλαστον καὶ ἑταιρικόν, to quote the scholiast at L 231. Its frequent appearance on vases really does not tell us whether or not the average Athenian couple had much use for it. Other references to this mode appear in contexts of rape, κάμπτων με καὶ στρέφων ὅλην διέφθορεν, bending me over and twisting me around, he ruined me, Perecr. 145.15, or violent sexual domination, like Theoria's by the Council in *Peace*: 896, τετραποδηδὸν ἑστάναι, 896 b, ἐς γόνατα κύβδ' ἱστάναι.

362. Compare Cratin. 301, where young girls are likened to three-legged tables loaded with food, and the euphemisms at Anaxil. 22.25 f. for positions in which a woman is penetrated while on all fours: τετράπους μοι γένοιτο, φησί, σκίμπους ἢ θρόνος,/εἶτα δὴ τρίπους τις, εἶτα φησί παιδίσκη δίπους, let me have a young girl, he says, a four-legger, or a hammock, or a sedan chair, and then a three-legger, and then, he says, a two-legger! (with the last position compare the joke at Eq 1384 ff., quoted in section 363, below).

363. κύπτειν is the natural position of the homosexual pathic; κίναιδοι were apparently called κυπτάται (Hsch.). Thus Cleon's threat at Eq 365 is intended, as the scholiast remarks, as a contemptuous reference to the Sausage-Seller's admitted profligacy: ἐγὼ δέ γ' ἐξέλξω σε τῆς πυγῆς θύραζε κύβδα, "I'll drag you out, bent double, by your ass." Socrates' pathic disciples are οἱ σφόδρ' ἐγκεκυφότες (N 191, cf. T 236), and Cleisthenes κἀκόπτετ' ἐγκεκυφώς at R 425, that is (1) bent over, he smote himself from grief and (2) he was buggered as he bent over. At Eq 1384 ff., where Demus is urged to enjoy himself with a young boy, we must understand κύπτειν: κἄν που δοκῇ σοι, τοῦτον ὀκλαδίαν πόει, "and if you want, make a folding-chair of him." The scholiast rightly explains, τοῦτον· τὸν παῖδα. παίζει δέ, περαίνειν καὶ κύφειν ποίει. The joke plays upon ὀκλάζειν, to squat, used of horses crouching to let their rider mount (*LSJ* s.v. II). See preceding section.

364. ἀποστρέφειν at Eq 263 is a metaphor from wrestling but has a secondary meaning in the context, namely Cleon turning his victims around and twisting them into positions for enforced buggery. Compare the threats of the Relation against Agathon and his servant at T 59 ff. See section 338, above.

364a. διαστρέφειν is used as a sort of refrain in Eup. 7 Dem. (from *Demes*) and has been interpreted as a reference to homosexual assault, a meaning that can be made to fit the three situations in which the word appears.

Other scholars argue for a meaning closer to "torture" or "torment." For the obscene interpretation, see A. Mayer, *BPhW* 32 (1912): 830 ff., P. Maas, ibid., pp. 861 ff., C. Jensen, *Hermes* 51 (1916): 321 ff., W. Schmid, *Philol.* 93 (1939): 414, J. Demiańczuk, p. 44; against: A. Körte, *Ber. Sachs. Akad.* 71 (1919): 6, pp. 25 ff., E. Wüst, *Philol.* 91 (1936): 114 f., J. M. Edmonds, *Mnem.* Ser. 3, 8 (1940): 1 ff., K. Plepelits, *Die Fragmente der Demen des Eupolis* (Diss. Vienna 46: Verlag Notring, Vienna, 1970), pp. 35 ff. I do not think our present evidence sufficient to decide the matter but note the following: the unquestionably obscene meanings of στρέφειν and ἀποστρέφειν (especially in section 364, above); the presence in priapic contexts of homosexual rape as a punishment (H. Herter, *RVV* 23 [1932]: 209 f., *APlan.* 261, Catullus 16); the possible obscene meaning of διεστραμ-μένος at Eup. 276.3; the prefix δια-, used also in, for example, διασποδεῖν, διαμηρίζειν, κτλ.

365. σιμός, in the sense of bent upwards or concave (cf. Plu. 2.139B), probably indicates κύπτειν. Thus in Fr 74 μέσην ἔρειδε πρὸς τὸ σιμόν we translate, "drive at her uphill" (a reference based on the contours of the acropolis); note the double entendres in μέσος and ἐρείδειν (q.v.). The same double meaning on this feature of the acropolis appears at L 288 of the men's assault on the barricaded women; their storming of the acropolis is often compared metaphorically to sexual intercourse in this play. At Philipp. Com. 1 ἀποσιμῶσαι means τὸ ἐπικῦψαι καὶ τὴν πυγὴν προτ-εῖναι γυμνήν, bending over and thrusting out the rear end naked; thus Thryallis, at Alciphr. 1.39, shows off her πυγή: ἀπεδύσατο τὸ χιτώνιον καὶ μικρὸν ὑποσιμώσασα τὴν ὀσφῦν. . . she hiked up her shift and wiggling her loins a little. . . .

Kissing

366. Kissing merits a place in a discussion of obscene language because in Attic Comedy kissing often has a definitely obscene tone. The various types of kisses are treated as an aspect of sexual congress which can be made as titillating and comical as modes of intercourse.

367. φιλεῖν and κυνεῖν are the standard terms for erotic kissing in Greek, and they appear frequently in Aristophanes. κυνεῖν: P 709, Av 141 (homosexual), L 797, 923, R 543, 755; φιλεῖν: A 1200 ff., Eq 946, V 608, Av 671, 674, L 840, 871, 890, 923, 1036, T 1190, 1191, E 181, 647, 650, 910. Although the substantive φίλημα appears in Aeschylus (*Fr.* 135), Sophocles (*Fr.* 537), Euripides,[113] and elsewhere in comedy, [114] Aristoph-

113. *IA* 679, 1238, *Suppl.* 1154, *Andr.* 416.
114. Pl Com. 46.5, Nicophon 8.

anes does not use it at all, preferring to specify certain kinds of kisses appropriate for prostitutes and other figures of lasciviousness, and thus more likely to raise a laugh than any ordinary kiss. For the cheering and comical effects of a whore's expert kissing-technique, see the description at Ephipp. 6, where open-mouthed kisses are compared to the gaping of young sparrows, and the dramatization of Elaphium's expertise with the archer at T 1190 ff.

368. τὸ περιπεταστόν is the kiss "with inside lip,"[115] literally "spread out," at A 1201. We hear of biting connected with this mode at A 1209.[116]

369. τὸ ἐπιμανδαλωτόν is the tongue-kiss, named after the μάνδαλος, door-bolt (schol. A 1201): A 1201. Compare μανδαλωτόν at T 132. This method of kissing is called καταγλώττισμα at N 51 (Strepsiades' over-sophisticated wife) and T 131 (as being especially stimulating, as at T 1192). The passage at V 607 ff., in which Philocleon's daughter kisses her father this way in order to capture with her tongue the three-obol piece he carries in his mouth, is meant to be warm and humorous, not disgusting, as some commentators have found it.

370. At Telecl. 13 this kiss is called τὸ γιγγλυμωτόν, after γίγγλυμος, door-hinge, perhaps (like μάνδαλος) referring to the open mouth (cf. Hsch. s.v.).

371. The image of intertwining tongues probably lies behind Fr 30 Dem.,[117] ἔκυσα νῦν ἐνταῦθ' ἐγὼ ταύτην δοκῶν/φορμὸν πλέκειν, now I kissed her there, and it was like weaving a wicker basket.

372. δρεπτόν, the plucking kiss (Telecl. 13), is clearly a variety of tongue-kissing.

373. ἰσχνίδες (Hsch.) probably refers to tongue-kissing, but may also involve puckering the lips.[118]

374. παιδάριον (Eust. 1880.61) is a little boy's or girl's kiss, that is, without the tongue.

375. σκιμβασμός (Hsch.), the limping kiss (?), is obscure.

376. σύστομος (Telecl. 12) describes the "mouth-to-mouth" kiss.

377. χύτρα (Eunic. 1) describes a kiss in which the ears are grasped like jug-handles (cf. *LSJ* s.v. II).

378. The kisses at Ephipp. 6 are like fledgling sparrows being fed.

379. καταγλωττίζειν can mean "tongue-kiss into silence" as well as merely tongue-lash. This vulgar and violent image is twice used of Cleon: A 380 (note the surrounding sexual imagery), Eq 352.

---

115. Shakespeare, *WT* 1.2.286.
116. For which see Luc. *Luc.* 32.
117. See schol., Taillardat (n. 52, above), pp. 104 f.
118. Hsch. glosses ἄγκυραι, ἰσχνάδες.

Fellatio

Fellatio was a favorite subject of the iambic poets and the Sicilian comic school, from what we can tell from fragmentary evidence, both as a way to insult a male enemy and to describe the skills of flute-girls or hetaerae. It continued to be both an erotic and a scurrilous *topos* throughout classical literature, particularly in epigram and iambic poetry.[119] The situation in comedy is similar.

380. Whereas κύπτειν/κυπτάζειν, to bend (down) over, appears to have been the standard term for fellatio in earlier poetry, there is only one instance of this usage in comedy, the pun at L 17, where a woman reports on the duties of housewives: ἡ μὲν γὰρ ἡμῶν περὶ τὸν ἄνδρ' ἐκύπτασεν; κυπτάζειν means both "busy herself" and "go down on [the phallus]," a joke on wifely lechery. As we saw earlier (section 361, above), this term is used in comedy rather than of a certain mode of sexual intercourse.

381. λεσβίζειν/λεσβιάζειν is virtually the *vox propria* for fellatio in the comic poets. Like Englishmen and Americans, who attribute shameless lovemaking techniques to the gay French, the Attic poets seem to have attributed the invention and practice of fellatio to the luxurious Lesbians: cf. Theopomp. 35,

> ἵνα μὴ τὸ παλαιὸν τοῦτο καὶ θρυλούμενον
> δι' ἡμετέρων στομάτων
> εἴπω σόφισμ', ὅ φασι παῖδας Λεσβίων
> εὑρεῖν.

[Not to mention that old technique, much repeated by mouth, which they say the Lesbians invented.]

Compare the schol. at V 1346, Pherecr. 149, Strattis 40.2, 41. In Aristophanes λεσβίζειν/λεσβιάζειν is used thrice: (1) of Philocleon's flute-girl (V 1346), whom he rescues μέλλουσαν ἤδη λεσβιεῖν τοὺς συμπότας, about to suck off the banqueters;[120] (2) of Euripides' Muse, who Dionysus maintains in a damning double entendre, οὐκ ἐλεσβίαζεν, οὔ (R 1308): that is, she never sang in Lesbian modes like those of Terpander imitated by Aeschylus, and she never performed fellatio; and (3) at E 920, where the young girl insults the hag, δοκεῖς δέ μοι καὶ λάβδα κατὰ τοὺς Λεσβίους, "As I see it, you put the L in Lesbianism." Here λάβδα is probably

119. See the numerous citations collected by Grassmann (chap. 1, n. 70, above), pp. 3 ff., 14 ff., 18 f., 25 f.

120. The performance of fellatio upon the guests was perhaps one of the "duties" of flute-girls and other female objects of amusement who were present at banquets: P 853 ff., V 1346, Alexis 49, Nicophon 17.

onomatopoetic, delivered by the actor, we may be sure, in a salacious and exaggerated manner.[121] Fellatio was a favorite insult in the rich ancient literature of *vetula-Skoptik*.[122]

382. λείχειν, later a common term for fellatio,[123] appears of Theoria at P 853 ff.,[124]

> Τρ. εἰωθυῖ' ἀεὶ
> παρὰ τοῖς θεοῖσιν ἀμβροσίαν λείχειν ἄνω.
> Οι. λείχειν ἄρ' αὐτῇ κἀνθάδε σκευαστέον.

[*Tr:* Up there with the gods she's always been accustomed to lick ambrosia.

Sl: Well, she'll have to get used to licking here, too!]

λείχειν is deliberately used by Trygaeus for ἐσθίειν, to set up the servant's coarse joke.[125]

383. References to the mouth often imply fellatio: thus Kinesias is told of his wife (L 855), ἀεὶ γὰρ ἡ γυνή σ' ἔχει διὰ στόμα, "your wife always has you on her lips," and the young man at E 1107, referring to his impending sexual bout with the three hags, wishes to be buried ἐπ' αὐτῷ τῷ στόματι τῆς εἰσβολῆς, at the very mouth of entry, implying again the sexual stock-in-trade of old ladies. Strattis' τῷ στόματι δράσω, I'll do you by mouth (40.2) is more explicit; cf. schol. V 1346.

383a. Compare the terms στοματεύειν[126] and γλωττοδεφεῖν (cf. CA 32 Dem.).

384. For (ἀπο) μυζουρίς, suck-tail (-phallus), see the references at CA 1352.

385. προσαυλεῖν, to pipe a tune, appears to be an obscene pun on fellatio at Nicophon 17, an exhortation to a flute-girl: ἀλλ' ἴθι προσαύλησον σὺ νῷν πτισμόν τινα, "blow us a winnowing-song." πτισμόν here plays upon πτίσσειν in the meaning "hull"[127] or "pound in a mortar";[128] cf. πτισάνη, peeled barley, and πτισάνης, one who hulls.[129] Thus the image is similar to

121. The reading λαβδᾶν, proposed by T. L. Agar in *CQ* 13 (1919): 19, is rightly dismissed by Coulon (chap. 4, n. 24, above), p. 28. See Phot., Frisk (n. 1, above), s.v. λάπτω.

122. See Grassmann (chap. 1, n. 70, above), pp. 18 ff., Hor. *Ep.* 8, 12.

123. Brecht (chap. 1, n. 62, above), p. 54; compare αἰσχρολοιχός at Eust. 518.52, Latin *lingere* (Mart. 12.55.13).

124. The image suggests the gods at their banquet (see n. 120, above).

125. For κωμῳδολοιχεῖν see n. 75, above.

126. Hsch. s.v. λεσβιᾶν.

127. Pherecr. 183; cf. Fr 339.

128. D.L. 9.59, Luc. *Herm.* 79.

129. For αὐλός used to refer to bodily parts, see *LSJ* s.v. 2, 3, 4; αὐλίσκος means the penis at Ptol. *Tetr.* 187, schol. Opp. *H.* 1.582, Anon. *In Ptol Tetr.* 157.

that of λέπειν (sections 288, 290, above). Another reading might be to interpret πτισμόν as a play on πτύειν, to spit out, with reference to ejaculation,[130] although this is less likely.

386. There are few references to men as fellators. The speaker at Strattis 40 certainly is, as is the πόρνος of Alexis 242, whose kiss would be offensive to his lover. In Aristophanes the well-known example is Aristyllus, who (predictably) also has a kiss people avoid (E 647). At Pl 314 he is ὑποχάσκων: as the scholiast remarks, διὰ τὴν αἰσχρουργίαν αὐτοῦ ἀεὶ ἐκεχήνει.

387. At both places there is a strange reference: at E 648 it is said that one who should kiss Aristyllus would smell of mint (καλαμίνθης), and at Pl 313 there is a reference to excrement (μινθώσομεν). Both of these are usually interpreted simply as references to dung, the first by pun (μίνθη/μίνθος) and the second directly. But since it is the oral-genital and not the anal side of Aristyllus with which we are dealing, we may suspect a phallic pun. P. Kretschmer in 1923 tried to establish a connection between μίνθη, *menta* and *mentula*,[131] and concluded that μίνθη must have been a *Deckname* for the phallus in Greek, although he could find no direct evidence that this was so. In these two jokes on Aristyllus the fellator, we may have just such evidence in puns.

388. One further joke is R 423 f., where it is said that Cleisthenes ἐν ταφαῖσι πρωκτὸν/τίλλειν ἑαυτοῦ καὶ σπαράττειν τοὺς γνάθους, which means (1) beats his jaws in grief and (2) fellates. The joke can only have this reference.

389. See also sections 246 and 290, above.

Cunnilingus

389. Ariphrades, a devotee of this kind of lovemaking, is the object of three savage descriptions unmatched anywhere else in the remains of comedy for coarseness and scabrous detail. As far as Aristophanes was concerned, Ariphrades was not only πονηρός, not only παμπόνηρος, but the inventor of a new kind of πονηρία, namely τὸ γλωττοποιεῖ (Eq 1281 ff.), which is described in lines 1284 ff.[132] This claim that Ariphrades "invented" cunnilingus reappears at V 1280 ff., and his practice thereof is further elaborated at P 883 ff., E 129, and at Fr 63. Ariphrades' "invention" is the subject of long and provocative discussion in an article by E. Degani.[133]

130. Cf. ἀπόπτυστον δρόσον (*secreta muliebria*) at Eq 1285, in a description of cunnilingus.
131. "Mythische Namen," *Glotta* 12 (1923): 105 ff.
132. With μολύνων καὶ κυκῶν in line 1286 compare μοιμύλλειν at Hippon. 124.
133. See further E. Degani, "Arifrade l'anassagoreo," *Maia* 12 (1960): 190 ff.

390. γλωττοκομεῖον, tongue-case, is a playful term for the cunt: Eub. 142, Lysipp. 5, Timocl. 2.[134]

391. λείχειν, lick, was apparently a standard term:[135] Eq 1285, Fr 409 (διαλείχοντα), Eup. 52.2 (περιλείξας), schol. P 883 (λείκτης).[136]

392. Culinary terminology understandably furnishes cunnilingus humor. In Aristophanes all such references but one come from *Peace*: like the second speaker at Eup. 52, Smoeus' dish-licking at E 847 is a double entendre for cunnilingus, τὰ τῶν γυναικῶν διακαθαίρει τρύβλια. Compare Trygaeus' exhortation to the Council at P 716 f., ὅσον ῥοφήσεις ζωμὸν ἡμερῶν τριῶν,/ὅσας δὲ κατέδει χόλικας ἐφθὰς καὶ κρέα, how much *juice* you will slurp down during those three days, how many *boiled sausages* and *cutlets*! and Ariphrades' potential behavior at line 885: τὸν ζωμὸν αὐτῆς προσπεσὼν ἐκλάψεται, falling upon her he'll lick up her *juice*. A subtler reference is the "bottom-grass posset" (κυκεῶνα βληχωνίαν) which Hermes prescribes for Trygaeus (712) as a cure for too much Opora (fruit/sex).[137]

393. There may be a pun involving cunnilingus in τράγοι δ᾽ ἀκρατιεῖσθε, in the scurrilous chorus of Pl 295, where the scholiast notes the habit goats have of licking their genitals: these "goats" are, of course, symbolic of contemporary debauchees (ἀπεφωλημένοι).

394. Two further jokes on cunnilingus and "breakfast" (see preceding section) are Cantharus 8, where a man declares that he will breakfast "in the Isthmus" (see section 143, above), and E 470, where Chremes advises Blepyrus to comply with his wife's orders in order to "make love and eat breakfast all at once" (ἵν᾽ ἀριστᾷς τε καὶ κινῇς ἅμα), an obvious double entendre.

395. Other ancient terminology that might be comic includes σκερός and σκερόλιγγες (Hsch.); σκύλαξ (Hsch.);[138] and φοινικίξιν (Eub. 142).[139]

---

134. Cf. schol. P 883; see also A. Lobeck, *Phrynichi Eclogae* (Leipzig, 1820), pp. 99 f.

135. Cf. Latin *lingere* (Mart. 7.67.17), *ligurire* (Suet. *Tib.* 45).

136. Cf. also Teucer ap. *Cat. Cod. Astr.* 8(4).196.

137. The surface meaning is κυκεών as medicine for colic resulting from the over-consumption of fruit. Here Opora symbolizes (as often) both the fertility of the earth and the ideal sex partner: Trygaeus is both her lover and her harvester. See H. Fränkel, *Wege und Formen frühgriechischen Denkens* (Munich, 1955), pp. 45 ff.

138. For this habit of dogs see Suda s.v. κυνάμυια.

139. Gal. 12.249, Luc. *Pseudol.* 28, Hsch. s.v. σκύλαξ, *EM* 235.46, schol. P 883.

6 Scatological Humor

Xezein

396.
$$\chi\varepsilon\zeta\eta\tau\iota\tilde{\omega}\nu$$
$$\mu\alpha\kappa\rho\grave{\alpha}\nu \ \beta\alpha\delta\acute{\iota}\zeta\omega\nu \ \pi\omicron\lambda\lambda\grave{\alpha} \ \delta' \ \grave{\iota}\delta\acute{\iota}\omega\nu \ \grave{\alpha}\nu\grave{\eta}\rho$$
$$\delta\acute{\alpha}\kappa\nu\omega\nu \ \tau\grave{\alpha} \ \chi\varepsilon\acute{\iota}\lambda\eta, \ \pi\alpha\gamma\gamma\acute{\varepsilon}\lambda\omicron\iota\acute{o}\varsigma \ \grave{\varepsilon}\sigma\tau' \ \grave{\iota}\delta\varepsilon\tilde{\iota}\nu.$$

This "perfectly hilarious" vignette, from Eubulus' *Cercopes* (53.4 ff.), of a man hard-pressed, oozing (see section 400, below), and biting his lips as he looks for a place to relieve himself, contains most of the limited comic possibilities inherent in defecation as a dramatic device. We are simply invited by the poet to laugh at someone revealed in his embarrassing dependence upon the most ignoble of bodily needs. No spectator can feel anything but merry superiority to the plight of such a character, whose rising desperation serves merely to degrade him further and thus increase our amusement. In a sense, defecatory jokes and routines are the purest kind of obscene comedy, in that a normally hidden aspect of a comic figure's life can be observed and enjoyed publicly without distraction from its lowliness. Defecation is indeed one aspect of our lives that must always be hidden (unlike sex), and must always be thought inappropriate in any social context whatever (see the discussion of the psychological dynamics of the excremental processes above, pp. 52 ff.). Sexual jokes can rarely be reduced to such a low level because sex is so important and so complex a part of our lives; defecation is a remarkably uncomplex process. Its only comic potential (aside from the fact that merely to mention defecation constitutes an automatic exposure and raises a laugh) may be said to involve the tension of pain or discomfort, followed by an ignominious relief of that tension. Someone who comes upon the stage for the purpose of dramatizing defecation must necessarily be in pain or in fear of pain, at least until relief is achieved. The fact that the pain is intense but perfectly

harmless adds to the basic humor of exposure. The worst possible outcome
for a comic figure in this situation is that he will soil himself or someone
else.

397. It is not surprising, then, that defecation in Old Comedy appears
only as a kind of low farce with little flexibility. That it was extremely
popular is indicated by passages like that of Eubulus quoted in the previous section, and by the prologue of *Frogs*, where Xanthias tries to initiate
some jokes on τὰ εἰωϑότα (l. 1), that is, defecation humor "at which the
audience will always laugh" (l. 2). Although Dionysus (speaking for the
poet) expresses revulsion at such cheap comedy, Xanthias manages to
develop a climax-joke involving the various stages of crepitation: πιέζομαι,
I'm hard-pressed (l. 3), ϑλίβομαι, I'm squeezed (l. 5), χεζητιᾷς, you're
about to shit (l. 8), ἀποπαρδήσομαι, I'll fart out (l. 10). Xanthias informs
us that such poets as Phrynichus, Lycis, and Ameipsias regularly employed
this kind of humor. But Aristophanes declares his contempt. As early as
the parabasis of *Clouds*, Aristophanes had proclaimed himself superior to
these lowly devices and to the poets who used them, and, in truth, although
we find in his plays many incidental references to the humor of defecation
farce, there are only a small number of scenes of any length that exploit
it dramatically, and when these occur it is invariably for thematic purposes
(outlined in chap. 3) which transcend the merely farcical: these are the
prologue of *Peace*, certain sections of *Frogs*, and Blepyrus' extended defecation scene in *Ecclesiazusae*.

398. We shall describe the uses of defecation comedy under several major
headings. It is interesting to note that the characters involved in these contexts or the persons referred to therein are invariably lowly (rustic and/or
vulgar) or in some way worthy of harsh insult (comical foreigners or the
victims of personal attack). Scatological humor in comedy is much more
restricted to certain lowly types of character than sexual humor, which
often appears in noble roles—for example, in the glorification of the
countryside or the praises of peace. Scatological humor, on the other hand,
remains quite ignoble.

399. *Urgency.* As in the Eubulus passage (section 396, above), χεζητιᾶν is
the standard term; χέζειν itself is an "altererbtes volkstümliches Wort"
(Frisk, s.v.) found almost exclusively in Old Comedy. This word is explicitly condemned, along with its attendant contortions, by Aristophanes (R 8).
Its two other appearances, outside the Blepyrus-scene (E 313, 345, 368),
are (1) at Av 790 ff.: anyone who should be caught χεζητιῶν at the theater
could, if he had wings, fly out, relieve himself, and return easily. Other
reasons given for this kind of avian escape are eating and adulterous
fornication—a nice trio of basic bodily drives; (2) at N 1386 ff.: the crude

Strepsiades complains of having been locked indoors and thus forced to soil himself out of desperation.

400. *Soiling oneself or one's clothes* is, of course, closely connected to the motif of urgency: Av 790 ff., N 1386 ff. ἐξιδίειν, to sweat/to ooze excrement, in the *Birds* passage is not unique in this meaning:[1] cf. R 237 ἰδίει ("sudat prae labore et ita cacaturit," [He sweats from strain and is therefore about to shit] Blaydes, ad loc.), Eub. 53.5 The comical picture of a hard-pressed character frantically looking for his shoes may have been popular in comedy, to judge from Eq 888 f. and E 344 f. A certain Patrocleides (Av 790) seems to have been known as ὁ χεσᾶς, the shitter, on account of his soiled clothing (see the schol., Poll. 5.91). Philocleon's aged incontinence leads to similar difficulties at V 1127 ff.: old people are especially prone to this kind of embarrassment (see section 420, below).

401. *Constipation* is closely related to the motif of urgency. In Aristophanes it occurs only in the Blepyrus scene of *Ecclesiazusae*. Interesting are two sexual jokes connected with constipation: at E 355 we hear that an ἀχράς, prickly-pear, is blocking Blepyrus' σιτία (excrement: P 137 ff., 163, 723 f.); this sets up a joke on buggery involving an ἀνὴρ ᾿Αχραδούσιος (punning on the deme Acherdous). At E 369 f., Blepyrus' call to Eileithyia to act as a midwife perhaps serves to emphasize the sudden exchange of sexual roles by man and wife. It is also in this most scatological of Aristophanic comedies that we hear of one Antisthenes, who seems to have suffered comic ridicule on account of his chronic constipation: E 367 f., 806 ff.

402. *Fear* often produces soiling. In Aristophanes see A 350 f., 581, Eq 900 f., 1056 f., V 627, N 295, P 241,[2] 1176, Av 65 ff., 1169, E 1061 f. The effects of the terrors of the underworld on Dionysus bring on the most extended exploitation of this kind of humor: R 308, 479, where the terrified Dionysus' confession, ἐγκέχοδα· κάλει θεόν, "I've shat; call the god," parodies the sacral formula, ἐγκέχυται· κάλει θεόν, It [the libation] is poured; call the god (see the schol.). Jokes on Dionysus' plight continue throughout the scene (479–502). We may compare the terror of Peisetaerus and Euelpides at their first sight of the hoopoe's servant at Av 65 ff.

403. *Color* jokes, usually involving the word πυρρός (E 329, 1061 f., Eq 900 f.), refer to the tawniness of soiled clothing. There are many witty variations on this theme. Kinesias' πυρρίχην at R 153 is at once a martial dance and a defecatory one (compare the frightened messenger at Av 1169

1. As is maintained, most recently, by J. Taillardat, *Les Images d'Aristophane* (Paris, 1962), p. 168.

2. Polemos is ὁ κατὰ τοῖν σκελοῖν, rightly glossed by the scholiast as meaning ἀπὸ τῶν διὰ δειλίαν ἀποτιλώντων.

πυρρίχην βλέπων). One of Cleon's schemes is called by Demus a Πυρρά-
νδρου μηχάνημα (Eq 900), a reference to Cleon's ruddy complexion as well
as to the scheme's fecal nature. The hapax ὑπερεπυρρίασε at R 308 does not
mean "blush scarlet for another" (as in LSJ) but "soil oneself a little in
fear of another." The ξουθὸς ἱππαλεκτρυών (P 1177) flees from fear and is
therefore tawny; compare the pun a line earlier on Κυζικηνικόν to describe
the color of the dye. The threat at T 570, to make a woman excrete the
sesame-cake she had eaten, plays on the tawny color of sesame: compare
the parallel joke at Eup. 163.3, σησαμίδας δὲ χέσει, shit sesame-cakes, and
see Athen. 14.646F, Plaut. Curc. 294 f. χρυσός, gold, can also be used in
this meaning: the Persian king who took eight months to defecate spent
that time ἐπὶ χρυσῶν ὁρῶν, a reference to the fabled golden mountains
of Persia and to excrement itself (A 81 f.). Similarly, Dionysus, in bowel
difficulties, calls upon the "golden gods" (R 483), a play upon ritual
language.[3]

404. *Heavy burdens or exertions* activate the bowels and cause soiling: thus
the Sausage-Seller nearly soils himself under the weight of his oracles (Eq
998) and Dionysus' rowing causes oozing defecation (R 237 f.) as well as
a long series of noisy explosions.

405. *Striking* someone often produces defecation, and one who threatens
bodily harm will often mention this reaction to strengthen his threat: thus
the fearful slave at Eq 69 f. and the terror of the young men at E 1060 ff.,
and the threats made by Philocleon (V 941), Cleonice (L 440), the Relation (T 570), the hypothetical father-beater (E 640). At Av 68 ᾿Επικε-
χοδώς, the name by which Peisetaerus introduces himself to the hoopoe's
servant, puns on χέζειν with reference to cowardice.

406. References simply to *befouling someone* are uniformly vulgar, reflecting the low characters of the befouler and the befouled. The buffoonish
Strepsiades much appreciates the story of the γαλεώτης that defecated on
Socrates as he stood gazing at the heavens, lost in thought (N 171 ff.).
Strepsiades himself is involved in self-defilement at N 411, in his story
about the burst bladder: compare the similar mishap of Dicaeopolis with
the λάρκος at A 350 f. The defiling of public monuments appears several
times: sometimes it is a bird that defiles (Av 1054, 1117), sometimes
human beings like Philocleon, who habitually defiles the statue of Lycus
(V 394), or the throngs who use the temple of Zeus the Savior as an
outhouse (Pl 1184). The most notorious offender of this type was the
dithyrambist, Kinesias, most blasphemous of men (Athen. 12. 551F), de-

3. See the discussion of gold in myth and cult by H. Lorimer in *Greek Poetry and Life:
Essays Presented to Gilbert Murray* (Oxford, 1936), pp. 14 ff. Freudian connections between
gold and the excremental processes are irrelevant, I think, to the joke here.

filer of all monuments, particularly the small ones dedicated to Hecate that stood outside homes (schol. R 153, 366). Apparently Kinesias' habit was a popular source of humor in later Aristophanic comedy: R 153, 366, E 329 f. For the clever excremental parody of certain Homeric battle-scenes at A 1168 ff., see E. Borthwick in *Mnem.* 20 (1967) 412 f. Further references to the theme of befouling another person include R 1075, Fr 152.3, Alc. Com. 4.

407. A rather childlike fascination with excrement appears in several jokes exaggerating the *size of the feces*. Blepyrus' production (E 351) is compared to a long rope, and the number eight appears in similar exaggerations at Eq 70 (ὀκτοπλάσιον χέζομεν) and A 81 ff., where the wealthy and debauched Persian king spends eight months defecating and another whole month reclosing his anus.

408. *Bed-pans and potties* are favorite items in Old Comedy.[4] The common term was ἀμίς, required at banquets or meetings whenever one could not politely leave the premises: cf. Eup. 4 Dem., 351.5, Epicr. 5.4, Axionic. 7.1, CA 15.32 Dem., 375.2, Diph. 43.34 f. Note also the antics of the aged, and therefore incontinent, Philocleon at V 807 ff., 858, 935, 940, 946.

409. Another such article was the λάσανα (always plural), which seems to have been the trivet for a chamber pot. We hear of it in Aristophanes only in Fr 462, but often elsewhere: Cratin. 49, Pherecr. 88, Eup. 224, Pl Com. 116.

410. From Eup. 46 (= Poll. 10.45) we learn that δίφρος and διφρίσκος were euphemisms for λάσανα, suggesting perhaps that that word, like ἀμίς, had an impolite tone. The euphemism used by women was σκάφιον (Eup. 46). This distinction lies behind the recognition of the Relation as an imposter by the assembled women: at T 633 the Relation, when asked as a test what was done at the previous meeting, invents some plausible answers, among them that the bibulous Xenylla asked for the σκάφιον, which is correct. But, ignorant of the euphemistic usage of that word, he goes on to remark that she asked for the σκάφιον because there was no ἀμίς, thus betraying himself as a man: only men have the ἀμίς. There is also perhaps a practical difference between the two articles: the ἀμίς is partly closed with an opening near the top for the penis; a woman would very probably have had strategic difficulties in using such a vessel.

411. σκωραμίς (E 371), a combination of σκῶρ and ἀμίς, is an Aristophanic invention designed to express Blepyrus' quintessentially degraded situation. Trygaeus degrades the arms-merchant by turning his breastplate into a bedpan (P 1228: cf. ll. 1235 ff.).

412. References to *outhouses* use the common terms κοπρών (P 99, T

4. For technical details see the notes of van Leeuwen and Fritzsche at T 633.

485, Eub. 53.2, 66.3, CA 868), κοπρία (Strattis 43), or λαύρα (P 99, 158).
None of these seems to have possessed an improper tone. ἄφοδος (E 1059,
Antiph. 40.5; cf. ἀφοδεῦσαι at Pl Com. 5) and ἰπνός (Pl 815; for the pun
see Blaydes, ad loc.; Fr 353: cf. Poll. 5.91, Hsch.; ἰπνεύω in *IG*² 4.15
probably means "relieve oneself"[5]) are of course more euphemistic. These
references occur in only two contexts: (1) the prologue of *Peace*, where it is
essential that all privies be closed, and (2) when a character is making a
polite excuse to leave, as at T 485, E 1059.

Scatophagy and Related Humor

413. Scatophagous humor in Aristophanes has two functions: to insult
(sections 414–17) and to refer to anal intercourse (sections 418–19).

414. Scatophagous insults are frequently hurled at Cleon: at P 48 he is
said to eat σπατίλη,[6] a play on σπάτος, the hides and leather of Cleon's
lowly trade, and τιλᾶν, to excrete. In P 47 ff. Aristophanes implies that his
dung-beetle "represents" Cleon. At Eq 899 Cleon is said to be an ἀνὴρ
Κόπρειος, a reference to pederasty (compare E 317). With Cleon as
βορβοροτάραξις, churner of filth, at Eq 309 and hurler of ἀπειλὰς βορβορ-
οθύμας, filthy-minded threats, at P 753, compare Hipponax 135b (βορβορόπη, filth-hole) and *Batr.* 230 (βορβοροκοίτης, lying in filth). Compare also
the "sea of βόρβορος" and the σκῶρ ἀείνων, eternal shit, which await evil
persons in the Aristophanic underworld (R 145 f.), an idea Aristophanes
had used in *Gerytades* (150), where the poet's enemies had to swim in a
river of diarrhoea.[7]

415. The crude Carion, who found that the god Asclepius did not react
even to the particularly foul odor of his crepitations, calls him a σκατοφάγος: the scholiast's idea that this is a reference to an actual diagnostic
technique of ancient physicians (he mentions Hippocrates) does not seem
to be the appropriate explanation of the joke here: Carion's epithet is a
gratuitous insult intended to shock his lady companion, as it does (Pl 706).

416. The joke at E 595, in which Praxagora says to her husband, κατέδει
πέλεθον πρότερός μου, seems to refer to a fable or colloquial expression of
some kind. van Leeuwen, ad loc., suggests that it means "only when eating
dung may you interrupt me"; van Daele, ad loc., sees an allusion to death,
which seems less likely. Perhaps Ussher, ad loc., is correct in maintaining
that the expression is not abusive or threatening but "simply the statement

---

5. I am grateful to Professor Zeph Stewart for this reference.

6. Diarrhoeic excrement, according to Hp. *Acut.* 28.

7. For allusions outside comedy to the folk-myth of underworld excrement, cf. Pl. *Ph.*
69e, *Rep.* 363d, 533d; D.L. 6.39.

of a fact: 'you're very keen to anticipate,' she tells him, 'even if I eat dung you'll be before me' (a case where few others would rush in)."

417. Scatophagous references to animal excrement are used to indicate especially low behavior. At N 1431 f. Strepsiades turns the logic of his son back on him by maintaining, in typically crude fashion, that if Pheidippides follows the cocks in father-beating, why not also sleep on a perch and munch dung? Pheidippides replies that not even Socrates would do that, filthy as he is. The diet of the dung-beetle in *Peace* includes animal dung, an item used by Aristophanes to designate buffoonishness and rusticity: thus at A 1026 a farmer says that he was raised ἐν πᾶσι βολίτοις (a surprise for ἀγαθοῖς). Similarly, Cleon is said to practice his trade among τοῖς βολίτοις at Eq 658. The Empusa who so terrifies Dionysus (R 295) is imagined by Xanthias to have one leg made of cow dung.[8] Cratinus' βόλιτα χλωρά (39) is of unknown context but seems to be an example of life in the country. Dogs and pigs are scatophagous, according to the slave at P 24, but not as dainty about their disgusting fare as the monstrous dung-beetle. For a similar reference to goats, see Creobyl. 7.2. ὀνίδες, ass-droppings (P 4), are part of the beetle's fodder, too, since dung-beetles were supposed to have sprung from ass dung.[9] With thematic reference to such filthy repasts in the prologue, the chorus at P 790 calls bad poets σφυράδων ἀποκνίσματα, little balls of sheep/goat dung (schol., Hsch). Compare the insult in Eup. 16, σφυράδων πολλῶν ἀναμεστή, full of many shit-balls. Eupolis elsewhere calls someone ἀποπάτημ' ἀλώπεκος, fox-shit (284). Similarly, an old man in Menander is μυόχοδος, mouse dung (430).

418. There are many references to dung in contexts of buggery; the word used is almost always a form of κόπρος. κοπροφορήσω σε (Eq 295) is a threat by the Sausage-Seller to bugger Cleon; at V 1184 κοπρολόγῳ means "debauchee" as well as *vidangeur* (van Daele). At P 9 ἄνδρες κοπρολόγοι must have the same reference, considering the joke in lines 11 f. After the apotheosis of the dung-beetle, we hear (P 724) that he will eat "Ganymedes' ambrosia," a reference to Olympian pederasty. The Spartan ambassador who wants κοπραγωγῆν (L 1174) contrasts his anal desires with the vaginal predilections of the Athenian prytanis, who wants γεωργεῖν (1173). Compare Pl Com. 222, κοπραγωγοὺς γαστέρας. We might also cite Juv. 9.43 ff., the most extended use of this motif:

> an facile et pronum est agere intra viscera penem / legitimum atque illic hesternae occurrere cenae? / servus erit minus ille miser qui foderit agrum / quam dominum.

8. Compare the ὀνοσκελέαι, female sea-monsters who devour travelers at Luc. *VH* 2.46.
9. See Blaydes, ad loc. and line 82, where Trygaeus calls his foul Pegasus κάνθων.

The segmentation pun at P 42, Διὸς καταιβάτου,[10] may refer to Zeus as
pederast,[11] although the insult need not have a specific sexual reference
(compare ὦ βδεῦ δεσπότα, CA 28).

419. Two scatophagous references to anal intercourse are heterosexual
(L 1174, discussed in the previous section, is actually a pederastic joke
despite its heterosexual reference): (1) at Pl 304 the debauched Philonides
and Lais are said to indulge in this kind of lovemaking: she persuades him
μεμαγμένον σκῶρ ἐσθίειν,/αὐτὴ δ' ἔματτεν αὐτοῖς, to eat shit-cakes she'd
made for them; that is, for Philonides and his companions; for the image
see section 446, below. We may compare Antiph. 126, where Cyprian
Aphrodite's affection for pigs leads her to transfer their scatophagous
habits to bulls; the exact references in the joke are unclear. (2) The young
swain of the lecherous old lady of Pl 1024 is said to eat her τἀφόδια, a pun
on τὰ ἐφόδια (travel-money) and τὰ ἀφόδια (excrement),[12] a clear reference
to anal intercourse.

Urination

420. Urination is specifically mentioned only infrequently, usually with
reference to incontinent old men: thus the scurrilous remarks about the old
and bibulous Cratinus' κῴδιον, pillow (Eq 400) and "flow" (ῥεύσας, Eq
526 with schol.), the problems of Philocleon (V 807 ff., 858, 935, 940, 946,
1127 f.), the chorus of old men in *Lysistrata* (402, 550), the Relation at T
611 f., and the ἐξώλης γέρων of Eup. 45.

421. To urinate on someone was to defile him, of course: thus Carion's
friend fears that the newly dominant women will κατουρήσουσί μου (E
832), that is, treat him like nothing. Similarly, the impotent poets of R 95
can merely defile Lady Tragedy (προσουρήσαντα), they cannot through a
genuine union (cf. Eq 517) produce live offspring, as can the manly and
fertile poet (γόνιμος) sought by Dionysus. Purely farcical are Philocleon's
defiling of Lycus' statue (V 394); the jokes about giving the dung-beetle a
drink (P 49); the (presumed) banquet-scene in Aristophanes' *Dramata*
(269), in which someone, perhaps Heracles, cannot find his ἀμίς and must
use a pitched jar instead: compare the gods' behavior after too much wine
in Hermipp. 82.1 f.; and Strepsiades' childish and typically rustic notion
that rain is Zeus passing water through a sieve (N 373).

10. Zeus who walks on high/shit-walker; the sexual meaning of βαίνειν/βατεῖν may also
be present.
11. Cf. ὀπισθοβάτης at *AP* 12.33.2.
12. Cf. E 1059, Hp. *Acut.* 30, Arist. *Mir.* 830a22.

Πέρδεσθαι

422. Much of what was said of excremental humor also applies to the humor of crepitation, which is extremely frequent in comedy. Indeed, the noise and odor of gas being expelled from the bowels is considered to be universally and unconditionally humorous, and can be found in virtually all slapstick comedy. As L. Radermacher remarks, "Man muss sich wundern, wie zahlreich die Möglichkeiten sind, die er [Aristophanes] besitzt, um auch aus der πορδή einen Schlager zu gestalten."[13] Undoubtedly the breaking of wind could be counted on to raise a laugh when all else failed. Unlike jokes about excrement, crepitation always has a gay, harmless tone, and sometimes even a neutral one. It never approaches the harsh tone and base level of excremental humor despite its essentially low and farcical dramatic dynamics.

423. Crepitation is used to designate *rusticity and vulgarity*. Strepsiades' ridiculous comparison of his own noisy defecation to thunderclaps (N 293 ff., 389ff.) marks him as a rustic clown. Socrates, who characteristically takes up the lowly comparison to illustrate a scientific principle, shares in the comic degradation.[14] The similarly rustic Silenus in Euripides' *Cyclops* (327 f.) makes the same joke. Carion's windy behavior in the temple of Asclepius is specifically condemned as ἄγροικον and γέλοιον (Pl 697 ff.), as is Xanthias' nauseating routine in the opening of *Frogs*. The man who breaks wind ἐκ δεξιᾶς(a parody of omen-taking) at Eq 639 is καταπύγων, and therefore εὐρύπρωκτος (and debauched);[15] compare the asinine Cephisodorus at Timocl. 16.8 περὶ τὸ βῆμ' ἐπέρδετο (see sections 425 and 429, below). The Sausage-Seller's crepitation jokes at Eq 902 are called βωμολοχεύματα by Cleon. Without doubt, the word ἀποπάρδαξ (CA 82) was meant to express similar disparagement.

424. Like defecation, crepitation can be used to designate *fear*. The *vox propria* is βδύλλειν/βδύλλεσθαι, a word built on βδεῖν. There is a fine crescendo at N 1133, where Strepsiades confesses, δέδοικα καὶ πέφρικα καὶ βδελύττομαι, "I tremble and shiver and fart out in fear!" Similarly, L 354

---

13. "Πορδή," *RE* 22.235. For full citations and discussion see E. Lenaiou (C. Charitonides), 'ΑΠΟΡΡΗΤΑ (Thessaloniki, 1935), pp. 204 ff. and R. Hošek, *Lidovost a lidové motivy u Aristofana* (Prague, 1962), "Zu Aristophanes Plutos 176," *SPFB* 91 (1960): 89 ff.

14. Dover's notion (*Clouds*, ad loc.) that πορδή and βροντή (*βορντη) may actually have been pronounced similarly is hardly necessary to explain the humor here: breaking wind loudly is amusing whatever the vocabulary used to describe it, and Strepsiades' etymologizing becomes all the more humorous if the two words are *not* that similar.

15. See section 459, below, and compare the sneezes at *Od.* 17.451 and Xen. *An.* 3.2.9.

and Pl 700 refer to characters who break wind in terror (cf. Pl 699 ἀπέπαρδον). βδύλλειν with a direct object ("to break wind in fear of") appears at Eq 224, L 354. βδεῖν itself is used absolutely at P 1077 and Pl 693. πέρδεσθαι never appears in a context of fear, except perhaps at V 1177, where the reference is probably to an incident of unknown nature from the *Lamia* of Crates (cf. Crates 18, E 78): see now M. G. Bonanno, *Studi su Cratete Comico* (Padua 1972), 102 ff.

425. Crepitation by rich and overfed people can express *arrogance*: at Pl 176 the rich general Agyrrhius is said to break wind because he is constantly overfed.[16] So also Lamius (E 78), a joke which probably alludes to the incident involving Lamia at V 1177 (see preceding section). For Cephisodorus at Timocl. 16.8, where the comparison with asses is explicit, see sections 423, 429.

426. The expression of *glee or friskiness* is the point of Philocleon's behavior at V 1305, ἀνήλλετ', ἐσκίρτα, 'πεπόρδει, he jumped and frisked and farted (like an ass, 1306), and that of the joyful Coryphaeus at P 335. ἥδομαι γὰρ καὶ γέγηθα καὶ πέπορδα καὶ γελῶ, "for I'm gleeful, I'm gay, I fart and I laugh!"

427. Crepitation from *contentment, laziness, or happiness* is quite frequent: thus Cleon lazes away at Eq 115, πέρδεται καὶ ῥέγκεται (there may also be an allusion to overfedness as well: see section 425, above), as do Pheidippides at N 9 (in contrast with his anxious father's insomnia) and Blepyrus at E 464, σὺ δ' ἀστενακτὶ περδόμενος οἴκοι μενεῖς, but you'll stay at home, farting away without a care. Dicaeopolis breaks wind from boredom (A 30) and later on makes a joke that has caused difficulties of interpretation:[17] A 254 ff.,

> ὡς μακάριος
> ὅστις σ' ὀπύσει κἀκποήσεται γαλᾶς
> σοῦ μηδὲν ἥττους βδεῖν, ἐπειδὰν ὄρθρος ᾖ

Blaydes, ad loc., understands a coital context: since brides are fearful, and breaking wind can express fear, the joke must lie in a comical description of defloration. But ἐπειδάν surely expresses general action and not a specific incident. The most reasonable (and humorous) explanation is that of the scholiast, who explains βδεῖν as a surprise; we may assume that the expected word was βινεῖν. Thus we may render "Blessed is the man who gets you, daughter, and produces from that union some kittens just as good as you are when it comes to . . . farting in the morning" (that is, instead of

16. Blaydes, ad loc., thinks the reference is to the habits of well-fed asses. R. Hošek (n.13, above) would place Pl 176 in our section 427.

17. See the acute but inadequate discussion of H. Erbse, "Zu Aristophanes," *Eranos* 52 (1954): 76 ff.

making love in the morning, they will laze and snore). Perhaps βδεῖν was suggested here for two additional reasons: (1) γαλῆ was a slang term for girls (cf. V 1185) and (2) γαλαῖ were animals notorious for laziness and lasciviousness[18] as well as for possessing particularly noxious crepitations (Pl 693).

428. The latter passage from *Plutus* emphasizes the *foul odor* of crepitation, an attribute of ventral wind which one supposes is always implicit in comic references but which is very rarely explicitly stated: cf. also the βδόλος at CA 781.

429. One can express *contempt* by breaking wind in the direction of someone else. The terms are καταπέρδεσθαι and προσπέρδεσθαι. There seems to be no difference in nuance between the two. At V 618 Philocleon's wine-flask (ὄνος) makes a gurgling sound which Philocleon interprets as a contemptuous crepitation (κατέπαρδεν): note κεχηνώς (617) and the pun on ὄνος, ass. Similarly, the mattock-maker at P 547 breaks wind at the sword-maker, and Blepsidemus does likewise for Poverty at Pl 618; cf. also Epicr. 11.28. All of the latter have καταπέρδεσθαι. προσπέρδεσθαι appears in the same meaning at R 1074, Sosip. 1.12, Damox. 2.39.

430. Crepitation, with its attendant noisiness, was much used for the purely farcical humor of describing the various stages of *incipient defecation*. Thus, throughout Trygaeus' perilous flight heavenward, when it was particularly hazardous to distract the beetle's attention from its flight upwards by emitting odors or excrement, Trygaeus has attacks of indigestion. The language at P 175, ἤδη στρέφει τι πνεῦμα περὶ τὸν ὀμφαλόν, "already a certain wind is churning up around my navel," is echoed frequently elsewhere in comedy: T 484 στρόφος μ' ἔχει τὴν γαστέρα "A churning possesses my belly"; Pl 1131 ὀδύνη σε περὶ τὰ σπλάγχν' ἔοικέ τις στρέφειν, "A certain distress seems to be churning at you in your innards"; Fr 462 τί μου στρέφει τὴν γαστέρα; "What's churning my belly?"; Antiph. 177.3 f., ἐὰν δ' ἄρα/στρέφῃ με περὶ τὴν γαστέρ' ἢ τὸν ὀμφαλόν, "If my belly or my navel starts to churn"; Damox. 2.25 ff. στρόφοι καὶ πνευμάτια, "churning and windiness." All of this suggests that such descriptions were a standard part of the comic poet's repertoire.

431. For emphasis on *windiness and noise* the following passages will be instructive: Strepsiades' thunder-making at N 386 ff., which probably included loud imitations of farts produced offstage (not by the actor himself: the mask would make that impossible); the stomach disorders of Eq 626 and 701; the πρωκτὸς λαλητικός, babbling ass-hole, of Eq 1381 f.;[19] the

---

18. Semon. 7.53, Theoc. 15.28.

19. Cf. Cratin. 6.3, Eub. 107.1, O. Crusius, *Die Mimiamben des Herondas*[2] (Leipzig, 1926) at Herod. 2.44.

jokes on the flatulent crackling of the flute-players at A 863 ff.;[20] and the
extended contest between the frogs' croaks and Dionysus' antiphonal
crepitations in *Frogs* (237 f., 250 f., 255, 261 f., 264 ff.).[21] Many of these
motifs are encapsulated in Eubulus' riddle (107), which is worth quoting
here:

> ἔστι λαλῶν ἄγλωσσος, ὁμώνυμος ἄρρενι θῆλυς,
> οἰκείων ἀνέμων ταμίας, δασύς, ἄλλοσε λεῖος,
> ἀξύνετα ξυνετοῖσι λέγων, νόμον ἐκ νόμου ἕλκων·
> ἓν δ' ἐστὶν καὶ πολλά, καὶ ἂν τρώσῃ τις ἄτρωτος.

[There is a tongueless babbler, the same for men and women, steward of
its own kind of wind, hairy but sometimes smooth, speaking nonsense to
the sensible, frequently sliding from key to key. It is one thing and many,
and if you stab it it remains whole.]

432. An obscene mutation, also referring to noisiness, of such proverbial
expressions as παρὰ κωφὸν διαλέγειν, to speak to a deaf person (Greg. Cypr.
3.32), is CA 50 παρὰ κωφὸν ἀποπαρδεῖν, to fart at a deaf person.

433. Garry Wills[22] suggests ways in which αὐλοί could produce elaborate
sound effects to accompany crepitation in comedy. There can be no doubt
that such sound effects were employed. We have already cited the βομβαύ-
λιοι of A 863 ff., where such effects were produced onstage, and N 386 ff.)
where they were produced offstage. Cf. further the βομβυλιός (cf. N 160 ff.)
whose sound is like crepitations and whose name derives from the same
onomatopoeia as the vessel of the same name: its gurgling sound resulted
from a narrow mouth called the πυγή.[23] For βόμβος as a musical term, see
E. Borthwick in *CQ* 17 (1967) 154 and the riddle of Eubulus quoted in
section 431, above (l. 3). Wills plausibly suggests that the sound effects
accompanying Dionysus were produced by a βομβυκίας κάλαμος (Thphr.
HP 4.11.3); compare the description of Pan in R 230, ὁ καλαμόφθογγα
παίζων, playing on the tuneful reed.

434. *Strain and effort* produce crepitation. Dionysus' rowing (an un-

20. See the schol., Starkie at ll. 863 and 866. Dicaeopolis dubs their song τὸν πρωκτὸν
κυνός (863), probably a witty turn on what seems to have been an insult directed at the
blear-eyed. Cf. E 255, Luc. *Asin. ad fin.*, and see P. Junghanns, *Die Erzählunstechnik von
Apuleius* (Leipzig, 1932), p. 36, n. 1.

21. κεκράξομαι = πέρδεσθαι, a play on the frogs' *vox* of l. 258. The most thorough and
persuasive account of the frogs in *Frogs* is G. Wills, "Why are the Frogs in the *Frogs?*"
Hermes 97 (1969): 306 ff. For doubts, see the note by D. M. MacDowell in *CR* 22 (1972):
3 ff.

22. *Art. cit.*, p. 315.

23. Eub. 107.25, Herod. 2.44.

wonted strain on the fat and lazy god: cf. R 21 ff., 200, 740) brings on his gastric troubles initially (221 f.) and leads to crepitation (237 f.) which continues throughout the scene with rising speed, volume, and intensity. Xanthias' efforts at the beginning of the play also lead to flatulence. The short, fat man at R 1091 ff. breaks wind from the exertion of running; L. Radermacher is correct in denying the blows he receives from the amused spectators have anything to do with his flatulence.[24] Strain and effort may also be the comic basis for μεσοπέρδην (CA 1078), a play on the wrestling term μεσοφέρδην.

The Hindquarters

435. ἀρχός (rectum or anus: *LSJ* s.v. II) appears in the invented name Κολέαρχος, sheath-rump (pathic) at CA 1047.

436. ἕδρα, seat, is a euphemism, and had a respectable tone in serious literature.[25] In Aristophanes (N 1507 and T 133) the word is given a wry and buffoonish coloration.

437. θύρα, gate, seems to be a vulgar term for the anus and is always used with reference to pederasty. At E 316 f.,

> ὁ δ᾽ ἤδη τὴν θύραν
> κρούων ἐπεῖχ᾽ ὁ Κόπρειος οὗτος

[This *Coprean* fellow keeps banging at my gate.]

the Coprean is a personification of the prickly pear blocking Blepyrus' defecation; κρούων (see section 305, above) gives the personification a homosexual meaning. Similarly, at E 361 an Ἀχραδούσιος (the pear again) βεβαλάνωκε τὴν θύραν (see section 41, above). Similar jokes on this *vox* are Apollod. Com. 13.9 (all orators are pederasts) and Eur. *Cyc.* 502.

438. θριγκός, fence, seems to be an invented double entendre at T 59 ff., where the Relation twists obscenely the paratragic terminology of Agathon's servant:

> ὃς ἕτοιμος σοῦ τοῦ τε ποιητοῦ
> τοῦ καλλιεποῦς κατὰ τοῦ θριγκοῦ

---

24. "Volkstümliche Schwankmotive bei Aristophanes," *WSt* 35 (1913): 193 ff.; Radermacher thinks that the man blows out the lamp as a prank, quoting the proverbial saying, "Alles ist eine Wissenschaft, sagte der Teufel, und blies die Altarlichter mit dem Hintern aus."

25. Hdt. 2.87, Hp. *Aph.* 5.22, Arist. *HA* 633^{b}8, Simon. *Eq.* 9, Theoc. 24.111, Luc. *VH* 1.23, Thphr. *Ch.* 27.

συγγογγύλας καὶ συστρέψας
τουτὶ τὸ πέος χοανεῦσαι.

The lines mean, "I'll smelt this penis of mine in your back gate," i.e. bugger you.[26]

439. At N 676 θυεία στρογγύλη is surely the round mortar (anus) into which the pestle (penis) is inserted. ἐν θυείᾳ στρογγύλῃ γ᾽ ἀνεμάττετο means "kneaded his dough in a round mortar," that is, buggered.[27] Dover's objections (ad loc.) are not decisive against this natural interpretation, and his solution—that the line refers to masturbation—is unsatisfactory. His only argument is an appeal to stage action, which cannot of course be documented. He cites "the two-handed grip favored by (e.g.) the satyr on the London black-figure cup B 410 (*JHS* 85 [1965], pl. vi*b*)" as the gesture behind our joke, but surely what we see on vases is highly stylized and not in conformity with natural masturbatory gestures, which are one-handed. Besides, the satyrs on vases are usually ostentatiously readying themselves for intercourse and are not really masturbating. As for Dover's notion that anal intercourse was "too much taken for granted by the Greeks to be an object of riducule *per se*," it is hoped that the following chapter will demonstrate the contrary. Aristophanes and the other comic poets never miss an opportunity for just such ridicule; indeed, there seems to have been no lack of opportunity.

440. For ἰσθμός see section 143, above.

441. For ἰσχάς, dried fig, see chap. 2, n. 137.

442. κόλον, the large intestine, refers to the rectum in the pederastic puns on κόλοις/κολᾷ and ἐγκοληβάζειν at Eq 263 and 455 f.; see chap. 3, n. 21.

443. For κόλπος, gulf, see section 203, above.

444. κοχώνη, the perineum,[28] almost always refers to anal intercourse: thus the debauched young Sausage-Seller at Eq 424, 483 f.; the "argonaut" who "sails" the κοχῶναι at Fr 544 (see section 266, above); Fr 482; the description of buggery at Eup. 77.3 f. At Eub. 97, Eup. 156, and Crates 27, it seems merely to mean "hindquarters"; at Theopomp. 78, it is a nickname for a hag.

444a. προχῶναι meaning "the buttocks" appears at Archipp. 41.

445. κυσός meaning "the male anus": see chap. 2, n. 123.

446. μᾶζα, kneaded dough, refers to the anus at P 11 f.:

26. The scholiast's explanation is correct: ὡς εἰς χόανον τὸν πρωκτὸν ἐμβαλεῖν. For the image cf. Hp. *Ep.* 23, where θριγκὸς ὀδόντων means "mouth."

27. So Blaydes, ad loc., A. Willems, *Aristophane* (Paris-Brussels, 1919), 1: 397, Taillardat (n. 1, above), p. 70. Cf. Hsch. αὐτομάττιτα (from μάττειν), glossed as σπέρμα ἀνδρός, a reference, one assumes from the prefix, to masturbation.

28. Hp. *Epid.* 5.7 (sg.); *Mul.* 2.131 (pl.); schol. Eq 422; Suda.

ἑτέραν ἑτέραν δός, παιδὸς ἡταιρηκότος·
τετριμμένης γάρ φησιν ἐπιθυμεῖν.

[Give me another turd-cake, and yet another—this one from a buggered boy: the dung-beetle says he likes them well kneaded.]

The same image, with reference to a woman, is that of Pl 305 (quoted in section 419, above).

447. ὄζος, a knot or eye from which a branch or twig springs (*LSJ*), is an image used to describe the anus at V 1376 f., where Philocleon and his son make anatomical jokes about the purloined flute-girl:

Βδ. ὁ δ᾽ ὄπισθεν οὐχὶ πρωκτός ἐστιν οὑτοσί;
Φι. ὄζος μὲν οὖν τῆς δᾳδὸς οὗτος ἐξέχει.

[*Bd.* Isn't this thing back here an ass-hole?
Ph. No, that's simply the branch-hole of the torch sticking out.]

MacDowell, ad loc., gives only the literal meaning, "a branch of the torch." Similar images involving ὄζος appear in technical writers: "ear" (Emp. 99) and "squinty eye" (Thphr. *HP* 1.8.4) are examples.

447a. The anus as a squinty eye is the image behind the joke at N 193, ὁ πρωκτὸς εἰς τὸν οὐρανὸν βλέπει, his ass-hole's peering at the sky!

448. ὄρρος, rump, appears at P 1239 and R 222. Both references are to sore backsides. ὀρροπύγιον, tail-feathers or tail-end,[29] appears in a quasi-technical sense at N 162 (of an insect's tail) and V 1075 (of the wasps').

449. πρωκτός was the *vox propria* for the anus in comedy and has an exclusively male (and therefore usually homosexual) reference (see sections 203 f., above). Its low tone assured that even in the absence of a joke its mere mention could be counted on to raise a laugh: thus its purely gratuitous occurrences at Eq 381, 640, 721, N 164, V 431, 604, 1035, 1173, P 172, 758, 1237, T 248, and so forth.

450. πυγή (and τὰ πυγαῖα, buttocks, at Archipp. 41), on the other hand, is not found very frequently in comedy at all, and certainly not nearly as often as the ubiquitous πρωκτός. Unlike the latter, πυγή occurs outside comedy regularly, often with no more vulgarity of tone than English "rump."[30] Also unlike πρωκτὸς, πυγή refers as often to women as to men, and except for the stock term κατάπυγων, only twice occurs with a homosexual meaning: (1) Eq 1368 with deliberate salaciousness in the diminu-

29. Arist. *HA* 504ᵃ 32, 618ᵇ 33, *al.*
30. Thus compounds like ἀντίπυγος (Arist. *HA* 540ᵃ14), ὀξύπυγος (*Hippiatr.* 14), πλατόπυγος (Str. 4.4.1, of boats), πυγαῖος (Hdt. 2.76, Hp. *Art.* 57, 78), πυγαλγίας (Str. 14.1.20), πύγαργος (Hdt. 4.192), πυγή (of land, Eust. 310.2), πυγηδόν (Arist. *PA* 659ᵃ20), παλιμπυγηδόν (ibid.), πυγόριζα (Hsch.), πυγολαμπίς (Arist. *HA* 523ᵇ21), πυγοσκελίς (Hsch.), and so on.

tive πυγίδιον; (2) R 1070, also in the context of wearing down the rump by rowing. The verb πυγίζειν (like πρωκτίζειν at T 1124) is used by the barbarian archer at T 1120 ff. to achieve some variation in his smutty language; the meaning, of course, is "to bugger."[31] Occasional comic compounds involving πυγή are found outside Aristophanes with a homosexual meaning.[32]

451. πύλη, gateway, at Anaxandr. 33.17 certainly has the double meaning of anus:

> ἥδε γὰρ δαμάζεται
> ἐφθοῖς προσώποις ἰχθύων χειρουμένη,
> ἄγουσ᾽ ὑπ᾽ αὐτὰ σώματ᾽ ἀρίστου πύλας,
> ἀσύμβολον κλίνειν τ᾽ ἀναγκάζει φύσιν.

[This art (e.g. the fisherman's) contributes to love's conquest with all manner of boiled fish, leading our very bodies to the threshold of a meal/the Best, and makes Nature take a free place at table.]

Here ἀρίστου plays upon some proper name, perhaps Εὐρύτου (Jacobs, cited by Kock); compare the similar joke on εὐρυπρωκτία at D.L. 6.59 involving Εὐρυτίων. For φύσις see section 27, above.

452. πύλος at Eq 54 f. seems to be a double entendre for the anus:

> καὶ πρώην γ᾽ ἐμοῦ
> μᾶζαν μεμαχότος ἐν πύλῳ Λακωνικήν.

[And just the other day when (1) I was kneading my bread Laconian-style in Pylos, (2) I was kneading my Laconian *loaf* in a gate . . .]

The μᾶζα Λακωνική is, of course, the slave's phallus (compare the action at N 676). Contributing to the humor is a pun on μάττειν/μάχεσθαι. For πύλος = cunt, see section 142, above.[33]

453. ταῦρος, bull, usually the phallus or the female member, can also indicate the hindquarters: Eust. 259.3, 527.44, 906.60, 1871.43 = ὄρρος,

---

31. See Theoc. 5.41, *AP* 9.317.

32. δωσίπυγος (Suda s.v. ἀφέλεια), δασύπυγος (Schol. Theocr. 5.112), λεπτόπυγος (Schol. Eq 1365), λισπόπυγος (Phryn. *PS* p. 86B, Poll. 2.184).

33. There is probably a further pun on πύλῳ/πυέλῳ. For the obscene meaning of the latter word, cf. Athen. 15.695E:

> πόρνη καὶ βαλανεὺς τωὐτὸν ἔχουσ᾽ ἐμπεδέως ἔθος·
> ἐν ταὐτᾷ πυέλῳ τόν τ᾽ ἀγαθὸν τόν τε κακὸν λόει.

[The whore and the bathman have one thing in common: they lave both the good man and the bad in the same trough.]

τὸν περὶ τοὺς γλουτοὺς τόπον. This usage is reflected in such comic terms for aggressive (as opposed to pathic) homosexuals as Κένταυρος(= ὁ κεντῶν τὸν ὄρρον, Eust. 1910.10; = παιδεραστής, Hsch.) and λάσταυρος (*AP* 12. 41.4 = aggressive homosexuals; cf. Eust. 259.4 *al.* = the hairy-rumped; Phryn. 173 Rutherford = ἐπὶ τοῦ καταπύγονας; Theopomp. Hist. 217 (a) = κίναιδος). κένταυρος at N 346 and 350 also refers to aggressive homosexuals.

454. τράμις, the perineum, appears in the ludicrous depilation of the Relation at T 242,[34] elsewhere with a pederastic meaning: τερπότραμις (Telecl. 66), διάτραμις (Stratt. 74),[35] not to mention Hipponax 114a, Archilochus 283. That it could mean simply "anus" is clear from Hsch., Luc. *Lex.* 2, Ruf. *Onom.* 101.

454a. τράχηλος, neck, seems (although I find no other example) to indicate the anus at R 19 f., where Xanthias is complaining that overexertion is causing him to fart:

> ὢ τρισκακοδαίμων ἆρ' ὁ τράχηλος οὑτοσί,
> ὅτι θλίβεται μέν, τὸ δὲ γέλοιον οὐκ ἐρεῖ.

[O this wretched *neck* of mine, so hard-pressed and yet unable to say anything laughable! (that is, fart: see lines 1–6).]

For τράχηλος used for various parts of the body, see *LSJ* s.v. II.

455. Several proper names are used to indicate the anus: Aristodemus (Fr 231, Cratin. 151) seems to have won this unflattering distinction on account of his debauchery,[36] as is likely also in the case of Execestus (CA 24), Theodorus (CA 310), and Timesianax (Hsch. s.v. 'Αριστόδημος). *Batalos,* accepted by Taillardat (n. 1, above), p. 70, into this category to refer to a distinguished flautist of that name (schol. Aeschin. 1.126.2), seems, rather, to be a word simply meaning "anus" (Harpocr. 44.9) which was used as a scurrilous epithet of debauchees or stammerers (a reference to crepitation):[37] βαταλίζεσθαι meant to wiggle the hindquarters,[38] and βατεῖν (βαίνειν) "to mount."[39]

34. Not, with Coulon, ad loc., the πρωκτός: see E. Fraenkel, *Beobachtungen zu Aristophanes* (Rome, 1962), pp. 116 f.

35. Unless the figure in question is an old lady with a gaping *podex* [anus], along the lines of Hor. *Ep.* 8.5. See Poll. 2.184, Hsch.

36. Schol. Luc. *Alex.* 4.

37. Demosthenes was apparently so smeared: Aeschin. 2.99, D. 18.180.

38. *Hippiatr.* 30 (of horses).

39. *AP* 317 (cj.), Theoc. 1.87.

7   Homosexuality

The aim of this chapter is to give an account of a complex cultural phenomenon solely through the eyes of Attic comic poets; it is hoped that their
evidence and viewpoints concerning homosexuality will shed light on this
subject about which all too little has been written, and that the material
analyzed here will provide some clues for the unraveling of the knotty
problems facing researchers who deal with broader questions than can be
dealt with in this book.[1]

Homosexuality was a universally recognized sexual option throughout
the ancient world, particularly in Dorian areas, where it seems to have had
a religious, ethical, and legal sanction and to have been more a part of a
man's everyday public life than was the case in Athens. The evidence does
not enable us to determine whether or not homosexual behavior was actually more frequent in Dorian areas than in Attica, but we may be sure
that in Athens it lacked the built-in nobility and social status it enjoyed
elsewhere, particularly by the middle of the fifth century.

The available evidence points to a certain Athenian nervousness regarding all types of homosexual encounters. Solon's laws concerning homosexuality, for which our chief source is Aeschines' speech *Against Timarchus,* attempted to regulate its practice and to protect Athenian citizens
from sexual abuses: slaves could not indulge in homosexuality willingly or

1. Those interested in a more general consideration of homosexuality in ancient Greece
may consult the following works: E. Bethe, "Die dorische Knabenliebe," *RhM* 62 (1907):
438 ff.; G. Devereux, "Greek Pseudo-homosexuality and the Greek Miracle," *Symb.
Oslo.* 42 (1968): 69 ff.; K. J. Dover, "Classical Greek Attitudes To Sexual Behavior,"
Arethusa 6 (1973): 59 ff., and "Eros and Nomos," *Inst. Class. Stud. Bull. Univ. Lond.* 11
(1964): 31 ff.; E. Eyben, "Antiquity's View of Puberty," *Latomus* 31 (1972): 677 ff.;
W. K. C. Guthrie, *Socrates* (Cambridge, 1971), pp. 70 ff.; W. Kroll, "Kinaidos," *RE* 21
(1921): 459 ff., and "Knabenliebe," *RE* 21 (1921): 897 ff.; H. Reynan, "Philosophie und
Knabenliebe," *Hermes* 95 (1967): 308 ff.; W. Schmid (chap. 1, n. 28, above), p. 22, n.
4 and p. 34, n. 5.

unwillingly or frequent the palaestras; free persons could not be prostituted or violated; and fathers were encouraged to protect their sons from seduction by employing guardians to watch out for their best interests, at least until they reached an age at which they could make intelligent decisions regarding the conduct of their lives. Nevertheless, it is clear that homosexual love flourished despite its less than noble public status: not only the evidence of comedy but also the enormous number of black- and red-figure vases with homosexual themes that appear up to the end of the fifth century attest to the popularity of homosexual love affairs, as do such celebrated names as Harmodius and Aristogeiton, Themistocles, Aristeides and Stesileus, and Sophocles as φιλομεῖραξ (*FHG* 2.64).

From Aeschines' speech it is possible to perceive something of the code of behavior that surrounded the carrying out of such affairs. Love affairs between men and boys or between two grown men could, depending on circumstances, be licentious and depraved or noble and chaste. If a man conducted the affair high-mindedly, without any kind of payment and out of proper regard for his lover's beauty and σωφροσύνη, then no one could blame him for satisfying his desires. But if a man prostituted himself for payment or made a habit of surrendering his body or pursuing young men for purely sensual purposes, then he could legitimately be called to account for lewdness. Obviously, there can be no cut-and-dried moral categories; like all matters sexual, this is an area in which many subtle shades of moral judgment are apparent; and the literature of comedy, allowing for its exaggerations and distortions, can teach us much about them.

Before we examine the presentation of homosexuality in comedy we must briefly develop several important points, mentioned in chapter 2 (pp. 52 ff.), which will be helpful in differentiating Greek homosexuality from the homosexuality of modern culture. As we remarked earlier, the Greeks showed a pronounced tendency to attach the greatest importance to (indeed, to glorify) the sexual *instinct* itself rather than the particular *object;* consequently they were much freer than modern men to vary sexual objects on their relative merits. Greek culture, unlike modern cultures, imposed on adult males no limitations as to the choice of sexual objects per se, and the only "perversions" remarked by the comic poets (reflecting, we may be sure, community opinion) are cases in which sexual acts other than vaginal intercourse, otherwise perfectly acceptable, are pursued to excess (see Cratin. 152, for example) or practiced in an inappropriate setting. As K. J. Dover remarks,[2] "The middle-aged peasant who is the common type of comic hero and whose values are implicit throughout comedy is a sensual opportunist who is prepared to take any pleasure for

2. "Eros and Nomos," n. 1, above, p. 39.

its own sake." Whether or not the average, happily married Athenian adult actually did indulge in the kind of multifarious sexual opportunism so frequently practiced by comic heroes, the fact remains that any and all sexual outlets were available to him should he choose to pursue them.

It is not difficult even from our limited evidence to understand the adult Greek male's easy sliding from one kind of sexual object to another and why his bisexuality probably caused him, on the whole, little anxiety of the kind modern homosexuals experience. For Greek men were expected by society to pass through predominantly homosexual stages of life on their way to full masculinity, marriage, and fatherhood. As young boys, they were pursued as ἐρώμενοι, love objects, by older boys and men and were expected to reciprocate these attentions with all the shyness, coyness, and modesty characteristic of all love games, including the American adolescent's pursuit of the opposite sex. (Instructive in this regard are Unjust Logic's harangue on youthful sexual decorum in *Clouds,* Pausanias' speech in Plato's *Symposium,* and Lysias' in the *Phaedrus.*) In later adolescence, a Greek youth might become an ἐραστής, lover, himself and pursue younger ἐρώμενοι. Finally, upon the assumption of manhood, he would arrange a suitable marriage, settle down into his role as father and citizen, and relegate homosexuality to a secondary role.

As an adult, the Greek male was predominantly heterosexual and his sexual responsibilities were primarily to his wife. Homosexual gratification became, with marriage, at best a marginal luxury, and in its distinctly secondary role did not usually become the focus of intense and lasting emotions of the kind we find exalted by Plato. Homosexual passion in Greece was a phenomenon of youth, as Callicles caustically remarks to Socrates in the *Gorgias,* and was, upon the advent of marriage and the rearing of children, expected to assume a role quite subordinate to adult heterosexuality.[3]

But homosexual drives were not shut off or denied in adulthood—they remained a powerful force and no shame was attached to their occasional gratification, provided the proper etiquette was observed. Thus the Greek male adult slid easily from one kind of sex object to another as a result of a natural and culturally sanctioned prolongation into adulthood of certain aspects of pubertal sexuality, especially the early adolescent's undifferentiated (and undifferentiating) sexual instincts. Comic terminology, in which words for the vagina and the anus, and vaginal and anal penetration, are very often identical, reflects this undifferentiatedness of the sexual drives.

Moreover, the comic terminology by which male and female bodies are

3. See also Pl. *Lgg.* 839b3–6, Lys. 3.4, etc.

erotically described (see pp. 53 ff., above) reflect another related feature of the bisexual personality, one we observe also in countless vase paintings and statues: namely, the preference of the Greeks for sexual objects which are sexually incompletely identified, not fully developed, and combine the physical characteristics of both sexes—women or girls who have trim, firm bodies with neat features (small breasts and hips like unripe fruit, and a minimum of pubic hair), and young, undeveloped boys who display the "feminine" mental qualities of shyness, coyness, modesty, and the need for instruction and assistance from older men. There is a constantly expressed preference for more or less ambiguously defined sexual characteristics, a preference reflecting well-known features of pubertal sexuality— namely, a decidedly narcissistic object-choice; the retention of the erotic cathexis of the anal zone (see pp. 53 ff.), the undifferentiatedness of the object-choice, and noticeable feelings of spontaneity and strangeness revealed by inordinate fascination with the phenomenon of erection.

Greek society encouraged its adult males to retain these adolescent traits into adulthood because the group ideal was the beautiful adolescent. Boys were encouraged in puberty to display homosexual interests and to reciprocate the attentions of older boys and adults, and retained these traits in manhood. Greek culture was an intensely male culture, preoccupied with youth and the ideals of youth. Not only in Sparta, where the ἐραστής was publicly responsible for the conduct of his ἐρώμενος, but also to a degree in Athens, the lover was a kind of father-surrogate and educator for his boyfriend, and the love of boys, even if infrequent, was considered to be more exciting and more rewarding than the routine love of one's wife or other women. As Devereux says, "The basic fact is not Greek (pseudo-) homosexuality, but a psychological and affective state, which made the Greek *capable* of complying with the cultural demand for homosexual behavior. This state . . . is that of adolescence, artificially prolonged into adulthood."[4]

Thus it is not too hard to see the great difference between Greek homosexuality, which was accepted by and fully integrated into society, and modern homosexuality, which is considered by society—not without reason—to be a perversion, a deviation from the socially enforced heterosexual pattern. All the energies of modern culture are devoted to the rearing of heterosexuals; homosexual leanings are assiduously discouraged from youth to adulthood and therefore can be nurtured by the individual only in defiance of society. Whereas Greek homosexuality is not a stable pattern in life, but only a phenomenon of puberty later integrated into adult heterosexual life, modern homosexuality tends to be a lasting pattern

4. N. 1, above, p. 90.

which establishes itself as a perversion early in childhood and gives way with great difficulty (if at all) to heterosexual "normality" in later life. Modern homosexuality becomes a compulsion leading inevitably to anxiety and even neurosis; Greek homosexuality, on the contrary, remained only a temporary resort (see, for example, *Lysistrata*), purely sexual in nature, and thus did not normally become a device for alleviating anxieties. Finally, there is no evidence that Greek homosexuality was normally fused with or placed in the service of nonsexual aggressive drives, or that it was ever antihedonistic or less pleasurable than vaginal intercourse, as modern homosexuality commonly seems to be. When these characteristics of true perversion occurred in Greece—as in the case of devoted pederasts, pathics, or transvestites (discussed below)—they were criticized not for their homosexual passions but only for what was considered to be unhealthy exclusiveness and a refusal to accept the normal range of sexual possibilities open to Greek male adults. Therefore, Heracles, when Dionysus confesses that he has been smitten by desire (R 52 ff.), tries to guess, *more tragico*, who the object of the god's desire might be: his first guess is a woman, then a boy, then a man, and finally Cleisthenes, who as an effeminate does not qualify for any of the recognized sexual categories.

456. The order in which Heracles mentions these four types of love-object in fact corresponds to their relative social acceptability, at least in the view of the poets of comedy. Heterosexual relations, whether with wife, flute-girl, courtesan, or slave, were of course a normal part of Greek male adulthood and could hardly be the target of mockery unless accompanied by some sort of perversion. Aristophanes never makes heterosexuality the basis for ὀνομαστὶ κωμῳδεῖν, personal ridicule, but on the contrary very often treats it with some seriousness and even nobility, most notably in *Peace* and *Lysistrata*. There can be no doubt that heterosexuality is presented in comedy as the normal sexual state; part of every hero's triumph, along with unlimited eating and complete freedom from social restraints, is unabashed and uninhibited access to the opposite sex; the healing through fantasy of a war-torn polis usually includes general heterosexual indulgence accompanied by themes of universal fertility.

457. Homosexuality, on the other hand, rarely appears in comedy without some pejorative coloration. The audience is invited to laugh self-consciously, and usually derisively, at the exposure of what was a common but somewhat embarrassing fact of Athenian sexual life in the fifth century. At best, homosexuality (in the form of the occasional enjoyment of a boy) is presented as a harmless vice; at worst (in the case of grown men who are fond of other men or who are actually effeminate), it is made to represent and exemplify corruption, decadence, shamelessness, wickedness, or "perversion". Never is it presented in a sympathetic light, never are we encouraged to look beyond its purely physical and sensual aspects to the more idealized view that we find in the writings of Greek philosophers. A modern analogy would be our own society's ambivalent feelings about alcoholism: nothing is more prevalent in America and most of northern Europe than the drinking of alcohol, and yet everyone admits that drinking is harmful, dangerous, and often degrading, not to mention illegal or rigorously circumscribed in certain areas. No one takes a drink without some sign of self-consciousness, and no form of joke, save sexual, is more popular in comedy. As with Athenian homosexual humor, modern humor regarding alcohol boasts as many slang terms as sexual humor itself.

Pathics

458. Of all the types of homosexual humor in comedy by far the most common is the abuse of pathics, evidently the most risible kind of homosexual. It would seem that homosexual surrender was potentially more harmful to one's good name than homosexual pursuit. Nearly all terms of abuse that refer to homosexuality refer to passive homosexuality. A commonplace in comedy is the contention that all Athenians (that is, the audience) are pathics;[5] Athens herself is ἡ Κεχηναίων πόλις (see section 464, below), the gapers' city (Eq 1263). A running joke in Aristophanes and other comic poets holds that most successful statesmen are those with the widest πρωκτοί: witness the discussion concerning the degraded beginnings of the Sausage-Seller's dizzying career at Eq 424 ff., 876 ff.; at Eq 879 f. Cleon is said to have "put a stop to" οἱ κινούμενοι simply to prevent the development of future rivals to his power. And Agyrrhius' career was going nowhere until he became a pathic: now he is an important official (E 102 ff.). Eupolis complains (100) that Athens has fallen under the sway of μειράκια βινούμενα, and Plato Comicus remarks (186.5) that anyone who becomes a pathic will of course become a rhetor as well.

459. The most striking comic working-out of this alleged pattern in Athenian public life is, of course, the rise of the Sausage-Seller. In a wonderfully ambiguous passage, the Sausage-Seller himself reports his maiden speech to the Βουλή (Eq 638 ff.):

$$\text{ταῦτα φροντίζοντί μοι}$$
$$\text{ἐκ δεξιᾶς ἐπέπαρδε καταπύγων ἀνήρ.}$$

5. A 79, 104, 635 (cf. also *LSJ* s.v. χαῦνος II, χαυνόω II), Eq 1263, 1367, P 11 and schol., 101, N 1084 ff., Fr 694.

κἀγὼ προσέκυσα· κᾆτα τῷ πρωκτῷ θενὼν
τὴν κιγκλίδ᾽ ἐξήραξα κἀναχανὼν μέγα
ἀνέκραγον . . .

[As I was mulling over these things, a pathic fellow farted on the right.
I bowed reverently, then ramming at the bar with my ass I burst in,
and, gaping wide, broke forth . . .]

We notice that his speech is prompted by an appropriate Athenian omen,
not a sneeze but the crepitation of a pathic. The words used to convey the
beginning of the address are all double entendres for εὐρυπρωκτία: τὴν
κιγκλίδα puns on the coital jerking named after the κίγκλος (see section
360, above); ἀναχανών plays on gaping in its pathic sense; and ἀνέκραγον
plays on the meaning "break wind" (see chap. 6, n. 21). The Sausage-
Seller qua rhetor seems indistinguishable from the Sausage-Seller qua
pathic; the authority of a politician's voice depends on the width of his
πρωκτός.

All of this bating of the audience is good-natured and takes place in a
venerable comic tradition. On the individual level, however, the strongest
Schimpfwörter in comedy derive from passive homosexuality.

460. εὐρύπρωκτος, the most common, seems not to have developed into
a more general term of abuse but to have retained its homosexual meaning. It is used only with reference to those whose πρωκτοί have been widened by constant buggery and who are on that account depraved or evil.[6]
The use of εὐρύπρωκτος to insult the audience in Clouds (1083 ff.) does
not imply that the term was being used simply to mean "wicked" but in
fact meant to assert that Athenians actually were pathics all.

461. The related word λακκόπρωκτος, cistern-arse, seems to have been
more general in its applicability. Strepsiades uses this word of his son (N
1330), who is anything but a pathic; at Eup. 351.4 λακκοπρωκτία is used of
wine-drinking in the morning; and in Cephisodor. 3 by a slave insulting
his master.[7]

462. καταπύγων is often used as a general term of abuse: two characters in Aristophanes' Banqueters were ὁ σώφρων and ὁ καταπύγων (N
529), the good man and the bad man. Such seems to be the tone of its use
at A 664, N 909, of women at L 137, 776 and in Fr 130, Cratin. 241. Other
appearances are distinctly homosexual: A 79, Eq 638 f. (see section 459,
above), N 1023, V 84, 687, T 200 (note the παθήμασιν of l. 201).

6. A 716, 843, Eq 721, N 1084 (a humorous reference to ῥαφανίδωσις), 1090–99, V
1070, T 200, Eub. 120.7 f.

7. Compare λακκοσχέας (Luc. Lex. 12, Poll. 2.172, Ruf. Onom. 107), λακκόπεδον (Poll.
2.172, Ruf. Onom. 106, Aristag. 6), λακκοσκαπέρδας (CA 1362)—all referring to pathics.

463. The opposite of the gaping πρωκτός is one that is στενός, narrow or closed. Thus the comic word στενόπρωκτος (Phot.) and the Sausage-Seller's crude joke at Eq 719 ff. (with which compare, in a nonhomosexual sense, N 161, E 367):

> Πα. δύναμαι ποεῖν τὸν δῆμον εὐρὺν καὶ στενόν.
> Αλ. χὦ πρωκτὸς οὑμὸς τουτογὶ σοφίζεται.

[*Pa:* I'm able to make the city now wide, now narrow.
SS: Even this ass-hole of mine knows that trick!]

464. The verb χάσκειν is often used in the abuse of pathics: the Athenians are χαυνόπρωκτοι (A 104), χαυνοπολίτας (A 635), κεχηναῖοι (Eq 1263). Certain young men are οἱ ἐν Χάοσιν (A 604), a joke that is repeated of Cleon at Eq 78.[8] By itself the verb seems to be a standard one with which to describe the widened state of pathics' πρωκτοί: Eq 380 f., 641,[9] V 1493, L 629 (where λύκος κεχηνώς, gaping wolf, is a humorous reference to Spartan pederasty. The expression is proverbial [*LSJ* s.v. 1] but here λύκος = pederast, as in *AP* 12.250.2; cf. Pl. *Phdr.* 241d).[10]

465. To have a smooth and white skin (rather than a manly suntan) meant effeminacy. The generally pale appearance of such men was concentrated in jokes on their rear-ends (as in English slang of our own day), resulting in terms like λευκόπυγος (Alex. 321)[11] and λευκόπρωκτος (Call. Com. 11.2). λευκός is a standard epithet of pathics (e.g. E 428; cf. *LSJ* s.v. λευκός II.1.c); Photius preserves the proverb, οὐδὲν λευκῶν ἀνδρῶν ὄφελος, [there's no good use for pale men.][12]

466. The opposite of the white-rumped were the hairy-rumped, the μελάμπυγοι or δασύπρωκτοι (Pl Com. 3). These men are virile, manly, and usually heterosexual.[13] Thus Myronides and Phormio at L 802 are para-

---

8. Cf. the scholiast: ἅμα δὲ τοὺς εὐρυπρώκτους διασύρει διὰ τὸ χαίνειντὸν πρωκτκόν. Van Leeuwen objects (ad loc.): "Immo vel nimis severum morum magistrum se praestabat Cleon." Nevertheless he admits that in the very next line Cleon is a thief (Κλωπιδῶν). We must not hold the scurrilities of comic poets to the factual level. In fact, Aristophanes often accuses Cleon of homosexual offenses: see sections 472–18, 479–4, below.

9. For χάσκειν referring to crepitation, see V 617.

10. For χάσκειν in a nonhomosexual sense, cf. N 161, E 367. A. Willems, *Aristophane* (Paris-Brussels, 1919), 2: 420 f., sees a reference to χαυνόπρωκτος in χαία at L 91 f., implying that the Corinthian girl is "une callipyge" (compare Pl 149–52). If this is true, Aristophanes may be making a reference to the notoriously free sexual habits of the Corinthians.

11. Glossed as meaning ἄνανδρος; λευκόπυγοι are glossed by Photius as δειλοί. Cf. also Hsch., Eust. 863.29, Suda, schol. at L 803.

12. For ἀργοναύτης in Fr 544.2, see section 266, above.

13. The only exception in Aristophanes appears to be λάσιοι at N 349, which refers, ap-

digms of manliness and strength, and the Agathon whom the Relation mentions as ὁ μέλας, ὁ καρτερός (T 31) is quickly differentiated from the Agathon shortly to appear onstage. This use of μελάμπυγος appears throughout Greek literature, from Archilochus onward.[14]

467. In general, a small phallus and a large rear-end (as opposed to a wide πρωκτός), like those of athletic youths we see displayed on vase-paintings, meant manliness and anal integrity: N 1014, 1018, Eub. 11.2. A large phallus and a small rear end (well-worn by buggery rather than well-muscled by exercise) meant idleness and pathic depravity: N 1014, 1018, R 1070. Thus the ὑπόλισπα πυγίδια at Eq 1368 refer to εὐρύπρωκτοι as well as to the "worn rumps" of deckhands: ἄπυγος seems to indicate pathic lechery.[15]

468. μολγός, apparently a Tarentine word for "hide" or βόειος ἀσκός, was a *Schimpfwort* in comedy similar to καταπύγων:[16] the image seems to be that of leather toughened by repeated rubbing (buggery). The word means "pathic" at Eq 963 (a reference to the Sausage-Seller made by Cleon), and Fr 56 Dem. (μολγόν σε ποιήσω = κινήσω) and Fr 694 (all Athenians are μολγοί).[17]

469. Identical to μολγός are the terms κόλλοψ, the tough chine of beef,[18] and λωγάς, the dewlap of oxen.[19] Compare the Latin *scortum*, hide, which can mean both prostitute and homosexual.[20] Perhaps κασαλβάς, whore, and the related words κασαλβάζειν, κασωρῖτις, etc. are connected with κασῆς, hide, in the same metaphor.[21] While these terms are used in comedy

---

parently, to aggressive homosexuality. Cf. δασύς = manly as opposed to effeminate at T 160. There is, however, no evidence to support the view of Th. Hopfner, *Das Sexualleben der Griechen und Römer* (Prague, 1938), p. 242, that "haarige Leute galten überhaupt als geil" [hairy people were considered especially lascivious]. For other hairy-rumped aggressors, see section 281–10, above.

14. Archil. 178, Hdt. 7.216, Luc. *Pseudol.* 32, Schol. *Il.* 24.315.

15. Pl Com. 184.3; compare the monkey-woman in Semon. 7.76. For the worn anus, cf. Poll. 2.184, Suda s.v. λίσποι, Phryn. *PS* p. 86B.

16. The Suda glosses as μοχθηρός. The explanation in Poll. 10.187, τὸ ἄπληστον, and the Suda's alternatives (ὁ βραδύς, ὁ τυφλός, οἱ ἐξαμέλγοντες καὶ κλέπτοντες τὰ κοινά) are clumsy guesses.

17. Brunck's suggestion that μολγός refers to fellatio, the connection being with ἀμέλγειν, to milk/suck/let suck (middle voice), is rightly denied by J. Taillardat, "Comica," *Rev. Ét. Gr.* 64 (1951): 14 ff.

18. Eub. 11.3, Pl Com. 186.5, CA 1048. Cf. also Diphil. 43.22, *AP* 12.42, Hsch., *AB* 102.33.

19. Suda = πόρνη; Hsch. s.v. λωγάλιον glosses ἀστράγαλοι ἢ πόρνοι.

20. M. Hammerström, "De vocibus scorti, scrattae . . . ," *Eranos* 23 (1925): 106 f.

21. See H. Frisk, *Griechisches etymologisches Wörterbuch* (Heidelberg, 1960–72) s.v. κασαλβάς, κασῆς.

chiefly with reference to female debauchees,[22] at least several uses may have a homosexual reference: Eub. 11.3 οἱ κόλλοπες = homosexuals; CA 1048 κολλοποδιώκτας = active pederasts; Diph. 43.22 κόλλωψι μαστροποῖς = debauched panderers.

470. Holding up the middle finger meant, as it still does, that the recipient of the gesture was a pathic. This insulting gesture has the same force as the word καταπύγων (which Phot. glosses as ὁ μέσος δάκτυλος) and can be used as an all-purpose expression of enmity and contempt. The technical term for this gesture was σκιμαλίζειν (A 444, P 549);[23] καταδακτυλικός is also used (Eq 1381).[24] Strepsiades' buffoonish game with his finger at N 653 f. disrupts his lesson and annoys Socrates, who considers anyone who would make such a gesture to be σκαιός and ἀγρεῖος, rustic and perverse (N 655).

471. The term σιφνιάζειν (CA 1142, Fr 912?) meant actually to poke someone's πρωκτός with the finger; the purpose was the same as that of the gesture discussed in section 470, above.

Pathic Κωμῳδούμενοι

472. The list of individuals attacked by comic poets as pathics is substantial; a detailed perusal will reveal most of the scurrilous nuances connected with this vice and considered so humorous by the audience.

1. Agathon: see section 479–1, below.

2. Agyrrhius—E 102 ff.: a γυνή; cf. Pl 176 (crepitation as a sign of εὐρυπρωκτία, as at Eq 638 ff.).

3. Alcibiades[25]—A 716: εὐρύπρωκτος; cf. Fr 554 (born in the archonship of "Phalenias"), CA 1063, Eup. 158. Also an adulterer (Pherecr. 155, Eup. 158, 351, CA 3).

4. Amynias—N 686 ff.: a γυνή and draft-dodger; V 466: κομηταμυνίας (see section 483, below); V 1267: a descendant of Crobylus, a play on κρωβύλος, an effeminate hair-style (cf. also Hermipp. 71).[26]

5. Amynon—E 364 f.: τῶν κατὰ πρωκτὸν δεινός ἐστι τὴν τέχνην, an expert in all matters concerning the ass-hole.

6. Androcles—Cratin. 263: ἡταιρηκότα, debauched.

7. Antimachus—N 1022 f.: full of καταπυγοσύνη.

8. Antisthenes—E 366 ff.: an expert on widening anal στενάγματα, narrows.

22. Eq 1285, E 1106, Fr 478, Hermipp. Com. 71.
23. Cf. D.L. 7.17, *PLond.* 1821.308.
24. Cf. schol. Eq 1381, P 549, Phryn. *PS* p. 83B, *AB* 48.23.
25. See now R. Littman, "The Loves of Alcibiades," *TAPA* 101 (1972): 263 ff.
26. See MacDowell at V 74.

9. Ariphrades—Eq 1287: ξυνὼν Οἰωνίχῳ, bed-mate of Oeonichus, in addition to his taste for cunnilingus. Cf. V 474 f. (of Bdelycleon).

10. Aristodemus—Fr 231: μιαρὸς καὶ καταπύγων εἰς ὑπερβολήν, polluted and pathic in the extreme. His name was synonymous with πρωκτός.

11. Aristomedes—Timocl. 1.3, 2.3 Dem. (?).

12. Autocles—Timocl. 2.1 Dem. (?).

13. Callias—see section 479–6, below.

14. Callistratus—Eub. 11: has a πυγὴ μεγάλη καὶ καλή, big, beautiful rump; Eub. 107.5: a walking πρωκτός.

15. Chaereas' son—V 687 ff.: μειράκιον κατάπυγον, pathic young man; Philocleon imitates his effeminate gait.

16. Chaerephon—Fr 573: νυκτὸς παῖς, son of the night.

17. Cleisthenes—see sections 480–88, below.

18. Clearchus (?)—CA 1047: called Κολέαρχος (see section 435, above).

19. Cleocritus—Av 877 (with schol.): γυναικίας καὶ κίναιδος, effeminate and debauched; cf. Eup. 124.

20. Cleon—A 664: λακαταπύγων; P 48: by implication a κοπρολόγος; Eq 380 f.: κεχηνότος, his πρωκτός being a comic substitute for his στόμα; P 758: he has the πρωκτός of a camel (i.e. wide and smelly);[27] Eq 876 ff.: one of the κινούμενοι (rhetors). These references do not mean that Cleon was actually a pathic; they are merely scabrous insults brought on by the poet's personal dislike of Cleon.

21. Cleonymus—N 672 ff.: feminine in gender, who ἐν θυείᾳ στρογγύλῃ γ᾽ ἀνεμάττετο (i.e. buggered: see section 439, above), a play on the κάρδοπος involved in Socrates' quibbles over gender.

22. Demochares—Archedic. 4 (a professional fellator).

23. Epigonus—E 167: identified in the audience as a woman.

24. Evathlus—Fr 411: εὐρύπρωκτος.

25. Execestus—CA 24: his name used to mean πρωκτός.

26. Geron—E 848 ff.: dressed effeminately and giggling with his boy-friend.

27. Gnesippus—Cratin. 97: a character in *Malthakoi*.

28. Gryttus—Eq 877: prosecuted by Cleon for pathic pederasty.

29. Leagrus— Pl Com. 64: has the soft shanks of a "eunuch cucumber" (i.e. ripe and seedless).

30. Lycurgus—Cratin. 30: follows behind women carrying a δίφρος (lady's potty) and an effeminate robe.

31. Melanthius and sons—Callias 11: μάλιστα λευκόπρωκτοι, especially

27. Cf. V 603 f., Hor. *Ep*. 8.5 f., Strattis 74 (= Poll. 2.184), Hsch. s.v. διάτραμις. διερρωγὼς τὴν τράμιν.

white-assed. (a play on their name); cf. Eup. 164: κίναιδος.

32. Melesias—N 686: feminine in gender.

33. Nicias—E 427 f.: a young man εὐπρεπής and λευκός "like Nicias" jumps up and advocates turning the city over to the women.

34. Philoxenus—V 84: καταπύγων; N 686: feminine in gender; Eup. 235: θήλεια; Phryn. Com. 47: πόρνος, male whore.

35. Prepis—A 843: just to touch him meant to be infected by εὐρυπρω-κτία.

36. Sebinus—R 427: a *Redender Name* (βινεῖν), not a real person, as has been supposed (for example, by W. Schmid [chap. 1, n. 28, above], p. 22, n. 4).

37. Smicythus—Eq. 969: called Smicythe (cf. *IG* I.139).

38. Sostratus—N 678: called Sostrate.

39. Straton—the habitual companion of Cleisthenes: A 122, Eq 1373 f. Fr 407.

40. Theodorus—CA 310 f.: his name meant πρωκτός, and he was nicknamed πελεθοβάφ.

41. Timarchus—CA 298: πόρνοι μεγάλοι called Τιμαρχώδεις from the notorious ἡταιρηκώς, Timarchus (cf. Hsch. s.v. Δημοκλεῖδαι).

42. Xenophon—Cratin. 53: καταπυγοσύνη; called a mouse on account of his lechery.

Active Pederasty

473. Humor involving active pederasty is far less frequent and less intense than that which plays upon the vices and foibles of pathics and effeminates, who surrender to rather than initiate homosexual intercourse. The reason for this seems to be that there was no particular shame involved in seeking outlets for one's homosexual drives as long as one did not make it the ruling passion of one' sexual life, and as long as one was careful not to involve boys or young men whose company would be denied by their parents or guardians.[28]

474. References to boy-love are often no more pejorative than references to heterosexual love: one of Peisetaerus' utopian dreams is a city where he might actually be encouraged to take his pleasure with high-born boys rather than being punished by their fathers (Av 137 ff.); Philocleon very much enjoys looking at naked boys (V 578); and both Demus (Eq 1385) and Dicaeopolis (A 1102, 1121) possess a boy as well as women as part of their triumphs.

28. See P. G. Maxwell-Stuart, "Strato and the Musa Puerilis," *Hermes* 100 (1972): 216.

475. But men who loiter around the palaestra waiting to seduce young boys are always condemned, though not subjected to the abuse and harsh humor reserved for pathics and effeminates. It is felt that grown men should spend their time on more grown-up pursuits and should not pester young men with their lusts. Thus Socrates and his followers are obliquely criticized at N 179[29] for spending idle hours at the palaestra engaged in various disreputable activities. Aristophanes must (for obscure reasons) deny having tried to seduce boys at the palaestra in the parabases of both *Wasps* (1025 ff.) and *Peace* (762 f.). The palaestra was, of course, associated with athletics, and the young men who exercised there were expected to be healthy and wholesome;[30] professional pathics usually frequented sleazier places, such as the agora,[31] the bath-houses,[32] or the area around Lycabettus (Theopomp. Com. 29).

476. Much of the active pederastic humor in Aristophanes derives from making fun of the nobles for their sexual behavior. Close pederastic relationships with boys, complete with all the trappings of a love affair, had been very much an accepted part of the nobles' style of life in aristocratic times, and the practice continued throughout Aristophanes' day, as is clear in the passionate Third Speech of Lysias, as well as in the names of the hundreds of *kaloi* memorialized on Attic *Lieblingsvasen,* most of them from the upper classes and including not a few archons, *strategoi,* politicians, and Socratics.[33] But the average democratic playgoer of Aristophanes' day must have looked at these affairs with cynicism and amusement, just as he looked with amusement at the odd doings of all men in authority: intellectuals, politicians, nobles, gods. Part of the fun of Old Comedy was the identification of the "average" people in the audience with the self-assertive and authority-debunking heroes on stage. The comic poets were quick to exploit this sensitive side of the nobility for its humorous potential. There is even some reason to believe that Aristophanes' attacks on the nobles' παιδικά led to some attempt at censorship on their part (V 1025 ff.).

477. Aristophanes wrote according to the cynical principle of CA 12, οὐδεὶς κομήτης ὅστις οὐ ψηνίζεται; this means, in essence, that every noble

---

29. The scholiast remarks, διαβάλλει αὐτὸν ὡς περὶ τὰς παλαίστρας τῶν παίδων ἔνεκεν διατρίβοντα.

30. Cf. N 1054, R 729, 1070, Fr 637.

31. Eq 181, 218, 293, 636, 1257, 1259, 1335, 1373, 1375 ff., N 991, 1003, 1055, T 578.

32. Eq 1060, N 837, 991, 1054.

33. See D. M. Robinson and E. I. Fluck, *A Study of the Greek Love Names* (Baltimore, 1937), pp. 36 ff., 66 ff.; W. Schmid (n. 1, above), p. 22, n. 4, p. 34, n. 5. Aristophanes pokes fun at such inscriptions at A 144, V 98 f.

is a pederast and that none of their fine words or lofty traditions can change the somewhat naughty character of a passion no different from the ones everyone has. The κομήτης Hieronymus at N 348 is called ἄγριος and grouped with the λάσιοι (aggressive pederasts), and Unjust Logic takes pains to identify a κομήτης in the audience as just as much an εὐρύπρωκτος as any other Athenian (N 1101). Aristophanes' cynical view regarding the nobles' homosexual relationships is particularly clear in the dialogue between Carion and Chremylus at Pl 153 ff.: Chremylus tries to differentiate youthful pathics according to motive and social class. Some do it for money and are therefore πόρνοι, common whores, while some do it for ἐρασταί and receive respectable gifts like silver, horses, or hunting dogs.[34] Carion, on the other hand, feels that buggery is an evil whatever the traditions and euphemisms the nobles bring forth to disguise it, and here we must accept Carion as the spokesman for the poet. Young men who take gifts in return for sexual favors are never any better than πόρνοι,

> αἰσχυνόμενοι γὰρ ἀργύριον αἰτεῖν ἴσως
> ὀνόματι περιπέττουσι τὴν μοχθηρίαν,

[For they are perhaps ashamed to take plain silver, so they cover up their wickedness with fine names.]

478. The speeches of Just Logic in *Clouds* may be taken in part as a humorous portrayal of what Aristophanes considered to be the sexual hypocrisy of the upper classes.[35] Just Logic sets himself up as the spokesman for the ἀρχαία παίδευσις (961 ff.),[36] the good old days when young men were modest and shy, exercised constantly and learned wholesome things, unlike the brazen, flabby, wide-arsed, and insolent youth of the present day, who take as their model the καταπύγων, Unjust Logic (909). In his speech Just Logic harangues his audience on the virtues of sexual continence and modesty, but falls into such anatomical and erotic detail that his own unchaste drives are apparent to all: his own vision of throngs of well-muscled, bronzed young men has inspired in him the kinds of lust that would be found in the most sexually aggressive member of the audience. This, of course, proves to be a tremendous psychological victory for Unjust Logic: what good are the elaborate rituals of pursuit and capture constructed by the nobles when it is apparent that the goal is τὸ βινεῖν

34. Av 705 ff., R 148; cf. Isaeus 10.25, Xen. *Mem.* 1.3.11, *Oec.* 2.7.

35. See the comments of K. J. Dover, *Aristophanic Comedy* (Berkeley and Los Angeles, 1972), pp. 114 f.

36. Note Demus's comment (Eq 1387) about the boy the Sausage-Seller has offered him: μακάριος εἰς τἀρχαῖα δὴ καθίσταμαι.

in any case? It is much healthier simply to let our desires have free play and not to try to repress them or pretend that they are something other than what they really are, namely τὰς φύσεως ἀνάγκας, the urges of "nature" (1075). In other words, Unjust Logic strips away the veil of Just Logic's double standard—which holds that it is proper to pursue boys but improper for them to play along without the trappings of an affair (cf. Pl. *Symp.* 182a ff.)—urging instead that everyone display his desires openly and that all young men readily comply without going to the outmoded trouble to be coy. This lesson is brought home to Just Logic in a very vivid fashion when Unjust Logic proves to his opponent that everyone in the audience, from the highest class to the lowest, is an εὐρύπρωκτος; Just Logic has no choice but to admit the bankruptcy of his aristocratic sexual notions and to desert to the enemies' camp with the cry (1103), ἡττήμεϑ', ὦ κινούμενοι.

479. The list of active pederasts ridiculed by name in comedy is very brief:

1. Agathon—T 254: his clothes smell of little boys' penises (Agathon is otherwise purely pathic).

2. Alcibiades—Fr 907: called κυσολάκων, a pederast (λακωνίζειν). The homosexual practices of the Spartans were notorious in Athens,[37] as were Alcibiades' noble, and therefore laconizing, tendencies.

3. Autocleides—cf. Timocles's *Orestautocleides*, Harpocr. s.v., Aeschin. 1.52.

4. Cleon—Eq 263: violates his victims anally; Eq 963 f.: a ψωλός all the way to his pubis, i.e. totally a pederast.; V 1284 ff.: Cleon violates Aristophanes figuratively.[38] These are all figurative uses of the image of anal penetration and are not meant to imply that Cleon was a pederast in real life. Anal rape is often the equivalent of a beating or some other violent humiliation of an opponent: cf., for example, the Sausage-Seller (Eq 364) or the Relation (T 59 ff.).

5. Hieronymus—see section 477, above.[39]

6. Meletus—Fr 114 (= schol. Pl *Apol.* 18b): ὡς Καλλίαν περαίνοντος. Perhaps also at Eup. 163.

7. Phaeax—Eq 1377 ff.: a clever speaker, περαντικός and κρουστικός (see sections 244 and 305 above).

8. Phaenippus—A 603: Τεισαμενοφαινίππους πανουργιππαρχίδας (active pederasts: see section 277, above).

---

37. Cf. V 474 f., L 620 ff., 629, 1105, 1148, 1174, Fr 338; Pl Com. 124, Eup. 352.1.
38. See chap. 5, n. 103, above.
39. Cf. Aeschin. 1.52 and schol., Harpocration s.v.

9. Teisamenus—see under Phaenippus, above.

10. Xenophantes' son—N 349 f.: a hairy, aggressive pederast compared to a κέντανρος (see section 453, above).

Effeminacy

480. Lowest in respectability and most ridiculous of all homosexuals in comedy are the effeminates, men who actually dress as women and who are, in addition, promiscuous pathics. Most of the many special characteristics of effeminates are to be found in the scenes in *Thesmophoriazusae* featuring Agathon and Cleisthenes, the most notorious effeminates in Aristophanes. Jokes connected with this vice appear throughout comedy. The major motifs are the following.

481. *Doubtful sex.* This motif occurs mostly in one-line jokes or sudden incidental references, and always refers to Cleisthenes: Strepsiades sees him in clouds that look like women (N 355); Peisetaerus complains that in Athens a woman goddess holds the πανοπλία while Cleisthenes holds the κερκίς (Av 829 ff.); Heracles is unsure where to place him sexually (R 57); and Cleisthenes himself, dressed as a woman, proclaims his effeminacy in *Thesmophoriazusae* in no uncertain terms (574 ff.):[40]

φίλαι γυναῖκες, ξυγγενεῖς τοὐμοῦ τρόπου,
ὅτι μὲν φίλος εἰμ' ὑμῖν, ἐπίδηλος ταῖς γνάθοις.
γυναικομανῶ γὰρ προξενῶ θ' ὑμῶν ἀεί,

[Dear women, relations of mine through style of life, my clean jaws show clearly that I am your friend: for I'm mad about women and always strive to protect your interests.]

482. *Transvestism.* Agathon and Cleisthenes are dressed as women throughout *Thesmophoriazusae,* and this ludicrous sight inspires the earthy Relation to react most colorfully to their appearance, voicing without doubt the amusement and surprise of the audience. From the descriptions he gives, we learn that comic effeminates were dressed in an odd combination of male and female clothing. Naturally, it is funniest to the audience to see a man dressed enough like a woman to be taken for one (T 137), but not so completely as to obscure his true sex. At T 97 f. Agathon is said to look like a whore, and in the Relation's paratragic outburst at T 130 ff. we learn that Agathon carries such incongruous items as the lyre

40. Cf. T 192, 268, 863, etc. for derisive words compounded in γυναικ- and referring to effeminacy. A complete list of such words can be found in *LSJ* s.v. γυναικάδελφος through γύννις.

and a woman's robe, skins and a snood, a λήκυϑος and a στρόφιον, a sword and a mirror. Other outlandish items of clothing are reviewed for the audience's amusement during the sex-change of the Relation (T 250 ff.).

483. *Hair-style.* Effeminates and pathics, like nobles and Spartans, wear their hair long and often curled: κίκιννοι at V 1068 are equated with εὐρυπρωκτία and with λειότης in Fr 218.[41]

484. *Depilated anus.* As courtesans depilate their cunts, so effeminates depilate their πρωκτοί : Cleisthenes at A 119, R 424, Agathon (and the unfortunate Relation) at T 218 ff.; cf. Eub. 107.2. CA 1340, 1346.

485. The practice of *removing hair* by means of hot pitch is alluded to at Alex. 264.1 (πιττοκοπούμενος, which is also the title of a play by Philemon [Poll. 7.165]) and CA 339.6 f., κιναίδους πεπιττοκοπημένους.

486. *Softness.* Effeminates are said to be smooth, soft, and white (unlike the hard and hairy: T 31, 159 f.; see section 466, above). The word λεῖος is the standard epithet;[42] ἁπαλός, usually used of women,[43] is applied to Agathon at T 192.

487. *Shaving.* All effeminates shave their faces smooth: Agathon at T 191, 216–48, Fr 326; Cleisthenes at Eq 1373 f., T 235, 575, Fr 407; cf. Alex. 264.1, CA 1340, 1346.

488. *Promiscuity.* Effeminates are supposedly willing to submit to anyone (L 621, 1092, T 35, 153, 157 f., 200 f., R 48, 57). Cleisthenes, despite his promiscuity, is often paired with one Straton,[44] and in the scurrilous chorus at R 427 he is made to lament for "Sebinus the Anaphlystian," an obscene *redender Name* (βινεῖν, ἀναφλᾶν).

Autoerotic Behavior

489. *Male masturbation* in comedy does not seem to bear the kind of harsh ridicule reserved for homosexual behavior but is considered more a type of ἀγροικία. Thus one of Strepsiades' crude buffooneries is his masturbation in bed (N 734).[45] All other references to masturbation in Aristophanes concern slaves or foreigners. Perhaps the crudest routine in

---

41. Cf. also N 349, V 466, 1267.
42. Fr 218, Eup. 338, Cratin. 10, Pl Com. 59, Theoc. 5.90.
43. Av 668, L 418, E 902.
44. A 118 f., Eq 1374, Fr 407.
45. Dover's comment, ad loc., that it is "a common assumption of vulgar humor that an adult male cannot be in bed alone and awake for long without masturbating," sounds more like a common assumption of the English public schools than one of classical Athens, for which there is no evidence at all.

Aristophanes occurs in the conversation between two slaves who open *Knights* (24 ff.), where the acceleration of their word-game on μολῶμεν/ αὖτο and their fear of being "flayed" are made the basis for a series of jokes about masturbation. The foreigner, Datis, famous for masturbating at noon (instead of making love?) sings a malapropian song at P 291, ὡς ἥδομαι καὶ χαίρομαι κεὐφραίνομαι, in which the middle voice of the verbs implies self-gratification rather than the innocent joy intended by the speaker. Such unwitting crudity was apparently dubbed "Datism."[46]

490. The masturbatory *redender Name* 'Αναφλύστιος, linked with the pederast "Sebinus" (see section 488, above) in the scene of Cleisthenes' pathic grief at R 428, and appearing again, more self-consciously, at E 979 f., may indicate that masturbation was humorously connected with the more comical types of homosexuality (cf. Pl Com. 59). It is interesting to note that personifications of this kind in English are feminine (e.g. "Mary Five-fingers"). Note also that in *Lysistrata* masturbation, along with pederasty (1092, 1113, etc.), was one of the last resorts of the men when deprived of their women (1090, 1099), and the same is true of the women's state in *Ecclesiazusae* (705 ff.). Eubulus similarly lists masturbation along with pederasty as a last resort of the men who fought at Troy (120.5).[47]

491. *Female masturbation* is mentioned only to satirize the lechery of women: μισηταὶ δὲ γυναῖκες ὀλίσβοισιν χρήσονται, lecherous women use dildoes, as Cratinus remarks (316). The ὄλισβος was the *penis coriaceus* (αἰδοῖον δερμάτιον),[48] about eight fingers long (L 109, about six inches), and said to be an Ionian import.[49] It was used by women, according to the comic poets, whose constant need of sexual input was momentarily frustrated by the absence of husbands (or, less charitably, the absence of adulterers, mule-drivers, or slaves. See, in addition to the passage from *Lysistrata* [n. 48, above], the scene in CA 5 Dem. in which two women contemplate the use of dildoes and slaves for sexual gratification, and compare Eup. *POxy.*, 2741, *Fr.* IB, col. ii[iii], 20 ff.). The word ὄλισβος

46. See the schol., Hdn. *Philet.* p. 443, Suda s.v.
47. Other appearances of masturbation, of unknown context, suggest that the motif was popular in stage-business and farcical jokes: Fr 36; Pherecr. 204 ἀποτυλοῦν (cf. *AB* 423); Eup. 61 ἀναφλασμός (see Phot., Suda, Zon. s.v.). See also Luc. *Peregr.* 17, Poll. 2.176, Hsch., Phot. s.v. ἀναφλᾶν; ἀναφαθάλλειν (cf. Pl Com. 59, Phryn. *PS* p. 12B, Hsch., *AB* 9.6); χειρομαχεῖν (*AP* 12.22, cf. χειρουργία at L 672); Μεσοτρίβας, a play by Blaesus, which may have had to do with this vice (Athen. 3. 111C).
48. Schol. L 109. Cf. L 110 σκυτίνη 'πικουρία, a phrase said to parody συκίνη 'πικουρία and which reappears at Strattis 54; cf. σκύτινα χηλεύειν at Eup. 388.
49. L 108 ff., Herod. 6.58. In CA 5.15 f. Dem. we learn that ὄλισβοι could be flesh-colored.

was undoubtedly vulgar, perhaps deriving from ὀλισθεῖν, to slip/glide along.

492. The comic characteristics of the motif of female masturbation are therefore very different from those surrounding male masturbation, which was purely farcical and not tendentious. In *Lysistrata* the women's use of dildoes is on a par with their adulterousness (107 ff.), bibulousness, and general lechery. When the women are without men they must "skin the skinned dog" (L 158: see section 117, above), although τὰ μεμιμημένα are all φλυαρία compared with the real thing (L 159, CA 5.7 Dem.). With *Lysistrata* we may compare the woman who owns the articles in Fr 320, from the *Second Thesmophoriazusae*, along with several ὄλισβοι (l. 13).[50] Masturbation has a slightly different tone in the insults the young woman hurls at her older rival in E 890 and 916: there it signifies the aging hag's inability to snare young men.

50. See sections 12, 70, 101, 147, 150, 154, and 158 for other such articles in this catalog.

Appendix: The Theory of Dorian Influences in the Development of Attic Comedy

The theory, put concisely by G. Norwood,[1] is as follows:

In fifth-century Athens the comic actor's costume included the phallus and huge padding of the stomach and posterior: the first item is attested by passages of Aristophanes, and all three by numerous vase-paintings. Comedy being Dionysiac, we are to understand this costume as that attributed to the attendants of Dionysus. But we know that the Athenian idea of the Dionysiac costume was not that just described: on Attic vases the god's male followers are always silenus-satyrs with the tail and ears of horses. On the other hand, Dorian Greeks regularly portrayed these attendants as human with phallus and padding. Firstly, such attire (as South Italian vases show) was used by the *phylakes*—actors in Italian farce—who often appear as companions of the god. Secondly, dancers thus padded are seen on Chalcidian and Spartano-Cyrenaic vases. Thirdly, they are found above all on the vases of Corinth: it is certain that the Dionysiac thiasos was imagined during the seventh and sixth centuries in Corinth as entirely human, with padding and phallus. The upshot is that the actors of Athenian Old Comedy regularly wore a costume displaying the physical peculiarities of Peloponnesian attendants on Dionysus, peculiarities entirely foreign to the Attic conception of the thiasos. They are a Peloponnesian element added to, but never completely coalescing with, the genuinely Attic chorus that normally appeared in animal masquerade.

There has been a recent tendency, however, to modify or deny this formulation. L. Buschor has shown that padded Dionysiac dancers of the

---

1. G. Norwood, *Greek Comedy* (London, 1931), pp. 9 f.

"Dorian" type existed in Attica from at least the first half of the sixth century, and probably represent a genuine Attic substratum.[2] Besides, Körte's thesis depends on an absolute distinction between the purely lyric choruses and the Dorian actors.[3] But we cannot make such a sharp distinction, especially in view of Aristotle's plausible derivation of comedy "from those leading off the phallic songs" (*Poet.* 1449ª 11), which certainly implies a *dramatic* development out of the lyric choruses themselves. Moreover, it is extremely difficult to imagine when and how such a fusion could have come about. The admittedly unorganic nature of Old Comedy need not be accounted for by such an improbable fusion.

It was H. Herter who most forcefully suggested that the entire development took place in Attica out of purely Attic components:[4] instead of an "ausserliche Kontamination" he saw "eine organische Entwicklung der attischen Komödie, die . . . ihre wesentlichen Vorbedingungen in sich selber trug."[5] These internal elements were in fact a chorus and actors *both* serving in the ithyphallic κῶμος of the Dionysiac cults. G. Giangrande has strengthened Herter's view by arguing that the pre-Greek *phlyakes*, so common in Dorian regions, existed from prehistoric times all over Greece, including Attica. There, however, they were suppressed and hidden from view by the emerging Dionysus-cult, which took hold in Attica much earlier than in Dorian areas.[6] This is why padded, phallus-bearing figures *seem* to flourish only in the Peloponnese and Southern Italy. The impulse to reactivate these dormant figures in Attica will have come about through the initiative of Aristotle's ἐξάρχοντες.[7]

On the negative side, L. Breitholz has dealt a mortal blow to the elaborate and confident hypotheses built up over the years around Körte's original intuition. His learned arguments systematically destroy each scrap of circumstantial evidence that had been used to postulate the existence and describe the nature of "Dorian farce." All that remains is the possibility that some form of mimetic activity may have taken place outside Attica, but certainly not with the characteristics of "einem scherzhaften Ensembledrama mit gesprochenem Dialog,"[8] and in any case not before the fifth century. That is, no evidence enables us to say that any form of non-Attic drama could have influenced the development of comedy

2. E. Buschor, "Satyrtänze und frühes Drama," *SB* (Vienna, 1943), p. 5.
3. *RE* 21 (1921): 1219.3 ff.
4. Herter (n. 44, above).
5. Ibid., pp. 36 ff.
6. Giangrande, n. 44, above.
7. H. Herter, "Phallophorie," *RE* 38 (1938): 1677.10 ff.
8. Breitholz, op. cit., p. 17.

in Attica before the fifth century. There is every reason to believe that
Old Comedy, like tragedy, was a native Attic product. Earlier we tried
to sketch a probable course of development for the obscenity of Old Comedy
along these lines; for the moment we must consider the argument
that the obscenity of Old Comedy derives from non-Attic sources.

We must begin by acknowledging certain hard facts about the literary
evidence (1) all the evidence concerning Dorian farce is late and doubtful;
(2) the later the evidence the more biased it is in favor of everything
Dorian;[9] and (3) not a single line, title, or description of any such farce
remains—an odd circumstance considering its supposed international
influence. As for the authors themselves, Susarion seems to be completely
legendary and Ecphantides cannot be localized.[10] Creatures like Maison
are stock types from later farces and not authors. Thus, one need waste
no time juggling hypotheses that have been constructed on flimsy deductions
based on phantom evidence. Instead we are forced back on two
potential sources of information: (1) references in Old Comedy to "Megarian
humor" and (2) the fragments of Epicharmus and Sophron.

The *locus classicus* for the former is the prologue to *Wasps* (54–66):

> φέρε νῦν, κατείπω τοῖς θεαταῖς τὸν λόγον,
> ὀλίγ᾽ ἄτϑ᾽ ὑπειπὼν πρῶτον αὐτοῖσιν ταδί,
> μηδὲν παρ᾽ ἡμῶν προσδοκᾶν λίαν μέγα,
> μηδ᾽ αὖ γέλωτα Μεγαρόϑεν κεκλεμμένον·
> ἡμῖν γὰρ οὐκ ἔστ᾽ οὔτε κάρυ᾽ ἐκ φορμίδος
> δούλω διαρριπτοῦντε τοῖς θεωμένοις,
> οὔϑ᾽ Ἡρακλῆς τὸ δεῖπνον ἐξαπατώμενος,
> οὐδ᾽ αὖϑις ἐνασελγαινόμενος Εὐριπίδης·
> οὐδ᾽ εἰ Κλέων γ᾽ ἔλαμψε τῆς τύχης χάριν,
> αὖϑις τὸν αὐτὸν ἄνδρα μυττωτεύσομεν.
> ἀλλ᾽ ἔστιν ἡμῖν λογίδιον γνώμην ἔχον,
> ὑμῶν μὲν αὐτῶν οὐχὶ δεξιώτερον,
> κωμῳδίας δὲ φορτικῆς σοφώτερον.

[Come, let me address the audience. First, by way of preface, a few

9. The bias of Aristotle has been excellently treated by G. Else, *The Origins and Early
Form of Greek Tragedy* (Cambridge, Mass., 1967), chap. 1, especially pp. 23 ff., in the area
of tragedy. As for Aristotle's comic theories, Aristotle himself admits that he knows little
about the subject (*Poet.* 1449b1), and his nod toward Dorian claims seems more philosophically
than historically founded. Else thinks, in *Aristotle's Poetics: The Argument* (Cambridge,
Mass., 1957), p. 122, that his disapproval of iambic satire and the abusive tone of
Archilochus, Hipponax, and Cratinus may have led him to look all the more favorably
on the harmless humor of such writers as Epicharmus as the originators of comedy.

10. Discussion in Breitholz, op. cit., pp. 71 ff.

words of caution: do not expect anything exceedingly grand, or jokes snitched from Megara. There will not be a pair of slaves tossing the audience nuts from a basket, no Heracles cheated out of a supper, no degrading portrayal of Euripides, and as for Cleon, even if luck should bring him some kind of success, we shall refrain from again making hash of him. This is just a bit of sensible advice, no cleverer than you are yourselves but much wiser than you will in find vulgar comedy.]

The passage says that the audience should not expect anything too grand, but neither should they expect "a joke snitched from Megara" (there is surely a play on μέγα—Μεγαρόθεν). The scholiast on line 57 gives two explanations of this remark: (1) certain Megarian dramatic poets are ἀμούσων and ἀφυῶς διασκωπτούντων, and (2) Megarians in general are always joking and laughing in a buffoonish and vulgar way (φορτικῶς). That the latter is the likelier interpretation is undeniable: γέλως does not mean "dramatic presentation," or even "literary production," but a laugh or a joke.

Those who use this passage to substantiate the existence of Megarian farce point to the two examples of Megarian humor that follow: nut-throwing slaves and Heracles cheated of his supper. (Presumably, the inclusion of Euripides and Cleon in the play would make it λίαν μέγα, like *Knights*.) Both of these jokes are given as typical Megarian jokes, undeniably, but it is far from certain that these jokelike motifs were taken from a Megarian *stage,* that they were *dramatic* motifs. In fact they were nothing of the kind: they were "dramatic devices which only Megarians would find amusing." Slaves throwing sweets was a common enough *captatio benevolentiae* on the Attic stage that Aristophanes would hardly need to associate them with a Megarian drama in order to condemn them as buffoonish (cf. P 959 ff, Pl 795 ff.). As for Heracles, there is nothing to associate him more closely with Megara than with any other place in Greece. His popularity extends back into Mycenaean times, before there *were* Dorians in Greece. And although he was especially popular in Dorian areas, where most of his adventures took place, we cannot for that reason assume any theatrical use of his legends and personality without further evidence.[11] No Dorian representation of Heracles on phlyax vases goes back further than the time of Middle Comedy, and for all of them we can suggest specific scenes from Attic drama as possible inspiration.[12]

On the other hand, Heracles always had many cult-places in Attica

11. The fragments of Epicharmus (in which Heracles figures prominently) do not have the character of farce, but at most are mythological travesty.

12. T. B. L. Webster, "South Italian Vases and Attic Drama," *CQ* 42 (1948): 15 ff.

(greatly outdistancing in this respect such homebred heroes as Theseus), and is very often represented on protoattic pottery. He was a popular figure in satyr drama, and only a little less popular in tragedy (*Prometheia, Alcestis, Trachiniae, Heracles, Philoctetes,* to name a few). After only occasional appearances in pre-Aristophanic comedy (the *Busiris* of Cratinus is the only specific example), Heracles became extremely popular: Pherecrates' Ἀνθρωφηρακλῆς, Nicochares' Ἡρακλῆς γαμούμενος, Ἡρακλῆς χορηγός, Archippus' Ἡρακλῆς γαμῶν, and Plato's Νὺξ μακρά, not to mention Aristophanes' *Birds* and *Frogs*. The scholiast at P 741 states that Ἡρακλῆς πεινῶν was so common a theme that even the poets grew sick of it (ἄχθεσθαι); cf. Cratin. 308. For Heracles cheated of his supper, there is a marvelous sophistication of this stock "Megarian" joke by the distended and frustrated Kinesias at L 928, ἀλλ' ἦ τὸ πέος τόδ' Ἡρακλῆς ξενίζεται, "But this poor cock's being fêted no better than Heracles!".

Thus Heracles the clown, as in the case of the nut-throwers, can be viewed as a native dramatic invention; we need not seek to explain Aristophanes' condemnation of playwrights who rely on stale Heracles jokes and cheap crowd-pleasing tricks by looking outside the conventions of the Attic stage itself.

That Megarian was a strong *Schimpfwort* in Attic ears seems quite clear.[13] Such clownish jokes as we find, for instance, in *Frogs* and *Acharnians* are fit "only to make the children laugh"[14] and are hence Megarian. Megara was thought of as "ein gerngrosses, dummstolzes Krähwinkel [an upstart, stupidly arrogant backwater],"[15] whose people were stupid, vulgar, and despicable: παναγεῖς γενεάν, πορνοτελῶναι, Μεγαρεῖς δειλοί, πατραλοῖαι (Philonides 5). Thus the foul and ludicrous scheme of the Megarian in *Acharnians* is Μεγαρικά τις μαχανά (738), an example of what Eupolis condemns as σκῶμμ' ἀσελγὲς καὶ Μεγαρικὸν σφόδρα, a lewd and very Megarian joke (244). That the Athenian comic poets would seek to excuse their use of such low humor by claiming it for the Megarians is understandable enough; as Wilamowitz puts it,[16] "Gewiss its das die wahre Komikerlogik. Aber die Megara liegt eben in der Vorstellung der Athener: diese Komödie wird nicht in Megara gespielt, sie

---

13. See the impressive collection of citations assembled by Starkie, *Wasps,* at V 57, and cf. Wilamowitz's amusing discussion, "Die megarische Komödie," *Hermes* 9 (1875): 319 ff.

14. P 50. Cf. Thphr. *Ch.* 9, Luc. *Gymn.* 22. For critiques by Aristophanes of such low humor, see N 537 ff., V 54 ff., R 1 ff., 16 ff., 354 ff.

15. Wilamowitz (n. 13, above), p. 327.

16. Ibid., p. 331.

spielt in Megara" [That is the true logic of Comedy. But Megara lay only in the imagination of the Athenians: this comedy was not played *in* Megara, it was played *on* Megara].

Bibliography

Editions and Commentaries

Aristophanes' Plays

Blaydes, F. *Aristophanis Comoediae. Annotatione critica, commentario exegetico et scholiis Graecis instruxit* (Halle, 1880–93).

Cantarella, R. *Aristophane. Le Commedie. Edizione critica e traduzione* (Milan, 1949–64).

Coulon, V. *Aristophane. Texte établi par V. Coulon et traduit par H. van Daele* (Paris, 1923–30). Quotations from Aristophanes appearing in this book are, unless otherwise indicated, taken from Coulon's text.

Dover, K. J. *Aristophanes Clouds* (Oxford, 1968).

Henderson, J. *Aristophanes Lysistrata* (Oxford, 1987; repr. 1990).

MacDowell, D. M. *Aristophanes Wasps* (Oxford, 1971).

Radermacher, L. *Aristophanes' Frösche. Einleitung, Text und Kommentar.*[2] With additions by W. Kraus (Vienna, 1954; reprinted 1967).

Sommerstein, A. H. *Aristophanes* (Warminster/Chicago, 1980————).

Starkie, W. *Aristophanes Acharnians* (London, 1909).

Ussher, R. G. *Aristophanes Ecclesiazusae* (Oxford, 1973).

van Leeuwen, J. *Aristophanis Comoediae. Cum prolegomenis et commentariis edidit* (Leyden, 1893–1906).

von Wilamowitz-Moellendorff, U. *Aristophanes Lysistrate* (Berlin, 1927).

Willems, A. *Aristophane. Traduction avec notes et commentaires critiques* (Paris/Brussels, 1919).

Fragments of Attic Comedy

Bergk, Th. In Meineke [below], 2, 2: 993–1224.

Bonanno, M. G. *Studi su Cratete Comico* (Padua, 1972).

Demiańczuk, J. *Supplementum Comicum* (Krakow, 1912; reprinted 1967).

Edmonds, J. M. *The Fragments of Attic Comedy* (Leyden, 1957–61).

Kaibel, G. *Comicorum Graecorum Fragmenta*, vol. 1 (Berlin, 1899).

Kassel, R. and Austin, C. *Poetae Comici Graeci* (Berlin/N.Y., 1983————).

Kock, Th. *Comicorum Atticorum Fragmenta* (Leipzig, 1880–88). Quotations from comic fragments are, unless otherwise noted, taken from Kock.

Meineke, A. *Fragmenta Comicorum Graecorum* (Berlin, 1840–57).

Scholia

Dubner, F., *Scholia Graeca in Aristophanem, cum prolegomenis grammaticorum* (Paris, 1877).

Other Authors and Texts

Allen, T., Halliday, W.; Sikes, E. *The Homeric Hymns*[2] (Oxford, 1963).
Audollent, A. *Defixionum Tabellae* (Paris, 1904).
Diehl, E. *Anthologia Lyrica Graeca.*[3] Rev. by R. Beutler (Leipzig, 1949–52).
Diels, H., and Kranz, W. *Die Fragmente der Vorsokratiker* (Zürich/Berlin, 1964).
Gentili, B. *Anacreon* (Rome, 1958).
Lasserre, F., and Bonnard, A. *Archiloque* (Paris, 1958).
Lobel, E., and Page, D. *Poetarum Lesbiorum Fragmenta* (Oxford, 1955).
Masson, O. *Les Fragments du Poète Hipponax* (Paris, 1962).
Nauck, A. *Tragicorum Graecorum Fragmenta.*[2] Suppl. B. Snell (Hildesheim, 1964).
Olivieri, A. *Frammenti della Commedia Greca e del Mimo nella Sicilia e nella Magna Grecia*[2] (Naples, 1946–47).
Pearson, A. C. *The Fragments of Sophocles* (Cambridge, 1917).
Rutherford, W. G. *Phrynichus* (London, 1881).
Seaford, R. *Euripides Cyclops* (Oxford, 1984).
Steffen, V. *Satyrographorum Graecorum Fragmenta*[2] (Poznań, 1952).
Treu, M. *Archilochos* (Munich, 1959).
West, M. L. *Iambi et Elegi Graeci* (Oxford, 1971–72).

Reference Works

Chantraine, P. *Dictionnaire Étymologique de la Langue Grecque* (Paris, 1968–).
Ernout, A., and Meillet, A. *Dictionnaire Étymologique de la Langue Latine*[4] (Paris, 1960).
Frisk, H. *Griechisches etymologisches Wörterbuch* (Heidelberg, 1960–72).
Gelzer, Th. "Aristophanes," *RE Supplbd.* 12 (1971): 1391 ff.
Hoffmann, O. *Griechische Dialekte* (Göttingen, 1891–98).
LSJ: Liddell, H. G., and Scott, R. *A Greek–English Lexicon.*[9] Rev. by Sir Henry Stuart Jones and R. McKenzie (Oxford, 1940).
Nilsson, M. *Geschichte der griechischen Religion*[3] (Munich, 1967).
RE: Pauly, A., and Wissowa, G. *Real-encyclopädie der classischen Altertumswissenschaft* (Stuttgart, 1894–). References to *RE* refer to column numbers.
Roscher, W. H. *Ausführliches Lexicon der griechischen und römischen Mythologie* (Leipzig, 1884–1937).
Schmid, W. *Geschichte der griechischen Literatur* (Munich, 1929–46).
Schwyzer, E. *Griechische Grammatik* (Munich, 1934–53).
ThLL: Thesaurus Linguae Latinae (Leipzig, 1900–).
Walde, A., and Hofmann, J. *Lateinisches etymologisches Wörterbuch*[3] (Heidelberg, 1938–56).

Books and Articles

Adams, N. *The Latin Sexual Vocabulary* (Baltimore/London, 1982).
Agar, F. L. "Notes on the *Ecclesiazusae* of Aristophanes," *Classical Quarterly* 13 (1919): 12 ff.
Andre, J. "Sur certains noms de plantes latins," *Latomus* 15 (1956): 299 ff.
Arnott, P. *Greek Scenic Conventions* (London, 1962).

Arrowsmith, W. "Aristophanes' *Birds*: The Fantasy Politics of Eros," *Arion*, n.s. 1/1 (1973): 119 ff.

Bartolucci, A. "Hipponacteae Interpretatiunculae," *Maia* 16 (1964): 243 ff.

Beare, W. "The Costume of the Actors in Attic Comedy," *Classical Quarterly* 4 (1954): 64 ff.

———. "Aristophanic Costume Again," *Classical Quarterly* 7 (1957): 184 f.

———. "Aristophanic Costume: A Last Word," *Classical Quarterly* 9 (1959: 126.

Bérard, C. et al. *A City of Images. Iconography and Society in Ancient Greece*, transl. D. Lyons (Princeton, 1990).

Bergler, E. "Obscene Words," *Psychoanalytic Quarterly* 5 (1936): 226 ff.

Berk, L. *Epicharmus* (Groningen, 1964).

Bethe, E. "Die dorische Knabenliebe," *Rheinisches Museum* 62 (1907): 438 ff.

Blau, A. "A Philological Note on a Defect in Sex Organ Nomenclature," *Psychoanalytic Quarterly* 12 (1943): 481 ff.

Blaydes, F. *Adversaria in Comicorum Graecorum Fragmenta* (Halle, 1890).

Boardman, J. *Eros in Greece* (London, 1978).

Borthwick, E. "Three Notes on the *Acharnians*," Mnemosyne 20 (1967): 409 ff.

———. "Some Problems in Musical Terminology," *Classical Quarterly*, n.s. 17 (1967): 145 ff.

Bowie, T., and Christenson, C. V. *Studies in Erotic Art* (New York, 1970).

Bowra, C. M. "A Love-Duet," *American Journal of Philology* 79 (1958): 376 ff.

Brecht, F. *Motiv- und Typengeschichte der griechischen Spottepigramms, Philologus Supplementband* 22 (1930).

Breitholz, L. *Die dorische Farce* (Uppsala, 1960).

Brown, L. "Noses at Aristophanes *Clouds* 344?" *QUCC* 43 (1983): 87–90.

Buchheit, V. "Feigensymbolik im antiken Epigramm," *Rheinisches Museum* 103 (1960): 200 ff.

Buffière, F. *Eros adolescens. La pédérastie dans la Grèce antique* (Paris, 1980).

Calame, C., ed. *L'Amore in Grecia*[3] (Rome, 1985).

Calder, W. M. "An Unnoticed Obscenity in Aristophanes," *Classical Philology* 65 (1970): 257.

Caldwell, R. *The Origin of the Gods: A Psychoanalytic Study of Greek Theogonic Myth* (Oxford, 1989).

———. "Psychoanalysis," in *Approaches to Greek Myths*, ed. L. Edmunds (Baltimore, 1990): 342–89.

Cartledge, P. "The Politics of Spartan Pederasty," *PCPS* 27 (1981): 17–36.

Charitonides, C. *ΑΠΟΡΡΗΤΑ* (Thessaloniki, 1935).

Cole, S. G. "*Gynaixi ou themis*: Male and Female in the Greek *Leges Sacrae*," *Helios* 17 (1991) (forthcoming).

Coulon, V. "Beiträge zur Interpretation des Aristophanes," *Rheinisches Museum* 105 (1962): 10 ff.

Croiset, M. *Histoire de la littérature grecque*[3] (Paris, 1913).

Davies, M. I. "The Tickle and Sneeze of Love," *AJA* 86 (1982): 115–18.

Degani, E. "Arifrade l'anassagoreo," *Maia* 12 (1960): 190 ff.

———. "Insulto ed eschrologia in Ar.," *Dioniso* 57 (1987): 31–47.

Denniston, J. D. "Technical Terms in Aristophanes," *Classical Quarterly* 21 (1927): 113 ff.

Deubner, L. *Attische Feste* (Berlin, 1932).

Devereux, G. "Greek Pseudo-Homosexuality and the Greek Miracle," *Symbolae Osloenses* 42 (1968): 69 ff.

DeVries, K. *Homosexuality and the Athenian Democracy* (forthcoming).

Di Marco, M. "'Ερεβοδιφῶσιν, paronimia e lusus osceno in Aristofane *Nub.* 192 sg.," *QUCC* 55 (1987): 55–58.

Dodds, E. R. *The Greeks and the Irrational* (Berkeley, 1964).

Dover, K. J. *Greek Homosexuality* (Cambridge MA, 1978).

———. "Greek Homosexuality and Initiation," in *The Greeks and their Legacy. Collected Papers II* (Oxford, 1988): 115–34.

———. *Aristophanic Comedy* (Berkeley and Los Angeles, 1972).

———. "The Poetry of Archilochus," in *Archiloque*, Fondation Hardt, *Entretiens sur l'antiquité classique* 10 (Geneva, 1964): 183 ff.

———. "Notes on Aristophanes' *Acharnians*," *Maia* 15 (1963): 6 ff.

———. "Aristophanic Scholarship," *Lustrum* 2 (1957): 52 ff.

———. "Classical Greek Attitudes to Sexual Behavior," *Arethusa* 6 (1973): 59 ff.

———. "Eros and Nomos," *Bulletin of the Institute for Classical Studies, University of London* 11 (1964): 31 ff.

Dracoulides, N. *Psychanalyse d'Aristophane* (Paris, 1967).

duBois, P. *Sowing the Body. Psychoanalysis and Ancient Representations of Women* (Chicago, 1988).

Edmonds, J. M. "The Cairo and Oxyrhynchus Fragments of the *Demoi* of Eupolis," *Mnemosyne*, ser. 3, 8 (1940): 1 ff.

Edmunds, L. "Ar. *Vesp.* 603–4," *AJP* 99 (1978): 321–24.

Ehrenberg, V. *The People of Aristophanes. A Sociology of Old Attic Comedy*[2] (Oxford, 1951).

Elliott, R. C. *The Power of Satire: Myth, Ritual, Art* (Princeton, NJ, 1960).

Ellis, K. et al. *Caught Looking. Feminism, Pornography and Censorship* (New York, 1986).

Else, G. F. *The Origins and Early Form of Greek Tragedy* (Cambridge, Mass., 1967).

———. *Aristotle's Poetics: The Argument* (Cambridge, Mass., 1957).

Erbse, H. "Zu Aristophanes," *Eranos* 52 (1954): 76 ff.

Εὔιος Ληναίου (alias C. Charitonides). 'Απόρρητα (Thessaloniki, 1935).

Evans-Pritchard, E. "Some Collective Expressions of Obscenity in Africa," *Journal of the Royal Anthropological Institute of Great Britain and Ireland* 59 (1929): 311 ff.

Eyben, E. "Antiquity's View of Puberty," *Latomus* 31 (1972): 677 ff.

Farnell, L. R. *Cults of the Greek States* (Oxford, 1896).

Ferenczi, S. "Über obszöne Worte," *Schriften zur Psychanalyse* (Frankfurt-am-Main, 1970), 1: 59 ff. (Also in Jones, E., below.)

Fernandez, J. G. "Parerga II, 2," *Emerita* 31 (1963): 135 f.

Fluck, H. *Skurrile Riten in griechischen Kulten* (Endingen, 1931).

Foley, H., ed. *Reflections of Women in Antiquity* (New York, 1981).

Forberg, F. C. *Manual of Classical Erotology* (Manchester, 1884, repr. New York, 1966).

Foster, B. O. "Notes on the Symbolism of the Apple in Classical Antiquity," *Harvard Studies in Classical Philology* 10 (1899): 39 ff.

Foucault, M. *The History of Sexuality*, vols. I–III. Trans. R. Hurley (New York, 1978, 1985, 1986).

Fraenkel, H. *Wege und Formen frühgriechischen Denkens* (Munich, 1955).

Frazer, J. G. *The Golden Bough*[3] (New York, 1935).

Freud, S. *Jokes and their Relation to the Unconscious*. Trans. J. Strachey (New York, 1960).

———. *Gesammelte Werke* (London, 1940–).

———. "The Antithetical Sense of Primal Words," *Collected Papers* (London, 1924–50), vol. 4, pp. 184 ff.

———. *The Complete Introductory Lectures on Psychoanalysis*. Trans. J. Strachey (New York, 1966).

———. *The Basic Writings of Sigmund Freud*. Trans. A. A. Brill (New York, 1938).

———. "The Acquisition of Fire," *Collected Works*. Standard edition (London, 1753–), vol. 22, pp. 187 ff.

———. *Three Essays on the Theory of Sexuality*. Trans. J. Strachey (New York, 1962).

———. "Anal Erotism and Castration," *Collected Works* (as above), vol. 17, pp. 72 ff.

Froehde, O. *Beiträge zur Technik der alten attischen Komödie* (Leipzig, 1898).

Gerber, D. "Eels in Archilochus," *QUCC* 16 (1973): 105–9.

———. "Archilochus, Fr. 119 West," *Phoenix* 29 (1975): 181–4.

———. "Archilochus, Fr. 42 West," *QUCC* 22 (1976): 7–14.

———. "The Female Breast in Greek Erotic Literature," *Areth.* 11 (1978): 203–12.

Gerhard, G. "Iambographen," *RE* 9 (1916): 651 ff.

———. *Phoinix von Kolophon* (Leipzig, 1909).

Giangrande, G. "The Origin of Attic Comedy," *Eranos* 61 (1963): 1 ff.

Golden, M. "A Double Pun in Aristophanes, *Lys.* 1001," *CQ* 32 (1982): 467–68.

———. "Slavery and Homosexuality at Athens," *Phoenix* 38 (1984): 308–24.

Gorsen, P. *Das Prinzip Obszön. Kunst Pornographie und Gesellschaft* (Reinbeck bei Hamburg, 1969).

Grasberger, L. *Die griechischen Stichnamen* (Würzburg, 1883).

Grassmann, V. *Die erotischen Epoden des Horaz. Literarischer Hintergrund und sprachliche Tradition* (Munich, 1960 = *Zetemata* 39).

Grene, D. "The Comic Technique of Aristophanes," *Hermathena* 50 (1937): 87 ff.

Griffith, J. G. "Ληκύθιον ἀπώλεσεν: A Postscript," *Harvard Studies in Classical Philology* 74 (1970): 43 f.

Grotjahn, M. *Beyond Laughter: Humor and the Subconscious* (New York, 1966).

Guthrie, W. K. C. *Socrates* (Cambridge, 1971).

Halperin, D. M. *One Hundred Years of Homosexuality* (New York/London, 1990).

———, Winkler, J. J., and Zeitlin, F. I. (eds.) *Before Sexuality* (Princeton, 1990).

Hammerström, M. "De vocibus scorti, scrattae . . . ," *Eranos* 23 (1925): 104 ff.

Henderson, J. "The Cologne Epode and the Conventions of Early Greek Erotic Poetry," *Areth.* 9 (1976): 159–79.

———. "Older Women in Attic Old Comedy," *TAPA* 117 (1987): 105–29.

Henderson, J. "Greek Attitudes Toward Sex," in Grant, M., and Kitzinger, R., eds. *Civilization of the Ancient Mediterranean II* (New York, 1988): 1249–63.

————. "A Note on Aristophanes' *Acharnians*, 834–35," *Classical Philology* 68 (1973): 289 f.

————. "The Lekythos and *Frogs* 1200–1248," *Harvard Studies in Classical Philology* 76 (1972): 133 ff.

————. "Sparring Partners: A Note on Aristophanes, *Ecclesiazusae* 964–965," *American Journal of Philology* 96 (1975).

Hendrickson, G. L. "Archilochus and the Victims of His Iambics," *American Journal of Philology* 46 (1925): 101 ff.

Heraeus, W. "Προπεῖν," *Rheinisches Museum* 70 (1915): 1 ff.

Herter, H. *Vom dionysischen Tanz zum komischen Spiel. Die Anfänge der attischen Komödie* (Iserlohn, 1947).

————. "Phallos," *RE* 38 (1938): 1681 ff.

————. *De dis atticis Priapi similibus* (Bonn, 1926).

————. "Die Soziologie der antiken Prostitution," *Jahrbuch für Antike und Christentum* 3 (1960): 70 ff.

————. *De Priapo, Religionsgeschichtliche Versuche und Vorarbeiten* 23 (1932).

Hewitt, J. "The Image in the Sand," *Classical Philology* 30 (1935): 10 ff.

Hofmann, H. *Sexual and Asexual Pursuit: A Structuralist Approach to Vase Painting* (London, 1977).

Holzinger, C. *De Verborum Lusu apud Aristophanem* (Vienna, 1876).

Hopfner, Th. *Das Sexualleben der Griechen und Römer* (Prague, 1938).

Hošek, R. *Lidovost a lidové motivy u Aristofana* (Prague, 1962).

————. "Zu Aristophanes Plutos 176," *Sborník Prací Filosofické Fak. Brnenské Univ. Rada archeol. klas. Brno* 91 (1960): 89 ff.

Housman, A. E. "Praefanda," *Hermes* 66 (1931): 402 ff.

Hyde, H. M. *A History of Pornography* (London, 1964).

Iungius, C. L. *De vocabulis antiquae comoediae atticae quae apud solos comicos aut omnino inveniuntur aut peculiari notione praedita occurrunt* (Amsterdam, 1897).

Jensen, C. "Zu den Demen des Eupolis," *Hermes* 51 (1916): 321 ff.

Jocelyn, H. D. "A Greek Indecency and its Students: *Laikazein*," *PCPS* n.s. 26 (1980): 12–66.

Johns, C. *Sex or Symbol: Erotic Images of Greece and Rome* (Austin, 1982).

Jones, E., trans. *Sex in Psychoanalysis* (Boston, 1916).

Keuls, Eva C. *The Reign of the Phallus: Sexual Politics in Ancient Athens* (New York, 1985).

Killeen, J. F. "The Comic Costume Controversy," *Classical Quarterly* 21 (1971): 51 ff.

————. "Sappho: Fragment 111," *Classical Quarterly* 23 (1973): 198.

Kirk, G. S. "A Fragment of Sappho Reinterpreted," *Classical Quarterly* 13 (1963): 51 f.

Koch-Harnack, O. *Knabenliebe und Tiergeschenke* (Berlin, 1983).

Körte, A. "Archäologische Studien zur alten Komödie," *Jahrbuch des archäologischen Institut* 8 (1893): 6 ff.

————. "Komödie," *RE* 11 (1921): 1207 ff.

Körte, A. "Zu neueren Komödienfunden," *Berichte über die Verhandlungen der Sächsischen Akademie der Wissenschaften zu Leipzig* 71 (1919): 6. I.

Koster, S. *Die Invektive in der griechischen und römischen Literatur* (Meisenheim am Glan, 1980).

Krenkel, W. "Masturbation in der Antike," *Wissenschaftliche Zeitschrift der Wilhelm-Pieck-Universität Rostock* 28 (1979): 159–78.

———. "Fellatio and Irrumatio," *ibid.* 29 (1980): 77–88.

———. "Tonguing," *ibid.* 30 (1981): 37–54.

Kretschmer, P. "Mythische Namen," *Glotta* 12 (1923): 105 ff.

Kroll, W. "Kinaidos," *RE* 11 (1921): 459 ff.

———. "Knabenliebe," *RE* 11 (1921): 897 ff.

Lambin, G. "Dans un rameau de myrte," *REG* 92 (1979): 542–51.

Lang, M. *The Athenian Agora 21: Graffiti and Depinti* (Princeton, 1976): 11–15.

Langlotz, E. *Aphrodite in den Gärten* (Heidelberg, 1954).

Latte, K. "Schuld und Sünde in der griechischen Religion," *Archiv für Religionswissenschaft* 20 (1920–21): 254 ff.

———. "Hipponacteum." *Hermes* 64 (1929): 384 ff.

Lattimore, R. "Notes on Greek Poetry," *American Journal of Philology* 65 (1944): 172 ff.

Lawrence, D. H. *Pornography and Obscenity* (London, 1929).

Lenz, F. "Catulliana," *Rivista di cultura classica e medioevale* 5 (1963): 62 ff.

Licht, H. *Sittengeschichte Griechenlands* (Zürich, 1927–28).

Littman, R. "The Loves of Alcibiades," *Transactions and Proceedings of the American Philological Association* 101 (1972): 263 ff.

Lloyd-Jones, H. Review of *The Maculate Muse* in *CP* 71 (1976): 356–59.

Lobeck, A. *Phrynichi Eclogae* (Leipzig, 1820).

Maas, P. "Zum neuen Eupolis," *Berliner Philologische Wochenschrift* 32 (1912): 861 f.

MacDowell, D. M. "The Frogs' Chorus," *Classical Review* 22 (1972): 3 ff.

MacCary, W. T. "Philokleon Ithyphallos. Dance, Costume and Character in the *Wasps*," *TAPA* 109 (1979): 137–47.

Madeiros, W. *Hipponactea* (Coimbra, 1969).

Marcadé, J. *Eros Kalos: Essay on Erotic Elements in Greek Art* (Geneva, 1965).

Marcovich, M. "*ΜΕΓΑΣ* is not Mutuniatus," *Classical Philology* 66 (1971): 262.

———. "Sappho Fr. 111: Anxiety Attack or Love Declaration?" *Classical Quarterly* 22 (1972): 29 ff.

Maxwell-Stuart, P. G. "Strato and the Musa Puerilis," *Hermes* 100 (1972): 215 ff.

Mayer, A. "Zu den neuen Fragmenten des Eupolis," *Berliner Philologische Wochenschrift* 32 (1912): 830 ff.

Mazon, P. "La Farce dans Aristophane," *Revue d'histoire du théâtre* 3 (1957): 7 ff.

McLeish, K. "*PHYSIS*: A Bawdy Joke in Aristophanes," *CQ* 27 (1977): 76–79.

Meder, A. *Die attische Demokratie zur Zeit des peloponnesischen Kriegs im Lichte zeitgenössischen Quellen* (Lengerich, 1938).

Mertner, E., and Mainusch, H. *Pornotopia: Das Obszöne und die Pornographie in der literarischen Landschaft* (Frankfurt-am-Main, 1970).

Meyer, G. *Die stilistische Verwendung der Nominalkomposition im Griechischen, Philologus Supplbd.* 16 (1923).

Meyer, M. "Delta Praehistoricum," *Philologische Wochenschrift* 49 (1929): 91 ff.

Mitsdörffer, W. *Die Parodie euripideischer Szenen bei Aristophanes* (diss. Berlin, 1943).

Murray, G. *Aristophanes* (Oxford, 1933).

Nissen, T. "Zu Alkman Frgm. 95 Diehl," *Philologus* 91 (1936–37): 470 ff.

Norwood, G. *Greek Comedy* (London, 1931).

Oeri, H. *Der Typ der komischen Alten in der griechischen Komödie* (Basel, 1948).

Page, D. "Archilochus and the Oral Tradition," in *Archiloque,* Fondation Hardt, *Entretiens sur l'antiquité classique* (Geneva, 1964): 119 ff.

Parker, H. "Love's Body Anatomized: The Ancient Erotic Handbooks and the Rhetoric of Sexuality," in Richlin (forthcoming).

Parker, R. *Miasma: Pollution and Purification in Early Greek Religion* (Oxford, 1983).

Partridge, E. *Shakespeare's Bawdy* (London, 1968).

Pascucci, G. "KINHTIAN," *Atene e Roma,* n.s. 4 (1959): 102 ff.

Patzer, H. *Die griechische Knabenliebe* (Wiesbaden, 1982).

Pease, A. "Caeli Enarrant," *Harvard Theological Review* 34 (1941): 163 ff.

Pickard-Cambridge, A. W. *Dramatic Festivals of Athens*[2] (London, 1968).

Plepelits, K. *Die Fragmente der Demen des Eupolis* (diss. Vienna: Verlag Notring, 1970).

Pohlenz, M. "Die Entstehung der attischen Komödie," *Nachrichten von der Gesellschaft der Wissenschaften zu Göttingen,* Philol.-Hist. Klasse (1949): 38 ff.

Pomeroy, S. *Goddesses, Whores, Wives and Slaves: Women in Classical Antiquity* (New York, 1975).

Preston, K. *Studies in the Diction of the Sermo Amatorius in Roman Comedy* (University of Chicago Libraries, 1916).

Radermacher, L. "Πορδή," *RE* 22 (1953): 235 ff.

———. "Volkstümliche Schwankmotive bei Aristophanes," *Wiener Studien* 35 (1913): 193 ff.

Rapp, A. "*Aves* 507," *Rheinisches Museum* 88 (1939): 191.

Reynan, H. "Philosophie und Knabenliebe," *Hermes* 95 (1967): 308 ff.

Richlin, A. *The Garden of Priapus: Sexuality and Aggression in Roman Humor* (New Haven/London, 1983).

———, ed. *Pornography and Representation in Greece and Rome* (forthcoming).

Robinson, D. M. "A New Logos Inscription," *Hesperia* 27 (1958): 74 ff.

———; Fluck, E. *A Study of the Greek Love Names* (Baltimore, 1937).

Rohde, E. *Der griechische Roman und seine Vorläufer*[3] (Leipzig, 1914).

Rosen, R. *Old Comedy and the Iambographic Tradition* (American Classical Studies 19: Atlanta, 1988).

Rosenbaum, J. *Geschichte der Lustseuche im Altertume* (Halle, 1882).

Rousselle, A. *Porneia: On Desire and the Body in Antiquity.* Trans. F. Pheasant (Oxford, 1988).

Ruck, C. "Euripides' Mother. Vegetables and the Phallus in Aristophanes," *Arion* 2 (1975): 13–57.

Rusten, J. "*Wasps* 1360–1369. Philokleon's τωθασμός," *HSCP* 81 (1977): 157–61.

Schmid, W. "Zu Eupolis' *Δῆμοι*," *Philologus* 93 (1938): 413 ff.

Schreckenberg, H. *Ananke* (Munich, 1964).

Seager, R. "Aristophanes *Thesm.* 493–496 and the Comic Possibilities of Garlic," *Philol.* 127 (1983): 139–42.

Segal, C. P. "The Character and Cults of Dionysus and the Unity of the *Frogs*," *Harvard Studies in Classical Philology* 65 (1961): 207 ff.

Sergent, B. *Homosexuality in Greek Myth.* Trans. A. Goldhammer (Boston, 1986).

Shapiro, A. "Eros in Love: Pederasty and Pornography in Greece," in Richlin (forthcoming).

Siems, K. *Aischrologia. Das Sexuell-Hässliche im antiken Epigramm* (diss. Göttingen, 1974).

Sperber, H. "Über die Einfluss sexueller Momente auf Entstehung und Entwicklung der Sprache," *Imago* 1 (1912): 405 ff.

Spyropoulos, E. ""*Όνεια πράγματα*. Aristophane, *Cavaliers* 1399," *Hellenica* 33 (1981): 3–13.

Stone, L. "On the Principal Obscene Word of the English Language," *International Journal of Psychoanalysis* 35 (1954): 30 ff.

Stone, L. M. "The Obscene Use of *ΜΕΓΑΣ* in Aristophanes," *AJP* 99 (1978): 427–32.

———. *Costume in Aristophanic Comedy* (New York, 1981; repr. Salem, 1984).

Strauss, L. *Socrates and Aristophanes* (New York, 1966).

Süss, W. *Aristophanes und die Nachwelt* (Leipzig, 1911).

———. "Zur Komposition der altattischen Komödie," *Rheinisches Museum* 63 (1908): 12 ff.

Sutton, R. F. Jr. *The Interaction Between Men and Women Portrayed on Attic Red-Figure Pottery* (diss. Chapel Hill, 1981).

———. "Pornography and Persuasion on Attic Pottery," in Richlin (forthcoming).

Syl, S. "Mention d'un saurien dans les Nuées (v. 170 sqq) d'Aristophane et ses rapports avec les mystères d'Eleusis," *RPhA* 3 (1985): 107–32.

Taillardat, J. *Les Images d'Aristophane* (Paris, 1962).

———. "*Ποσθαλίων* et *Ποσθαλίσκος* (Ar. Thesm. 292)," *Revue de Philologie* 35 (1961): 249 f.

———. "Comica," *Revue des Études Grecques* 64 (1951): 14 ff.

Taplin, O. "Phallology, *Phlyakes*, Iconography and Aristophanes," *PCPS* 34 (1988): 92–104.

Thielscher, P. "Zu *κωλῆ* bei Aristophanes *Nub.* 989 und 1018," *Philologische Wochenschrift* 57 (1937): 255 f.

Thierfelder, A. "Obscaenus," *Navicula Chilonensis. Studia Philologica F. Jacoby Oblata* (Leyden, 1956): 107 ff.

Thomas, W. *Primitive Behaviour* (New York, 1937).

Thompson, D. *A Glossary of Greek Fishes* (London, 1947).

Trencsenyi-Waldapfel, J. "Eine äsopische Fabel und ihre orientalischen Parallelen," *Acta Antiqua Acad. Scient. Hungaricae* 7 (1959): 317 ff.

Truesdale, J. *A Comic Prosopographia Graeca* (Menasha, Wisconsin, 1940).

Vaio, J. Review of *The Maculate Muse* in *Gnomon* 51 (1979): 692–94.

Vaio, J. "Aristophanes' *Wasps*: The Final Scenes," *Greek, Roman and Byzantine Studies* 12 (1971): 335 ff.

———. "The Manipulation of Theme and Action in *Lysistrata*," *Greek, Roman and Byzantine Studies* 14 (1973): 369 ff.

van der Valk, M. "Observations in Connection with Aristophanes," in *KOMOIDO-TRAGEMATA. Studies in Honor of W. J. W. Koster* (Amsterdam, 1967): 125 ff.

von Blumenthal, A. *Die Schätzung des Archilochos im Altertume* (Stuttgart, 1922).

———. "Beobachtungen zu griechischen Texten," *Hermes* 74 (1939): 96 ff.

Von Erffa, C. *AIΔΩΣ, Philologus Supplbd.* 30 (1937).

von Salis, A. *De doriensium ludorum in Comoedia Attica vestigiis* (Basel, 1905).

von Wilamowitz-Moellendorff, U. "Lesefrüchte," *Hermes* 59 (1924): 249 ff.

———. "Die megarische Komödie," *Hermes* 9 (1875): 319 ff.

Watkins, C. "La famille indo-européenne de grec ὄρχις: linguistique, poétique et mythologie," *Bulletin de la Société de Linguistique* 70 (1975): 11–25.

Weber, L. "ΣΥΚΑ 'ΕΦ' 'ΕΡΜΗΙ," *Philologus* 74 (1917): 96 ff.

———. *Anacreontea* (diss. Göttingen, 1892).

Webster, T. B. L. "South Italian Vases and Attic Drama," *Classical Quarterly* 42 (1948): 15 ff.

———. "Attic Costume: A Reexamination," *Ephemeris Archaeologica* (1953–54): 192 ff.

———. "Some Notes on the New Epicharmus," *Serta Philologica Aenipontana* (Innsbruck, 1961): 85 ff.

Wehrli, F. *Motivstudien zur griechischen Komödie* (Basel, 1948).

West, M. L. *Studies in Greek Elegy and Iambus* (New York/Berlin, 1974).

Whitehorne, J. E. G. "Rowing with Two Oars at Aristophanes, *Ecclesiazusae* 1091," *Hermes* 117 (1989): 363–66.

Whitman, C. H. *Aristophanes and the Comic Hero* (Cambridge, Mass., 1964).

Wills, G. "Phoenix of Colophon's *KOPΩNIΣMA*," *Classical Quarterly* 20 (1970): 112 ff.

———. "Why are the Frogs in the *Frogs*?" *Hermes* 97 (1969): 306 ff.

Winkler, J. J. *The Constraints of Desire* (New York/London, 1990).

Winkler, J., and Zeitlin, F., eds. *Nothing to Do with Dionysos? Athenian Drama in its Social Context* (Princeton, 1990).

Wit-Tak, Th. de. *Lysistrata: Vrede, Vrouw, en Obsceniteit bij Aristophanes* (Groningen, 1967).

———. "Obscenity in the *Thesm.* and *Eccl.* of Aristophanes," *Mnemosyne* 21 (1968): 4 ff.

Wright, F. *Feminism in Greek Literature from Homer to Aristotle* (London, 1923).

Wüst, E. "Διαστρέφειν bei Eupolis," *Philologus* 91 (1936): 114 f.

Zeitlin, F. I. "Travesties of Genre and Genre in Aristophanes' *Thesmophoriazusae*," in Foley (1981): 169–217.

———. "Cultic Models of the Female: Rites of Dionysus and Demeter," *Arethusa* 15 (1982): 129–57.

———. "Playing the Other: Theater, Theatricality, and the Feminine in Greek Drama," in Winkler/Zeitlin (1990): 63–96.

Zielinski, Th. *Die Gliederung der altattischen Komödie* (Leipzig, 1885).

Pictorial and Plastic Art

Since this book explores verbal phenomena only I have included no plates and have referred to pictorial and plastic art only when it strengthens the conclusions drawn from textual evidence. Readers interested in examining Classical Greek artifacts of a sexual or scatological nature will find collections in H. Licht, *Sittengeschichte Griechenlands* (Zürich, 1927–28), and in J. Marcadé, *Eros Kalos* (Geneva, 1965); see also the works cited on p. ix, note 8.

Addenda, Corrigenda, Retractanda

(Boldface numbers correspond with the section-numbers of Chapters 4–7.)

The fragments of Attic Comedy should now be read in R. Kassel and C. Austin, *Poetae Comici Graeci* (Berlin/New York, 1983—), together with their annotations.

Introduction

x–xi

For costuming in general see Stone (1981), who is undecided about whether comic choreutai as well as actors could be ithyphallic (101–2), in spite of, for example, Kratin. *Dionysalexandros*, whose chorus is unthinkable without the phallos. A new piece of evidence is a late fifth-century Attic red figure calyx-krater, published by J. R. Green, *Greek Vases in the J. Paul Getty Museum* 2 (1985) 95–118, which depicts an aulos-player and two dancers costumed as birds who wear short drawers to which erect phalloi are attached; one of the dancers is reproduced on the cover of Sommerstein's edition of *Birds* (Warminster/Chicago, 1987). Green argues that the vase illustrates *Birds* (some grounds for caution are given by Sommerstein, *Birds* 6 and Henderson at *Lys.* 799–800), while Taplin (1988) 93–96 thinks they may be the two Logoi from the original *Clouds*, costumed as fighting cocks. In my view, the aulos-player at least indicates that the dancers are choreutai, so that the vase may be taken as evidence that comic (like satyric) choreutai could, when appropriate, be ithyphallic. For speculations about the optical and musical dynamics of comic drama see MacCary (1979).

Chapter 1

2–3

We still need to refine our definition of the boundaries of the Greek semantic category "obscene." Classical Greek lexicographers, unlike their

Roman (Richlin [1983] 1–31) and modern counterparts, included obscene words alongside other words and had no separate category for them: one finds only explanatory paraphrase (X = a certain body-part or act) and κακεμφάτως ("in a base/bad sense") to characterize metaphors. At the same time, classical literary genres show distinct stylistic discrimination across a broad spectrum of aeschrologic language: Koster (1980) has investigated this spectrum in the language of invective and Parker (forthcoming) has uncovered a basic taxonomy in Hellenistic sex-manuals.

In addition, obscenity was not a moral category for classical Athenians, but a generic one (allowed/demanded on special festive occasions and in certain genres of art associated with them, e.g., comedy, iambos, drinking-bowls) and a social one (a status- and gender-marker). Thus, as Dover (1978) 143 n. 13 points out, my use (e.g., p. 210) of words such as "evil" and "wicked" (rather than "worthless" or "useless") is inappropriate.

No form of sexuality, at least before Plato, was considered in any way "unnatural"; it is more accurate to speak of what was conventional or unconventional: Dover (1978) 60, 100–1, 154, 165–70; Parker (1983) 99–100; Winkler (1990) 20–22; cf. Hdt. 1.61.1 (Peisistratos, not wanting to impregnate his wife, ἐμίσγετό οἱ οὐ κατὰ νόμον). For Greek terminology covering the category "taboo" (none of which refers to obscenity) see Parker (1983) 328–31.

The feelings of shame, guilt and inhibition that characterized Athenian sexuality differed in important respects from our own, but were not demonstrably less "muddled." More subtle formulations can be found in Dover (1978), index at "inhibition," and Winkler (1990). Parker (1983) 74–103 discusses the points at which sexuality was considered incompatible with the sacred and was regulated by the community. "Such rules," he writes,

> have nothing directly to do with morality ... nor is it easy to see them as expressions of a strong internalized feeling that the sexual act is degrading or disgusting.... An aura of shame does indeed surround sexuality, but its source seems to be embarrassment about bodily functions rather than guilt. It is within the general structure of respectful behaviour and decorum that these rules find their place.... The insulation of sex from the sacred is merely a specialized case of the general principle that sexual activity, like other bodily functions, requires disguise in formal contexts (75–76).

Thus sexual offenses are breaches of social not moral rules: "It is only among the possessors of 'honour' (full citizen rights) that they are out of place. Offenders are not exiled or put to death but deprived of 'honour' and forced to find a place amid the flotsam of foreignness and vice that laps around the citizen body" (96). From the point of view of the adult male citizen, to avail oneself of this flotsam (unchaste women and boys) carried no dishonor or penalty so long as the safety and honor of his own family, and his reliability as a citizen, were not thereby compromised. Among the public vehicles of such dishonor or penalty was the comic festival, where the effect of sexual accusation lay somewhere between doing something about disruptive but otherwise unactionable gossip and doing nothing about it: see Henderson in Winkler/Zeitlin (1990) 295–96. It would be interesting to know the attitudes of the "silent majority" who were not adult male citizens (including the "flotsam"), but these are perhaps irrecoverable.

9

We are no longer in a position to verify Aristophanes' claim to be less vulgar than his rivals, but one ancient critic at least thought him less vulgar than Kratinos (Platon. *diff. char.* 1 p. 6 Koster = Ar. test. 79 K-A).

12–13

I no longer hold the view that what was said or portrayed at the comic festivals was all in fun in the sense that it could have had no impact on the social and political life of the polis as a whole, or that anyone was fair game for comic ridicule. Comic festivals were an organic institution of the democratic polis in its fifth-century form and played a distinctive role in its social regulation; comic poets show systematic bias in their choice of people to satirize and not to satirize; and they were not exempt from the rules governing other kinds of public/official discourse: see Henderson in Winkler/Zeitlin (1990) 271–313.

13–17

On obscenity, humor, and women's cults see Zeitlin (1981, 1982, 1985) and Winkler (1990) 188–209. "It is possible that, for the more frankly hedonistic rites, purity will not have been required; but the contrast between the intrinsic dignity of religious activity, and the possibly disreputable character of actual rites, presumably meant that the Greeks sometimes purified themselves in respectful preparation for acts they would have been ashamed to perform in everyday life," Parker (1983) 78–79. For a different approach to women and sexual pollution see A. Carson, "Putting Her in Her Place: Women as Dirt in Ancient Society," in Halperin/Winkler/Zeitlin (1990).

Other aspects of aeschrology in cult are discussed by Rusten (1977) and Syl (1985).

17–23

For the iambos generally see Rosen (1988) and West (1974), who notes (17) that "obscenity is always cast in the form of ritual strife and abuse". Note, however, that the first-person speakers of iambos can sometimes speak (like characters in drama) in fictive identities rather than *in propria persona*. For euphemism preferred to obscenity in the archaic epode see Henderson (1976). For the recently discovered erotic poem by Arkhilokhos known as the Cologne Epode I use D. L. Page's text in *Supplementum Lyricis Graecis* (Oxford, 1974) S478.

Add to the lists:

αὐλόc = drinking-straw and penis in A 42: Gerber (1976), who adds Strattis 3 (αὐλοτρύπηc), *AP* 11.221, 12.215, 216.

δέχομαι [receive] = admit sexually: A 189, Sem. 7.48–49, cf. A 331 δέκτρια.

εἴλειν: read εἴλεcθαι.

ἐπείcιον = pubis: A 40, 67.11(?).

μηρῶν μεταξύ [between the thighs]: A 66.

μύρτον: also A 32.

{καὶ} τὴν ῥῖνα καὶ τὴν μύξαν ἐξαράξαcα [after she beat my nose and my mucus/wick]: H 22 (cf. West [1974] 143), perhaps referring to manual sex? For ῥίc = penis cf. S. fr. 171 (see on pp. 26–27 below) and probably also *Nu.* 344; cf. Davies (1982) 117, Brown (1983).

Σινδικὸν διάcφαγμα [Sindic sluice-gate] = vagina: H 2a. cίφωνι λεπτῶι τοὐπίθημα τετρήναc [having pierced her/his lid (vagina or anus) with my/his thin siphon]: H 56, cf. E. *Kykl.* 439–40 with Seaford (1984).

cτάζουcιν ὥcπερ ἐκτροπήιον cάκκοc [they drip like a bag of sour wine]: H 57, cf. West (1974) 142.

τρώζειν: read τιτρώcκειν.

From the Cologne Epode, where the speaker apparently ejaculates outside the girl's vagina (whether or not he first penetrates her is unclear), add:

3 ἰθύειν [drive straight on] = a pun ("make straight")? Cf. ἰθύφαλλοc.
15 τὸ θεῖον χρῆμα [the divine thing] = "sexual intercourse" (Hesych. π 839) or perhaps "marriage."
21 θριγκόc [coping] = area around the clitoris; or anus (cf. Ar. *Th.* 60)?
21 πύλοι [gate] = vagina or anus.

23–24 *cχήcω...ἐc ποη[φόρουc] κήπουc* [I will hold a course to the grassy gardens] = end up at/on the pubis.

43 *λαβεῖν* [grab].

48 *ἐφάπτεcθαι* [seize hold of].

51 *ἀμφαφᾶν* [feel all around].

52 *λευκὸν ἀφῆκα μένοc* [I discharged my white force] = ejaculate.

Other sexual descriptions are:

A 23: a woman's capture of the speaker is like the capture of a city.

A 48 (and 49?): a drinking party with prostitutes, West (1974) 125.

A 51–54: Perhaps an encounter with one of Lykambes' daughters, see Henderson (1976) 162–63.

A 112: Not a wedding, as West (1974) 129–30—this is a city under attack—but a brothel-scene with young soldiers. For *Κουροτρόφοc* = bawd cf. Pl.Com. 174.7, Hom. *Ep.* 12, *AG* 6.318, Henderson (1987) 125–26.

A 113: The speaker chides his commander for being more valiant in bed than in battle, West (1974) 129–30; cf. *Ra.* 428–30.

H 22: see above.

Some poems of Anakreon ought to be noticed as examples of symposiac erotica: I cite D. A. Campbell's Loeb edition (II 1988):

346 Seduction of a boy; abuse of a girl or hetaira.

358 *χάcκειν* [gape] perhaps refers to fellatio (the girl is Lesbian) or to cunnilinctus: see Dover (1978) 183.

399 *δωριάζειν* [play the Dorian] = of a woman showing herself naked.

408 Seduced girl compared to a fawn, cf. the Cologne Epode.

417 Lover as horseman.

446 Abusive terms for whores: *πανδοcία* (generous giver), *λεωφόροc* (public highway), *μανιόκηποc* (with lust-mad garden = vagina), *πολύυμνοc* (much-sung).

For symposiac iconography see F. Frontisi-Ducroux and F. Lissarague, "Ambiguity and Ambivalence in the "Anakreontic" Vases: A Dionysiac Inquiry," in Halperin/Winkler/Zeitlin (1990).

26–27

The language of satyr-dama, though never obscene, is less chaste than was here characterized and deserves a study of its own. Seaford (1984) provides a thorough analysis for E. *Kykl.* and F. Lissarague discusses "The Sexuality of Satyrs" in Halperin/Winkler/Zeitlin (1990).

For example, *τὸ φαλακρόν* [the bald thing] was apparently used instead of φαλλός to mean a boy's (hairless) penis: A. *Dikt.* 787–88 (of young Perseus) τὸ μιλτόπρεπτον φ. [his red-tipped bald thing], cf. 31 ποσθοφιλής; S. fr. 171 Mette (a boy) τὴν ῥίνά μ' εὐθὺς ψηλαφᾶι κἄνω φέρει τὴν χεῖρα πρὸς τὸ φ. [straightway stroked my nose (= penis) and moved my/his hand to his bald thing], *Ikhn.* 368 Mette παύου τὸ λεῖον φ. ἡδονῆι πιτνάς [stop merrily fluttering your smooth bald thing]. In E. *Kykl.* 227 (Polyphemos describing Silenos) πληγαῖc πρόcωπον (μέτωπον Tyrwhitt) φαλακρὸν ἐξωιδηκότα [his bald countenance/mask swollen from blows], φ. punningly refers to Silenos' stage-phallos (with "blows" alluding to masturbation?).

Other examples from E. *Kykl.*:

2 δέμαc (cf. **18**).
169 ὀρθόc and τουτί deictic ~ phallos.
171 ὀρχηcτύc ~ ὄρχειc.
184 αὐχήν ~ penis (cf. on **15**, below).
185 ἐκπτοεῖν of erotic arousal.
326 τέγγειν ~ ejaculate.
327–28 πέπλον κρούειν/κτυπεῖν ~ masturbation.
439–40 cίφων ~ penis, here "widowed" (cf. Ar. *Lys.* 956 of an "orphaned" penis).
495–502 (wine and sex spoken of in mystical/religious terms).
502 θύρα ~ vagina.
516 δροcερῶν ἔcωθεν ἄντρων ~ the vagina of a concupiscent bride.
589 πικρότατον οἶνον ~ semen.

Chapter 2

51–52

Fellatio when performed by a *man* was considered disgusting and degrading: note the abuse directed at (in addition to Aristyllos) Demokhares (Arkhedik. 4 = Polyb. 12.13.7) and Demosthenes (76 FGrH fr. 8, cf. Aiskhin. 2.23, 88), and the absence of male fellatio in vase-paintings; contrast cunnilinctus (in group sex on *ARV*² 113: Thalia Painter), which is often portrayed as enjoyable enough, though Ariphrades (despite other critical agenda underlying Aristophanes' abuse) could be reviled for practicing it (*Eq.* 1276 ff.) and in Roman times Galen 12.249 Kühn could say that "we are more revolted" by cunnilinctus than by fellatio. Of oral sex generally Parker (1983) 100 concludes, "When performed by a woman such acts are not revolting, because woman is naturally degraded in relation to man; even when done by a man, it is only when combined with the absolute self-degradation of homosexual prostitution that they are sufficiently outrageous to become a focus for political abuse." For further recent bibliography see Krenkel (1980), Richlin (1983) 26–29 (on the Roman concept of *os impurum*), and Halperin (1990) 185 n. 73.

66–70

Spyropoulos (1981) discusses *Eq.* 1399 in light of the play's thematic association of obscenity with "dirty" politics.

Chapters 4–6

In these chapters I sometimes succumbed to a danger inherent in the glossarial method and about which I warn users: treating words apart from their dramatic contexts. In his review Vaio (1979) picked a good example, my treatment of the song in *Peace* 1127–39 (trans. Sommerstein):

> I rejoice, yes I rejoice,
> that I am free from helmets,
> free from cheese and onions.
> For I take no delight in battles,
> but in drinking deep
> by the fire in the company
> of friends, after kindling
> those of the logs
> which have dried best after
> being grubbed up in summer,
> toasting some chickpea
> and roasting acorn,
> and also kissing Thratta
> while the wife is in the bath!

The words for cooking and for the foods mentioned in this song have sexual meanings elsewhere and are distributed among five sections, cf. **44**, **165**, **344**, and **346** ("bake/roast my phallus in coitus"), but nowhere is the song considered as a whole. Had I done so, as Vaio 693 points out, I would have seen that this song pictures "a rustic drinking bout with male comrades, there being no mention of female companionship until lines 1138 f. (*kissing the maid, while the wife's in the bath*). Why talk of mere osculation at 1138, when you've just 'baked and roasted your phallus in coitus' at 1136 f.?"

Chapter 4

120–24

"The Greeks felt, however inarticulately, that the penis was a weapon, but a concealed weapon held in reserve," Dover (1978) 134 of the impression given by vase-paintings.

2. For *Th.* 254 see on **479** below. For the aesthetics of penis-size see Dover (1978) 125–35. For κωλῆν μεγάλην in *Nu.* 1019 (Dover's emendation μικράν has not found critical acceptance) see C. Austin, *CR* 20 (1970) 20, who argues that it is an interpolation and is followed by G. Mastromarco, *Aristofane I* (Torino 1983) (cf. his critical note, p. 89) but not by Sommerstein.

3. cάθη could indicate a large penis: Arkhil. 43, where someone's penis is likened to a donkey's, *AB* 394.5 ἀνδροcάθων/-cάθηc· μεγάλα ἔχων αἰδοῖα (referring to the cult of Priapos).

4–5. ἀπεψωλημένοc and ψωλόc are used to mean "with glans exposed" (by erection) and "circumcised": ψωλόc in both senses in *Av.* 504–7, circumcised in *Eq.* 964 (Kleon as Paphlagonian barbarian), *Pl.* 265–67; ἀπεψωλημένοc circumcised in *Akh.* 155–61. For circumcision generally see Dover (1978) 129–30.

6. Timokles wrote a play titled *Konisalos*.

10. Add Euboulos' play-title *Orthannes* (cf. Ar. fr. 325 with Kassel-Austin).

13ff. Add ῥίc [nose] = penis in *Nu.* 344 (see above on pp. 17–23); cf. Davies (1982) 117, Brown (1983).

15. Seaford at E. *Kyk.* 184 suggests adding S. fr. 756 (a satyr lusts after Herakles) ἀνακειμένωι μέcον εἰc τὸν αὐχέν᾽ εἰcαλοίμην.

16. A phallic meaning is unlikely in *Eq.* 1168–69, *Lys.* 365; the context of Euboul. 75 (from *Orthannes*) is suggestive but indecisive (see Kassel/Austin here and at Ar. fr. 325).

18. δέμαc means "body."

21. Stone (1978) reviews the passages in which μέγαc may refer to the penis or comic phallos and excludes *Ve.* 56–57 and 68–69 from the list.

25. τὸ cχῆμα παραφυλάξηι: perhaps "misguard (take advantage of) our posture."

30. Another omission of an expected obscenity (πρωκτόν) is *Av.* 443.

42. Di Marco (1987) sees a play on ἐρέβινθοc in ἐρεβοδιφῶcιν, *Nu.* 192–93.

45. For the controversy about ληκύθιον ἀπώλεcεν in *Ra.* 1198–248 see D. Bain, *CQ* 35 (1985) 31–37, who concludes (as I still do) against a phallic interpretation.

48. *ϲτύομαι τριέμβολον* probably envisages a "prow" stout enough to ram thrice without failure (cf. **49**).

58. For the erotic use of this skolion see further Henderson on *Lys.* 630–31.

60. Add *Ve.* 27 and 823 (pl.).

73. For *ὄρχεις* see Watkins (1975).

82. D. Bain, *JHS* 104 (1984) 210 argues against reference to the testicles here.

84. The uses of *ἵπποϲ* cited here point to the female; the white horse of *Lys.* 191–92, if it has an erotic tone, seems to evoke the Amazons rather than the penis.

104. The foot as a displacement for the phallus is very common as a structural symbol in myths and folktales, most notoriously in the story of Oidipous (swollen/knowledgeable foot/phallus).

111. On depilation see M. Kilmer, *JHS* 102 (1982) 104 ff., D. Bain, *LCM* 7 (1982) 7 ff.

115f. *ὕϲϲαξ* or *ὕϲϲακοϲ* in *Lys.* 1001 is attested in a Doric iambos, *Lyr. Adesp.* 974 Page *εἶμ' ὅτ' ἀπ' ὑϲϲάκω λυθεῖϲα* (context?). See further Golden (1982), who discuses the etymological play on (*τὸ*) *ϲάκοϲ* "shield" and (*ὁ*) *ϲάκοϲ* "haircloth sack."

118. For the priapic name *Κύνν⟨ε⟩ιοϲ* cf. Ar. fr. 325 with Kassel/Austin.

125. Note that the myrtle was sacred to Aphrodite, cf. G. W. Elderkin, *CP* 35 (1940) 387 ff. "Myrtle berry" (as opposed to myrtle bush) might also have designated the clitoris. For the Harmodios-skolion see Lambin (1979), Henderson on *Lys.* 630–31.

146. In *Lys.* 414–18 *δακτυλίδιον* refers to the anus (too narrow), just as in the previous anecdote (408–13) *τρῆμα* refers to the vagina (too wide), Henderson ad loc.

157. In Eupolis 56 (= 64 K-A) *εὐτρήϲιοϲ* was an epithet applied to Autolykos.

164. "If there were one reference to veneral disease in Old Comedy, there would be several hundred; Aristophanes knew no more of the pox than of astrology, or Christianity (see Housman ap. Fraenkel on Aesch. *Ag.* 6)," Lloyd-Jones (1976) 358.

184ff. *πελλάνα Lys.* 996, which must refer to vagina or anus, may be a hapax (the speaker is Lakonian), or a play on a proper name or toponym. Coulon suggests emending to *τὰν πελλάν* [their milkbowls].

184. *δέλτα παρατετιλμέναι* means "trimmed in the shape of a delta": the wives' pubic hair must be carefully trimmed since it is to be visible through their diaphanous clothing (Henderson ad loc.). Reference to the pubis itself would require the definite article.

192. *μυωνιά* "is not well rendered by 'she is all cunt': a mouse's nest has many different apertures, and one remembers how Theodote 'most ungratefully murmured against the parsimony of nature,'" Lloyd-Jones (1976) 358.

196. Psychoanalytic critics think that the cχιcτή όδός, the intersection of three roads where Oidipous met Laios (S. *OT* 733, and still so called today), symbolizes the female (ultimately maternal) genitals/womb in their cathected ("oedipal") aspect. This interpretation, supported by the structural role played in the myth by the cχιcτή όδός, gains further support from the parallels for cχιcτός in an explicitly sexual sense.

200ff. For breasts see further Gerber (1978).

203. In *Lys.* 1170 "the Melian Gulf" refers to the vagina not the anus (which the Spartans have already opted for, 1163), Henderson ad loc.

Chapter 5

205. The force and usage of βινεῖν has been debated in a series of articles in *LCM*: C. Collard, 4 (1979) 213–14; H. D. Jocelyn, 5 (1980) 65–67, 6 (1981) 45–46; A. H. Sommerstein, 5 (1980) 47; J. Henderson, 5 (1980) 243; D. Bain, 5 (1982) 111. I no longer think that βινεῖν invariably connoted "violent and/or illicit intercourse," though in all instances it can be translated by "fuck." That it had obscene force, however, is assured by its use for climactic effect (*Av.* 793 ff., *Th.* 206, *Ek.* 228); when it is used in the presence of a spouse it expresses exasperation rather than affection (*Lys.* 934, *Ek.* 525). Its attestation for Solon (Hesych. β 322) was probably drawn from an iambic poem rather than a public notice, but in any case Solon cannot be used to exemplify fifth-century usage any more than can Menander, who also used βινεῖν (frr. 397.11 K-T, 138.8 Austin). Even "primary" obscenities vary in usage over time; it is my impression that for Americans "fuck," though still obscene, has become less shocking in polite discourse than it was when I wrote this book.

213. With n. 12: Jocelyn (1980), following Heraeus and Housman, demonstrates that λαικάζειν (always used absolutely in securely transmitted passages) means "behave like a λαικάς" (one who fellates), an act appropriate only for whores and slaves; when attributed to citizen males this was an insult parallel to those referring to submission to anal penetration (as *Akh.* 79). To the list of references to irrumation Seager (1983) adds *Th.* 493–96.

222. Read βιάζεcθαι.

237. Whatever εἰc ταὐτὸν μολεῖν means we cannot translate "go into her."

240. For παιδικά [playmate] = eromenos see Dover (1978) 16–17; two comic examples (Kratin. 258 and Eup. 327) use this term to refer to a girl "but in both the language may very well be humorous and figurative" (Dover).

249. For ὕβρις as sexual aggression see Dover (1978) 35–39.

250. For χάρις/χαρίζειν as gratification of an erastes cf. ¡Pl. *Smp.* 182a.

252–53. Words denoting work in sexual contexts: πονεῖν Arkhil. 42, Alex. 237; ἐργάτις Arkhil. 208; ἐνεργεῖν Eup. 266, Theokr. 4.61, Alkiphr. 3.19.9, 4.14.4; ἔργον Ἀφροδίσιον Sem. 7.48; see further Gerber (1975). For ὑπουργεῖν as gratification of an erastes cf. Pl. *Smp.* 184d, X. *Hiero* 1.37, 7.6.

259. See Whitehorne (1989).

301. In *Pax* 896b πλαγίαν καταβάλλειν should mean "throw her down sideways." For the question of the line's authenticity (it is preserved only in R) see Sommerstein ad loc.

322. For "grating" add ἀνακνᾶν (masturbation) in Ar. fr. 36 (37 K-A); κατακνίζειν and κνισμός (sexual arousal) in *Pl.* 973–74; κνέωρον (**131**); cf. Dover (1978) 123, Davies (1982).

336. The symbolic equation urine ∼ semen is well attested in myths (cf., e.g., the name and function of the sky-father Ouranos).

362. In Kratinos 301 tables are likened to girls, and Anaxil. 22 alludes to the riddle of the Sphinx.

366–79. For the connection between kissing and drinking see Seaford on E. *Kykl.* 172; for tonguing Krenkel (1981).

183–86

See on 51–52, above.

395. Euboul. 142 φοινικιστής.

410. In *Av.* 1552 it seems that Peisetairos palms off on Prometheus the unwelcome task of carrying off the δίφρος (see Sommerstein ad loc.).

415. σκατοφάγος is here probably used as glossed by Σ ad loc.: ἀναίσθητος [crude/unrefined], cf. Men. *Sam.* 427 with Austin's note: "an interesting exception to the general tendency noted by H. at the top of p. 40," Lloyd-Jones (1976) 359.

419. "at Antiph. 126, the scatophagous habits commonly attributed to cows in Cyprus are explained by the hypothesis that Aphrodite has transferred to them the habits usually attributed to pigs because in her Cyprus cults the pig is a sacred beast," Lloyd-Jones (1976) 359.

438. θριγκός referring to "some area or other of the lower human trunk" (Jocelyn [1980] 38) is now attested for Arkhilokhos (S 478.21). Jocelyn suggests that *Th.* 59 ff. may threaten irrumation (cf. 1. 57), but Agathon's phrase cυγγογγύλας καὶ cυcτρέψας is used in *Lys.* 973–79 (Kinesias of his wife Myrrhine) to set up a joke about (apparently) vaginal penetration.

439. I am now inclined to interpret *Nu.* 675–76 as referring to masturbation, cf. Dover (1978) 139, Sommerstein ad loc.

Chapter 6

400. Edmunds (1978) interprets the πρωκτός "too dirty to be washed clean" in *Ve.* 603–4 as referring to Philokleon's incontinent defecation and flatulence.

Chapter 7

This chapter must be read, corrected, and adjusted in light of Dover (1978), Halperin (1990), Winkler (1990), and DeVries (who provides a full review of the iconographic record). Shapiro (forthcoming) discusses the male "pinup" in vase paintings. I ought to have noted that neither in the comic poets nor in our other sources is there allusion to any category of Athenian males that would correspond to our category "gay": for reasons see Halperin (1990) 18 ff., 41 ff. Against current models for an "initiatory" homosexuality in classical Greece see Dover (1988). For oral and anal rape as punishments meted out to defeated enemies and adulterers see D. Fehling, *Ethologische Ueberlegungen auf dem Gebiet der Altertumskunde* (Munich 1974) 18–26, Dover (1978) 105, Jocelyn (1980) 63 n. 290, Richlin (1983) 140–41, 150, 215, 221. For the ways in which the sexual behavior of citizen males was overseen in classical Athens see Winkler (1990) 45–70.

Note that no mention of female homosexuality (for which see Dover 171–84) is attested in comedy.

204

For Dorian homosexuality see Dover 185–96.

458ff. "It must be emphasized that when a comic poet uses such words as *eurupröktos, lakkopröktos* and *katapūgon* of a named person (e.g., *Clouds* 1023, *Wasps* 687), we do not know whether it is important to him that the audience should interpret the word as a charge of passive homosexuality rather than as a charge of worthlessness, inferiority or shamelessness in general," Dover (1978) 143.

465. Men. *Sik.* 200 μειράκιον ... λευκόχρων. For vase-paintings see Dover (1978) 76–81.

476. On *kalos*-vases see Dover (1978) 114–24.

478. On φύσις and *natura* = "genitals" McLeish (1977) rejects an obscene meaning, but see now Winkler (1990) 217–20.

479. "There is no passage of comedy which demonstrably ridicules or criticizes any man or any category of men for aiming at homosexual copulation with beautiful young males or for preferring them to women," Dover (1978) 137. Comic poets criticized only excessive or otherwise improper behavior. Of my candidates on pp. 218–19:

1 In *Th.* 254 the point is that Agathon, who is wearing a dress, is male: the diminutive ποcθίον [pricklet] is contemptuous.
2 Alkibiades was portrayed by contemporaries as sexually unrestrained in every way, and his assimilation to Spartans further conditions this portrayal as unattic.
3 Autokleides' sexual hybris need not have included active pederasty.
4 Kleon is aggressive toward everybody and here is portrayed (very figuratively) not as a pederast but as raping adult men, an expression of dominance, cf. *Akh.* 519–20 (with Dover [1978] 204).
5 (and 10) By characterizing Hieronymos Xenophantou (*PA* 7556) as a shaggy centaur (cf. **453**) Ar. does seem to allude to predatory pederasty. But; as in the case of Alkibiades, this characterization criticizes not pederasty itself but Hieronymos' excessive behavior, and it need not exclude the predatory pursuit of females as well; cf. Dover (1978) 37–38, 138.
6 Ar. fr. 114 may as well have ridiculed Kallias as Meletos.
7 The context rather suggests that men like Phaiax are being called passive.
8 (and 9) In *Akh.* 603 Ar. ridicules Phainippos and Teisamenos merely for featherbedding in office.

In *Ve.* 1023–28 and *Pax* 762–63 Ar. defends himself against rumors that he conceitedly thought his celebrity would bring sexual success and that he had taken bribes from jealous erastai to slander the eromenoi in his comedies.

486. Men. *Sik.* 201 (μειράκιον) ὑπόλειον.

487. Men. *Sik.* 201 (μειράκιον) ἀγένειον, 264 ἐξυρημένον.

489. For masturbation see Dover (1978), Krenkel (1979), and note that masturbation, one of the characteristic attributes of satyrs, was often exploited in satyr-drama. (n. 45) "Actually, I first encountered [this assumption] in a reveille-call used among American GIs in Italy in 1943 ['drop your cocks and grab your socks'?], and heard it again in the film *Kes*, where the speaker is a Barnsley miner," Dover (1978) 98 n. 73.

491. For female homosexuality see Dover (1978) 173–84.

Index of Specially Discussed Passages

Index of Greek Words

255

σκινδακίσαι, σκινδαρεύεσθαι, σκινδαρίσαι,
   σκινθίζεσθαι: 176
σκοτοβινιᾶν: 62
σκυτάλα: 123
σκύτινος: 221.48
σκῶμμα: 9, 15, 106
σκώπτειν: 15
σκῶρ: 26, 35, 36, 192
σκωραμίς: 102, 191
σόφισμα: 183
σπαθᾶν: 73, 171
σπαράττειν: 185
σπασμός: 111
σπατάγγης: 142
σπατίλη: 192
σπερματίας: 125.94
σπλεκοῦν: 35, 154
σποδεῖν: 172
στέναγμα: 213
στενόπρωκτος: 211
στενός: 211
στηνιοῦν: 14
στόμα: 183, 184
στοματεύειν: 184
στρέφειν: 176, 180, 197
στρόβιλος: 124, 170
στρογγύλη: 200, 214
στρουθίας: 129
στρουθός: 129
στρόφος: 197
στύειν: 35, 85, 112, 121, 154, 158, 164
στῦμα: 112, 116
συβίνη: 152
συγγίγνεσθαι: 8, 159
συγγογγύλειν: 200
συγκαθεύδειν: 161
συγκαταδαρθεῖν: 160
συγκατακεῖσθαι: 160
συγκατακλίνεσθαι: 160
συγκλέπτειν: 156.25
συκάζειν: 135
Συκᾶς: 134
συκάστρια: 135
συκῆ: 23, 118
σύκινος: 22
συκίς: 118
συκολογεῖν: 65, 135
σῦκον: 118, 135
συκόπρωκτος: 134.137
Συκοτραγίδης: 21
συκοφαντεῖν: 135
συκοφάντρια: 135
σύμβολον: 124
συμμείγνυσθαι: 156
συμπαίστρια: 157

συμποιεῖν: 158
συμφέρειν: 161
συναρμόζειν: 119
συναρπάζειν: 156
συνεῖναι: 159, 214
συννήχεσθαι: 164
συνοικεῖν: 65
συνουσία: 159
σφραγίς: 124
σῦς: 132.130
σύστομος: 182
συστρέφειν: 200
σφίγξ: 132.127
σφυράδες: 193
σχῆμα: 117
σχίζειν: 147
σχισταί: 147
σχοίνιον: 130
σωλήν: 25
σώφρων: 9

Ταυροπόλος: 133
ταῦρος: 127, 133, 202–03
τέμαχος: 144, 178
τερπότραμις: 203
τετραίνειν: 114, 141–42
τετραποδηδόν: 169, 180
τετράπους: 180
τιλᾶν: 22, 192
τίλλειν: 22
Τιμησιάναξ: 203
τιτθίον: 148–49
τιτθός: 148
τιτίς: 147
τιτρώσκειν: 176
τόρος: 124, 142.179
τράγημα: 144, 178
τράμις: 21, 22, 128.112, 203
τράχηλος: 203
τρῆμα: 141–42
τρία/τρίς: 121
τρεβαλλοποπανόθρεπτος: 121.77
Τρίβαλλος: 121.77, 176.108
τρίβειν: 27, 126, 176
τριέμβολος: 85, 121, 164
τρικέφαλος: 113, 121
τρίορχος: 21, 121, 125
τρίπους: 180
τροπωτήρ: 124
τρύβλιον: 143, 186
τρυγᾶν: 65, 167
τρυμαλιά: 142.180
τρυμαλίτες: 142.180
τρύξ: 174
τρύπανον: 142.179

General Index

Agriculture
—symbolism from, 45–47
—terminology from: for male genitals, 117–20; for female genitals, 134–36; for breasts, 148–49; for sexual congress, 166–69
Anal sex, 51–54
Animals: as symbols, 48; for male genitals, 126–29; for female genitals, 131–33
Anus: cathexis of, 53–54; terms for, 199–203
Archilochus, 18–23
Aristophanes' plays: A, 57–62; Eq, 66–70; N, 70–78; V, 78–82; P, 62–66; Av, 82–86; Th, 86–91; L, 93–99; R, 91–93; E, 99–104; Pl, 104–7

Birds: as symbols, 46–47, 50; for male genitals, 128–29; for female genitals, 147
Breasts, 38, 148–49
Buttocks, 149–50, 199–203

Circumcision, 110–11, 118
Cookery: in sexual symbolism, 142–44. See also Foods; Heat
Costuming, iii, 111; as thematic device, 82, 87–89, 98–99
Countryside: and sexuality, 58–61, 64–66, 72–73
Cracks: and female genitals, 147
Crepitation, 195–99; sound effects for, 198
Cults. See Iambic poetry; Obscenity
Cunnilingus: in iambic poetry, 22; in Greek life, 51–52; in comedy, 185–86

Demeter: cults of, 13–15
Demonstratives, 117
Dionysus: cults of, 15–17
Dorian Farce, ii, 23–26, 223–28
Dreaming, 37–38, 41–43, 45

Eating: and sex, 47–48, 52, 60–61, 174. See also Cookery; Foods
Effeminacy: as theme, 88–89. See also Homosexuality
Eleusinian Mysteries, 16–17
Epicharmus, 24–26
Erection, 36, 44, 49, 110–12, 115–16
Euphemisms, 54–55, 101; for male genitals, 112–17; for female genitals, 133–34; for sexual congress, 154–61
Excrement: valuation of, 54; as theme, 63–64, 69–70, 74–75, 92, 102, Ch. 6, passim; and urgency, 188–89; soiling clothes, 189; and constipation, 189; and fear, 189; color of, 189–90; and exertion, 190; and violence, 190; soiling others, 190–91; vessels for, 191–92. See also Scatology; Scatophagy
Exhibitionism: in iambic poetry, 22

Fellatio: in iambic poetry, 22; in Sicilian Comedy, 25; in Greek life, 51–52; in comedy, 153–54, 157, 159, 167–68, 183–85
Female secretions, 145–46
Fish. See Sea animals
Flowers. See Agriculture
Flying: as sexual metaphor, 49–50
Foods: as symbols, 144. See also Cookery; Eating; Heat

Gates: symbolizing female genitals, 137–39
Genitals: terms for in iambic poetry, 19–20; in Sicilian Comedy, 25; in satyr-drama, 27; symbols for, 44–50; male, 108–30; female, 130–48

Heat: and sexuality, 47–48, 177–78. See also Cookery; Eating
Herodotus, 4–5